Global Environmental Governance

NEW HORIZONS IN ENVIRONMENTAL AND ENERGY LAW

Series Editors: Kurt Deketelaere, *Professor of Law, University of Leuven, Belgium and University of Dundee, Scotland and* Zen Makuch, *Reader in Law, Barrister, Imperial College, London, UK*

Environmental law – including the pressing considerations of energy law and climate change – is an increasingly important area of legal research and practice. Given the growing interdependence of global society and the significant steps being made towards environmental protection and energy efficiency, there are few people untouched by environmental and energy lawmaking processes.

At the same time, environmental and energy law is at a crossroads. The command and control methodology that evolved in the 1960s and 1970s for air, land and water protection may have reached the limit of its environmental protection achievements. New life needs to be injected into our environmental protection regimes – perhaps through the concept of sustainability in its environmental, economic and social forms. The same goes for energy policy and law, where liberalisation, environmental protection and security of supply are at the centre of attention. This important series seeks to press forward the boundaries of environmental and energy law through innovative research into environmental and energy law, doctrine and case law. Adopting a wide interpretation of environmental and energy law, it includes contributions from both leading and emerging international scholars.

Titles in the series include:

Myths and Realities of Business Environmentalism
Good Works, Good Business or Greenwash?
Kurt A. Strasser

European Emissions Trading in Practice
An Economic Analysis
Stefano Clò

Conservation, Biodiversity and International Law
Alexander Gillespie

Comparative Ocean Governance
Place-Based Protections in an Era of Climate Change
Robin Kundis Craig

Environmental Governance of the Great Seas
Law and Effect
Joseph F.C. DiMento and Alexis Jaclyn Hickman

Conservation on the High Seas
Harmonizing International Regimes for the Sustainable Use of Living Resources
Simone Borg

Global Environmental Governance
Law and Regulation for the 21st Century
Louis J. Kotzé

Climate Law in EU Member States
Towards National Legislation for Climate Protection
Edited by Marjan Peeters, Mark Stallworthy and Javier de Cendra de Larragán

International Law and Freshwater
The Multiple Challenges
Edited by Laurence Boisson de Chazournes, Christina Leb and Mara Tignino

Global Environmental Governance

Law and Regulation for the 21st Century

Louis J. Kotzé

Faculty of Law, North-West University, South Africa

NEW HORIZONS IN ENVIRONMENTAL AND ENERGY LAW

Edward Elgar

Cheltenham, UK • Northampton, MA, USA

Published by
Edward Elgar Publishing Limited
The Lypiatts
15 Lansdown Road
Cheltenham
Glos GL50 2JA
UK

Edward Elgar Publishing, Inc.
William Pratt House
9 Dewey Court
Northampton
Massachusetts 01060
USA

A catalogue record for this book
is available from the British Library

Library of Congress Control Number: 2012938076

MIX
Paper from
responsible sources
FSC® C018575

ISBN 978 1 78100 252 0

Printed and bound by MPG Books Group, UK

For Klaus Roman Z.

Contents

Abbreviations

APEC	Asia-Pacific Economic Cooperation Forum
ASEAN	Association of Southeast Asian Nations
AU	African Union
CBO(s)	Community based organization(s)
CDP	Carbon Disclosure Project
CERN	European Organization for Nuclear Research
CITES	Convention on International Trade in Endangered Species of Wild Fauna and Flora
COP(s)	Conference(s) of the Party(ies)
EC	European Commission
ECJ	European Court of Justice
EMAS	European Eco-management and Audit Scheme
EMS	Environmental Management System
EU	European Union
FAO	Food and Agricultural Organization
GEF	Global Environment Facility
GRI	Global Reporting Iniative
IAEA	International Atomic Energy Agency
ICANN	Internet Corporation for Assigned Names and Numbers
ICC	International Criminal Court
ICJ	International Court of Justice
ICLEI	International Council for Local Environmental Initiatives
ILO	International Labour Organization
IMF	International Monetary Fund
IMO	International Maritime Organization
INECE	International Network for Environmental Compliance and Enforcement
ISO	International Organization for Standardization
IUCN	International Union for Conservation of Nature
IUCN AEL	International Union for Conservation of Nature Academy of Environmental Law
MNCs	Multinational corporation(s)
NGO(s)	Non governmental organization(s)
OECD	Organization for Economic Co-operation and Development

SADC	Southern African Development Community
UN	United Nations
UNCSD	United Nations Commission on Sustainable Development
UNECE	United Nations Economic Commission for Europe
UNEP	United Nations Environment Programme
UNFCCC	United Nations Framework Convention on Climate Change
WHO	World Health Organization
WSSD	World Summit on Sustainable Development
WTO	World Trade Organization

Acknowledgements

This book was made possible through the generous financial assistance of the Alexander von Humboldt Foundation. My sincere thanks to the Humboldt Foundation for its financial and professional support. The greater part of the book was written during an extensive research stay at the Max Planck Institut für ausländisches öffentliches Recht und Völkerrecht, Heidelberg, Germany, and the manuscript was finally concluded during my term as the IUCN Academy of Environmental Law Visiting Professor at the Faculty of Law, University of Ottawa, Canada. I wish to thank all of these institutions for accommodating me and for their generous support and hospitality.

I am also indebted to professors Jonathan Verschuuren, Gerrit van der Waldt, Benjamin Richardson, Ulrich Beyerlin, and Thilo Marauhn for their guidance and helpful comments on earlier versions of the manuscript. All views expressed herein and all errors remain my own. Finally, my sincere thanks to Ben Booth, David Fairclough and the team at Edward Elgar Publishing for their extraordinary publishing and editorial assistance.

Preface

This book is an attempt to interrogate the concept of contemporary global environmental governance from a legal perspective. I am an environmental lawyer and am often uncomfortable with engaging with extra-legal concepts such as governance. The idea of writing this book accordingly arose from a personal need to better understand the concept of governance in the environmental regulatory domain, and more specifically to understand what governance is and what role governance and (environmental) law play in contemporary forms of global environmental regulation. Political scientists have written extensively on the concept of governance, including its manifestation in the form of global governance. Some have even reflected on the concept of global environmental governance. At the same time, various environmental law scholars have dedicated extensive volumes to international environmental law, which is how environmental lawyers usually perceive the manifestation of global environmental governance. Understandably, in the latter instance, the focus is a strictly legal one and as a result the link between governance and law in the environmental regulatory domain often remains unclear. Moreover, while other environmental lawyers have promisingly included references to environmental governance in their work, I have found it hard to lay my hands on a single source which brings together governance theory, environmental regulation and law from a meta-theoretical point of view.

While writing this book much has become clear to me with respect to the role of governance, its connections with law, and the collective role of these two phenomena in global environmental regulation. While many questions concerning the foregoing vexing issues remain unanswered, I express the hope that the book will provide a point of departure for environmental lawyers, helping them to engage more comfortably and critically with the concept of environmental governance.

Louis J. Kotzé
Potchefstroom, South Africa
February 2012

1. Introduction

> The drama of global environmental change and the extent to which environmental problems threaten to overwhelm our existing forms of political and economic organization make it particularly tempting to devise new schemes of how the world ought to be organized: to put forward arguments about desirable reforms in the way in which states negotiate and co-operate; to argue that sustainability requires both a radical redistribution of the world's wealth and a new form of global democratization.[1]
>
> (Andrew Hurrell, 1995)

1. A BRIEF ACCOUNT OF A LONG HISTORY

People depend on the environment for their survival because they rely on environmental goods, services and conditions to sustain life and because they are part of the environment. In the words of Godden and Peel:[2] 'our knowledge of the world is mediated through the frame of concepts, language and terminology that we employ to describe and analyse the environment – which includes ourselves.' It would clearly be in our best interests not to engage in and perpetuate the self-destructive practices which are eroding the world's ecological capital, which feeds us, or to perpetuate our ever-increasing human-centred socio-economic demands. Yet, despite the clear logic of this symbiotic relationship and the implied thresholds and restrictions it presumably imposes, Hurrell's 'drama of global environmental change' is becoming more tragic every day, and we are gradually bringing about our own demise.[3] As Pelletier[4] puts it:

---

1 Hurrell, Andrew (1995), 'International Political Theory and the Global Environment' in Ken Booth and Steve Smith (eds), *International Relations Theory Today*, Cambridge: Polity Press, 150–51.

2 Godden, Lee and Jacqueline Peel (2010), *Environmental Law: Scientific, Policy and Regulatory Dimensions*, Melbourne: Oxford University Press, 57.

3 Among the many publications in this repect see Winchester, Brian N. (2009), 'Emerging Global Environmental Governance', *Indiana Journal of Global Legal Studies*, **16**(1), 7–23 at 7–9.

4 Pelletier, Nathan (2010), 'Of Laws and Limits: An Ecological Economic Perspective on Redressing the Failure of Contemporary Global Environmental Governance', *Global Environmental Change*, **20**, 220–28 at 220.

> Contemporary industrial society consumes a continuous and accelerating throughput of material and energy resources ... These resources are transformed, through the application of various technologies, into the diverse economic goods and services that fuel the metabolic processes of social production and reproduction, as well as a wide range of waste products. Thus, industrial society hinges on access to a material base that is both generous with regards to resource supplies and forgiving in terms of waste assimilation.

It is, however, also true that people have been seeking for many years to regulate their relationship with the environment mainly with a view to maximizing their benefits and arguably to a lesser extent with a view to avoiding or at least postponing their own demise. For this purpose they have designed societal constructs which generally speaking have as their primary objectives to influence, order or control behaviour, to 'shape the flow of events',[5] and ultimately to solve certain societal problems primarily by means of regulatory interventions such as rules (or norms) expressed in terms of laws.[6] These rules are in turn executed and enforced by a myriad of actors by way of numerous processes and mechanisms which are popularly referred to as regulation or governance. The deterioration of the environment has been and is increasingly regarded as a major societal problem that requires regulatory intervention if we are to sustain life on earth. Indeed, environmental problems are also social problems because they affect society: 'environmental problems are not just naturally revealed, they are – like conceptions of wealth, knowledge, and politics – socially constructed.'[7]

Regulatory interventions with respect to the environment are not new phenomena.[8] Braithwaite and Drahos[9] trace some of the first forms of envi-

---

[5] Parker, Christine *et al.* (2004), 'Introduction' in Christine Parker *et al.* (eds), *Regulating Law*, Oxford: Oxford University Press, 1–2.

[6] The need for rules that create order in society is gloomily explained by Fuller as follows:

> To say that man can reshape himself by rules is to confess that he is a creature who has to put a halter on himself before he can live safely with his fellows. If this is something no other animal can do, it is something no other animal needs to do, for mankind is the only species that chooses its own kind as its preferred prey.

Fuller, Lon L. (1968), *Anatomy of the Law*, New York: Frederick Praeger Publishers, 3.

[7] Hempel, Lamont C. (1996), *Environmental Governance: The Global Challenge*, Washington: Island Press, 52.

[8] The words environmental problems or issues could mean many things and admittedly refer to many manifestations, temporal scales and degrees of severity. At a very tangible level, environmental problems relate to contaminated air, water and soil, climate change, species extinction and loss of biodiversity, for instance. At a more general theoretical level, they refer to the uncontrolled deterioration of ecological

ronmental regulation to Greece in the 6th Century BC, when Solon the Lawgiver proposed measures banning agriculture on steep slopes with a view to combating soil erosion. These measures, ancient as they may be, were obviously intended to change or influence behaviour and arguably involved or were intended to involve some rule-making or norm creation and mechanisms to enforce compliance with these rules.

Of course, there have been many subsequent attempts to influence the behaviour of people in their environment. The history of environmental regulation is well-trodden scholarly ground and literature abounds with detailed elaborations.[10] While this body of literature is too comprehensive to summarize here, the milestones of environmental regulation can be grouped into three distinct phases, according to Bodansky.[11] A survey of these phases suggests that there is a clear correlation between how society perceives environmental problems (as being complex and severe, as opposed to being simple and non-threatening) and the manner in which and the extent to which society responds to these environmental problems. A society that perceives environmental problems as complex and particularly challenging and threatening will attempt to devise comprehensive (and often complex) strategies which in its view would be sufficient to address the complexities and deal with the threats that environmental problems pose. Less complex problems would require less complex and comprehensive interventions.

Bodansky terms the period stretching from the latter part of the 19th Century to the middle of the 20th Century as the 'conservationist stage'. This period was characterized by a strong national or country-specific focus and, as the name suggests, was primarily concerned with nature conservation. The focus was distinctly domestic and was often limited to the protection of fauna

---

capital caused by social and economic demands resulting in the ecological system's losing its integrity and its ability to support itself and human beings in a state of health and well-being. This is so from both a quantitative and a qualitative point of view. See also Esty, Daniel C. (2007), 'Global Environmental Governance' in Colin I. Bradford and Johannes F. Linn (eds), *Global Governance Reform: Breaking the Stalemate*, Washington, DC: Brookings Institution Press, 109.

9 Braithwaite, John and Peter Drahos (2000), *Global Business Regulation*, Cambridge: Cambridge University Press, 256.

10 See, for example, Birnie, Patricia, Alan Boyle, and Catherine Redgwell (2009), *International Law and the Environment* 3rd edn, Oxford: Oxford University Press, 48–58; Bodansky, Daniel (2010), *The Art and Craft of International Environmental Law*, Cambridge, Massachusetts: Harvard University Press, 18–36; Hierlmeier, Jodie (2002), 'UNEP: Retrospect and Prospect – Options for Reforming the Global Environmental Governance Regime', *Georgetown International Environmental Law Review*, **14**, 767–805.

11 Bodansky, Daniel (2010), *The Art and Craft of International Environmental Law*, Cambridge, Massachusetts: Harvard University Press, 22.

and flora and their habitats.[12] Nature conservation was a straightforward regulatory issue which required few complex interventions because at the time it was not deemed sufficiently complicated to merit detailed, intricate regulatory interventions.

With increased air, soil and water pollution (notably because of industrial pollution and the pollution of the seas through oil spills), the 'pollution prevention and regulation stage' soon followed and it enjoyed widespread popularity in the 1960s and early 1970s. The United Nations (UN) Conference on the Human Environment, which was held in 1972 in Stockholm, is considered a crucial part of the first collective response, as having awoken worldwide environmental consciousness, and as constituting 'the major catalyst in the emergence of international environmental law'.[13] The United Nations Environment Programme (UNEP) was established, various multilateral environmental agreements were concluded, and a plethora of state and non-state environmental organizations were created as institutional responses to pollution problems in particular, as these had gradually become international concerns.[14] Thus, in addition to an expanded regulatory focus, this period saw a gradual shift from a national, country-focused approach to a supra-national one; an approach which simultaneously involved fast-growing, clearly discernible and more detailed supra-national responses and regulatory interventions specifically with respect to environmental pollution and, more generally, with respect to environmental protection.

---

12 As part of the domestic legal response in many countries, nature conservation was mostly accomplished by means of legislation, common law and customary law.

13 Bodansky, Daniel (2010), *The Art and Craft of International Environmental Law*, Cambridge, Massachusetts: Harvard University Press, 28 *et seq*. The United Nations Conference on the Human Environment was the first of several global environmental conferences to be convened. While many commentators are sceptical about the impact of these conferences on the success of environmental regulation efforts and the improvement of environmental quality, their overall contribution to the global environmental governance efforts should not be underestimated. As Haas points out:

> UN conferences contribute to governance and sustainable development by establishing and reinforcing ... constructivist themes in international relations [including, for example, processes of socialization, education, persuasion, discourse and norm incalculation] ... international conferences seldom have direct causal influences on member states' behavior, but their outputs are part and parcel of this broader process of multilateral governance and may contribute to stronger and more effective environmental governance by states.

Haas, Peter M. (2002), 'UN Conferences and Constructivist Governance of the Environment', *Global Governance*, 8, 73–91 at 74.

14 Kanie, Norichika and Peter M. Haas (eds) (2004), *Emerging Forces in Environmental Governance*, Tokyo: United Nations University Press, 1–2.

10 years later, in 1982, the UN General Assembly adopted the World Charter for Nature; in 1987 the World Commission on Environment and Development (the Brundtland Commission) popularized sustainable development[15] by means of its report, *Our Common Future*;[16] and 1992 saw the hosting of the second major global environmental conference, the UN Conference on Environment and Development in Rio de Janeiro. The UN World Summit on Sustainable Development (WSSD) diligently continued with the sustainability topic in 2002 in Johannesburg. As a follow up to all the foregoing conferences, the next major global environmental meeting is the United Nations Conference on Sustainable Development (otherwise referred to as Rio+20) which took place in Rio de Janeiro in June 2012. The official objective of the conference is 'to secure renewed political commitment for sustainable development, assess the progress to date and the remaining gaps in the implementation of the outcomes of the major summits on sustainable development, and address new and emerging challenges'.[17] Notably, this conference's central theme and focus remain 'sustainable development' and within this context, the issue of the green economy, as a 'new and emerging challenge' will be of central importance.

Realizing that the satisfaction of human needs (mostly socio-economic needs) is subject to the limits of available environmental resources, the regulatory focus in this period continues to be predominantly on the interplay between economic, social and environmental concerns and on finding ways to better ensure a balance between these considerations. Not surprisingly, Bodansky[18] describes this period as the 'sustainable development phase',

---

15 While the term 'sustainable development' is the one most often used in literature, I prefer instead to use the term 'sustainability'. The term 'sustainable development' in my view is often abused by some to legitimize socio-economic development and because of this 'forced' linkage with development (which usually implies socio-economic development), 'sustainable development' reflects only limited ecological considerations. The term 'sustainable development' is therefore not adequately representative of ecological interests and is much narrower in focus than the term 'sustainability', which at least in theory could better accommodate ecological interests. For similar views see among others Pinto, Moragodage C.W. (1995), 'Reflections on the Term Sustainable Development and its Institutional Implications' in Konrad Ginther, Erik Denters and Paul J.I.M. De Waart, *Sustainable Development and Good Governance*, Dordrecht: Martinus Nijhoff Publishers, 72–89; and generally, Bosselmann, Klaus (2008), *The Principle of Sustainability: Transforming Law and Governance*, Aldershot: Ashgate.

16 World Commission on Environment and Development (1987), *Our Common Future*, Oxford: Oxford University Press.

17 United Nations, http://www.uncsd2012.org/rio20/about.html [accessed 25 February 2012].

18 Bodansky, Daniel (2010), *The Art and Craft of International Environmental Law*, Cambridge, Massachusetts: Harvard University Press, 30–35.

which sees intensified institutionalization of environmental regulation at various levels and further proliferation of environmental institutions and actors. While it is especially at the international level that treaty regimes mushroom at an impressive rate and the number of state and non-state actors involved with environmental regulation increases exponentially, this period is also characterized by an equally comprehensive development of national and regional environmental laws and environmental agencies. As with the pollution prevention and regulation stage, the scope, depth and complexity of the recognized environmental problems also increase and, as a result, so too do the perceptions of environmental problems and the corresponding regulatory responses to them.

2. ENVIRONMENTAL GOVERNANCE AS CONTEMPORARY REGULATION IN THE 21ST CENTURY

Notably, the 'sustainable development stage' also concerns itself with the institutional framework for sustainable development which signals the world's growing awareness that matters of government and governance are increasingly important in environmental regulation. Thus, with the latter focus on ways to render development more sustainable, especially through a comprehensive institutional response, it is possible to discern a fourth stage in addition to Bodansky's three-staged development continuum of environmental regulation described above. This fourth stage of environmental regulation arises from the 'sustainable development stage', it exists in parallel with the 'sustainable development stage', and it could be termed the 'environmental governance stage'. As with other societal problems and regulatory areas that require society's attention (for example, the economy and trade),[19] the term 'governance' has slowly but surely entered onto the environmental regulatory scene, with the result that the 'sustainable development stage' has progressed to the governance level, as it were. The 'environmental governance stage' is therefore a continuation and result of, and a reaction to the 'sustainable development stage', because it emerges as a strategy to mediate the conflicts that arise from sustainable development in a globalized world. In other words, environmental governance, or the need to 'govern' the balance between social, economic and environmental considerations, arises from the nature of the disaggregated global context, including the condition of the states of which it consists. On the one hand, the state supports, offers incentives for, and itself

[19] 'Corporate governance' and 'financial governance' are two examples.

actively pursues economic development, and it would not want excessive regulation to slow this economic development and prevent the achievement of financial prosperity. On the other hand, for its own future survival the state cannot allow environmental degradation to continue unabated in the name of economic prosperity. Neither can it ignore the social protest against unabated socio-economic development at the cost of ecological capital. It is within this conflicted reality of sustainable development that the need for environmental governance arises, first on the state level and therefore in the global context.

It would be difficult to pinpoint an exact time at which environmental governance first surfaced as a concept. What is clear, as is argued elsewhere in this book,[20] is that the idea of governance is as old as humanity itself and, more importantly, that governance grew from the globalization maelstrom in an era which increasingly acknowledges the need to develop descriptive umbrella terms more closely suggesting complex contemporary societal concerns. Governance is a notoriously post-modern, vague, and 'globalized' concept, and has even been described as 'fuzzy'[21] and 'slippery', yet 'innocent'.[22] With governance being added to the environmental regulatory mix, the phrase 'environmental governance' thus gradually found its way into the discourse to describe, for example, the need to better understand social interaction with the environment, the effects of human behaviour on the environment, and ways to better respond to environmental problems in an ever more complex world where the importance of national boundaries is less pronounced, the role of the once all-powerful state is gradually changing, non-state actors are becoming increasingly influential in policy making and execution, and environmental problems are intensifying at a rate and with a degree of complexity hitherto unknown. One such example of complex environmental problems with global reach is climate change and the entire climate governance regime which has been developed as a response to the 'problems' created by climate change. The climate governance regime consists of numerous laws and guidelines, actors, institutions, processes and mechanisms at the local, national, regional and international levels, which collectively focus on interrelated and highly complex issues ranging through nature conservation, pollution regulation, water resources, food security, desertification, humanitarian issues, migration, financial markets, and state and human security, to name just a few of the relevant issues. Considered thus, it is possible to suggest

---

20 See Chapters 2 and 3.

21 Finkelstein, Lawrence S. (1995), 'What is Global Governance?', *Global Governance*, **1**, 367–72 at 367.

22 Harlow, Carol (2005), 'Deconstructing Government?' in Tom Ginsburg and Robert A. Kagan (eds), *Institutions and Public Law: Comparative Approaches*, New York: Peter Lang Publishing, 143.

that environmental governance is fourth-generation environmental regulation and a contemporary societal response to highly complex environmental problems in a globalized world where problems of nature conservation, the regulation of environmental pollution, and sustainability all converge globally.

The growing prevalence of the notion of environmental governance can easily be discerned in the literature, and environmental lawyers can scarcely be forgiven for not having noticed its recent proliferation.[23] The term adorns the covers of an increasing number of books and it boldly allures potential academic audiences to scholarly gatherings all over the world. Courses on the topic (increasingly multi-disciplinary in nature) are replacing traditional courses on environmental law at numerous higher education institutions and it increasingly forms the focus of various research projects. Its popularity suggests that environmental governance today seems to be what sustainability was in the latter part of the 20th Century, because it permeates virtually the whole of modern environmental discourse.

3. THE CONFUSING CONCEPTUAL LABYRINTH OF ENVIRONMENTAL GOVERNANCE

Yet despite its popularity considerable uncertainty surrounds the nature of the concept. A compelling theoretical description and understanding of the concept remains elusive, especially from the perspective of environmental law. Many seem to use the concept but in various different ways and contexts, and for different purposes. This suggests that continuity, certainty and at least

---

[23] As illustration, the following are examples of some publications related to the theme: Young, Oran R. (ed) (1997), *Global Governance: Drawing Insights from the Environmental Experience*, Cambridge, Massachusetts: MIT Press; Kanie, Norichika and Peter M. Haas (eds) (2004), *Emerging Forces in Environmental Governance*, Tokyo: United Nations University Press; Chambers, Bradnee W. and Jessica F. Green (eds) (2005), *Reforming International Environmental Governance: From Institutional Limits to Innovative Reforms*, Tokyo: United Nations University Press; Kotzé, Louis J. and Alexander R. Paterson (eds) (2009), *The Role of the Judiciary in Environmental Governance: Comparative Perspectives*, Alphen aan den Rijn: Kluwer Law International; Young, Oran R. (1994), *International Governance: Protecting the Environment in a Stateless Society*, Ithaca, NY and London: Cornell University Press; Esty, Daniel C. (2007), 'Global Environmental Governance' in Colin I. Bradford and Johannes F. Linn (eds), *Global Governance Reform: Breaking the Stalemate*, Washington, DC: Brookings Institution Press; Myint, Tun (2003), 'Democracy in Global Environmental Governance: Issues, Interests, and Actors in the Mekong and the Rhine', *Indiana Journal of Global Legal Studies*, **1**(10), 287–314; Akhtarkhavari, Afshin (2010), *Global Governance of the Environment: Environmental Principles and Change in International Law and Politics*, Cheltenham: Edward Elgar Publishing.

some form of agreement on its core content is lacking. It is also unclear whether environmental governance has achieved any normative status and if it actually provides any meaningful framework to allow for systematic analysis of issues pertaining to environmental regulation. It is not clear whether it is used as an analytical concept, a political and legal programme (in the normative sense), or both. It is also unclear what the term 'governance' implies for the regulation of environmental issues in the legal domain, what the implications of differing conceptions of the 'environment' would be for regulation, and what the role of (environmental) law is in the governance scheme of things. If these critical theoretical issues are left unattended, environmental governance could potentially suffer the same fate as 'governance' (its root concept), in the sense that it could become a popular buzzword with indeterminate meaning and therefore dubious analytical and normative value.[24] As Curtin and Dekker[25] warn:

> It cannot however at this stage in the debate be excluded that the notion of 'governance' in the sense it is currently being used will prove no more than a convenient 'catch-phrase' in vogue in a particular context whose days are numbered by zapping politicians (and bureaucrats) whose attention quickly turns to a newer, trendier, 'sound-byte' [sic] to catch their fluid ideas.

More particularly, despite their increased interest in and focus on the topic, environmental lawyers are apparently hesitant at best or unable at worst to understand, systematically to describe, and justifiably to concretize the notion of environmental governance; if the latter achievement is at all possible. The reasons for this are many and varied. In 2009 Fisher *et al*[26] raised questions about the maturity, methodology, and quality of environmental law scholarship. The authors identify a non-exhaustive list of four methodological challenges which in their view contribute to the existing 'dearth of critical analysis' in environmental law, which they see as leading to the production of

---

24 According to Curtin and Dekker: 'the content of the concept of "governance" is not only rather indeterminable but strongly varies in different contexts as well'. Curtin, Deidre M. and Ige F. Dekker (2005), 'Good Governance: The Concept and its Application by the European Union' in Deidre M. Curtin and Ige F. Dekker (eds), *Good Governance and the European Union: Reflections on Concepts, Institutions and Substance*, Antwerp: Intersentia, 5.

25 Curtin, Deidre M. and Ige F. Dekker (2005), 'Good Governance: The Concept and its Application by the European Union' in Deidre M. Curtin and Ige F. Dekker (eds), *Good Governance and the European Union: Reflections on Concepts, Institutions and Substance*, Antwerp: Intersentia, 20.

26 Fisher, Elizabeth *et al.* (2009), 'Maturity and Methodology: Starting a Debate about Environmental Law Scholarship', *Journal of Environmental Law*, **21**(2), 213–50 at 228.

environmental law scholarship of questionable quality. One of these challenges is 'the heavy reliance in environmental law on a diverse range of governance arrangements'.[27] They explain that:

> The methodological challenge raised by governance regimes is that such [governance] regimes require [environmental law] scholars to take a 'more diverse view of state authority and its exercise' but, in doing so, it is not clear what form such a 'diverse view' should take and how it differs from existing scholarly approaches. *Indeed, the concept of governance is much admired and referred to in worshipful tones but rarely scrutinised and deconstructed by environmental law scholars.*[28]

The theory of 'governance' and its increased prevalence in the environmental law domain is therefore one of the methodological challenges which makes environmental law scholarship in the authors' view 'darn difficult as an intellectual enterprise'. This is so because, *inter alia*, governance is a catch-all term; it deals with legal and non-legal issues; it involves novel forms of authority; issues of environmental governance are not confined only to environmental law, but also require a broader trans-disciplinary legal view that straddles the traditional boundaries of environmental law; and environmental governance derives from a multi-disciplinary foundation, which suggests that while it contains some legal elements it also heavily relies on a range of other disciplines (for example, ecology, ethics, sociology, politics and economics).[29] Considering this sobering reality, one can scarcely blame environmental lawyers for restricting their theoretical-analytical interactions with environmental governance to worshipful references instead of thoroughgoing scholarly analysis.

To concede defeat, however, would be tantamount to ignoring valid arguments that urge us to engage more fully with important theoretical concepts which are foundational to contemporary environmental law and regulation. Notably, ignorance would also result in a missed opportunity for seeking clarity on 'fuzzy' yet theoretically significant descriptive scientific terms which are important for informing our analytical endeavours and regulatory

---

27 The others include the speed and scale of regulatory change; inter-disciplinarity; and the multi-jurisdictional nature of environmental law regimes. Fisher, Elizabeth *et al.* (2009), 'Maturity and Methodology: Starting a Debate about Environmental Law Scholarship', *Journal of Environmental Law*, **21**(2), 213–50 at 228–43.

28 Fisher, Elizabeth *et al.* (2009), 'Maturity and Methodology: Starting a Debate about Environmental Law Scholarship', *Journal of Environmental Law*, **21**(2), 213–50 at 235. Emphasis added.

29 Fisher, Elizabeth *et al.* (2009), 'Maturity and Methodology: Starting a Debate about Environmental Law Scholarship', *Journal of Environmental Law*, **21**(2), 213–50 at 235–9.

responses as we attempt to deal effectively with contemporary environmental problems. As Finkelstein[30] argues, '[I]t is not wrong to wish to understand ... phenomena [such as governance]'; indeed it seems imperative to do so if one intends to make any meaningful contribution to the environmental discourse and cause. Important as they have been for the development of environmental regulation, and critical as they remain for regulatory efforts, the world has now moved beyond the nature conservation, pollution regulation and sustainability phases to the more complex and all-encompassing environmental governance phase of regulation which, for reasons set out throughout the course of this book, is better able to address environmental problems in a globalized world today.

4. AN UNCOMFORTABLE MARRIAGE

Environmental governance is a central concern of modern regulation in the legal context and it is becoming increasingly important and relevant for lawyers, legal discourse and, more specifically, the environmental law sub-discipline. Yet it is a concept which fits uncomfortably in the legal domain and as such it is one which requires to be more closely scrutinized. In addition to those already offered there are other reasons for looking closely at the concept of environmental governance.

First, environmental governance derives from the governance paradigm, which is an extra-legal concept but which is nevertheless interesting and relevant to lawyers, because it contains some legal elements and characteristics which could have legal effects. Governance, therefore, because it is a construct of social science that deals with regulation, is very close to law. In a sense, lawyers have always busied themselves with issues of governance, but only recently have environmental lawyers been forced to grapple with issues of governance in the environmental context. While this does not mean that environmental lawyers would necessarily be more comfortable or even better equipped to venture into scientific fields unknown to them and littered with quasi-legal landmines, it does suggest that lawyers require a better understanding of the interplay between legal, quasi-legal and non-legal concepts in the regulatory arena which, in the environmental field, often have a definite reciprocal relationship and interdependence and collective applicability to environmental problems. Moreover, as a prerequisite to the foregoing, lawyers must be able to understand the concept of governance and how it manifests in

30 Finkelstein, Lawrence S. (1995), 'What is Global Governance?', *Global Governance*, **1**, 367–72 at 368.

the environmental and legal context, which is by no means an easy task. Kooiman[31] helpfully captures the complexity and incredibly wide scope of the governance phenomenon as follows:

> ... governance of and in modern societies is a mix of all kinds of governing efforts by all manner of social-political actors, public as well as private; occurring between them at different levels, in different governance modes and orders. These mixes are societal 'responses' to persistent and changing governing 'demands', set against ever growing societal diversity, dynamics and complexity. Governing issues generally are not just public or private, they are frequently shared, and governing activity at all levels (from local to supra-national) is becoming diffused over various societal actors whose relationships with each other are constantly changing.

The varying contexts in which the phrase is used and the different meanings ascribed to it, as is illustrated later in this book,[32] suggest that environmental governance similarly is a highly complex construct which is equally vague, diverse and dynamic. Its increased popularity despite this theoretical confusion thus requires us to attribute a more concrete and uniform meaning to it for the sake of terminological consistency and clarity.

Second, the evolution of environmental regulation requires a broader view from environmental lawyers because '[T]oday law is no longer centre stage but simply one instrument among others in the environmental regulator's toolkit.'[33] Conversely, governance has the potential to broaden legal perspectives on environmental law-making, implementation, enforcement and regulation. Clearly, the changing face of environmental problems gives rise to many divergent and highly complex social, economic and ecological challenges which law alone cannot solve, but which instead demand a wider descriptive context, infused by multi- and trans-disciplinary perspectives where 'conventional boundaries between disciplinary areas of study are dissolving and reforming as interdisciplinary areas focused on broader topics like regulation or governance'.[34] The governance concept fulfils a specific scientific function in this respect because it can act as a useful bridging concept (*Brückenkonzept*) between different disciplines.[35] It could therefore function as a theoretical

---

[31] Kooiman, Jan (2003), *Governing as Governance*, London: Sage Publications Limited, 3.

[32] See Chapter 3 and further.

[33] Gunningham, Neil (2009), 'Environmental Law, Regulation and Governance: Shifting Architectures', *Journal of Environmental Law*, **21**(2), 179–212 at 179.

[34] Godden, Lee and Jacqueline Peel (2010), *Environmental Law: Scientific, Policy and Regulatory Dimensions*, Melbourne: Oxford University Press, 2.

[35] Schuppert describes governance as possesing the ideal characteristics to act as this bridging concept because it can connect various sub-disciplines and discourses as well as their scientific results:

bridge to traverse disciplinary boundaries in instances where it is both useful and necessary to marry unlikely partners with a view to seeing scientific problems through a common lens and to finding answers to problems posed in a multi-disciplinary context. The environment poses many such problems to society, which cannot be solved by law alone. The multiplicity, scope, depth and nature of environmental problems today are such that their solutions require a comprehensive multi-disciplinary approach, ranging from the natural sciences to the humanities. Governance could act as a bridging concept between law, political science, environmental sciences, management theory and sociology, for instance, enabling us to find answers to questions and solutions for problems related to the environment. Governance, or more specifically, environmental governance, connects these disciplines, and if understood and properly employed it could be useful to lawyers who seek to understand and solve complex contemporary environmental problems.

Third, the nature, scope and complexity of environmental problems and the concomitant responses devised in the political regulatory milieu have changed to such an extent that 'environmental governance, though sometimes touted as a "best" solution to multiple problems, may be most suited to dealing with "wicked" problems of such complexity that few if any other options seem viable'.[36] Climate change is one example of the many multi-dimensional and complex environmental problems which require a comprehensive, hybrid approach to devise regulatory solutions that consist of a whole range of legal and non-legal norms, processes, actors, and mechanisms at various levels.[37]

> ... der Governance-Begriff [ist] ein geradezu idealer Kandidat, um als *Brückenbegriff* zwischen den Disziplinen zu fungieren, wobei wir unter Brückenbegriffen ... solche Begriffe verstehen, die die Eigenschaft haben, verschiedene disziplinäre Fachdiskurse und ihre Ergebnisse miteinander zu verkoppeln, also auf einander zu beziehen und nicht einfach nur in berührungsloser Parallelität nebeneinander zu führen.

Schuppert, Gunnar Folke (2007), 'Was ist und wozu Governance?', *Die Verwaltung: Zeitschrift für Verwaltungsrecht und Verwaltungswissenschaften*, **40**(1), 463–511 at 506.

36 Gunningham, Neil (2009), 'Environmental Law, Regulation and Governance: Shifting Architectures', *Journal of Environmental Law*, **21**(2), 179–212 at 210.

37 Young emphasizes the issue of complexity in regulating environmental problems such as climate change:

> When we turn to the complex environmental problems that confront us now (for instance, climate change or the loss of biological diversity), moreover, the barriers to the achievement of effective governance are far more severe than they appear to be in the simple scenarios commonly used to illustrate the basic logic of collective action. It is often difficult to frame the problems to be solved appropriately, much less to design and operate governance systems that are both acceptable to all the major actors involved and likely to prove effective in practice.

As the complexity of environmental problems increases, so too do the complexity and variety of the regulatory responses, making the need to find collective terms to properly describe and understand these regulatory responses that answer to environmental complexity even more pressing. Governance, and indeed, environmental governance, is a way of approaching complexity in regulating human behaviour and the multiple effects of human behaviour on the environment. If environmental governance constitutes the contemporary fourth-generational manifestation of environmental regulation, then its content and conceptual underpinnings should be understood and described for the sake of promoting theoretical clarity and improving the practical application of the theory to everyday environmental problems.

Fourth, in the current globalized world, traditional forms of regulation are giving way to newer, more flexible forms of regulation that collectively resort under the terminological umbrella of governance. The term 'governance' suggests that there has been a 'shift away from a certain traditional mode of governing associated with [the term] "government"';[38] it is experimental and innovative; decentralized and more diverse; more flexible and revisable; it allows for improved participation and the coordination of multiple levels of government; and it fosters greater deliberation.[39] Contemporary governance arguably is everything that the orthodox state-centred, Westphalian concept of government is not, and environmental governance is an example of such a new form of governance, as is argued later in the book.[40] Gunningham[41] describes 'new environmental governance' as follows:

> This enterprise involves collaboration between a diversity of private, public and non-government stakeholders who, acting together towards commonly agreed (or mutually negotiated) goals, hope to achieve far more collectively, than individually. It relies heavily upon participatory dialogue and deliberation, devolved decision-making, flexibility rather than uniformity, inclusiveness, transparency and institutionalised consensus-building practices.

Young, Oran R. (1994), *International Governance: Protecting the Environment in a Stateless Society*, Ithaca, NY and London: Cornell University Press, 18.

38 Armstrong, Kenneth and Claire Kilpatrick (2007), 'Law, Governance, or New Governance? The Changing Open Method of Coordination', *The Columbia Journal of European Law*, **3**(13), 649–77 at 651.

39 Trubek, David M. and Louise G. Trubek (2006), *New Governance and Legal Regulation: Complementarity, Rivalry, or Transformation*, University of Wisconsin Law School Legal Studies Research Paper Series No 1022, 5–6 available at http://papers.ssrn.com/sol3/papers.cfm?abstract_id=908229 [accessed 4 January 2012].

40 See Chapters 3–6.

41 Gunningham, Neil (2009), 'Environmental Law, Regulation and Governance: Shifting Architectures', *Journal of Environmental Law*, **21**(2), 179–212 at 203.

The author concurs with the opinion that environmental governance is an evolving concept and that its precise architecture remains open to debate. While we might be familiar (comfortable even) with the Westphalian concept of government and its traditional, state-centred characteristics and elements, the same cannot necessarily be said of governance and its application in specific contexts such as the environment. The reality and inevitability of the development of 'new' forms of regulation in an era of globalization therefore would require a more complete and precise description of the characteristics of these new forms of regulation as they pertain to the environment in the 21st Century.

Fifth, from an abstract theoretical point of view, there is a need to transpose the environmental governance construct into the sphere of legal thinking for the sake of creating a frame of reference for those who use it. This is especially true if the purpose of the transposition is to better understand our increasing need to consolidate scientific and governance activities in the environmental field in a more systematic and exact way. Environmental governance could then serve as an aid in the theoretical consideration, interpretation and the systematization and clarification of the vague, ambiguous, general, fluid, amorphous mass of regulatory arrangements which cumulatively resort under the broad banner of environmental governance. Mindful of Young's[42] warning that we are running the risk of 'choking on the cascade of conceptual distinctions social scientists have devised to frame questions and guide analysis concerning interactions between human users and natural resources and environmental services', it seems an opportune moment not necessarily to expand on these but rather to carefully reflect on existing concepts such as environmental governance with a view to clarifying them and navigating the conceptual labyrinth we find ourselves in. This should allow for the creation of an appropriate scientific frame of reference for environmental lawyers that could guide them in their efforts to understand and solve increasingly complex environmental problems.

Sixth, lawyers have an irresistible urge to define the concepts with which they work. This need for definition arguably arises from the fact that lawyers often busy themselves with issues of liability, which is an exercise that requires an estimation and description of boundaries, limits and scope. This requires law and the interpretation of laws to be exact, consistent and clear. Law is also about language and the meaning of words, which is a further consideration in lawyers' propensity for definition:

42 Young, Oran R. (2007), 'Rights, Rules, and Common Pools: Solving Problems Arising in Human/Environment Relations', *Natural Resources Journal*, **1**(47), 1–16 at 1.

> Definition, as the word suggests, is primarily a matter of drawing lines or distinguishing between one kind of thing and another, which language marks off by a separate word. The need for such a drawing of lines is often felt by those who are perfectly at home with the day-to-day use of the word in question, but cannot state or explain the distinctions which, they sense, divide one kind of thing from another.[43]

Or in Scholte's[44] words:

> Definitions fundamentally shape descriptions, explanations, evaluations, prescriptions and actions. In other words, they affect our entire understanding of a problem. If a core definition is slippery, then the knowledge built upon it is likely to be similarly loose and, in turn, the policies constructed on the basis of that knowledge can very well be misguided.

Lawyers thus tend to define concepts with a view to clarifying ambiguities for the sake of uniformity and ultimately to enhance legal certainty. They also seek to define concepts with a view to understanding what it is they are working with. The manner in which lawyers would define environmental governance and the theoretical sub-components thereof (notably including the environment, governance and law), would also inform the design of regulatory legal interventions that seek to direct human behaviour towards the environment. For lawyers, the urge to define environmental governance is therefore almost intuitive.

5. THE PURPOSE OF THIS BOOK

The foregoing observations are meant to describe the motivation behind the writing of this book. They might understandably be considered as verging on the edge of ivory tower pomposity and hence as being the justification for yet another futile exercise in semantics. One cannot, however, ignore the fact that uncertainty is often cited as the main culprit and sometimes the excuse for the failures of our regulatory efforts in the environmental domain.[45] While 'uncertainty' in this context obviously signifies scientific uncertainty, it is reasonable

---

43 Hart, H.L.A. (1994), *The Concept of Law* 2nd edn, Oxford: Clarendon Press, 13–14.

44 Scholte, Jan Aart (2000), *Globalization: A Critical Introduction*, London: Macmillan Press, 42.

45 Bodansky, Daniel, Jutta Brunnée and Ellen Hey (2007), 'International Environmental Law: Mapping the Field' in Daniel Bodansky, Jutta Brunnée and Ellen Hey (eds), *The Oxford Handbook of International Environmental Law*, Oxford: Oxford University Press, 7.

to expect that normative and analytical uncertainty concerning the conceptual underpinnings of the foundational theoretical constructs of modern environmental regulatory efforts would only augment our regulatory failures.[46] It is in this context that the purpose of this book must be understood: it is an attempt to understand environmental governance; to situate 'governance' in the environmental regulatory domain, and to understand the role of law as part of the environmental governance effort. The book therefore seeks to provide a point of departure that should enable environmental lawyers to engage more critically with environmental governance. In doing so, its central aim is to aid environmental lawyers to scrutinize environmental governance and to attempt to understand the interplay between law, governance and the environment.

6. GLOBAL ENVIRONMENTAL GOVERNANCE

It is entirely likely that the nature of environmental governance could be described in a variety of different ways and from a number of different perspectives. One could, for example, describe the concept as it manifests nationally in a specific country, regionally as it occurs in the structures of the European Union (EU), or internationally as it manifests in supra-national structures such as those of the UN. Yet, considering the realities of fourth-generational environmental regulation, the interconnected nature of the environment, the global nature of contemporary environmental problems, and the collective global regulatory responses to these problems, it seems more useful to focus on the global aspects of environmental governance or, to put this differently, to focus on *global environmental governance*.

While global environmental governance includes international or supra-national environmental governance, it also concerns itself with the effects of and relationships between national and supra-national governance. It should be noted that global environmental governance is not exclusively international. 'Global' in this context is something of an all-inclusive term which refers to governance occurring simultaneously at various levels and executed by various state and non-state actors through a multitude of 'hard' and 'softer' legal arrangements. An extended view of the 'global' thus allows one to consider general trends in an interconnected, globalized world where there is considerable causality in their occurring at one level and their having

46 Biermann, Frank (2007), '"Earth System Governance" as a Crosscutting Theme of Global Change Research', *Global Environmental Change*, **17**, 326–37 at 329–30.

trans-level repercussions.[47] In other words, global environmental governance describes governance that is supra-national, but also governance that occurs at all other levels as well, through the agency of state and non-state actors. While the sub-national and national remain important for domestic interventions, the world has become less local and has taken on a decidedly global character which permeates the regulatory responses to environmental problems that occur everywhere and affect everyone. Clearly then, the term 'global' is used here to signify its spatial characteristics and as a causal category which applies in the context of globalization.

In most cases today, because the environment is a holistic integrated phenomenon that demands a global, universal, or holistic view, one must also approach environmental problems in an equally holistic, integrated or global manner. The notion of the Anthropocene provides a useful point of departure for an analysis of the 'global' in the context of a holistic environment and the global environmental governance paradigm, because it relates to the ways in which to change and make an impact on human behaviour. The term 'Anthropocene' describes the geological time period in which people dominate the earth and influence it to the extent that the dynamics and functioning of the earth are being changed.[48] Viewing the global environmental *problématique* through the lens of the Anthropocene is a new approach that contributes to our 'understanding of nature and society as a governable domain'; it provides an integrated and holistic opportunity for the 'reinvention of the boundaries between nature and society and the political space for government intervention'.[49] Indeed, it seeks to understand 'the planetary life-support system as an integrated whole',[50] with the result that the holistic character of the Anthropocene could be considered as a semantic precondition for global regulatory interventions, including global environmental governance. For example, climate change is truly a global problem with global repercus-

---

47 A very tangible example here is the important role that national governance organizational units play in transposing international legal obligations into national laws to the extent that '[N]ational administrative bodies serve as the nodes of transnational environmental policy frameworks.' Haas, Peter M. (2002), 'UN Conferences and Constructivist Governance of the Environment', *Global Governance*, **8**, 73–91 at 85.

48 For a more elaborate survey of the Anthropocene see Zalasiewicz, J. *et al.* (2011), 'The Anthropocene: a New Epoch of Geological Time?', *Philosophical Transactions of the Royal Society*, **369**, pp. 835–41.

49 Lövbrand, Eva, Johannes Stripple and Bo Wiman (2009), 'Earth System Governmentality Reflections on Science in the Anthropocene', *Global Environmental Change*, **19**, 7–13 at 7, 8.

50 Lövbrand, Eva, Johannes Stripple and Bo Wiman (2009), 'Earth System Governmentality Reflections on Science in the Anthropocene', *Global Environmental Change*, **19**, 7–13 at 7.

sions; what happens at the sub-national and national levels affects the supranational and *vice versa*. It affects people, water, land, the air, fauna, flora, and cultural and social issues, and everything else, in all countries. Climate change and its effects cannot therefore be viewed from an exclusively domestic point of view and based on a single environmental medium. For the same reasons climate change is also not an exclusively international environmental problem. Instead, regulating climate change involves all levels of governance and a widely diverse range of state and non-state actors at all of these levels; and it provides a hybrid mix of legal, financial and other quasi-legal environmental governance mechanisms including for example emission limits, carbon trading schemes and voluntary initiatives. It also provides for a multitude of normative legal arrangements at all of these levels. It is therefore an example of a truly global manifestation of environmental governance in the Anthropocene. Yet other less obviously global environmental problems fit equally well under the umbrella of global environmental governance in the Anthropocene. The pollution of a river in a specific country could have transboundary effects, and it could affect the resilience of communities, a fact which could in turn have devastating socio-economic and health consequences for a country. Because of the interconnectivity of the world, these events could also affect other countries and/or people in other countries. To be sure, in the context of the Anthropocene, the idea of a holistic environment and an encompassing conception of the global, today arguably few environmental problems do not resort under the umbrella of global environmental governance.

Focusing on global environmental governance thus helps one to understand the complexity of the governance phenomenon as it manifests in the context of globalization in the environmental regulatory domain, and it simultaneously provides the opportunity to distil generic insights on the content, purpose and objective of the societal construct of environmental governance. Notably, a focus on global environmental governance acknowledges the interconnected, universal, holistic and transnational facets, characteristics and problems of a globally conceived environment, and it informs the type, content, extent and design of regulatory responses to these globally conceived environmental problems. The current globalized age, the realities of the Anthropocene and the global environmental *problématique* demand nothing less.

7. A MULTI-DISCIPLINARY APPROACH

Due to the complexities of the nature of the concept, any study that purports to contribute to clarifying global environmental governance cannot, from a methodological point of view, confine itself to the boundaries of the law. Earlier in this chapter the case was made that environmental governance is diverse, multi-faceted and amorphous; qualities which raise daunting methodological challenges. Any attempt to describe global environmental governance must also borrow from non-legal but nevertheless law-related disciplines such as political science. While political scientists are far better equipped to pronounce on global environmental governance from their own perspective, this book will attempt to view global environmental governance from an environmental lawyer's perspective and through a political science lens insofar as the latter is necessary and possible. Undoubtedly, global environmental governance can also be described from various other disciplinary perspectives, such as those of economics and management theory. (In the latter instances it is frequently referred to as 'environmental management'.) This book, however, focuses on only the political science and legal domains, given the already large scope of the enquiry and the undeniable symbioses between law, politics and governance on the one hand, and political science's ability to inform conceptual theoretical frameworks dealing with global regulation on the other.

This multi-disciplinary approach is both intuitive and logical because, as Laferrière and Stoett[51] remind us: '[F]ew serious scholars or policy makers believe, in our day and age, that the connection between environmental problems and international relations ... can be ignored.' Moreover, from a methodological point of view, Slaughter[52] suggests that:

> ... seeing familiar terrain from an unfamiliar angle is often the key to unlock legal creativity. [It] is analogous to shifting intellectual gears, allowing the analyst to incorporate different sets of assumptions about what he or she is actually observing and what the likely outcome will be.

The complexity of environmental problems today is such that it demands a high level of legal creativity, which in turn would require environmental lawyers to wander onto unfamiliar disciplinary terrain as this book does.

8. THE USE OF TERMS AND CONCEPTS

This chapter deliberately does not include a section dealing with the definition and clarification of terms and concepts. Those terms and concepts that are important for the global environmental governance paradigm and that are part

---

[51] Laferrière, Eric and Peter J. Stoett (2006), 'Introduction: Exploring International Ecopolitical Theory' in Eric Laferrière and Peter J. Stoett (eds), *International Ecopolitical Theory: Critical Approaches*, Vancouver: UBC Press, 3.

[52] Slaughter, Anne-Marie (2001), *Recueil des Cours, Collected Courses of the Hague Academy of International Law, 2000: International Law and International Relations*, The Hague: Martinus Nijhoff Publishers, 192.

of the discourse are instead explored throughout this book. However, for the sake of consistency it is useful to point out at this stage that the terms 'governance' and 'regulation' are used interchangeably as meaning the same thing unless the contrary is indicated. The term 'global' refers not only to the international level of governance (as some commentators tend to use it), but throughout this book includes the national, regional and international levels of governance. The 'global' is thus considered to be a space or a context rather than a level. Unless indicated otherwise, the term 'law' is similarly used in its widest sense to include traditional 'harder' or formal forms of state-made law such as treaties and statutes, and also 'softer' non-state yet law-like rules such as voluntary corporate standards and codes of practice. As Chapter 8 explains, the term 'environment' is used to denote a holistic and all-encompassing notion of the environment, which includes but is not limited to the natural environment and its resources; fauna and flora; the environmental media, consisting of water, the air and the soil; all forms of life, including biological and chemical processes; socio-cultural environmental properties; and the man-made environment.

9. OBJECTIVES AND CHRONOLOGY

The previous sections highlighted the need for a comprehensive theoretical treatise on environmental governance, the production of which would no doubt be a daunting scholarly enterprise. This book is more modest in its aims in that it seeks to contribute to clarifying environmental governance by providing a synthesizing analysis of this concept as it manifests globally in the 21st Century in its fourth generational regulatory guise as global environmental governance. In doing so, it has eight specific objectives.

First, the study reflects in Chapter 2 on the phenomenon of globalization as an important informative setting and descriptive context for law, governance, environmental regulation and global environmental governance. It is argued in this chapter that global environmental governance on the one hand is a result of globalization and on the other, conversely, that it contributes to globalization. There is accordingly an inextricable link between globalization and global environmental governance and despite the general view that globalization is 'old hat' it remains a valuable interpretative setting that provides an important context for the sufficient appreciation of contemporary societal constructs and governance phenomena against the realities of a globalized world. This is so because globalization is changing our perceptions about governance and the manner in which we seek to devise and apply regulatory strategies to address global environmental problems. A focus on globalization also permits a broader view of global environmental problems and the link between globalized processes such as increased trade and consumption and the environment. Globalization as the context for global environmental governance is further useful to explain the rise of the global governance phenomenon, the changing role of the state, the emergence of global governance institutions, and the changing role of law in global (environmental) governance.

A second objective of this book is to describe and understand governance, because governance is a vague, amorphous and dangerously malleable concept. It has the potential to create and exacerbate theoretical uncertainty (as it does in the environmental governance and law context). Governance is a much debated and frequently investigated concept, as the burgeoning body of especially political science literature on the topic suggests. Because the mere repetition of this voluminous body of work would be pointless, this book instead aims to provide a broad understanding of governance which could be useful in the environmental regulatory context. It does so in Chapter 3 primarily by means of a multi-disciplinary literature review of the governance construct. The review aims to scrutinize the nature of governance and to establish those of its features and characteristics that would be useful in describing and understanding governance as it manifests in the global environmental context.

Third, proceeding from the description of globalization and governance, the book investigates and describes in Chapter 4 the manner in which governance manifests globally as global governance. It does so by unpacking the general theory of global governance and by focusing on some of its central features, including institutionalism and institutions, regimes, organizations, networks and the many actors involved in global governance. While it does not intend to exhaustively venture on the analytical theories and frameworks of international relations theory (this has been done extensively by others far better equipped to do so) this chapter does seek to provide a succinct review and description of the nature, parameters and foundational building blocks of global governance, and eventually the concept of global governance itself. The chapter is premised on the hypothesis that a comprehensive treatment of the theory of global governance as the fulcrum around which global environmental governance revolves would be key to formulating a proper understanding of global environmental governance.

Chapter 5 discusses the relationship between law and governance and the role that law plays in governance. It reflects on the social function of law, its relationship with other social constructs such as governance, and the manifestation of law in a globalized context. As it deals with the book's fourth objective, it is the primary aim of this chapter to highlight the constitutive, regulative and legitimizing role of law and its steering effect in governance, as well as the rise of more informal and 'softer' versions of non-state law and law-like rules in addition to formal or 'hard', state-based law. For the latter purpose, it extensively discusses the increased pluralization and hybridization of law and emphasizes that globalization and governance require a considerably extended view of law.

Departing from the theory of global governance contained in Chapter 4, Chapter 6 focuses on distinct aspects of global environmental governance. This chapter again highlights the 'globalness' of global environmental governance and it explains the difference between environmental management and environmental governance. As a foundation for the remainder of the chapter, it then seeks to provide a generic description of environmental governance, whereafter it investigates the orthodox legal doctrinal aspects, the public and private aspects, the hybrid aspects, and the multilevel aspects of global environmental governance.

A literature review of current manifestations of global environmental governance is conducted in Chapter 7. This part of the book essentially aims to map the definitional field of global environmental governance with a view to providing a consolidated description of the construct of global environmental governance.

Chapter 8 focuses on the role of regulatory norms, and more specifically law in global environmental governance. Here the study endeavours to fulfil its seventh objective by focusing on the function of law in relation to the environment and the broader global environmental governance effort. It specifically discusses how ideas of the environment influence our idea of law's functions in the context of global environmental governance. This chapter also investigates the steering, legitimizing and constitutive functions of law in relation to global environmental governance and law as a product of global environmental governance. In addition, the chapter investigates the role of 'softer' normative arrangements such as codes of conduct and guidelines as additional and increasingly influential forms of regulatory norms in the domain of global environmental governance. The chapter finally endeavours to provide an account of 'global environmental governance law', which it considers a recently emerging sub-discipline of law and a natural successor to international environmental law.

The final objective of this book is to draw from the insights distilled in the foregoing chapters with a view to proposing in Chapter 9 a consolidated and reconstructed theoretical description of global environmental governance. It concludes that global environmental governance has become a popular concept that has now gained widespread endorsement and is in common use. The concept is based on the pervasive concepts of governance and global governance, and the way it manifests today suggests that the term is used to describe and to make sense of the countless (and growing) institutional arrangements at the international, regional, sub-regional, national and sub-national levels that are responsible for responding to environmental problems. Global environmental governance is also normative to the extent that it consists of intricate political and diplomatic processes; a plethora of legal and law-like instruments such as treaties and their regimes; regional, sub-regional, national and sub-national laws and soft-law arrangements; numerous state and non-state actors; and a host of monitoring, research, information sharing, enforcement and dispute-resolution mechanisms. The primary objective of global environmental governance is to change behaviour with respect to the environment through the foregoing collective mass of institutional arrangements, with the long-term and overarching yet idealistic goal of achieving sustainability.

10. SOME CAVEATS

The book's approach and focus opens numerous angles of enquiry and critique. To fulfil its objectives described above, its approach is descriptive and the enquiry is a meta-theoretical one. The enquiry is also normatively biased towards a critique of environmental governance which is informed by an expectation that environmental governance *should* advance the goal of sustainability. Notably, this expectation figures strongly in a later description of the objectives of environmental governance, which it is argued, are of a pragmatic and idealistic nature.[53] While the pragmatic objective of environmental governance is to change human behaviour *vis-à-vis* the environment, it idealistically seeks to achieve the goals of sustainability.

Notably, this enquiry does not venture on *how* best environmental governance should achieve its objectives, nor does it propose strategies to ameliorate the current environmental governance response. Instead, it accepts that the current environmental governance is probably ineffective to the extent that it does not seem to be able to adequately achieve sustainability and comprehensively to change human behaviour towards the environment.[54] In other words,

---

53 See Chapters 6 and 9.

54 The majority of commentators situates the failures of environmental law and governance among various causes and consequences including: the fragmentary growth of international laws and their concomitant governance structures; the lack of compliance with and enforcement of environmental laws, norms and standards; the lack of or the inadequate participation of civil society in governance and law-making processes; a general lack of good governance practices; the continued prevalence of environmental injustice and the lack of access to justice; the lack of legitimacy of the actors and the democratic deficits in decision-making structures; the obstacles presented by state sovereignty, unilateral decision-making, abuse of authority and the serving of self-interests by states; the difficulties of holding private entities such as

environmental governance is ineffective to the extent that it does not answer to the dictates of what is perceived to be an effective governance system: '[A]n effective governance system is one that channels behavior in such a way as to eliminate or substantially to ameliorate the problem that led to its creation. A governance system that has little behavioral impact, by contrast, is ineffective.'[55] The book nevertheless attempts to provide a better conceptual understanding of environmental governance which should enable other commentators to expand on the important issue of effectiveness.

---

transnational corporations to account for their environmental wrongs; the lack of core ecological and ethical values; and the non-existence, and/or lack of adherence to and enforceability of universal, fundamental environmental rights. Among the many authorities on the failures of environmental governance, see, Chambers, Bradnee W. and Jessica F. Green (eds) (2005), *Reforming International Environmental Governance: From Institutional Limits to Innovative Reforms*, Tokyo: United Nations University Press; DeSombre, Elizabeth R. (2006), *Global Environmental Institutions*, New York: Routledge; Esty, Daniel C. (2007), 'Global Environmental Governance' in Colin I. Bradford and Johannes F. Linn (eds), *Global Governance Reform: Breaking the Stalemate*, Washington, DC: Brookings Institution Press.

55 Young, Oran R. (1994), *International Governance: Protecting the Environment in a Stateless Society*, Ithaca, NY and London: Cornell University Press, 30.

2. The contemporary context of globalization

> As slippery and easily polemicized a conception as globalization has become, it remains seemingly indispensable for the task of identifying several new, aggregative features of international reality that are not encompassed within such traditional categories of state, society or system of states and international institution or organized international community. The idea of globalization is needed to put an emphasis on the special contemporary relevance of forms of behaviour and challenges that have a global scope that cannot be comprehended or addressed adequately by state-centric approaches.[1]
>
> (Richard Falk, 1995)

1. INTRODUCTION

We live in the midst of a truly globalized age; one that is upsetting comfortable, often archaic, orthodox, and trusted notions of society, the state, law, the environment, the manner in which we address social problems (including environmental problems), and the way in which we regulate. While it could easily be described as yesterday's news, globalization remains relevant and indispensable for the task of identifying several new, aggregative features of international reality, as Falk suggests above. Therefore, as with many other contemporary social phenomena vested in a continuously changing and interdependent reality, a discussion of global environmental governance must, if it is to be current, also be situated in the wider context of globalization.

Globalization and governance are inherently intertwined: 'asking whether and how globalization is responded to is asking about governance'.[2] Questions of globalization necessarily concerns *global* governance, because '[G]lobal governance is ... about setting up global institutions that address the changes resulting from globalization.'[3] To be sure, globalization goes to the very heart

[1] Falk, Richard (1995), 'Environmental Protection in an Era of Globalization', *Yearbook of International Environmental Law*, **6**, 3–63 at 4.

[2] Kjær, Anne Mette (2004), *Governance*, Cambridge: Polity Press, 60.

[3] Kjær, Anne Mette (2004), *Governance*, Cambridge: Polity Press, 60.

of governance, because it is changing the landscape of governance. It implies a steady progression towards a new, hitherto undefined global order which affects person-to-person, person-to-the environment and environment-to-environment relationships and the way we contemplate these relationships. Globalization also influences the design of the social constructs that people have created to govern these relationships, including the social constructs of governance and law in a post-modern setting where traditional concepts of government, governance, environmental regulation, and the role of the state and non-state actors are changing fundamentally. In the words of Winchester:[4] '[W]e seem headed toward a new and as yet undefined global order, characterized in part by porous borders and power-sharing among states, non-state actors, and new geographic and/or functional entities.'[5]

More pertinently, globalization itself has environmental dimensions. It leads to a myriad of environmental problems and affects the way society addresses environmental problems. Some attribute the cause of and the increase in global environmental problems to globalization, because processes such as increased trade, the movement of goods and people, industrialization, and resource exploitation all have very tangible impacts on environmental quality and the quality of goods, and services.[6] Environmental problems also undeniably have become global because they are inextricably interconnected and have reciprocal and causal effects, ranging from the local to the supranational levels. The increased 'globalness' of environmental issues is further evidenced by the increased number of environmental challenges pertaining to the shared commons, as well as the global impact of certain complex environmental phenomena such as climate change. Conversely, local environmental problems such as deforestation and desertification are increasingly having an impact far beyond the national borders within which they occur. In this sense, then, environmental concerns and what we perceive as environmental problems, have become 'global'; a point which has already been made in Chapter 1. Global environmental governance is about responding to these changes and

---

4 Winchester, Brian N. (2009), 'Emerging Global Environmental Governance', *Indiana Journal of Global Legal Studies*, **16**(1), 7–23 at 22.

5 Some are of the opinion that 'fundamental precepts upon which international governance was founded, notably the Westphalian system of nation-states and state sovereignty, as well as the state-centeredness of international organizations and institutions are inadequate to meet all the challenges of globalization, and a few are even becoming irrelevant in effect'. Badrinarayana, Deepa (2007), *A New Environmental Order: Laying the Legal and Administrative Foundation for Global Environmental Governance* (S.J.D. dissertation, Pace University School of Law, November) at 8–19 available at http://digitalcommons.pace.edu/cgi/viewcontent.cgi?article=1007&context=lawdissertations [accessed 14 March 2011].

6 See the discussion further below.

addressing the environmental problems resulting from and related to globalization. In other words, the realities of globalization give rise to the need for global environmental governance. At the same time, globalization offers an important context in which to understand governance as a societal response to complex contemporary environmental phenomena, because it is 'the fundamental context within which emerging forms of global environmental governance must operate'.[7]

The focus on the control over environmental problems has shifted from nation-states to supra-national institutions, regimes, and organizations, where not only states but also non-state actors play an increasingly important role in governance. In other words, globalization is changing the way we think about and approach the issue of governance in general and global environmental governance in particular. As Bodansky[8] explains:

> The process of globalization has put mounting strains on the state system. Environmental problems are increasingly escaping the control of individual states and international institutions have often been too weak to step into the breach. The result has been a 'decision-making deficit', an erosion in the ability of government to address environmental problems effectively.

It is against this more general background that this chapter investigates the phenomenon of globalization as giving rise to and as the context for global environmental governance, with a view to broadly illustrating the complicated *global* context in which environmental governance should be understood. The chapter first revisits the conceptual underpinnings of globalization. This section is followed by an investigation of the meaning and implication of 'global' as part of the globalization paradigm and as an important determinant of and context for global environmental governance. The next section focuses on the relationship between globalization and the environment. The discussion then turns to the relationship between globalization and global environmental governance, with the final section focusing on the relevance of globalization for regulatory norms (specifically law) in the context of global environmental governance.

---

7 Paterson, Matthew (1999), 'Interpreting Trends in Global Environmental Governance', *International Affairs*, **75**(4), 793–802 at 800.

8 Bodansky, Daniel (1999), 'The Legitimacy of International Governance: A Coming Challenge for International Environmental Law?', *American Journal of International Law*, **93**(3), 596–624 at 623.

2. SOME THOUGHTS ON '-ATIONISMS'

The study of globalization is a well-trodden field of scholarly enquiry. Nevertheless, establishing a core meaning for this term is by no means an easy task, considering the maelstrom of different descriptions which prevail in a complex multi-disciplinary setting.[9] It is, however, not the purpose of this chapter to provide a standard generally applicable definition. Moreover, it must be emphasized that the complexity of the phenomenon and the urgency of the need for a standard explanation and understanding of globalization should neither be overstated nor overestimated. In fact, the malleability of the term provides us with an opportunity to customize it to suit specific phenomena, contexts, and problems. It is a contextually rich concept which is simultaneously multi-faceted and possibly accommodative of a wide array of considerations that might influence the way we perceive contemporary social realities and social change. As Berman[10] puts it: 'the existence of many different visions of globalization is a fundamental part of globalization itself'. If vagueness therefore is globalization's greatest flaw, it is arguably also its greatest asset.

This chapter argues therefore that there can (or should) not be a uniform definition of globalization that satisfies everyone, because the concept will differ *inter alia* according to the specific scientific discipline that seeks to define it and the varying objectives of the act of definition.[11] Its chameleon-like nature is illustrated by the varying synonyms which often appear in globalization discourse and which frequently are used either as supplementary to globalization and/or as being specific manifestations of globalization. These

---

9 See further, Kumar, Vidya S.A. (2003), 'A Critical Methodology of Globalization: Politics of the 21st Century?', *Indiana Journal of Global Legal Studies*, **2**(10), 87–111 at 90–104.

10 Berman, Paul Schiff (2005), 'From International Law to Law and Globalization', *Columbia Journal of Transnational Law*, **43**(2), 485–556 at 552.

11 As Scholte states:

> ... if asked to specify what they understand by 'globalization', most people reply with considerable vagueness, inconsistency and confusion. Moreover, much discussion of globalization is steeped in oversimplification, exaggeration and wishful thinking. In spite of a deluge of publications on the subject, our analyses of globalization tend to remain conceptually inexact, empirically thin, historically and culturally illiterate, normatively shallow and politically naïve. Although globalization is widely assumed to be crucially important, we generally have scant idea what, more precisely, it entails.

Scholte, Jan Aart (2000), *Globalization: A Critical Introduction*, London: Macmillan Press, 1.

include liberalization, internationalization, unification, homogenization, transnationalization, supra-nationalization, universalization, deterritorialization, westernization, and modernization.[12] What most of these terms have in common is not only the '-ation' suffix but also, generally speaking, the fact that they imply that social processes are progressively traversing state borders and bypassing the traditional locus of state-centred regulation and control in a spontaneous, flexible, self-generating, and bottom-up way in an increasingly interconnected world.[13] They also impart the impression, to a greater or lesser extent, that globalization has at a minimum to do with 'the intensification of global interconnectedness, in which capital, people, commodities, images, and ideologies move across distance and physical boundaries with increasing speed and frequency'.[14] In other words, these terms imply that social processes are increasingly moving beyond the nation state, state boundaries and traditional actors in nation-state-centred systems of social ordering and regulation.

3. CHARACTERISTICS OF GLOBALIZATION

Mindful of Kumar's[15] cautionary note that 'it would be a difficult, if not indomitable, task to completely capture the multiplicity of meanings connoted by the term "globalization"', the remaining part of this section attempts instead a generic description of globalization's characteristics.

In its most basic form, globalization is 'a process of the world becoming a single place'.[16] Applied to different contexts it is, however, much more than this and could be 'the emergence and spread of a supra-national dimension of social relations' in institutional, ecological,[17] economical, normative and

---

12 Scholte, Jan Aart (2000), *Globalization: A Critical Introduction*, London: Macmillan Press, 15–16; Shams, Heba (2001), 'Law in the Context of "Globalisation": a Framework of Analysis', *The International Lawyer*, **35**(4), 1589–626 at 1592–3.

13 Ladeur, Karl-Heinz (2004), 'Globalization and Public Governance: A Contradiction?' in Karl-Heinz Ladeur (ed), *Public Governance in the Age of Globalization*, Aldershot: Ashgate, 5.

14 Berman, Paul Schiff (2005), 'From International Law to Law and Globalization', *Columbia Journal of Transnational Law*, **43**(2), 485–556 at 552.

15 Kumar, Vidya S.A. (2003), 'A Critical Methodology of Globalization: Politics of the 21st Century?', *Indiana Journal of Global Legal Studies*, **2**(10), 87–111 at 88.

16 Scholte, Jan Aart (1996), 'Beyond the Buzzword: Towards a Critical Theory of Globalization' in Eleonore Kofman and Gillian Youngs (eds), *Globalization: Theory and Practice*, London: Pinter, 43.

17 For present purposes it might suggest that environmental governance is itself becoming increasingly globalized, or becoming global because of globalization, espe-

psychological terms.[18] Kumar's compact survey of the different meanings of the term in the sociological, economic, legal, political, and social contexts is useful. Drawing from the work of various scholars, the author suggests that globalization in the foregoing contexts entails, for instance: increased social integration and the increased transnational autonomy of nation states; increased and more complex global decision-making; the connection of local strategies to supra-national concerns; a more pronounced concept of the world as a whole and thus of world unity; a growth in global trade and foreign direct investment, production and consumption; diminishing state sovereignty and the dilution of traditional concepts of the state and forms of regulation; increased inter-dependence between national economies; denationalization of political, economic and social activities; increased interconnectedness between societies; and a deepening phase of capitalism.[19] Mansbach[20] adds to this list what he calls various 'interrelated features of globalization', which in most instances correspond to and in others expand on those of Kumar. These features include: shrinking geographical distances and thus a diminishing role for territory; the spread of knowledge and skills and the expansion of political awareness and participation; the growth of capitalism and the emergence of a global market beyond state boundaries; the spread of a global culture; the spread of democracy; the expansion of global civil society; the growth of complex transnational linkages; the diffusion of global power; increased environmental degradation; the erosion of state autonomy and sovereignty; the increased spread of non-state identities; growing acceptance of the importance of human rights; and a changing definition and importance of security. In this sense, globalization describes the modern reality of a new, global world order. However, globalization as described here also relates to the effects or results of globalized processes. In other words, globalization refers to the processes of 'becoming global' and the results that these processes of 'becoming global' may possibly lead to. In the environmental context these may include, for

---

cially if one considers the growing body of 'global environmental law' as some call it. See, for example, Percival, Robert V. (2009), 'Fifteenth Annual Lloyd K. Garrison Lecture on Environmental Law: The Globalization of Environmental Law', *Pace Environmental Law Review*, **26**, 451–64, and the discussion in Chapter 8.

[18] Scholte, Jan Aart (1996), 'Beyond the Buzzword: Towards a Critical Theory of Globalization' in Eleonore Kofman and Gillian Youngs (eds), *Globalization: Theory and Practice*, London: Pinter, 46.

[19] Kumar, Vidya S.A. (2003), 'A Critical Methodology of Globalization: Politics of the 21st Century?', *Indiana Journal of Global Legal Studies*, **2**(10), 87–111 at 93–100.

[20] Mansbach, Richard W. (2010), 'Globalization, East Asia, and the Future of Global Politics' in Peter Yu Kien-hong, Emily Chow and Shawn S.F. Kao (eds), *International Governance, Regimes and Globalization: Case Studies from Beijing and Taipei*, Maryland: Lexington Books, 142–52.

example, increased risks of ocean pollution, the spread of alien invasive species as a result of increased world trade and shipping, and an increase in the number of resource-extracting multinational companies all over the world and their environmental impacts.

Shams[21] finds that globalization is mostly about change that occurs in a spatial sense, and that it therefore has a geographical connotation. It does not, however, operate exclusively in this geographic setting, since it also refers to social change when it is used to emphasize changing social relations, the diminishing role of the state in governance at the national and supra-national levels, and the extension of regulation beyond traditional modes of (mostly state-centred) governance. Globalization is thus part of the processes of social change where 'spatial change and its accompanying consciousness [are] core features of the process'.[22] Social change could refer to continuously changing patterns of human behaviour in society; a process which is itself fraught with complexities in the sense that social change can be fast or slow, incremental or comprehensive, revolutionary or cumulative. Clearly, then, globalization involves some form of spatial change and concomitantly manifests in the manner that people perceive the spatial changes that affect their social relationships and behaviour:

> Globalisation is a process of social change that is identified with and substantially triggered by a change in the space within which we conduct our social relations. Both the objective geographical change and the subjective consciousness of this change are defining elements of this process.[23]

Casting globalization in terms of social change is useful because it obviates the need to trace the exact point in time when globalization first emerged.[24] Social change is as old as time, it is currently happening, and it will always occur in future as long as people exist to perceive this change. In this sense, then, globalization is as recent as it is ancient. Nevertheless, the process is much more pronounced today than, say, a thousand years ago. This is because of various factors which are leading to a more interconnected world, such as the advent of efficient transnational telecommunications and the increase in international trade.

---

21 Shams, Heba (2001), 'Law in the Context of "Globalisation": a Framework of Analysis', The International Lawyer, **35**(4), 1589–626 at 1594–5.

22 Shams, Heba (2001), 'Law in the Context of "Globalisation": a Framework of Analysis', *The International Lawyer*, **35**(4), 1589–626 at 1595.

23 Shams, Heba (2001), 'Law in the Context of "Globalisation": a Framework of Analysis', *The International Lawyer*, **35**(4), 1589–626 at 1599.

24 In so doing one is able to sidestep the cumbersome debate on the exact historical origins of globalization. For a brief overview in this respect see Scholte, Jan Aart (2000), *Globalization: A Critical Introduction*, London: Macmillan Press, 19.

Whether this process of social change is old or new is perhaps less relevant than the realization that globalization does not replace existing social constructs such as law and governance, for example. Scholte[25] importantly notes in this respect that:

> ... globalization has not displaced deeper social structures in relation to production (capitalism), governance (the state and bureaucratism more generally), community (the nation and communitarianism more generally) and knowledge (rationalism) but globalization has prompted important changes to certain attributes of capital, the state, the nation and modern rationality.

In other words, globalization has changed only some social structures and constructs (for better or for worse), or certain attributes of these social structures. Globalization has also changed the way people perceive these structures and constructs and engage with them. It is therefore not a new phenomenon that seeks to replace deeply entrenched social structures such as law and governance, but rather a phenomenon which fundamentally influences these social structures and the manner in which people view and interact with them.

Globalization has also influenced the social structure of governance in relation to the environment in many ways. Its processes and their effects have a physical impact on the environment; it necessitates a change in the traditionally conceived and orthodox role of the state in a post-Westphalian (global) world and thus the manner in which the state plays a role in governing environmental issues; and it provides an analytical tool for better understanding social and environmental change in a new world order or a state of affairs with a view to also explaining the occurrence of certain phenomena and simultaneously informing the contextualization and design of responses to these phenomena. The latter point suggests that globalization is a lens through which to view the world and as such it is especially useful in our attempts to understand social realities and the responses by social structures to the effects of these social changes on human life. In terms of this view, globalization is not so much a process as it is a specific analytic perspective and a tool that one could use to analyse and understand contemporary societal phenomena. In the environmental context, globalization could thus assist us to understand the modern realities of global environmental change and those societal constructs, such as global environmental governance, that people create to address the problems stemming from globalized social realities. As a result, in addition to describing a process globalization is also a critical perspective that provides us with the opportunity to view and understand global environmental change and

---

25 Scholte, Jan Aart (2000), *Globalization: A Critical Introduction*, London: Macmillan Press, 8.

to appreciate more fully the way in which people are perceiving and attempting to govern global environmental issues.

4. DEFINING THE 'GLOBAL'

This book focuses on *global* environmental governance and the meaning of the term 'global' has already been briefly stated in Chapter 1. However, given its centrality to the present theme, some further elaboration of the meaning of 'global' in the context of globalization is merited here. As a point of departure, Paterson, Humphreys and Pettiford[26] helpfully point out that:

> ... it is in the conflict over how we understand 'global' that most differences of interpretation [of global environmental governance] arise ... this ranges from the use of 'global' in lieu of international ... through to the use of 'global' to mean deterritorialized ... These differences reflect a range of uses more general in academic and popular usages of the term, where global is variously taken simply as a synonym for international (the sum of things which occur across state borders), or as a description for those things which occur everywhere, through to more coherent conceptualizations of global as a distinct phase of capitalist development, or a spatial reorganization of politics involving a decline in the relevance of territory.

Considering the meaning of globalization as discussed earlier 'global', perhaps not surprisingly, has its roots in the setting of globalization. Global in this context could mean what Ford[27] calls an 'orthodox spatial definition', where it is used as a 'causal category' that posits: 'environmental degradation is global because it is caused by social, economic and political relationships and structures that are global'.[28] It is worth pointing here to the old but true cliché which holds that environmental problems know no boundaries. They are global: '[T]here is thus no single sense in which an environmental issue can be described as "international": it could be global, regional, transbound-

---

26 Paterson, Matthew, David Humphreys and Lloyd Pettiford (2003), 'Conceptualizing Global Environmental Governance: From Interstate Regimes to Counter-hegemonic Struggles', *Global Environmental Politics*, **3**(2), 1–10 at 4.

27 Ford, Lucy H. (2005), 'Challenging the Global Environmental Governance of Toxics: Social Movement Agency and Global Civil Society' in David L. Levy and Peter J. Newell (eds), *The Business of Global Environmental Governance*, Cambridge, Massachusetts: MIT Press, 307.

28 Ford, Lucy H. (2005), 'Challenging the Global Environmental Governance of Toxics: Social Movement Agency and Global Civil Society' in David L. Levy and Peter J. Newell (eds), *The Business of Global Environmental Governance*, Cambridge, Massachusetts: MIT Press, 307.

ary, domestic, or a combination of all or any of these.'[29] When considered in the context of globalization, this would entail that what occurs at the sub-national level could have an effect on what happens at the sub-regional, regional and international levels and vice versa. Global, thus described, therefore by implication refers to the local, national, regional and international both in a spatial and causal sense.

In addition, Ivanova[30] explains that 'governing human relations has become a complicated endeavor that has transcended the national and interstate scale and moved to a global level involving multiple actors across national borders and multiple levels of regulatory authority – from sub-national to supranational.' Global in this context refers to de-territorialization; it indicates, among others things, that governance can occur at all levels simultaneously. By implication, de-territorialization means that governments and states will not always be the sole actors involved in governance. Global therefore also implies multi-level and multi-actor governance where the state and government are often not the predominant role players and where the focus is shifting to the important contribution of non-state actors that operate on different levels and in other ways. To be sure, then, 'the word "global" is used as much for its geographical connotation as it is used for its omission of the state'[31] and for referring to the causal effects of globalized processes. When one considers the term 'global' in the environmental context, it becomes possible to employ it to describe a whole range of multi-level, reciprocal and interconnected environmental issues, governance levels and state and non-state actors, which manifest in a multi-level spatial (geographic) and causal setting that could be described as a complex, intertwined global mass.

5. THE ENVIRONMENT AND GLOBALIZATION

The literature is replete with analyses focusing on the relationship between globalization and the environment, and more specifically on the effects of globalization on the environment. While this section does not duplicate these

---

29 Birnie, Patricia, Alan Boyle and Catherine Redgwell (2009), *International Law and the Environment* 3rd edn, Oxford: Oxford University Press, 9. This is also because of the nature of the environment and environmental problems, which makes them hard to define in a legal-political context. See, further, Chapter 8.

30 Ivanova, Maria H., *Partnerships, International Organizations, and Global Environmental Governance* at 9 available at http://www.gppi.net/fileadmin/gppi/Ivanova_Article.pdf [accessed 11 March 2011].

31 Shams, Heba (2001), 'Law in the Context of "Globalisation": a Framework of Analysis', *The International Lawyer*, **35**(4), 1589–626 at 1626.

findings, for the purpose of context it is worth briefly reflecting on this relationship in addition to what has already been stated earlier in this chapter.

Keohane and Nye[32] point out that '[T]he oldest form of globalization is environmental: climate change has affected the ebb and flow of human populations for millions of years ... Today, human impact on global climate change could affect the lives of people everywhere.' 'Environmental globalism', as they call it, is therefore as relevant today as it was in earlier times, and when considered in the broader context of globalization, it is arguably responsible for coming into being of 'new' forms of environmental regulatory interventions and approaches such as global environmental governance. Duffy[33] reminds us in this respect that:

> Globalisation has meant that states and societies have been incorporated into complex global networks that have directly impacted on the environment and on the ability of states to manage natural resources at a local level ... Global politics is entering a new phase of turbulence where centralising and decentralising tendencies operate simultaneously and are fundamentally altering the identity and authority of an increasingly diverse number of [environmental] actors on the world stage. In short *the politics of everywhere affects the politics of everywhere else.*

An expansive definition of the 'environment', which this book proposes in Chapter 8, would by implication necessarily incorporate environmental concerns into the globalization paradigm. This is so because the global environment and its constitutive elements are in many ways the objects of globalization and are affected in one way or another by the processes of globalization and the resultant institutional responses that society is creating to address global environmental problems. When viewed as including planetary life-support systems such as the stratosphere, the environment has distinct global properties, which means that it could be affected by all things global. Additionally, in terms of a social ecological perspective, various anthropogenic ecological changes also have global environmental, political and social consequences.[34] This link is further explained by recent trends in (or characteristics of) contemporary globalization, all of which have an impact on the environment to a greater or lesser extent: globalization is changing the

---

32 Keohane, Robert O. and Joseph S. Nye (2002), 'Governance in a Globalizing World' in Robert O. Keohane (ed), *Power and Governance in a Partially Globalized World*, London: Routledge, 195.

33 Duffy, Rosaleen (2005), 'The Politics of Global Environmental Governance: the Powers and Limitations of Transfrontier Conservation Areas in Central America', *Review of International Studies*, **31**, 307–23 at 307. Emphasis added.

34 Scholte, Jan Aart (2000), *Globalization: A Critical Introduction*, London: Macmillan Press, 54.

business environment by dispersing production patterns all over the world; the nature of production processes and trade is changing and this places unprecedented strain on environmental resources; and the gains resulting from globalization are not distributed equally within and between countries, giving rise to environmental injustice that manifest as the so-called North-South divide.[35] In other words, globalization and its processes and the institutional responses to the effects of globalization are all fundamentally affecting the environment for the better or for the worse. This means that perhaps the most evident link between globalization and the environment lies in the impact that globalization has on the environment, its goods, quality, and services. Sonnenfeld[36] states:

> ... in this time of hyper-economic globalisation, which includes the acceleration of trade from the world's factories and farms into our homes and onto our dining tables, never before has the commoditised exchange and consumption of goods and services been so great – with large accompanying risks, health and environmental impacts, and regulatory strains, gaps, and gaping holes.

Sonnenfeld later notes that because of this, '[O]ur world of rapid social, institutional, and environmental change is desperately in need of new insights.'[37] One might intuitively speculate that environmental change is an important catalyst for and cause and effect of broader social change which, in turn, necessitates our developing new insights into and novel approaches to how people address environmental change through societal responses such as laws, governance institutions and other regulatory arrangements. While people cannot control nature, the environment, and natural processes, we are able to mitigate anthropogenic impacts on the environment and to adapt to changing social circumstances as a result of environmental change through the social constructs we design and implement. As this book argues in later chapters, law

---

35 OECD, *Environment and Globalisation: Background Report for Ministers – Meeting of the Environment Policy Committee at Ministerial Level, Environment and Global Competitiveness* [ENV/EPOC(2007)18/FINAL] 5–7 available at http://www.oecd.org/dataoecd/3/59/40511624.pdf [accessed 21 April 2011].

36 Sonnenfeld, David A. (2008), 'Globalisation and Environmental Governance: Is Another World Possible?', *Global Environmental Change*, **18**, 341–2 at 341. Kütting also confirms that: '[T]he global nature of environmental degradation can largely be linked to the rise of the fossil fuel economy and the decreasing distance of time and space in the relations between different parts of the globe ... These phenomena are intrinsically linked to the rise of modern capitalism.' Kütting, Gabriela (2004), 'Globalization and the Environment: Moving Beyond Neoliberal Institutionalism', *International Journal of Peace Studies*, **9**(1), 29–46 at 35.

37 Sonnenfeld, David A. (2008), 'Globalisation and Environmental Governance: Is Another World Possible?', *Global Environmental Change*, **18**, 341–2 at 341.

and governance are two essential components of this social institutional response.[38]

Paradoxically, globalization is both good and bad for the environment.[39] The logic is simple: on the one hand, globalization is manifestly bad for the environment if one considers that it causes increased resource exploitation, population growth and consumption, industrialization and trade. On the other, globalization is also good for the environment because it provides opportunities for increased global environmental awareness and reactive responses to global environmental problems, including the creation of non-state actors, regimes, institutions and organizations which must respond to global environmental problems.[40] Other 'positive' impacts of globalization on the environment include: the transfer and spread of more efficient, cleaner technologies and goods; cross-border environmental learning, capacity and norm building; a more efficient allocation of production means,[41] and the emergence of a more coherent order of global environmental governance law.[42] Globalization, its processes and their effects therefore not only create environmental problems but also provide opportunities and the means to address these problems. As a response and in tandem with these various non-sequential 'environmental events' have marked the last part of the 20th Century such as the rise of global environmental concern and awareness;[43] increased global environmen-

---

38 See Chapters 3–8.

39 The paradoxical effect of globalization is not peculiar and limited only to environmental issues. See further Lee, Robert and Elen Stokes (2009), 'Environmental Governance: Reconnecting the Global and Local', *Journal of Law and Society*, **36**(1), 1–10 at 1–2.

40 Blanco and Razzaque attribute the emergence of environmental concepts such as sustainable development and corporate social responsibility, and their growing importance and popularity to globalization. These concepts herald new thinking in environmental regulation and have 'enabled the emergence of a consensus on the limitations of continued growth and the need for an integration of sustainability models within the economic system'. Blanco, Elena and Jona Razzaque (2011), *Globalisation and Natural Resources Law: Challenges, Key Issues and Perspectives*, Cheltenham: Edward Elgar Publishing, 82.

41 Zarsky, Lyuba (1997), 'The Asia-Pacific Economic Cooperation Forum and the Environment: Regional Environmental Governance in the Age of Economic Globalization', *Colorado Journal of International Environmental Law and Policy*, **8**(2), 323–57 at 337.

42 See Chapter 8.

43 Environmental problems such as soil erosion, pollution, deforestation and over-fishing have not universally been perceived as problems or concerns which require a collective and co-ordinated response, but they are now seen to be such, mainly because human values, perceptions and consciousness have changed. Bodansky, Daniel (2010), *The Art and Craft of International Environmental Law*, Cambridge, Massachusetts: Harvard University Press, 19.

tal cooperation; and increased global environmental norm and regime creation. Globalization accordingly collectively describes the global context and response that has led to and continues to contribute to increased global environmental degradation, and it explains the increased supra-national awareness and cooperative global responses devised to address the threats to the global environment.[44]

6. GLOBALIZATION AND GOVERNANCE

Arguments concerning the relationship between globalization and the governance phenomenon usually follow three distinct yet complementary pathways. Proponents of the first contend that globalization provides an interpretative context for governance; a contemporary setting for the development and use of postmodern analytical terms that seek to explain social realities. The second and more dominant strand posits that globalization is transforming orthodox concepts of governance to the extent that the state (and coercive forms of hard law for the purpose of regulation) is increasingly playing a less central role. The third line of argument in the globalization-governance interplay is that globalization contributes to the steady growth in global bureaucratic machinery which aims to govern globalization, its processes and their effects. Globalization is thus an important source of global bureaucracy which in turn is an important ingredient of global governance. While this chapter has already briefly touched on some of these issues, it now proceeds to analyse the relationship between globalization and governance in greater detail.

6.1 A New Contextual Setting and Interpretative Context

Some commentators propose that globalization's 'globalness' and everything that it represents provide a vital interpretative context for understanding developments that have occurred in its wake.[45] Globalization has become an important 'part of the established conceptual vocabulary for addressing social relations on a global scale'.[46] In this sense, globalization 'fill[s] the "void" left

---

[44] Percival, Robert V. (2009), 'Fifteenth Annual Lloyd K. Garrison Lecture on Environmental Law: The Globalization of Environmental Law', *Pace Environmental Law Review*, **26**, 451–64 at 456–60.

[45] Falk, Richard (1995), 'Environmental Protection in an Era of Globalization', *Yearbook of International Environmental Law*, **6**, 3–63 at 4.

[46] Kofman, Eleonore and Gillian Youngs (1996), 'Introduction: Globalization – the Second Wave' in Eleonore Kofman and Gillian Youngs (eds), *Globalization: Theory and Practice*, London: Pinter, 1.

by the collapse of Cold War frameworks for understanding the world',[47] and illuminates our understanding of social change as far as governance is concerned.

As a result, globalization sets the contextual scene for the development of umbrella terms more in tune with today's society; terms with a fancier political ring to them; terms which, in the environmental context, collectively describe the need to better understand social interaction with the environment, the effects of human behaviour on the environment, and ways to better respond to global environmental problems. Global environmental governance, as was indicated in Chapter 1, is one of these concepts and institutional responses which seek to acknowledge that environmental issues and the way they affect people are a reality. Issues of global environmental change are also of special contemporary relevance and must be understood and explained by theoretical approaches that rise above contextually-constrained descriptions that are limited by a strong dependence on traditional concepts and approaches to regulation and concepts of the state, governance and normative regulatory mechanisms such as law.

6.2 A Reallocation of Authority and the Transforming State

The relationship between governance and globalization is further explained by the second more pronounced and popular view, which holds that globalization points to a new state of global governance, which Koskenniemi[48] calls 'the increasing management of the world's affairs by flexible and informal, non-territorial networks within which decisions can be made rapidly and effectively'. In this sense globalization is important for governance, since it 'invokes not government, but *governance*, a spontaneous process, pushed by private interests and actors in a thoroughly pragmatic process, accountable to no functional equivalent of a public realm but to an amorphous aggregate of stakeholders'.[49] Also, from a public international law perspective:

> The governance mindset proposes a new vocabulary to replace the law's antiquated one: globalization, ethics, democracy, market. These are words whose meanings it

---

[47] Kofman, Eleonore and Gillian Youngs (1996), 'Introduction: Globalization – the Second Wave' in Eleonore Kofman and Gillian Youngs (eds), *Globalization: Theory and Practice*, London: Pinter, 6. Dingwerth, Klaus and Philipp Pattberg (2006), 'Was ist Global Governance?', *Leviathan*, **34**(3), 377–99 at 396.

[48] Koskenniemi, Martti (2004), 'Global Governance and Public International Law', *Kritische Justiz*, **37**, 241–54 at 243.

[49] Koskenniemi, Martti (2004), 'Global Governance and Public International Law', *Kritische Justiz*, **37**, 241–54 at 243.

> [the governance mindset] can control due to its predominant position in the deformalised, fragmented and imperial institutions that manage its rationality-regimes.[50]

That globalization is increasingly contributing to enriching and concretizing the governance as opposed to the government mindset is also evident from the gradual erosion of the autonomous, all-powerful and sovereign Westphalian concept of the state. This is so because the concept of government is 'closely associated with the sovereign state even if it includes certain non-state forms of exercising political power'.[51] While government implies a certain measure of binding decision-making as part of a political process, governance denotes a 'softer' and more flexible approach in which private or non-state actors and forms of regulation play an important role. Governance in a globalized context is thus much less structured than orthodox government because it:

> ... takes up the new forms of permeability of the state, which establish themselves beyond the more structured relationships between state and society in the 'corporate state' which has stable relationships with large/major 'representative' organizations. The new paradigm of 'openness' of governmental decision-making procedures towards societal influences is much less structured than it used to be in the past.[52]

The foregoing suggests that, as mere concepts, government and governance have quite distinct meanings attributed to them. While the former implies a more coercive, strict and formal exercise of power and forms of regulation, the latter is usually perceived as being a softer, unstructured, private, more flexible and/or informal manner in which authority is exercised and society regulated; a point which is further explained in Chapter 3. It is primarily newly emerging patterns of networks of inter-relationships caused as a result of globalization that are responsible for the emergence of non-state agents and with them, softer and more informal forms of regulation in the form of governance.[53]

The foregoing suggests that in the context of globalization governance is a concept of institutional intervention that lacks concreteness. It is not concrete in the sense that it is deliberately open and flexible, and 'it takes into account

---

50 Koskenniemi, Martti (2004), 'Global Governance and Public International Law', *Kritische Justiz*, **37**, 241–54 at 252.

51 Ladeur, Karl-Heinz (2004), 'Globalization and Public Governance: A Contradiction?' in Karl-Heinz Ladeur (ed), *Public Governance in the Age of Globalization*, Aldershot: Ashgate, 10.

52 Ladeur, Karl-Heinz (2004), 'Globalization and Public Governance: A Contradiction?' in Karl-Heinz Ladeur (ed), *Public Governance in the Age of Globalization*, Aldershot: Ashgate, 10.

53 Berman, Paul Schiff (2005), 'From International Law to Law and Globalization', *Columbia Journal of Transnational Law*, **43**(2), 485–556 at 500–507.

that, both at national and at transnational level, there is no clear separation between public and private, and that forms of public and private ordering overlap and become exchangeable'.[54] Governance not only implies government (in concrete terms) but also supposes a mass of regulatory arrangements and actors operating on different levels. These arrangements are also relevant to the environment. Ellis and Wood[55] thus explain that the challenges resulting from ecosystem interdependence and globalization are significant challenges of governance because: '[T]here is no *government* at the international level consisting of centralised structures for the promulgation, implementation and enforcement of laws and policies, but there are governance structures that serve these ends'. The realities of global environmental problems are such that it would be difficult to speak of a global government for the environment, simply because, first, there is no such government and second, in the absence of such a world environmental government and in addition to the formal role of states, various flexible and open-ended non-state actors and their governance arrangements exist, which could be used instead of a powerful, coercive, centralized (world) government. This helpfully explains the emergence and existence of *global environmental governance* as a specific form of regulation that is to be preferred in the absence of a single *world environmental government.*

In the light of the foregoing, it is clear that globalization provides the modern setting for governance and in many respects has changed and is still changing the face of governance.[56] Globalization is the instigator of new forms of deformalized, private-public governance which manifestly challenge the traditional state-centred, nation-focused Westphalian model of governance, where the principle of state sovereignty reigns supreme. As a result, governance is gradually becoming multi-layered in the sense that '[A]uthority is increasingly diffused across substate ... and superstate ... agencies as well as

---

[54] Ladeur, Karl-Heinz (2004), 'Globalization and Public Governance: A Contradiction?' in Karl-Heinz Ladeur (ed), *Public Governance in the Age of Globalization*, Aldershot: Ashgate, 17.

[55] Ellis, Jaye and Stepan Wood (2006), 'International Environmental Law' in Benjamin J. Richardson and Stepan Wood (eds), *Environmental Law for Sustainability: A Reader*, Portland: Hart Publishing, 345.

[56] Campbell similarly finds that '[G]lobalization ... has dramatically changed the context in which environmental governance takes place.' Campbell, Laura B. (2004), 'The Effectiveness of the WTO and WIPO: Lessons for Environmental Governance?' in Norichika Kanie and Peter M. Haas (eds), *Emerging Forces in Environmental Governance*, Tokyo: United Nations University Press, 51. See also Hierlmeier, Jodie (2002), 'UNEP: Retrospect and Prospect – Options for Reforming the Global Environmental Governance Regime', *Georgetown International Environmental Law Review*, **14**, 767–805 at 777–8.

state organs',[57] and state sovereignty is concomitantly diminishing at a steady rate.[58] Yet this diffusion should not be overemphasized:

> ... globalization does not abolish the state, but transforms it by making it more permeable for the observation and registration of the discontinuous effects emerging in a world economy which can no longer be 'steered' by supposedly stable and continuous international treaties which allow for stable exchange between otherwise separate economies.[59]

In a globalized era, the state is therefore as relevant as it has always been; it is merely repositioning and reconfiguring its traditional work through a process of privatization and de-nationalization.[60] This transformation of state-centred governance is a phenomenon that is characterized by a disaggregated process of increased multilateralism, where non-state actors such as civil society are steadily obtaining increased autonomy from states to act with an unprecedented measure of influence in numerous regulatory processes.[61] This mix

---

[57] Scholte, Jan Aart (2000), *Globalization: A Critical Introduction*, London: Macmillan Press, 22.

[58] See, for example, Kütting, Gabriela (2004), 'Globalization and the Environment: Moving beyond Neoliberal Institutionalism', *International Journal of Peace Studies*, **9**(1), 29–46 at 32.

[59] Ladeur, Karl-Heinz (2004), 'Globalization and Public Governance: A Contradiction?' in Karl-Heinz Ladeur (ed), *Public Governance in the Age of Globalization*, Aldershot: Ashgate, 11.

[60] Sassen, Saskia (2004), 'De-nationalized State Agendas and Privatized Normmaking' in Karl-Heinz Ladeur (ed), *Public Governance in the Age of Globalization*, Aldershot: Ashgate, 51. Venter also suggests that the state will remain an essential, if not the most essential, actor at the global level, not least because the state is the only entity which can conceivably create a space to create law that aims to regulate international relations. Any pleas for its demise would thus be premature:

> Om die staat in die huidige tydsgewrig as 'n krimpende verskynsel te beskou wat hardnekkig vasklou aan sy soewereiniteit om die kragte van globalisering te weerstaan, is nie realisties nie. Diegene wat die staat voortydig afskryf neem nie die onontbeerlikheid daarvan in ag nie: dit bly steeds die belangrikste instelling wat 'n ruimte daarstel waarbinne reg geskep en toegepas word en waarop die volkereg as regulerende orde primêr tussen state van toepassing is.

Venter, Francois (2008), 'Die Staat, Staatsreg en Globalisering', *Tydskrif vir die Suid-Afrikaanse Reg*, **3**, 412–24 at 415.

[61] Scholte, Jan Aart (2000), *Globalization: A Critical Introduction*, London: Macmillan Press, 22. Lee and Stokes speak of hybrid forms of regulation, and new and multi-level governance in this respect. Lee, Robert and Elen Stokes (2009), 'Environmental Governance: Reconnecting the Global and Local', *Journal of Law and Society*, **36**(1), 1–10 at 3.

between state and non-state forms of governance is often described as hybrid governance, where the state and increasingly private or non-state parties play an important, often complementary role in addressing issues of global common concern.[62]

As Chapter 4 will explain, globalization is therefore a direct cause of global governance and its 'new' forms of hybrid, decentralized and deformalized regulation that now transcend the role of the hollowed-out state and it increasingly sees the emergence of a wide variety of non-state actors such as civil society and multinational corporations operating on multiple levels.[63] The term 'hollowed-out state' in this context is dramatic yet deliberate and instructive, because it suggests that state authority and influence are being transformed to some extent, together with the state's mandate, ability and capacity to steer from the top downwards. This would mean 'the ability of central government to give direction to society has been weakened'[64] and that the steering function of governance is increasingly derived from elsewhere to complement state-centred efforts. In short, in this sense globalization is about the reallocation of authority and about reconceptualizing and necessarily at the same time redesigning traditional manifestations of governance and the role of

---

62 See further, on the issue generally, Erman, Eva and Anders Uhlin (eds), *Legitimacy Beyond the State? Re-examining the Democratic Credentials of Transnational Actors*, Basingstoke: Palgrave Macmillan; and Chapters 4 and 6 of the present book.

63 In fact:

> While states may still be willing and able to re-assert their authority when private and hybrid governance systems stray too far from the goals of powerful governments, these new forms of governance currently engage in standard setting and regulation, policy coordination, knowledge generation and dissemination, and service provision.

Bernstein, Steven (2005), 'Globalization and the Requirements of "Good" Environmental Governance', *Perspectives on Global Development and Technology*, **4**(3/4), 645–79 at 648.

64 Kjær, Anne Mette (2004), *Governance*, Cambridge: Polity Press, 32. Kjær explains the term 'hollowing out' in this context as follows:

> The centre [central government] is becoming hollow because of three tendencies: (i) the core executive is losing or conceding capacities to societal actors; (ii) the core executive is losing or conceding its capacity to other state actors; and (iii) the core executive is losing or conceding capacities to supra-state entities ... The first two points refer to the state's internal hollowing out, while the latter refers to the state's external hollowing out. External hollowing out refers to the loss of authority that occurs because of globalization, that is, the global market makes economic decision-making less autonomous.

the state and non-state actors in governance. Globalization in this context is therefore about the transformation of the state and changing the face of global governance.

6.3 Globalization and Increased Bureaucracy

It has been explained that globalization is reconceptualizing governance (from the state-centred to the multi-layered and hybrid) within a specific context. Together with the hybridization of governance, globalization has concomitantly increased the bureaucratic element of global governance. Bureaucracy or administration is a necessary element especially of state-centred governance; it is what makes public governance work, as it were. According to Scholte:[65]

> Neither the diffusion of public-sector authority nor the growth of private-sector regulation has displaced bureaucracy as the underlying principle of modern administration. Under a structure of bureaucratism, governance is mainly conducted through large-scale, relatively permanent, formally organized, impersonally managed and hierarchically ordered decision-making procedures. The post-sovereign state, substate bodies, suprastate organs and nonstate regulatory agencies have all in the great majority of cases reproduced rather than challenged the general bureaucratic framework of administration. If anything, bureaucratism is more pervasive and stronger than ever in the present-day globalizing world.

This increase in global bureaucracy can be attributed among other things to the mushrooming of state and non-state governance rules, structures, governors and governance procedures on multiple levels, as was shown earlier. The transformation and aggregation of governance through globalization therefore means that an increasing number of sources of bureaucracy are being created and that a change in the foundation, nature, and concept of governance would mean not only a change in how the bureaucracy conducts itself but would also explain the cumulative growth of bureaucracy alongside the gradual expansion of governance. In other words: if globalization and its processes are understood to mean the impetus for exponential growth in the regulatory (governance) machinery that is used to govern global regulatory problems, then it must follow that globalization, because it leads to the establishment of various regulatory structures and various actors (themselves sources of and actors in bureaucracy), is also an important source of global bureaucracy. In this sense, the rise in and expansion of governance in terms of a burgeoning bureaucracy, especially in a global context, is not only a result of globalization but also simultaneously a cause of globalization.

---

[65] Scholte, Jan Aart (2000), *Globalization: A Critical Introduction*, London: Macmillan Press, 133.

6.4 Globalization and Governance: Reciprocity and the Sources of Mutual Growth

The foregoing reciprocity could be further explained as follows: while it is evident that globalization has caused fundamental changes in the way global governance is conceptualized and is occurring, it is also true that global governance, its processes, institutions and mechanisms are at the same time causing globalization or at least the conditions for globalized processes to thrive. It is especially regulatory frameworks created primarily by states, but increasingly also by non-state actors such as civil society, which provide fertile ground for globalization to flourish.[66] States and global non-state actors set rules with a view to regulating the issues stemming from globalization:

> There is no such thing as an unregulated social context, and no social change takes place in the absence of rules that stimulate, facilitate and confirm the transformations. In the case of globalization, too, various legal and institutional arrangements have played a key enabling role.[67]

It is these rules, institutions, organizations, and other governance arrangements that pave the way for further globalization. Evidently then, globalization requires governance arrangements (norms, institutions and so forth) to regulate its effects. These governance arrangements, in turn, increase globalization in many ways including, for example, through processes of standardization, removal, simplification and regulation of all kinds of barriers to global development and other barriers that are considered to hinder globalization. In sum, then, while globalization leads one to re-conceive governance in a global context, this reconceptualized or reconceived governance also simultaneously causes globalization.

7. GLOBALIZATION AND THE LAW

There is a very close relationship between globalization and the law, especially insofar as the law is part of the governance construct that aims to regulate soci-

---

[66] An example of this is the removal of trade barriers and the global regulation of trade by the World Trade Organization (WTO). Increased worldwide consumption and industrial growth requires an increase in trade to meet global demands, which are eventually all matters that must be governed by states through global non-state actors such as the WTO.

[67] Scholte, Jan Aart (2000), *Globalization: A Critical Introduction*, London: Macmillan Press, 101.

ety and human behaviour.[68] This is also true for globalization and environmental law. Environmental problems are global, as was indicated earlier. This means that the laws that apply to these problems and their effects transcend physical and political borders and thus have a global effect. For example, the causes of climate change can usually be traced to particular countries, i.e., to national jurisdictions, which means that they can be regulated by national laws. However, because the consequences of climate change are global one could reasonably expect that environmental laws at regional and international levels will also be applicable. To be sure, climate change as a global environmental problem is regulated by sub-national, national, sub-regional, regional and international laws, and there currently exists a burgeoning institutional framework situated within various legal regimes at all of these levels as a means to respond to climate change globally. These legal regimes create, for example, a multitude of governance institutions such as intergovernmental organizations, and they provide for the establishment and functioning of various actors, while spelling out numerous procedures and mechanisms related to regulating climate change. It is therefore possible to conclude that environmental law, insofar as it is used as a societal construct to regulate as part of the larger governance construct, is increasingly assuming a global character. At the same time environmental law is also contributing to the globalization of environmental regulation through the establishment of regulatory regimes, institutions, actors, processes and mechanisms. Conversely, supra-national legal regimes impose numerous obligations on states, especially with respect to the obligations they place on states to streamline their national legal regimes to conform to the international legal order. In this way, the national affects the international and the international affects the national.

It is also important to note in this context that the burgeoning body of environmental law, at all levels, is increasingly a product not only of formal political and state-centred law-making processes but also (not surprisingly, considering the changing role of the state brought about by globalization) of private or non-state rule-making. As Teubner[69] states:

> The focus in law-making is shifting to private regimes, that is, to binding agreements among global players, to private market regulation through multinational enterprises, internal rule-making within international organizations, inter-organizational negotiating systems, and worldwide standardization processes. The dominant sources of law are now to be found at the peripheries of law, at the boundaries with other sectors of world society that are successfully engaging in regional

68 See Chapter 5.

69 Teubner, Gunther (2004), 'Global Private Regimes: Neo-spontaneous Law and Dual Constitution of Autonomous Sectors' in Karl-Heinz Ladeur (ed), *Public Governance in the Age of Globalization*, Aldershot: Ashgate, 74.

> competition with the existing centres of law-making – national parliaments, global legislative institutions and intergovernmental agreements.

Quite evidently, globalization is expanding and diversifying the various sources of law across private and public divides in a manner which transcends all levels, spheres and modes of authority.[70] Often the norms that are created here are not considered 'hard', orthodox legal norms, but rather 'softer' rules and principles such as codes of practice, guidelines, and international soft-law instruments.[71] In this context globalization has a tangible and very direct influence on the cumulative expansion of normative arrangements as part of a process of change which is gradually transforming the way in which we govern through law. The implication of this in the environmental context is that environmental issues (be they sub- or supra-national) cannot continue to be regulated solely by means of a state-centred government situated in a single country and by means of laws that are derived only from orthodox sources and applied in the traditional sense. The global character of environmental problems, the expanding and diversifying range of sources and forms of (environmental) law and the changing face of the institutional framework responsible for addressing environmental problems cumulatively suggest that environmental governance in a globalized age is being transformed well beyond the traditional manner in which the world has been perceiving, conceptualizing and executing environmental regulation and the role of law and other normative mechanisms as part of this effort. These issues are further investigated in Chapter 8.

8. SUMMARY

The most straightforward way to understand globalization is to consider it as a process which leads to the world becoming one. Globalization is dramatically affecting the world, society, and the way that society would seek to regulate social interactions and human behaviour. Globalization is thus important for the governance of global issues:

---

[70] The traditional focus on normative systems that are promulgated exclusively by and among states is thus giving way to a more diversified view which ventures beyond the centrality of public, state-centred power and the sovereignty of the nation state as the primary sources of law. Berman, Paul Schiff (2005), 'From International Law to Law and Globalization', *Columbia Journal of Transnational Law*, **43**(2), 485–556 at 487–8.

[71] These could include, for example, voluntary 'soft' codes for corporate and investor behaviour such as the United Nations Global Compact, the United Nations Principles for Responsible Investment, and the Equator Principles.

> Globalization depends on effective governance, now as in the past. Effective governance is not inevitable. If it occurs, it is more likely to take place through interstate cooperation and transnational networks than through a world state. But even if national states retain many of their present functions, effective governance of a partially – and increasingly – globalized world will require more extensive international institutions. Governance arrangements to promote cooperation and help resolve conflict must be developed if globalization is not to stall or go into reverse.[72]

Environmental problems are part of a contemporary global reality that postulates interdependence and reciprocity; a social reality which is fundamentally different from that of a hundred years ago. More importantly, it is a reality which requires new global social constructs to govern human behaviour in a transformed society where globalization is exponentially increasing the number, scope, complexity and severity of environmental problems and the way in which society would seek to respond to these. This process has a profound impact on the environment, as it leads to many adverse environmental impacts. Yet it concomitantly gives rise to various global responses to those environmental problems.

Globalization therefore plays an important role in the environmental governance paradigm in the way that it acts as a lens through which to view contemporary changing spatial conditions, environmental change, and the effect of environmental change on society. It also provides society with the descriptive and analytical tools to understand these changes and to design appropriate institutional responses to global environmental change through global environmental governance. Clearly globalization's relevance for governance and global environmental governance is almost intuitive. These considerations collectively emphasize the need for global environmental governance:

> If a healthy environment is a global public good, in the sense that nobody can be excluded from enjoying it, the provision of such a good requires global coordination ... although the degree to which our planet is seriously threatened by environmental degradation is continuously debated, no one seems to argue against the need for global environmental governance.[73]

If globalization also means increased global activity, it follows that it is contributing in real terms to an increased need for regulation of these activities by means of a wide range of private and public actors, structures,

---

72 Keohane, Robert O. (2002), 'Governance in a Partially Globalized World' in Robert O. Keohane (ed), *Power and Governance in a Partially Globalized World*, London: Routledge, 245.

73 Kjær, Anne Mette (2004), *Governance*, Cambridge: Polity Press, 74.

processes and mechanisms in a multi-layered or multi-polar setting.[74] Globalization is therefore also changing the role of and the extent to which the state will be involved in addressing global environmental change. It is giving rise to the establishment of a widely diverse array of non-state actors who will increasingly act to address global environmental problems where the 'hollowed out' state cannot act. State and non-state actors will be inclined now to act collectively through a global form of environmental governance to respond to global environmental problems. This form of governance, which aims to collectively govern environmental problems in a globalized world, is global environmental governance.

[74] Taylor, Paul (2003), *International Organization in the Age of Globalization*, London: Continuum, 1.

3. Framing governance

> In the opening years of the 21st century the question of 'governance' has moved to the center of our political, economic, social, personal and religious lives. The most immediate and obvious reason for this is that the dominant institutions of contemporary societies – international law regimes, state governments, the global financial system and the corporate organization of economic life, educational and cultural institutions of all kinds – have lost their capacity to govern the spheres of human activity for which they are deemed responsible in such a way as to maintain the common good.[1]
>
> (Ronald Engel, 2010)

1. INTRODUCTION

The word governance invokes a certain sense of familiarity. It is often encountered in daily life; for example in the media, corporate boardrooms, the world of politics and power, in dealings with governments, state departments and government officials; in almost all instances where regulation occurs and where authority, in whatever form and whether emanating from state or non-state sources, is present and exercised. Governance has become a popular focus of scholarly analysis in many disciplines, especially the social and economic sciences (for example, public administration, business administration, and political science). As was argued in Chapter 1, the pervasive governance concept has also found its way into the environmental regulatory scene where environmental regulation in its fourth generational guise is termed environmental governance. To be sure, environmental governance, as its name suggests, is centrally concerned with the issue of governance.

For reasons explained in Chapter 1 it is, however, mostly the concept of governance which gives rise to theoretical and conceptual uncertainty with respect to the phenomenon of global environmental governance. The reticence of lawyers especially to fully engage with the governance concept might come

[1] Engel, Ronald (2010), 'Introduction' in Ronald J. Engel, Laura Westra and Klaus Bosselmann (eds), *Democracy, Ecological Integrity and International Law*, Cambridge: Cambridge Scholars Publishing, 2.

as a surprise, because there is an intuitive connection between law and governance: both are means to regulate human behaviour. Governance is concerned with regulation and law is an important societal construct used for regulation; in many ways law is the primary source of the authority necessary for governance; law establishes governance mechanisms and actors; and governance is intricately connected with the state, government and its agencies, all of which rely on law as a source of regulatory norms, authority and legitimation. Conversely, law is created by governance actors and processes, for example, by means of treaty making, and law is therefore as much a product of governance as it is a source of governance. Through non-state actors governance is also increasingly responsible for creating 'softer' non-state but law-like forms of norms which are used in the governance domain. Nevertheless, while lawyers are steadily being confronted by governance, they are not necessarily comfortable with using this construct in the legal domain for the simple reason that it is not a pure legal concept, but at most one which exudes some legal characteristics and one which is somehow connected with the law. Clearly, governance is what Ruiter[2] calls an 'extra-legal concept'.

Mostly though, governance is a vague and amorphous concept which is bedevilled by inconsistent use in a plural and multi-disciplinary setting. Governance is also multi-contextual and could be viewed, for example, from a geo-political perspective, a corporate perspective, a micro perspective such as project governance, and the governance of specific functional areas such as water governance and financial governance. It is often political and value laden and therefore deliberately vague, fluid and non-committal. It is open to interpretation and has even been described as a fad, an Anglicism that is often used to add to the complex social science repertoire (what Benz[3] calls a *Modeausdruck* (a fashionable term)).[4] It is for all of these reasons that one

2 An extra-legal concept is one which is used in non-legal language, yet nothing prohibits it from being part of a legal rule. Ruiter, Dick W.P. (2000), 'Legal Institutions as Systems of Legal Norms' in Oscar Van Heffen, Walter J.M. Kickert and Jacques J.A. Thomassen (eds), *Governance in Modern Society: Effects, Change and Formation of Government Institutions*, Dordrecht: Kluwer Academic Publishers, 351.

3 Benz, Arthur (2004), 'Einleitung: Governance-Modebegriff oder nützliches sozialwissenschaftliches Konzept?' in Arthur Benz (ed), *Governance- Regieren in komplexen Regelsystemen: Eine Einführung*, Wiesbaden, Germany: VS Verlag für Sozialwissenschaften, 12.

4 See also Schuppert, Gunnar Folke (2007), 'Was ist und wozu Governance?', *Die Verwaltung: Zeitschrift für Verwaltungsrecht und Verwaltungswissenschaften*, **40**(1), 463–511 at 463; Jann, Werner (2006), 'Governance als Reformstrategie- Vom Wandel und der Bedeutung verwaltungspolitischer Leitbilder' in Gunnar Folke Schuppert (ed), *Governance-Forschung*, Baden-Baden: Nomos Verlag, 21.

should take extra care when engaging with the concept;[5] it demands a certain measure of apprehension and even scepticism in theoretical analysis.[6] Engaging with the notion of governance nevertheless necessitates a conscious effort to revisit its theory and to situate it in the context of law with a view to creating some common ground as far as clarifying and understanding its minimum content is concerned. More importantly for the purpose of this book, it is necessary to re-examine the concept in an attempt to understand global environmental governance and to contextualize and explain governance in the global environmental regulatory domain.[7]

---

[5] Two further observations merit inclusion here. First, governance is of course not the only concept plagued by inconsistencies and vagueness. Concepts such as politics, sustainability, and law are equally clouded. Second, many of these concepts are vague and non-descript, not because the scientific domain within which they find themselves is vague, but because they deal with complex matters that require a measure of generalization and imprecise description. In fact, especially in the enviro-political context, vagueness could be a useful attribute because of 'constructive ambiguity', or as Pinto argues: 'often because the idea that first fired the collective imagination and mobilized legislative effort, was contained in some captivating phrase capable of widely different interpretations'. Pinto, Moragodage C.W. (1996), '"Common Heritage of Mankind": From Metaphor to Myth, and the Consequence of Constructive Ambiguity' in Jerzy Makarczyk (ed), *Theory of International Law at the Threshold of the 21st Century: Essays in Honour of Krzysztof Skubiszewski*, The Hague: Kluwer Law International, 250. Another reason for the illusiveness and ambiguity of the governance concept may be that, as Ocheje puts it: '[I]n a divided and multicultural world, "governance" is a value-laden concept, and this invariably militates against the emergence of a single universally acceptable definition.' Ocheje, Paul (1999), 'Exploring the Legal Dimensions of Political Legitimacy: A "Rights" Approach to Governance in Africa' in Edward Kofi Quashigah and Obiora Chinedu Okafor (eds), *Legitimate Governance in Africa: International and Domestic Legal Perspectives*, The Hague: Kluwer Law International, 165.

[6] Benz later warns that one should be sceptical of new concepts such as governance, which are suddenly used by many in various different ways but without any specific meaning attributed to them:

> Neuen Bezeichnungen sollte man mit Skepsis begegnen, vor allem dann, wenn sie plötzlich in aller Munde sind und in vielen Bereichen Verwendung finden, keiner aber so genau definieren kann, was eigentlich damit gemeint ist. Und all dies trifft für den Governance-Begriff zu.

Benz, Arthur (2004), 'Einleitung: Governance-Modebegriff oder nützliches sozialwissenschaftliches Konzept?' in Arthur Benz (ed), *Governance- Regieren in komplexen Regelsystemen: Eine Einführung*, Wiesbaden, Germany: VS Verlag für Sozialwissenschaften Wiesbaden, 12.

[7] The central hypothesis of this chapter therefore is that a sound understanding of the theory of governance is a prerequisite for the formulation of a basic theory of global environmental governance. See also Chapter 1.

It is against this general background that this chapter seeks first to retrace the historical roots of the governance concept. It then briefly surveys the plurality and diversity of governance with a view to explaining its modern day relevance, multidimensionality and the lack of a uniform definition. The discussion then proceeds to map the definitional field of governance by providing a critical survey of the concept as it has been described in literature. The purpose of this survey is to extract the central rationale behind governance and to propose a formulation of its core content. The final sections explain the difference between governance and government and reflects on the relationship between governance and some of its related concepts such as regulation, bureaucracy, management, and law.

2. A HISTORY OF GOVERNANCE

The etymological roots of governance can be traced back to the Greek verb *kybernân*, which means to pilot or to steer.[8] *Kybernân* is derived from the noun *kybernêtês*, which describes the helmsman of a war ship.[9] While *kybernân* had no specific political meaning, its Latin equivalents, *gubernare* and *regere* additionally describe the action of steering in terms of the state; a process which involves rule making, rule interpretation, rule application and enforcement and the sanctioning of non-compliance with rules. Thus, even in ancient times the term government was used to impart the notion of the steering or piloting of the state, just as a ship's helmsman would pilot and steer a ship. In the English language, steering, piloting and rule-making have, however, traditionally been expressed by means of the word *government* (which is not to be confused with governance, as is explained later), and it was only towards the end of the 20th Century that the Anglo-American concept of governance began to feature as an expression of disaggregated political steering; a semantic metamorphosis which has been mirrored and even set in motion by significant changes in political regulatory theories, especially in the context of globalization.[10]

8 Kjær, Anne Mette (2004), *Governance*, Cambridge: Polity Press, 3; Schneider, Volker (2004), 'Organizational Governance: Governance in Organisationen' in Arthur Benz (ed), *Governance- Regieren in komplexen Regelsystemen: Eine Einführung*, Wiesbaden, Germany: VS Verlag für Sozialwissenschaften, 176.

9 Schneider, Volker (2004), 'Organizational Governance: Governance in Organisationen' in Arthur Benz (ed), *Governance- Regieren in komplexen Regelsystemen: Eine Einführung*, Wiesbaden, Germany: VS Verlag für Sozialwissenschaften, 176.

10 Mayntz, Renate (2004), 'Governance im modernen Staat' in Arthur Benz (ed), *Governance- Regieren in komplexen Regelsystemen: Eine Einführung*, Wiesbaden, Germany: VS Verlag für Sozialwissenschaften, 66. See also Chapter 2.

In addition to these semantic and etymological developments, governance as a scientific concept was surprisingly not coined in the political sciences but in the field of economics, in the late 1970s, when it was used to collectively describe the institutional rules and management arrangements in companies and other business enterprises.[11] It was also at this time that there was a marked revival of the concept and its scientific utility. Governance in the economic context refers to company/corporate management and corporate administrative structures and processes, as well as the vertical and horizontal design of interactions in a company and the various actors in the company that have as their primary aim the reduction of transaction costs. (This is commonly referred to as corporate governance.)[12]

The concept of (corporate) governance then gradually found its way into the public-centred political governance realm (or government in its traditional sense) via international institutional economics, which is concerned with markets, federative and hierarchical organizations, contracts and commitments between private and public actors, as well as the manner in which cooperation occurs between these actors. It was specifically through the work of the World Bank in Sub-Saharan Africa during the 1980s that the concepts of 'good' and 'bad' governance (as meaning acceptable and unacceptable governance respectively) were coined, and as such, these events cumulatively marked the

---

11 Benz, Arthur (2004), 'Einleitung: Governance-Modebegriff oder nützliches sozialwissenschaftliches Konzept?' in Arthur Benz (ed), *Governance- Regieren in komplexen Regelsystemen: Eine Einführung*, Wiesbaden, Germany: VS Verlag für Sozialwissenschaften, 15; Mayntz, Renata (2006), 'Governance Theory als fortentwickelte Steuerungstheorie?' in Gunnar Folke Schuppert (ed), *Governance-Forschung*, Baden-Baden: Nomos Verlag, 14–15. More accurately, governance in the economic context is 'the means by which *order* is accomplished in a relation in which potential *conflict* threatens to undo or upset opportunities to realize *mutual* gains'. Williamson, Oliver E. (1996), *The Mechanisms of Governance*, New York: Oxford University Press, 12. See further, Trute, Hans-Heinrich, Wolfgang Denkhaus and Doris Kühlers (2004), 'Governance in der Verwaltungsrechtswissenschaft', *Die Verwaltung: Zeitschrift für Verwaltungsrecht und Verwaltungswissenschaften*, **37**, 451–73 at 452–3.

12 Engi, Lorenz (2008), 'Governance: Umrisse und Problematik eines staatstheoretischen Leitbildes', *Der Staat: Zeitschrift für Staatslehre und Verfassungsgesichte, deutsches und europäisiches Öffentliches Recht*, **47**, 573–87 at 573–4. Notably, it is also the concept of corporate governance with its decidedly institutional character that has subsequently led to the institutionalization of the governance concept in the public/political context. Mayntz, Renata (2006), 'Governance Theory als fortentwickelte Steuerungstheorie?' in Gunnar Folke Schuppert (ed), *Governance-Forschung*, Baden-Baden: Nomos Verlag, 15. For a detailed theoretical treatment of corporate governance in the governance context see Jürgens, Ulrich (2008), 'Corporate Governance-Anwendungsfelder und Entwicklungen' in Gunnar Folke Schuppert and Michael Zürn (eds), *Governance in einer sich wandelnden Welt*, Wiesbaden, Germany: VS Verlag für Sozialwissenschaften, 47–71.

first endorsement and support for the concept in a political context at the international level.[13]

During the 1990s governance increasingly featured in the globalization debate. It is in the context of increased global activity and the involvement of non-state actors in tandem with state actors that governance emerged as a prominent approach that seeks to optimize the regulation of interactions among and between these actors with a view to maximizing benefits and reducing costs.[14] In a sense, this was a natural progression and a logical development of a way to describe regulatory intervention which did not necessitate reinventing the wheel, but merely required the application of a conceptual approach developed earlier in the economic sciences to similar regulatory problems and externalities that arose in the political arena. The idea was that the world is a corporation and could be governed as one, as it were. Thus, the idea of governance that has its roots in the corporate context could be equally as relevant and applicable to political world affairs as it would be to a corporation.

The extrapolation of governance to the world political stage occurred in tandem with globalization, because the problems and new social realities caused by globalization required a new approach to regulating global phenomena and their impacts on society. It was especially through the work of the Commission on Global Governance and its report *Our Common Neighbourhood*, that the governance concept was steadily broadened and widely popularized.[15] The work of the Commission in many respects also served as the impetus for a steadily increased reliance on the governance concept by the UN and its agencies in the context of development politics. One of the most recent applications of governance as it manifests in the international political context is in the EU, where it describes multi-actor and multi-level governance. The term 'European governance' is now a popular and frequently recurring one.[16] Today, in addition to these higher level political

---

[13] Engi, Lorenz (2008), 'Governance: Umrisse und Problematik eines staatstheoretischen Leitbildes', *Der Staat: Zeitschrift für Staatslehre und Verfassungsgesichte, deutsches und europäisiches Öffentliches Recht*, **47**, 573–87 at 574. Governance was primarily used by the World Bank as a methodological tool which 'raised the question of the location of effective control and power in countries lacking in solid state structures'. Smouts, Marie-Claude (1998), 'The Proper Use of Governance in International Relations', *International Social Science Journal*, **50**(155), 81–9 at 82.

[14] See Chapter 2.

[15] Commission on Global Governance (1995), *Our Global Neighbourhood*, Oxford: Oxford University Press. Also see Chapter 4.

[16] See, for example, Jachtenfuchs, Markus (2008), 'Institutionelle Struktur und Governance in der EU' in Gunnar Folke Schuppert and Michael Zürn (eds), *Governance in einer sich wandelnden Welt*, Wiesbaden, Germany: VS Verlag für

developments, governance is also increasingly finding its way into the public administration domain, where it is used as a measure to improve public service delivery, specifically in the form of new public management.[17]

In sum, it is clear that governance is an ancient concept which has been used since its birth to convey the ideas of piloting, leading, directing, steering, and/or guiding. Its subsequent manifestations in the modern world similarly impart these ideas. In this respect, one observes a steady progression of governance as a scientific concept and a normative programme from its initial, infantile stages in an economic context to its current political manifestations. In political sciences governance now encapsulates, among other things: international relations between states, relations between states and non-state actors (such as international organizations) and between non-state actors *inter se*; the collective solving of social problems; power structures which are characterized by gradually diminishing sovereignty and hierarchy in these power structures; forms of control and steering by means of a mixture between cooperation and the exercise of coercive state power; communication, negotiations and guidelines as 'softer' forms of steering; and the dominance of processes over structures and the continuing change of these structures.[18] It is in this globalized context that the concept of governance is used as part of the global environmental governance paradigm to describe the different structures and forms of steering and coordination of the relations between a variety of actors with respect to the environment at variously different levels and in terms of many governance mechanisms.

Sozialwissenschaften, 383–400; Börzel, Tanja A. (2006), 'European Governance-nicht neu, aber anders' in Gunnar Folke Schuppert (ed), *Governance-Forschung*, Baden-Baden: Nomos Verlag, 72–94.

[17] Engi explains that governance in the context of new public management is essentially used as a reform concept which aims to improve public administration with respect to its inner workings and its relations with the outside world: '[Governance] bezeichnet diesbezüglich ein Reformkonzept, das insbesondere die Modelle des New Public Management insofern weiterentwickelt, als es neben den Binnenverhältnissen auch die Außenbeziehungen der Verwaltung verstärkt berücksichtig.' Engi, Lorenz (2008), 'Governance: Umrisse und Problematik eines staatstheoretischen Leitbildes', *Der Staat: Zeitschrift für Staatslehre und Verfassungsgesichte, deutsches und europäisiches Öffentliches Recht*, **47**, 573–87 at 575.

[18] Benz, Arthur (2004), 'Einleitung: Governance-Modebegriff oder nützliches sozialwissenschaftliches Konzept?' in Arthur Benz (ed), *Governance- Regieren in komplexen Regelsystemen: Eine Einführung*, Wiesbaden, Germany: VS Verlag für Sozialwissenschaften, 16–17.

3. THE MANY FACES OF GOVERNANCE

Governance is used in many scientific disciplines and contexts including, for example, political science, comparative politics, economics, international relations, public administration (where it focuses on bureaucracy in the Weberian sense), public policy, and increasingly law. It is a concept with as many definitions as there are commentators that write on it, with most of these working within specific disciplines and hailing from various perspectives and backgrounds. The following sections reflect on the plurality of the governance concept as it manifests in some of these sciences.[19]

3.1 A Multi-disciplinary, Multi-textual and Plural Setting

As a concept, governance's diversity, inconsistent terminological application, and lack of terminological clarity can be attributed to the breadth of its scope of application. Governance is a term which is applied in many different domains and the inevitable result is a chameleon-type concept which changes itself and is changed according to specific external considerations and needs. Hirst,[20] for example, lists at least five versions of governance, or five different areas in which it is used, including: governance in economic development and in the context of international development agencies such as the World Bank; governance in terms of international relations and international regimes; corporate governance or governance in private corporations; governance as new public management; and negotiated social governance, which is representative of networks, partnerships and various deliberative forms.

---

[19] In addition to there being many descriptions of the concept, governance is also not culturally neutral. This is evidenced by the fact that it is a concept which is difficult (and in some instances impossible) to translate into many languages. For instance, the French understanding of governance (*gouvernance*) is not the same as the Anglo-American understanding. There is no equivalent of the word in Afrikaans and the words *regulering/regering* (regulating or government) are often used instead. This is also the case in German, where the words *Steuerung/Regulierung* (steering, control or regulating) are used instead of governance. Because of these difficulties of translation and for the sake of consistency most languages seem to use the term *governance*. See further Friedrichs, Jörg (2004), 'The Neomedieval Renaissance: Global Governance and International Law in the New Middle Ages' in Ige F. Dekker and Wouter G. Werner (eds), *Governance and International Legal Theory*, Leiden: Martinus Nijhoff Publishers, 14–15.

[20] Hirst, Paul (2000), 'Democracy and Governance' in Jon Pierre (ed), *Debating Governance: Authority, Steering and Democracy*, Oxford: Oxford University Press, 14–19.

In its earliest guise, governance was used mostly to express the procedural aspects of government,[21] to the extent that it functioned as a derivative of the verb 'to govern'.[22] Other nuances include governance as meaning: the capacity to regulate; situations where authority is exercised; a mode of allocating values; and the emergence of rule-like systems and problem-solving mechanisms.[23]

It is evident that governance could mean many things and that it has many faces. Its content will vary in relation to the details of its application and the purpose for which it is used and the context in which it is used. In addition, the meaning of the term will also depend on which actors one chooses to include in one's concept of governance; how one chooses to view and describe these actors; the object of governance or the problems it aims to solve (i.e., whether they are to be found in the domain of the environment, trade, or economics, for example); the general purpose of a specific governance effort; the level of governance (local, national, regional or international); the instruments of governance, and so forth. It is therefore reasonable to expect that governance in the environmental context will have its own distinguishing characteristics and elements while it nevertheless will share some communalities with governance in other contexts, such as economic governance, trade governance, and corporate governance. It is nevertheless possible that the core purpose or rationale of governance would remain the same for all of these different applications in different contexts. This core purpose and rationale is explained further below.

3.2 Governance as an Analytical Perspective

Governance can manifest as a process and institution (in other words a normative concept or political programme), or as an analytical perspective.[24] The role of governance as an analytical perspective means that it provides one with

---

21 Mayntz, Renate (2004), 'Governance im modernen Staat' in Arthur Benz (ed), *Governance- Regieren in komplexen Regelsystemen: Eine Einführung*, Wiesbaden, Germany: VS Verlag für Sozialwissenschaften, 66.

22 Schneider, Volker (2004), 'Organizational Governance: Governance in Organisationen' in Arthur Benz (ed), *Governance- Regieren in komplexen Regelsystemen: Eine Einführung*, Wiesbaden, Germany: VS Verlag für Sozialwissenschaften, 176.

23 Rosenau, James N. (1992), 'Governance, Order, and Change in World Politics' in James N. Rosenau and Ernst-Otto Czempiel (eds), *Governance without Government: Order and Change in World Politics*, Cambridge: Cambridge University Press, 6–7.

24 Köck, Wolfgang (2006), 'Governance in der Umweltpolitik' in Gunnar Folke Schuppert (ed), *Governance-Forschung*, Baden-Baden: Nomos Verlag, 323–4.

the means to conceive, perceive, and appreciate, in other words, to understand and to explain something.[25] In this sense it is an 'analytical lens' which functions as an interpretative aid[26] to the extent that it could be used as a mental map to help make sense of contemporary global realities and societal problems.[27]

Because it is a concept used mostly in social (political) sciences, the object that governance as an analytical perspective attempts to understand and explain is social reality and why people behave as they do. It has been shown in Chapter 2 that governance owes much of its current popularity and prominence to globalization which, in turn, is a phenomenon that is constantly changing social reality. As an analytical perspective, it follows that it is, among other things, globalization, its problems and realities that governance aims to understand. These things include relations between states and between states and their subjects; the changing role of the nation state; the rise of civil society and the many private forms of governance and non-state actors; the increasing importance of hybrid public-private governance; and new forms of regulating behaviour, interaction, and working towards a shared purpose or common good.[28]

---

25 Benz explains that governance as an analytical perspective helps us to understand something; it provides us with the ability to work with and understand scientific issues which would have been impossible or difficult had we not had the analytical and explanatory assistance of the concept: '[E]inen Begriff zu haben, heißt etwas zu begreifen, heißt die Fähigkeit zu besitzen, einen Gegenstand der Erkenntnis wissenschaftlich verstehen und bearbeiten zu können. Genau dieses soll der Governance-Begriff leisten.' Benz, Arthur (2004), 'Einleitung: Governance-Modebegriff oder nützliches sozialwissenschaftliches Konzept?' in Arthur Benz (ed), *Governance- Regieren in komplexen Regelsystemen: Eine Einführung*, Wiesbaden, Germany: VS Verlag für Sozialwissenschaften, 14.

26 An analytical perspective could be described as:

> ... a pair of glasses whose different lenses allow us to view the distinct political, economic, and social characteristics and processes that shape world politics. These lenses act as filters, directing attention toward (and away from) certain kinds of actors and focusing discussion on certain kinds of questions. Through these theoretical lenses, we see different reflections, different explanations regarding which actors – states, individuals, class, gender – should figure most prominently in our understanding of international relations.

Pease, Kelly-Kate S. (2008), *International Organizations: Perspectives on Governance in the Twenty-First Century* 3rd edn, New Jersey: Pearson Prentice Hall, 1–2.

27 Pease, Kelly-Kate S. (2008), *International Organizations: Perspectives on Governance in the Twenty-First Century* 3rd edn, New Jersey: Pearson Prentice Hall, 5.

28 Engi emphasizes that governance fulfils the role of a common denominator in this respect by bringing together various phenomena and various conceptions of regu-

Turning to a more concrete example of governance as an analytical perspective, Bernstein[29] describes governance in the context of good global governance as follows:

> Governance, at any time and in any place, is the sum of collective understandings and discourse about *material capabilities*, *knowledge* (normative, ideological, technical and scientific), *legitimacy* (the acceptance and justification of the right to rule by relevant communities), and *fairness* (which, in our account, may include notions of accountability, representation, and responsibility, as well as distributive justice).

Governance, in Bernstein's view, is about the manner in which people endeavour to understand their ability to govern, knowledge with respect to the issues that require governance, the manner in which governance should occur, the acceptability of and support and authority for governance (legitimacy), and the way in which governance is conducted (fairness). This more abstract definition, understandably so in the context of good governance, does not necessarily focus on what governance is but rather on what governance should be and how we perceive our abilities to influence social reality, human relations and global change.[30] Ideally then, governance should provide people with the means to appreciate those material factors which would enable them to govern, knowledge of the governance process itself, and knowledge of what is to be governed, as well as an understanding of what sort of governance would be supported and accepted by people: governance

---

lation and regulatory actors into a single area of understanding. In this way, governance acts as a constant universal central core that relates to decision-making in private and public spheres:

> 'Governance' greift damit viele Erschreinungen auf, die als kooperatives und informelles Staats-und Verwaltungshandeln seit längerem beobachtet werden, und bringt sie sozusagen auf einen Nenner. Als Begriffskern lässt sich eine Enstcheidungsfindung in kollektiven Belangen ausmachen, die verläuft, in denen sich Staat und Private als prinzipiell gleichberechtigte Akteure begegnen.

Engi, Lorenz (2008), 'Governance: Umrisse und Problematik eines staatstheoretischen Leitbildes', *Der Staat: Zeitschrift für Staatslehre und Verfassungsgesichte, deutsches und europäisiches Öffentliches Recht*, **47**, 573–87 at 577.

29 Bernstein, Steven (2005), 'Globalization and the Requirements of "Good" Environmental Governance', *Perspectives on Global Development and Technology*, **4**(3/4), 645–79 at 652.

30 Globally, various mechanisms and initiatives are in place to measure the successes and failures of governance. These include, for example, the World Bank Governance Surveys, the World Governance Index, Sustainable Governance Indicators, the African Peer Review Mechanism, and the Worldwide Governance Indicators.

which is based on accountability, representation, responsibility, and distributive justice. Global environmental governance is also an analytical perspective insofar as it allows us to view global governance through an environmental lens. In this sense, global environmental governance would not be much different from good governance, because it would arguably also underscore the achievement of the ideals of good governance: transparency, democracy and participation, in particular, as far as environmental issues are concerned. It will, however, also focus on 'environmental' ideals such as achieving inter- and intra-generational equity, sustainability and the preservation of ecological integrity.

As an analytical perspective, in this sense governance plays a crucial role as part of our efforts to understand contemporary global realities and problems, and it guides us in our attempts to formulate a collective understanding, often expressed as ideals, the realization of which must be accompanied by normative forms of governance, as is explained hereafter. In this way, governance could, for example, be used to achieve the ideal of sustainability, if indeed one wishes to consider sustainability as an ideal of environmental governance.[31]

3.3 Governance as a Normative Concept

Normative manifestations of governance often have their roots in specific ideologies where, for instance, Western values and ideas such as transparency, participation, and democracy are equated with universal values, and where they then act as political programmes or goals for these programmes.[32] An example in this respect is good governance (again), where governance is used to describe ways to legitimize and optimize governance actors and processes, or ways to increase governance's ability to solve and efficiency in solving societal problems.[33] Good governance as a normative concept here differs from good governance as an analytical perspective, as described above, to the extent that it forms a more concrete political or normative programme to achieve the ideals of good governance. In other words good governance as an analytical perspective explains how we ideally wish to see governance and the

---

[31] See also Chapter 6.

[32] Köck, Wolfgang (2006), 'Governance in der Umweltpolitik' in Gunnar Folke Schuppert (ed), *Governance-Forschung*, Baden-Baden: Nomos Verlag, 324. On the issue of universal values see further De Wet, Erika (2006), 'The International Constitutional Order', *International and Comparative Law Quarterly*, **55**, 1–26.

[33] Benz, Arthur (2004), 'Einleitung: Governance-Modebegriff oder nützliches sozialwissenschaftliches Konzept?' in Arthur Benz (ed), *Governance- Regieren in komplexen Regelsystemen: Eine Einführung*, Wiesbaden, Germany: VS Verlag für Sozialwissenschaften, 25–6.

changes it must accomplish in society, and as a normative political programme it provides us with the means to achieve these ideals. Good governance was developed by the World Bank, and as a normative concept it is used as a set of criteria, guidelines and minimum requirements by means of which the World Bank decides whether or not to lend money to countries in the developing world. Clearly, the normative manifestations and forms of governance are reactions to existing or expected future regulatory problems.[34] As a normative concept governance then attempts to recognize, predict, and ultimately to solve the many consequences of social dynamics and address the manner in which human activities affect economies, other states, other people and, for our purposes, the environment. To do so, governance as a normative programme or concept will provide the institutional structures, organizations, regimes, actors and rules (mostly expressed by laws), for example, with which a country may achieve good governance. European governance is another example of a normative form of governance and it addresses regulatory challenges and problems resulting from increased regional integration in Europe, not only in the context of politics, but also in social, environmental and economic contexts.

In the environmental context, environmental governance is a recent normative concept which is a specific political programme that has emerged to address regulatory problems as far as the environment is concerned. It recognizes that environmental issues require regulation with a view to achieving an acceptable/sustainable standard of living, health and well-being in an environment of which the ecological integrity is intact. When applied to the global milieu, it is termed global environmental governance, which is a normative programme that focuses on regulating global environmental issues through various actors, at various different levels, and through numerous processes and mechanisms. While global environmental governance is often used as an analytical perspective, it is mostly used as a normative concept. The remainder of this book similarly focuses on governance, and thus also on environmental governance, as a normative concept, unless the contrary is stated.

It is worth noting that different normative forms of governance such as good governance, European governance and environmental governance are not necessarily mutually exclusive. They often overlap in the sense that all three could be used in a single instance for a single purpose. For example, one might thus use governance as a normative concept to address environmental problems within the EU by focusing on the improvement of transparency, the involvement of civil society, and accountability in decision-making (aspects of

34 Köck, Wolfgang (2006), 'Governance in der Umweltpolitik' in Gunnar Folke Schuppert (ed), *Governance-Forschung*, Baden-Baden: Nomos Verlag, 324.

good governance), which in turn affect the environment, people, and the economies of the EU Member States. The notion of 'good environmental governance in the European Union' seems therefore quite plausible and is now recognized in literature.[35]

3.4 Core Communalities

Despite its plurality, vagueness, contrasts, and the many ways in which it is used, it is possible to determine at least some degree of consistency and a measure of clarity with respect to governance's conceptual core, regardless of any additional nuances that might influence its meaning. First, governance has traditionally been associated with the state, government, political power and authority, rule-making and enforcement, and the process of ordering societies. Much of the foregoing has to do with politics and institutions which, in turn, relate to social behaviour. Kjær[36] points out that governance theory is manifestly grounded in institutionalism: in other words, governance theory has to do with 'formal and informal rules, behavioural codes and norms that constitute prescriptions ordering repeated, interdependent relations'. All this points to governance being centrally concerned with human agency in the institutional context, which means that it has to do with the ability of people to choose and to make decisions and to impose these decisions on themselves and other people by means of rule setting, rule interpretation, rule application and rule enforcement.[37] Governance is therefore about people steering or piloting activities or behaviour and having the ability to steer and pilot their own and other human activities and behaviour with the purpose of achieving some or other (often common) goal. In other words, governance is about people 'acting more or less deliberately in a fairly durable concert for the attainment of a considered complex of ends',[38] especially insofar as it embodies 'the purposeful generation of influence on the behaviour of actors to collectively improve sub-optimal outcomes'.[39] This goal or complex of ends has also been described as the 'overall process

35 Heldeweg, Michiel A. (2005), 'Good Environmental Governance in the EU: Lessons from Work in Progress?' in D.M. Curtin and R.A. Wessel (eds), *Good Governance and the European Union: Reflections on Concepts, Institutions and Substance*, Antwerp: Intersentia, 175–214.

36 Kjær, Anne Mette (2004), *Governance*, Cambridge: Polity Press, 8–9.

37 Kjær, Anne Mette (2004), *Governance*, Cambridge: Polity Press, 10.

38 Finer, Herman (1949), *Theory and Practice of Modern Government* Revised Edition, New York: Henry Holt and Company, 4.

39 Gehring, Thomas (1994), *Dynamic International Regimes: Institutions for International Environmental Governance*, Frankfurt am Main: Peter Lang, 481.

of regulating and ordering issues of public interest'.[40] Governance thus clearly intends to change human behaviour and provides the means for this with a view to achieving a specific outcome, whether good or bad, through a process of steering.

Second, the regulation and ordering of issues of common public interests take place to a greater or lesser extent in the context of politics and power, where, 'hard' state and softer, non-state forms of law play an important role. To be sure, power is arguably the common denominator of law, politics and governance, or as Hunt and Wickham[41] put it: '[G]overnance involves power ... and as such involves politics and resistance.' Politics can be explained as the 'use of social power' and power in relation to politics and regulation could simplistically be explained as: 'X has power over Y insofar as: (i) X is able, in one way or another, to get Y to do something (ii) that is more to X's liking, and (iii) which Y would not otherwise have done.'[42] Law is an example of a normative societal construct that could be used to 'get someone to do something' and it is employed in the governance setting as a social construct intended to regulate and to exercise power, also by means and as a result *inter alia* of political processes. Another view describes the relationship between politics, power and governance as follows:

> Where 'power' summarises the processes of the operation of various techniques of governance, 'politics' summarises the processes which have emerged and which continue to emerge, in myriad form, concerned with the contestation of power, that is, to be more precise, the contestation of techniques of governance.[43]

In other words, power is related to the process of governance and the way governance is performed, and politics is the process concerned with the struggles for superiority or victory in these governance processes. As far as the environmental aspect of politics, law and power is concerned, it is trite that politics is a powerful ingredient in the present environmental debate: '[E]cological thought ... is extensively devoted to the *problématique* of

---

40 Peters, Anne (2005), 'Global Constitutionalism in a Nutshell' in Klaus Dicke *et al.* (eds), *Weltinnenrecht: Liber amicorum Jost Delbrück*, Berlin: Duncker & Humblot, 537.

41 Hunt, Alan and Gary Wickham (1994), *Foucault and the Law: Towards a Sociology of Law as Governance*, London: Pluto Press, 80.

42 Goodin, Robert E. and Hans-Dieter Klingemann (1996), 'Political Science: the Discipline' in Robert E. Goodin and Hans-Dieter Klingemann (eds), *A New Handbook of Political Science*, Oxford: Oxford University Press, 7–8.

43 Hunt, Alan and Gary Wickham (1994), *Foucault and the Law: Towards a Sociology of Law as Governance*, London: Pluto Press, 82.

politics: the principles of sustainable community life.'[44] Hurrell[45] further reminds us in this respect that:

> The fragility of international society and the propensity of international relations to frustrate hopes for progress make it important to adopt a broad definition of the scope and purpose of political theory and to insist at the outset that normative conceptions of how we should tackle environmental challenges facing us be firmly anchored in a realistic appreciation of the possibilities of effective political actions.

While the political and power aspects of governance arguably manifest predominantly in the state (public) context, it is conceivable that private forms of governance exercised by non-state actors would similarly, if to a lesser degree, be characterized by the interplay between power and politics. The ideas of power and politics therefore do not necessarily always have to be considered in strict state context but could fit equally well in the private, non-state context. It is, for example, highly unlikely that global environmental non-governmental organizations (NGOs) such as Greenpeace would be immune from politics and power both in their internal governance and in exerting outside influence with a view to achieving their objectives. Moreover, non-state actors such as Greenpeace mainly attempt through their work to change behaviour towards the environment. Thus, if power and politics relate to getting someone to do something which he or she would not normally have done in the absence of a corrective or preventative intervention, then power and politics would also apply in the private, non-state context, where a non-state actor would attempt to change behaviour by using these.

A third and related commonality permeates various conceptions of governance, which is governance's central objective: to steer, regulate, control, direct or influence interactions.[46] Interactions must be broadly interpreted to

---

[44] Laferrière, Eric and Peter J. Stoett (2006), 'Introduction: Exploring International Ecopolitical Theory' in Eric Laferrière and Peter J. Stoett (eds), *International Ecopolitical Theory: Critical Approaches*, Vancouver: UBC Press, 4. Commenting on global environmental governance reforms, Hierlmeier stresses the connection between the environment and politics thus: '[A]lthough reformed legal arrangements are necessary, they alone will not be sufficient to overcome the environmental challenges of this generation. Ultimately, at the root of change lies the need for political will; only once institutional change is backed by popular and political support will tangible results be achieved.' Hierlmeier, Jodie (2002), 'UNEP: Retrospect and Prospect-Options for Reforming the Global Environmental Governance Regime', *Georgetown International Environmental Law Review*, **14**, 767–805 at 805.

[45] Hurrell, Andrew (1995), 'International Political Theory and the Global Environment' in Ken Booth and Steve Smith (eds), *International Relations Theory Today*, Cambridge: Polity Press, 129.

[46] Kooiman, Jan (2003), *Governing as Governance*, London: Sage Publications Limited, 11–13.

include interactions between multiple human actors; between various organizational units through which people act (such as organizations, networks and regimes);[47] and the interactions between people and non-human objects. The latter point is explained by Hunt and Wickham,[48] who understand governance to be 'any attempt to control or manage any known object. A "known object" is an event, a relationship, an animate object, an inanimate object, in fact any phenomenon which human beings try to control or manage.' A useful example here is the relationship between people and non-human environmental components,[49] between people themselves as far as the environment is concerned, and the subsequent many interactions which arise as a result of these relationships. Here governance is concerned with regulating people-to-people interactions and people-to-(non-human) environment interactions, where the process of governing could be described as:

> The totality of interactions, in which public as well as private actors participate, aimed at solving societal problems or creating societal opportunities; attending to the institutions as contexts for these governing interactions; and establishing a normative foundation for all those activities.[50]

While the meaning of 'interactions' is self-evident, it is important to note that interactions consist of processes and structures. Processes are understood to mean 'the outcome of the capacity of governing actors or entities to act', and the structures of interactions refer to 'the material, social and cultural contexts in which interactions come about'.[51] The governance perspective therefore consists of interactions, processes and structures, which means that it usually involves a multitude of people and structures (through which people are represented) by means of which people govern (for example, the citizens of a state who elect officials and create government departments), as well as the authority that the people and structures have to achieve a certain outcome, including the processes by means of which they achieve that outcome. In this context Kooiman further helpfully distinguishes between different modes of governance, which include self-governance, co-governance and hierarchical governance. These modes are not necessarily mutually exclusive but could co-exist

---

47 On regimes, organization and networks, see Chapter 4.

48 Hunt, Alan and Gary Wickham (1994), *Foucault and the Law: Towards a Sociology of Law as Governance*, London: Pluto Press, 78.

49 The phrase 'the non-human environment' encapsulates a necessary distinction if one assumes that people are also part of the environment, as is suggested in Chapter 8.

50 Kooiman, Jan (2003), *Governing as Governance*, London: Sage Publications Limited, 4.

51 Kooiman, Jan (2003), *Governing as Governance*, London: Sage Publications Limited, 13.

in a complementary fashion where appropriate and desirable. All three modes describe different ways of regulating interactions, regardless of where and how these interactions manifest and occur. While self-governance relates to the 'capacity of social entities to govern themselves autonomously',[52] co-governance essentially refers to collaborative governance shared between private and public actors such as public-private partnerships, co-management schemes, regimes and networks.[53] Hierarchical governance refers to the rational Weberian bureaucratic form of state-centred or public actor-dominated governance that one traditionally finds in the orthodox Westphalian model of governance.[54] A concrete example occurs where various state and non-state actors interact by means of negotiations, for instance, with a view to regulating the manner in which countries respond to an environmental problem. This is a task for global environmental governance, which would consist of the interactions between the citizens of numerous countries (represented through states and the representatives of states such as intergovernmental organizations) who seek to mitigate and adapt to the effects of climate change by negotiating a legal agreement acceptable to them (the *United Nations Framework Convention on Climate Change* (UNFCCC)[55] and the *Kyoto Protocol*);[56] and by means of which they commit themselves to creating various structures and institutions and mechanisms (the Treaty Secretariat, for example) which must oversee the implementation of the climate treaty regime. Non-state actors have an increasingly important role to play in this process by asserting themselves (often through NGOs) to influencing the creation of these structures and institutions. The structures and institutions now have the authority, by virtue of majority state consent and civil society support, to embark on a multitude of actions or processes to achieve the outcomes of the overall climate treaty regime.[57] These processes, structures and interactions are cumulatively termed

---

52 Kooiman, Jan (2003), *Governing as Governance*, London: Sage Publications Limited, 79.

53 Kooiman, Jan (2003), *Governing as Governance*, London: Sage Publications Limited, 96–114.

54 Kooiman, Jan (2003), *Governing as Governance*, London: Sage Publications Limited, 116–31.

55 *United Nations Framework Convention on Climate Change*, 31 I.L.M. 849 (1992)

56 Kyoto Protocol to the United Nations Framework on Climate Change, 37 I.L.M. 22 (1998).

57 This, however, does not necessarily mean that the process of creating the climate governance regime is legitimate and that the regime itself is legitimate. Legitimacy in international environmental law and governance is a contentious issue which is increasingly demanding its fair share of scholarly attention, as is attested by the extensive writings on the issue. Perez states: 'as more and more powers are trans-

'climate governance', which constitutes part of the broader global environmental governance paradigm. The climate governance regime thus described is an example of hierarchical governance with state actors assuming central roles. However, in tandem and as a result of globalization, the centrality of the state is gradually being tempered and diluted by the increased prominence of non-state actors, a point which is elaborated upon elsewhere in this book.[58] One can thus justifiably speak of the emergence of forms of co-governance as opposed to hierarchical governance and even self-governance where, for example, corporations are subscribing to voluntary environmental management programmes such as the ISO 14001 environmental management system (EMS) with a view to contributing, without state coercion, to climate mitigation and adaptation.

4. MAPPING THE DEFINITIONAL FIELD OF GOVERNANCE

Literature is replete with definitions of governance. The following sections offer a critical survey of how scholars use and understand governance as a scientific concept.[59]

4.1 Black-letter Dictionary Definitions

Standard dictionary definitions of governance are mostly concerned with governance in its orthodox state-centred manifestation. For example, the Oxford Dictionary of English defines the noun governance as 'the action or

---

ferred from state-level to transnational level, the detachment between these global legal networks and the traditional sources of legitimacy – the nation, the cultural unit – is becoming more problematical. The result is a deepening legitimacy crisis.' Perez, Oren (2004), 'The Many Faces of the Trade-Environment Conflict: Some Lessons for the Constitutionalisation Project' in Christian Joerges, Inger-Johanne Sand and Gunther Teubner, *Transnational Governance and Constitutionalism*, Oregon: Hart Publishing, at 241. See further on the issue of legitimacy Bodansky, Daniel (1999), 'The Legitimacy of International Governance: A Coming Challenge for International Environmental Law?', *American Journal of International Law*, **93**(3), 596–624; Stone, Christopher D. (1996), 'Locale and Legitimacy in International Environmental Law', *Stanford Law Review*, **48**(5), 1279–91; Bernstein, Steven (2005), 'Legitimacy in Global Environmental Governance', *Journal of International Law and International Relations*, **1**(1–2), 139–66.

58 See Chapters 4 and 6.

59 It should be noted from the outset that most of these descriptions have various commonalities that are related, making it difficult to divide them into distinct categories.

manner of governing a state, organization, etc.'[60] As a verb, governance manifests as 'to govern', which is defined as an activity to 'conduct the policy, actions, and affairs of (a state, organization, or people) with authority ... [to] control, influence, or regulate (a person, action, or course of events)'. In short, and as a minimum in its traditional guise as per this definition, governance means the regulation of a state's affairs and its people through political authority; a decidedly hierarchical orthodox Westphalian concept of governance. Governance is defined elsewhere as the '[E]xercise of authority; direction; [and] control' or the '[M]anner or system of government or regulation.'[61] The activity 'to govern' is defined *inter alia* as '[T]o rule or control by right or authority ... [t]o control or influence morally or physically ... [t]o exercise authority.'[62]

These dictionary definitions, while suffering from sensitivity to nuance as dictionary definitions often tend to do, suggest that governance, at least from a political perspective, means the collection of polity (institutions), politics (processes), and policy (the content and result of polity and politics).[63] In terms of these definitions, governance seems to focus on steering (*Steuerung*),[64] a concept which some argue includes both governance and

---

60 Soanes, Catherine and Angus Stevenson (eds), *Oxford Dictionary of English* 2nd edn revised, Oxford: Oxford University Press, 749.

61 Funk and Wagnalls (1965), *Collier's Standard Dictionary of the English Language: International Edition Volume One*, New York: Funk and Wagnalls Company, 546.

62 Funk and Wagnalls (1965), *Collier's Standard Dictionary of the English Language: International Edition Volume One*, New York: Funk and Wagnalls Company, 546.

63 Benz, Arthur (2004), 'Einleitung: Governance-Modebegriff oder nützliches sozialwissenschaftliches Konzept?' in Arthur Benz (ed), *Governance- Regieren in komplexen Regelsystemen: Eine Einführung*, Wiesbaden, Germany: VS Verlag für Sozialwissenschaften, 15.

64 The historically-derived description of governance as meaning steering or control today gives rise to some theoretical anomalies, especially when one attempts to apply the theory of steering or control to modern conceptions of governance. This is so because governance in a globalized context describes a non-hierarchical mixture of various public and private actors against the broader backdrop of the changing role of the state. As Engi points out, steering implies a steering subject and steering object, but in the modern plural and non-hierarchical conception of governance these steering subjects and objects are not well defined and thus not easily identifiable, if at all. It is accordingly often unclear who is steering and who is being steered. If governance entails the disappearance or merging of a steering subject and object, as it increasingly does, it is then the direct opposite of steering and rather coincides with 'being steered'. Instead of representing a further theoretical stage of development of the concept governance, it rather functions as a contra-concept. Engi, Lorenz (2008), 'Governance: Umrisse und Problematik eines staatstheoretischen Leitbildes', *Der Staat: Zeitschrift für Staatslehre und Verfassungsgesichte, deutsches und europäisiches Öffentliches Recht*, **47**, 573–87 at 579.

governing.[65] Whilst governing collectively refers to numerous activities by means of which actors (both private or public, or hybrid private-public) intend to guide, steer, control, or manage, governance instead refers to a certain set of patterns which emerges as a result of the activities involved with governing. Governance is therefore a direct result of governing activities in terms of which action is taken to steer, direct, control or manage. Thus viewed, governing leads to governance. The actors that govern make use of certain mechanisms such as rules of authority which could be encapsulated in and provided by law in the form of command and control mechanisms; voluntary mechanisms; self-regulatory mechanisms; and market-based mechanisms.[66] In this sense, the specific design and nature of the normative rule would also have an impact on the method and design of governance. For example, command and control regulation through statutory environmental provisions that provide *inter alia* criminal sanctions and licence conditions would be a decidedly state-centred and hierarchical form of governance, as opposed to a more flexible and non-state dominated legal framework that provides corporate actors with the opportunity to comply with environmental legislation by means of co- or self-governance.

In addition to dictionary definitions, descriptions of the concept of governance abound in scientific literature. These differ from author to author and from discipline to discipline. To date, there is no uniform and universally accepted definition of the governance concept which could be consistently applied in all the disciplines, a point which is illustrated by the analysis contained in the following sections.

4.2 Governance and the Poetic Promise of Happiness and Well-being

In his 1949 work entitled *Theory and Practice of Modern Government*, Finer[67] makes an important general and somewhat poetic statement about government which is instructive to our modern day conception of governance, especially because government as he described it then is no different from governance as we know it today:

---

65 Kjær, Anne Mette (2004), *Governance*, Cambridge: Polity Press, 41.

66 Kjær, Anne Mette (2004), *Governance*, Cambridge: Polity Press, 42–3. For a discussion of these instruments, see also Blanco, Elena and Jona Razzaque (2011), *Globalisation and Natural Resources Law: Challenges, Key Issues and Perspectives*, Cheltenham: Edward Elgar Publishing, 104–16.

67 Finer, Herman (1949), *Theory and Practice of Modern Government* Revised edition, New York: Henry Holt and Company, 6.

> Government is composed of patterns of human cooperation; the allocation and forms of authority; and procedure. That is its anatomy. Its soul lies in choosing between alternative objectives of happiness and choosing between duties and sacrifices, and effecting a proportion between them. It allows no complete rejections, but imposes a decision on a tolerable mixture of preferences, seeking and keeping power balanced against what other men and women are seeking; seeking, keeping and changing. The institutions of government are created and amended by men to enable them the better to attain what they believe to be their happiness and to fulfil what they surmise to be their duty.

Thus considered, intuitively speaking, it is easy to appreciate the central tenet of governance: to a greater or lesser extent it has to do, among other things, with regulating, controlling, manipulating, and steering social behaviour; with managing, exercising authority, directing and direction, influencing, reigning, swaying, correcting, coercing, compelling, enforcing, punishing, rewarding and organizing bureaucracy, politics, power, laws, rules, and commands. All of the foregoing is aimed at achieving a certain result. The words describe governance as a means to an end; namely the achievement of 'happiness' or rather satisfaction and well-being and the concomitant fulfilment of various (moral) duties to achieve the foregoing. Governance is mostly focused on people and the way that people cooperate through authority and various procedures to realize that authority. Finer's conception of governance suggests that it is also centrally concerned with enhancing human well-being (happiness) and that it seeks to identify objectives and to set out duties to be performed in the achievement of these objectives, often at the expense of some but to the benefit of others.[68]

4.3 The Commission on Global Governance

One of the most frequently cited definitions of governance is that of the Commission on Global Governance,[69] which describes it as:

> ... the sum of the many ways individuals and institutions, public and private, manage their common affairs. It is a continuing process through which conflicting or diverse interests may be accommodated and co-operative action may be taken. It includes formal institutions and regimes empowered to enforce compliance, as well

---

68 Throughout this process it is self-evidently impossible for governance to satisfy everyone all the time. As long as it is accepted (or tolerated) by the majority of people, the most it can wish to achieve is to balance disparate human needs and to fulfil these as far as possible to the extent that as many people as possible are satisfied by it in the process.

69 Commission on Global Governance (1995), *Our Global Neighbourhood*, Oxford: Oxford University Press, 2.

> as informal arrangements that people and institutions either have agreed to or perceive to be in their interest.

In the Commission's view, governance involves private and public institutions (supposedly meaning physical organizations such as intergovernmental organizations and government departments), and individuals working in these institutions. Governance is a management process which strives to continuously accommodate common interests among many actors, with a view to achieving and promoting the common good. It is not clear what the common good would be, but presumably it is what people perceive to be in their interest and to be to their benefit; for example, a better quality of life and an environment not harmful to health or well-being.[70] Of everything globally, the environment is perhaps the clearest manifestation of a common concern of mankind in which all people, including state and non-state actors, have a collective universal interest. At the heart of this common interest lies the need to survive in the wake of unsustainable resource exploitation and depletion, population growth, climate change, and unprecedented pollution in the midst of a world troubled by political instability, armed conflict and economic upheaval.

Governance also relates to institutional structures, including organizations and regimes flowing from these structures, and an array of widely defined informal arrangements (which could be anything that aims to achieve the steering objective of governance) that people employ in their efforts to manage their common affairs. That the focus of governance is on common affairs is significant because one has to ask if governance could also be used to manage affairs that are only important to one person or one group of persons and not to others. While an answer is not forthcoming from the Commission's definition, one could argue that in an interconnected global society individual, non-collective

---

[70] As Bryde states;

> The core of a constitutionalised international law is the general acceptance of a common interest of mankind that transcends the sum of individual state interests ... The recognition of common interests of mankind is of fundamental importance. The challenges facing mankind cannot be solved by balancing the interests between individual states. Solutions can only be found if common interests of mankind are recognised as paramount and all actors of international law are obliged to pursue a global policy programme.

Bryde, Brun-Otto (2005), 'International Democratic Constitutionalism' in Ronald St, John Macdonald and Douglas M. Johnston (eds), *Towards World Constitutionalism: Issues in the Legal Ordering of the World Community*, Leiden: Martinus Nijhoff Publishers, 107.

affairs could presumably have an influence on common affairs and interests and thus would require governance in equal measure as part of the collective effort to manage common affairs. Indeed, it is difficult to think of a case in the environmental context where the environmental interests of one state would not affect the interests of other states as well. This is because of the interconnected nature of the environment and the reciprocity and mutual causality of those who influence its condition.[71] Environmental issues are common issues because they affect the common good, especially and increasingly so in a globalized world. They lend themselves therefore particularly well to the governance paradigm, which aims to regulate activity with a view to promoting this common good or achieving a common objective.[72] In sum, governance is a management process for the Commission. It consists of private (non-state) and public (state) actors and institutions, and it provides the opportunity and means to take collective action to protect and promote common interests and affairs.

4.4 Steering Behaviour for Collective Gains

Related to the issues of the common good discussed above is the notion of 'steering the collective', which is similarly a central concern of governance. Leonard[73] defines governance as an 'accepted set of rules that guide actors' behavior in their endeavor to solve collective problems'; it is centred on the objective of 'steering'. Keohane and Nye[74] similarly state that governance is 'the processes and institutions, both formal and informal, that guide and restrain the collective activities of a group'. These rules, processes and institutions arguably include legal and non-legal rules and a range of social institutions which could be used to steer the behaviour of actors with a view to solving collective problems that are of concern to these actors. Governance therefore provides a roadmap containing the rules which should guide various

---

71 See also the discussion in Chapter 8.

72 It is true that where one element of the environment is affected, others will also be affected because of this. Where, for example, a state takes a decidedly one-sided decision not to commit to the obligations of the Kyoto Protocol because it would be in its singular economic interest not to do so, this decision will necessarily have an impact on all other states and all people living in the world, because the effects of climate change will be prolonged and possibly exacerbated if carbon emissions are not limited and reduced, even by one state.

73 Leonard, Eric K. (2005), *The Onset of Global Governance: International Relations Theory and the International Criminal Court*, Aldershot: Ashgate, 168.

74 Keohane, Robert O. and Joseph S. Nye (2002), 'Governance in a Globalizing World' in Robert O. Keohane (ed), *Power and Governance in a Partially Globalized World*, London: Routledge, 202.

actors, presumably private and public, in their efforts to solve collective problems. Again, the emphasis is on influencing, directing or changing human behaviour with a view to achieving common or collective objectives.

Benz[75] similarly describes the conceptual essence of governance as steering and coordination with the purpose of managing interdependencies that exist between and among various actors. Steering and coordination is based on institutionalized systems of rules which aim to control or direct human interaction. Governance provides for the design and functioning of interactions and the *modi* for collective actions such as networks or coalitions, as well as steering processes including, for example, coordination activities that now traverse increasingly fluid geographic and organizational boundaries (especially in regional context), including those traditionally strict boundaries between the state and society, which have become equally blurred.[76]

For Pierre,[77] governance:

> ... refers to sustaining co-ordination and coherence among a wide variety of actors with different purposes and objectives such as political actors and institutions, corporate interests, civil society, and transnational organizations ... governance could be said to be shorthand for the predominant view of government in the *Zeitgeist* of the late twentieth century. Governance, in this debate, is about how to maintain the 'steering' role of political institutions despite the internal and external challenges to the state. It is also, presumably, more palatable than 'government' which has become a slightly pejorative concept.

Betsill and Bulkeley[78] define governance along similar lines: 'it involves processes through which collective goals are defined and pursued in which the state (or government) is not necessarily the only or most important actor'. These authors emphasize, as the former two commentators do, governance's central purpose of steering, which aims to achieve collective co-ordination and coherence and common goals of and among different actors in a globalized world where the traditional role of the state is increasingly transforming – a

---

75 Benz, Arthur (2004), 'Einleitung: Governance-Modebegriff oder nützliches sozialwissenschaftliches Konzept?' in Arthur Benz (ed), *Governance- Regieren in komplexen Regelsystemen: Eine Einführung*, Wiesbaden, Germany: VS Verlag für Sozialwissenschaften, 25.

76 See also Heinelt, Hubert (2004), 'Governance auf lokaler Ebene' in Arthur Benz (ed), *Governance- Regieren in komplexen Regelsystemen: Eine Einführung*, Wiesbaden, Germany: VS Verlag für Sozialwissenschaften, 30.

77 Pierre, Jon (2000), 'Introduction: Understanding Governance' in Jon Pierre (ed), *Debating Governance: Authority, Steering and Democracy*, Oxford: Oxford University Press, 4.

78 Betsill, Michelle M. and Harriet Bulkeley (2006), 'Cities and the Multilevel Governance of Global Climate Change', *Global Governance*, **12**, 141–59 at 144.

point which is further explained in the following section. In this view governance is a modern metamorphosis of government. Its connotation is not as disparaging as the term government, and it is therefore more palatable.

4.5 The Club of Rome's *Leviathanesque* Perspective

For the Club of Rome[79] governance is:

> ... the command mechanism of a social system (and its actions), that endeavours to provide security, prosperity, coherence, order and continuity to the system. It necessarily embraces the ideology of the system ... It also includes the structure of the government of the system, its policies and procedures ... governance is the means to provide a stable equilibrium between the various centres of power. Seen in a broad sense, the concept of governance should not be restricted to the national and international systems, but should be applied to regional, provincial and local governments as well as to other social systems.

This definition is representative of an orthodox state-centred and hierarchical view of governance as a political phenomenon by means of which a government exerts control over its subjects in a social system. It is what Pierre above would describe as 'unpalatable' or pejorative. The idea of the Leviathan state as an all-powerful and conquering entity significantly deviates from an understanding of governance as a hybrid public-private construct which responds to continuously changing conditions in a globalized world, and the Club of Rome's definition is therefore unacceptable as an explanation of governance in a contemporary globalized context.[80] The definition remains useful, however, to the extent that it emphasizes the inevitability of the state's involvement in global governance, because it stresses the important point that the state remains a key ingredient, if not *the* key ingredient, in global governance, regardless of any movement towards 'governance without government'[81] in a globalized world.

---

[79] King, Alexander and Bertrand Schneider (1993), *The First Global Revolution: A Report by the Council of the Club of Rome*, Orient Longman, 114–15 [accessed at http://www.archive.org/details/TheFirstGlobalRevolution on 25 February 2011].

[80] The Leviathan, here, is a reference to Thomas Hobbes's seminal work *Leviathan or the Matter, Form and Power of a Commonwealth Ecclesiastical and Civil* (1651), where he argues for a strong central government with absolute power and an absolute sovereign as a means to achieve and perpetuate peace.

[81] On the issue of 'governance without government', see generally Rosenau, James N. (1992), 'Governance, Order, and Change in World Politics' in James N. Rosenau and Ernst-Otto Czempiel (eds), *Governance without Government: Order and Change in World Politics*, Cambridge: Cambridge University Press.

4.6 Governance as Transformative, Multi-level Hybrid Regulation

In sharp contrast with the Club of Rome's definition, Biermann *et al.*[82] understand governance generally to imply new forms of regulation that are increasingly non-state centred and less hierarchical. For them it is multi-level and includes a wide array of state and non-state actors. This implies the need for some measure of self-regulation, and increasingly involves public and private (state and non-state) cooperation in addressing societal problems:

> The concept of governance is mirrored in legal science, where scholars observe an evolution from an international law based on explicit state consent ... and from single to pluralist sites and actors of governance ... and to multilevel systems of governance and complex hybrid public-private international law systems ... from the local to international levels, the concept of governance is not confined to states and governments as sole actors, but is marked by participation of [a] myriad public and private non-state actors at all levels of decision-making, ranging from networks of experts, environmentalists and multinational corporations to new agencies set up by governments, such as intergovernmental bureaucracies.

The authors further indicate that it is possible to identify in some instances a distinct governance architecture, which consists of 'clusters of norms, principles, regimes and other institutions in any issue area'. The governance architecture 'conceptualizes the overarching system of public or private institutions, principles, norms, regulations, decision-making procedures and organizations that are valid or active in the issue area'.[83] In instances where a distinct cluster or grouping of norms, principles, regimes and institutions around a specific issue can be observed, one would be able to speak of an equally distinct governance architecture.

Extrapolated to the context of the environment (the environment being a specific issue area), it is therefore possible to identify global environmental governance as a distinct governance architecture that consists of normative rules (mostly in terms of 'hard' laws made by states, but increasingly – with the input of non-state actors – also 'softer' normative arrangements); principles (such as sustainability, the principle of 'no harm' and the precautionary and preventive principles);[84] more specific miscellaneous regulations which

---

[82] Biermann, Frank *et al.* (2010), 'Earth System Governance: A Research Framework', *International Environmental Agreements: Politics, Law and Economics*, **10**(4), 277–98 at 279.

[83] Biermann, Frank *et al.* (2010), 'Earth System Governance: A Research Framework', *International Environmental Agreements: Politics, Law and Economics*, **10**(4), 277–98 at 281.

[84] These principles exist because they have been created by means of legal-political processes and are mostly constituted in and by legal instruments such as treaties and legislation.

could be formal and/or informal; state and non-state organizations responsible for applying and monitoring normative rules and regulations, such as NGOs, intergovernmental organizations and environmental treaty secretariats; and decision-making procedures which mostly determine the manner in which these actors go about their everyday business to apply the substantive normative rules. These decision-making procedures could include, for example, the administrative rules and procedures of UNEP or those rules which govern the administration and bureaucracy of administrative bodies under the climate change treaty framework, such as the Secretariat situated in Bonn, Germany.

4.7 Governance as Cooperation, Interaction and Coordination

For Falkner,[85] governance is not merely synonymous with incidental cooperation:

> Cooperation requires the adjustment of individual behavior to achieve mutually beneficial objectives ... Governance, however, emerges out of a context of interaction that is institutionalized and of a more permanent nature. In a system of governance, individual actors do not constantly decide to be bound by the institutional norms based on a calculation of their interests, but adjust their behavior out of recognition of the legitimacy of the governance system. Cooperation may lead to governance, but more is required than the spontaneous convergence of ... interests.

In terms of this description, governance is concerned with achieving mutually beneficial objectives through cooperation and institutionalized interaction. Falkner sees cooperation as leading to governance; a view that differs from the more generally accepted idea that governance arises out of a need for cooperation among and between various actors. Nevertheless, actors' willingness to cooperate and to interact is motivated not only by their attempts to pursue their mutual interests. It also lies in considerations of legitimacy of the governance system to which they subscribe. This would mean that actors would be less inclined to cooperate and interact if they perceived a governance system as lacking legitimacy. Governance therefore is about cooperation and focuses on aligning and regulating the interactions between diverse actors and, as with most of the preceding descriptions, governance is about achieving mutual objectives where common interests are at stake. It represents, however, more than mere cooperation around common interests; it is mostly about adjusting human behaviour in an interactive setting where the achievement of common

[85] Falkner, Robert (2003), 'Private Environmental Governance and International Relations: Exploring the Links', *Global Environmental Politics*, **3**(2), 72–87 at 73.

goals is a primary concern and where various actors change their behaviour according to what they perceive to be legitimate and thus acceptable.

Closely related to Falkner's emphasis on governance as cooperation and interaction is governance's related coordination function. Schuppert,[86] for example, states that governance is centrally occupied with coordination; especially coordination of the activities and actions of a wide variety of state and non-state actors. These actors have different approaches to achieve the communal pursuit of collective issues, objectives and interests, and it is one of the primary tasks of governance to coordinate all of these activities. Governance thus viewed is about cooperation, interaction and the coordination of many actors and variables with a view to achieving a common goal.[87]

4.8 Governance as Formal and Informal Rules

According to Scanlon and Burhenne-Guilmin:[88]

> Governance can be described as the means by which society defines goals and priorities and advances cooperation; be it globally, regionally, nationally or locally. Governance arrangements are expressed through legal and policy frameworks, strategies, and action plans; they include the organizational arrangements for following up on policies and plans and monitoring performance. Governance covers the rules of decision-making, including who gets access to information and participates in the decision-making process, as well as the decisions themselves ... Most fundamentally, governance is a means to an end, not an end in itself.

Scanlon and Burhenne-Guilmin's description provides a broad juristic view of governance by emphasizing its procedural, substantive, and normative aspects as they are entrenched in law and other non-legal norms. It sees governance not as a result, but rather as a way of achieving a specific result which has been defined by a society in terms of goals and priorities. Part of this societal process is the setting of goals and priorities and the advancement of cooperation to achieve these goals. Governance occurs at all levels, including the international, regional, national, and local. It consists of broadly defined

86 Schuppert, Gunnar Folke (2007), 'Was ist und wozu Governance?', *Die Verwaltung: Zeitschrift für Verwaltungsrecht und Verwaltungswissenschaften*, **40**(1), 463–511 at 487.

87 The motivation and driver behind the willingness of actors to cooperate will be the desire to achieve a common goal or solve a common problem, provided the governance system is legitimate.

88 Scanlon, John and Francoise Burhenne-Guilmin (2004), 'Executive Summary' in John Scanlon and Francoise Burhenne-Guilmin (eds), *International Environmental Governance: An International Regime for Protected Areas*, Gland, Switzerland and Cambridge: IUCN, 2.

means and arrangements which are provided by rules ranging from formal legal rules to rules stemming from more informal arrangements such as action plans. Governance is also about the execution or enforcement of these rules by means of an organizational response. It is concerned not only with substantive rules and the decisions that are made in terms of these rules, but also with rules concerning procedural matters and how these decisions are made. The rules should thus determine both the content of decisions and the manner in which these decisions are made and the objectives of governance are achieved. This description emphasizes the hybrid normative characteristics of governance: that it consists of formal and informal rules which provide the substance of governance, as well as the procedural rules according to which the substantive objectives must be achieved.

4.9 Governance as an Institutional Response to Collective Problems

For Young,[89] governance at the most general level:

> ... involves the establishment and operation of social institutions (in the sense of rules of the game that serve to define social practices, assign roles, and guide interactions among the occupants of these roles) capable of resolving conflicts, facilitating cooperation, or, more generally, alleviating collective-action problems in a world of interdependent actors.

A comparable definition from Reinalda[90] suggests that: '[G]overnance thus refers to the solving of collective problems in a continuously changing public and private realm, stressing processes and institutional procedures and practices.' In the view of both authors, governance is an institutional response to collective problems and is therefore focused on problem-solving. This is accomplished by means of social institutions that have as their primary objective directing actor behaviour in such a way that conflicts are resolved, cooperation is facilitated, and collective problems that exist between interdependent actors are alleviated.[91] Governance is about the establishment

---

[89] Young, Oran R. (1994), *International Governance: Protecting the Environment in a Stateless Society*, Ithaca, NY and London: Cornell University Press, 15.

[90] Reinalda, Bob (1999), 'International Organizations as Sources of Political Change' in Kees Van Kersbergen, Robert H. Lieshout, and Grahame Lock (eds), *Expansion and Fragmentation: Internationalization, Political Change and the Transformation of the Nation State*, Amsterdam, The Netherlands: Amsterdam University Press, 116–17.

[91] Kooiman stresses the importance of interdependence in the governance realm:

> The governance approach also assumes that many of these inter-relations are

and operation of these social institutions; it is the sum of all of these social institutions and sets out the rules by means of which the game is to be played. The rules define social practices, assign roles, and guide interactions, and could include formal, 'hard' legal rules as well as informal, 'softer' rules. The institutional aspects of global governance are further explored in Chapter 4.

4.10 Governance as Spheres of Authority

Rosenau[92] describes governance at an abstract and generalized level to be:

> ... spheres of authority (SOAs) at all levels of human activity – from the household to the demanding public to the international organization – that amount to systems of rule in which goals are pursued through the exercise of control ... Governance, in other words, encompasses the activities of governments, but it also includes any actors who resort to command mechanisms to make demands, frame goals, issue directives, and pursue policies.

The aspect of 'control' is obviously central to Rosenau's understanding of governance. He explains that control:

> ... consists of relational phenomena which, taken holistically, comprise systems of rule. Some actors, the controllers [or the governors], seek to modify the behaviour and/or orientations of other actors, the controlees [or the governed], and the resulting patterns of interaction between the former and the latter can properly be viewed as a system of rule sustained by one or another form of control.[93]

Control is exercised in spheres of authority which range from the formal sphere of the state to the more informal sphere of the private sector (such as households) through formal and informal processes and institutions and systems of rule which aim to control or restrain human behaviour with the view to fulfilling a specific objective. Rosenau's emphasis on 'systems of rules' embraces the idea that governance is also based on some normative

---

> based on the recognition of inter-dependencies. No single actor, public or private, has the knowledge and information required to solve complex, dynamic and diversified societal challenges; no governing actor has an overview sufficient to make the necessary instruments effective; no single actor has sufficient action potential to dominate unilaterally.

Kooiman, Jan (2003), *Governing as Governance*, London: Sage Publications Limited, 11.

92 Rosenau, James N. (1997), *Along the Domestic-Foreign Frontier: Exploring Governance in a Turbulent World*, Cambridge: Cambridge University Press, 145.

93 Rosenau, James N. (1997), *Along the Domestic-Foreign Frontier: Exploring Governance in a Turbulent World*, Cambridge: Cambridge University Press, 146–7.

foundation which consists of rule-making, rule interpretation, rule application, and rule enforcement. Governance is thus characterized as having to do with authority and the ability to control, command or to restrain with the important objective of modifying the behaviour of people and human agencies (meaning the institutions by means of which humans act): '[T]he distinguishing and prime characteristic of any SOA [sphere of authority] involves the issuance of directives by its leadership and the compliance of its adherents.'[94] The ability to achieve this is thus derived from a specific sphere of authority. If authority is lacking there will be no governance, or at least governance will not be legitimate in the sense that it will not be accepted by the 'controlees' or the governed. Governance must thus be authoritative to be acceptable, which conceivably would mean that it must be legitimate, legal, have majority support, and so forth.

4.11 Common Characteristics

The broad divergence of the views on governance described above suggests that it is a highly fluid concept with many characteristics and aspects. Yet some commonalities permeate the different descriptions, and they could therefore be used collectively in an attempt to derive a core of meaning for the term. The following notions occur frequently in the above descriptions: governance arises where there is human activity; governance could be used to describe the objective of steering; governance is thus a social construct and an institutional response to steer human interaction with a view to achieving some common or collective goal or to solve a collective social problem; governance facilitates cooperation to achieve the foregoing; governance could be private and/or public, formal and/or informal; governance has a normative foundation embedded in rules which dictate its design, substantive content and procedural aspects; and governance requires some form of authority to be present, whether in a public and/or a private sense.

5. GOVERNANCE AND REGULATION

The concepts regulation and governance are often used interchangeably. Is there a difference between them? A functional, conceptual approach to regulation in and of society suggests that regulation consists of some form of stan-

---

[94] Rosenau, James N. (2009), 'Governing the Ungovernable: The Challenge of a Global Disaggregation of Authority' in Dries Lesage and Pierre Vercauteren (eds), *Contemporary Global Governance: Multipolarity vs New Discourses on Global Governance*, Brussels: P.I.E. Peter Lang, 254.

dard setting in society; ways for information gathering that enable continuous monitoring and knowledge about the state of the regulatory system; and the capacity to modify, shape or direct behaviour so that behaviour conforms to predetermined objectives or standards.[95] A narrow approach to regulation centres on the predominant role of the state in all of this, where it seeks to 'influence socially valuable behaviour which may have adverse side-effects by establishing, monitoring and enforcing legal rules'.[96] A broader conception sees regulation 'as encompassing all forms of social control, whether intentional or not, and whether imposed by the state or other social institutions'.[97] Considering the realities of globalization and its disaggregated effects on governance, it seems only logical to follow a more inclusive and comprehensive approach to regulation, namely one which includes traditional orthodox and less-traditional regulatory rules (including laws and other norms), and one which recognizes the participation and influence of numerous state and non-state actors at multiple levels in their efforts to exercise social control or influence behaviour. As another commentator puts it: 'governance, defined as any strategy, process, procedure, or programme for controlling, regulating or exercising authority over either animate or inanimate objects or populations, is regarded as being much broader than the traditional conception of state-centred regulation'.[98] Considering the very broad description of governance earlier in this chapter, regulation in this equally broad sense is thus mostly synonymous with governance, especially insofar as both regulation and governance have the purpose of influencing human behaviour in the pursuit of the collective interests and welfare of a community. The only conceivable difference between governance and regulation in the broad sense might be that governance is a more modern and socio-politically acceptable term than regulation, which instead is part of an older jargon. In a sense, the use of the word 'governance' is therefore more fashionable than the use of the word 'regulation'.

---

[95] Hood, Christopher, Henry Rothstein, and Robert Baldwin (2001), *The Government of Risk: Understanding Risk Regulation Regimes*, Oxford: Oxford University Press, 23.

[96] Morgan, Bronwen and Karen Yeung (2007), *An Introduction to Law and Regulation: Text and Materials*, Cambridge: Cambridge University Press, 3. This narrow approach is similar to the narrow meaning of government as opposed to governance. See the section below.

[97] Morgan, Bronwen and Karen Yeung (2007), *An Introduction to Law and Regulation: Text and Materials*, Cambridge: Cambridge University Press, 3–4.

[98] Swan, Peter (2002), 'Governing at a Distance: An Introduction to Law, Regulation, and Governance' in Michael Mac Neil, Neil Sargent, and Peter Swan (eds), *Law, Regulation and Governance*, Oxford: Oxford University Press, 11.

6. GOVERNANCE AND GOVERNMENT

There are important distinctions between governance and government, yet the two cannot be separated.[99] This is a distinction which reaches far deeper than mere semantics, one that is surprisingly less than obvious, and one that needs to be examined further to enable a better understanding of governance. In a general sense, government is a noun which usually signifies the physical structures and people responsible for governance. Whereas governance is used to describe the process of governing, government is an important ingredient in making governance happen, as it were. Young,[100] for example, describes the difference between governance and government as follows: 'governance systems ... are social institutions or sets of rules guiding the behavior of those engaged in identifiable social practices, and governments ... are organizations or material entities established to administer the provisions of governance systems'. In this sense, government has a physical institutional character which could, for example, consist of people, buildings, offices, ministries, and secretariats. From a legal point of view, government could relate to the legal structure of a state or organization, a form of political authority, or to the functionaries which are responsible for governance, i.e., the people and institutions which govern. Black's Law Dictionary, for example, defines government as:

> The structure of principles and rules determining how a state or organization is regulated ... The sovereign power in a nation or state ... An organization through which a body of people exercise political authority; the machinery by which sovereign power is expressed ... In this sense, the term refers collectively to the political organs of a country regardless of their function or level, and regardless of the subject matter they deal with.[101]

In this sense, government is used to describe the regulatory machinery of a state, including its government. It signifies 'the system by which a state or community is governed'[102] and therefore does not necessarily describe an action but rather a means (machinery) in terms of which regulation takes

---

[99] Detomasi, David Antony (2007), 'The Multinational Corporation and Global Governance: Modelling Global Public Policy Networks', *Journal of Business Ethics*, **71**, 321–34 at 321.

[100] Young, Oran R. (1994), *International Governance: Protecting the Environment in a Stateless Society*, Ithaca, NY and London: Cornell University Press, ix.

[101] Garner, Bryan A. (ed) (2004), *Black's Law Dictionary* 8th edn, Thomson West, St. Paul, 715–16.

[102] See the definition of government in Soanes, Catherine and Angus Stevenson (eds), *Oxford Dictionary of English* 2nd edn revised, Oxford: Oxford University Press, 749.

place; or the 'form by which a community is managed'.[103] It therefore also refers to the executive, legislative and judicial components of a state's government (otherwise referred to as the *trias politica*). In the environmental context the difference between government and governance in the foregoing sense is also obvious. For example, calls for a world environmental government (usually expressed in terms of a world environment organization based in the UN system) are common and many believe it to be a strategy to improve global environmental governance.[104] This would imply that the world environment organization would function as an environmental government which busies itself with matters of environmental governance. The world environment *government* would thus play an important role and be a crucial physical ingredient in global environmental *governance*.

A related and more dominant view on the difference between government and governance is nestled in the globalization paradigm, where government refers to the orthodox, traditional and hierarchical notion of formal Westphalian state-centred governance, while governance means the direct opposite, i.e., informal, flexible, hybrid and multi-level governance, or 'an emerging political strategy for states to redefine [their] role in society'.[105] Finkelstein[106] states that:

> While [governance] turns up often in scholarly discourse about how states relate to each other in the international system, little attention has been given to what it means. At least, it must be clear that it does not mean 'government', or we would say that instead. Since the international system notoriously lacks hierarchy and government, the fuzzier word governance is used instead.

Intuitively, when we speak of government we relate it to a nation state and its formal components, such as the national government of a state which consists

---

103 Funk and Wagnalls (1965), *Collier's Standard Dictionary of the English Language: International Edition Volume One*, New York: Funk and Wagnalls Company, 547.

104 See, for example, Swart, Lydia and Estelle Perry (eds) (2007), *Global Environmental Governance: Perspectives on the Current Debate*, New York: Centre for UN Reform Education; Biermann, Frank and Steffen Bauer (eds) (2005), *A World Environment Organization: Solution or Threat for Effective International Environmental Governance?*, Aldershot: Ashgate.

105 Pierre, Jon (2000), 'Introduction: Understanding Governance' in Jon Pierre (ed), *Debating Governance: Authority, Steering and Democracy*, Oxford: Oxford University Press, 2. For a discussion on the changing role of the nation state in this context, see also Dittgen, Herbert (1999), 'World without Borders? Reflections on the Future of the Nation State', *Government and Opposition*, **34**(2), 161–79.

106 Finkelstein, Lawrence S. (1995), 'What is Global Governance?', *Global Governance*, **1**, 367–72 at 367.

of executive, judicial and legislative authorities, and which purposefully influences the behaviour of the people living in that country by way of rule creation, rule interpretation and rule enforcement; in other words by means of public authority, top-down legal regulation, and through the state apparatus. Whereas government denotes the idea of centralized, hierarchical political power that is vested in some concrete form of state apparatus, governance lacks this hierarchy and is thus more open and flexible and could include non-state actors. The strict separation between public and private forms of governance is increasingly blurred, and 'forms of public and private ordering both overlap and become exchangeable'.[107] The term governance therefore not only describes the process of governing but also describes a change in how we perceive regulation today:

> The past twenty years have witnessed important changes in the ways in which government is exercised ... To capture these processes [of change], the term 'governance' was coined ... [It] points to a turn from a normative substantive conception of government exclusively tied to the national state based on constitutional and international law towards a functional characterization of governing activities. It embraces the possibility of a multiplicity of governance agents, who engage in new modes of exercising power.[108]

Continuing along the same line of argument, Ladeur[109] argues that governance

---

107 Ladeur, Karl-Heinz (2004), 'Globalization and Public Governance: A Contradiction?' in Karl-Heinz Ladeur (ed), *Public Governance in the Age of Globalization*, Aldershot: Ashgate, 17. See also Van Heffen, Oscar, Walter J.M. Kickert and Jacques J.A. Thomassen (2000), 'Introduction: Multi-level and Multi-actor Governance' in Oscar Van Heffen, Walter J.M. Kickert and Jacques J.A. Thomassen (eds), *Governance in Modern Society: Effects, Change and Formation of Government Institutions*, Dordrecht: Kluwer Academic Publishers, 4–5, who write that:

> ... changing attitudes towards the role of government have led to a remodelling of the boundaries between the public and private sectors. Governmental authority and the capacity of public administration systems to steer society are limited by the growing dependence of governmental actors on economic and social actors. This shift of balance has severe consequences for government institutions, decision making, implementation, management and organization.

108 Von Benda-Beckmann, Franz, Keebet Von Benda-Beckmann and Julia Eckert (2009), 'Rules of Law and Laws of Ruling: Law and Governance between Past and Future' in Franz Von Benda-Beckmann, Keebet Von Benda-Beckmann and Julia Eckert (eds), *Rules of Law and Laws of Ruling: on the Governance of Law*, Farnham: Ashgate, 1–2.

109 He specifically finds that:

> ... 'government' ... is closely associated with the sovereign state even if it includes

in the context of globalization describes a form of regulation which is characterized by 'new patterns of networks of inter-relationships' that is not only confined to nation-states any longer. Regulation is new in that it is more 'open', it 'takes up the new forms of permeability of the state'. This 'openness' of governance must be understood in terms of the concept of 'network governance'[110] which denotes 'coordination characterized by informal social systems rather than by bureaucratic structures'.[111] Governance therefore involves less formal bureaucratic state arrangements and instead relies on informal 'open' arrangements for coordination; it provides greater linkage of actors from different institutional levels; it involves a shift of power from orthodox and traditionally well-established levels and actors to organizations or individuals who now must link and coordinate different governance actors; and it entails a move away from hierarchy towards unstructured consultation, negotiation and 'softer' normative regulatory arrangements.[112] Formal governmental decision-making is also less structured, and its focus moves beyond state-centred concerns to focus on global interests. While these new governance processes are not necessarily entirely unstructured and 'chaotic', they are conducive to facilitating more adaptive, responsive, productive, heterarchical, decentralized forms of regulation.[113] In other words, governance describes a new form of bottom-up, 'horizontal' regulation and self-steering, as opposed to the top-down notion of government, where a society is 'vertically' steered by a national government.[114] In this sense, governance implies the existence of shifting *loci* and forms of authority which are diffusing 'upwards' to intergovernmental organizations such as the WTO, UNEP, and

---

> certain non-state forms of exercising political power [it] focuses on binding decision-making, at least as the outcome of a political process. The concept of 'governance', which might be criticized for its vagueness, also comprises, and not by chance, private forms of management.

Ladeur, Karl-Heinz (2004), 'Globalization and Public Governance: A Contradiction?' in Karl-Heinz Ladeur (ed), *Public Governance in the Age of Globalization*, Aldershot: Ashgate, 10.

110 For the role of networks in global governance, see Chapter 4.

111 Jones, Candace, William S. Hesterly and Stephen P. Borgatti (1997), 'A General Theory of Network Governance: Exchange Conditions and Social Mechanisms', *Academy of Management Review*, **22**(4), 911–45 at 911.

112 Coen, David and Mark Thatcher (2008), 'Network Governance and Multi-Level Delegation: European Networks of Regulatory Agencies', *Journal of Public Policy*, **28**(1), 49–71 at 50.

113 Ladeur, Karl-Heinz (2004), 'Globalization and Public Governance: A Contradiction?' in Karl-Heinz Ladeur (ed), *Public Governance in the Age of Globalization*, Aldershot: Ashgate, 10–11.

114 Kjær, Anne Mette (2004), *Governance*, Cambridge: Polity Press, 10–11.

transnational corporations; 'sideways' to global financial markets and social movements; and 'downwards' to various sub-national, mostly non-state, actors.[115]

It is thus clear that government is more formal than governance and that government and various other actors that can govern are involved in governance. Governance is therefore not restricted to governments only, although governments play a most important role in governance:

> Government is the subset that acts with authority and creates formal obligations. Governance need not necessarily be conducted exclusively by governments and the international organizations to which they delegate authority. Private firms, associations of firms, nongovernmental organizations (NGOs), and associations of NGOs all engage in it, often in association with governmental bodies, to create governance; sometimes without governmental authority.[116]

Government is an ingredient of governance: '[T]o use the term governance instead of government ... indicates that the state, or government, is only one of a multitude of agents exercising power from different sites and levels.'[117] Rosenau's[118] explanation is instructive in this respect:

> ... governance is not synonymous with government. Both refer to purposive behavior, to goal-oriented activities, to systems of rule; but government suggests activities that are backed by formal authority, by police powers to insure the implementation of duly constituted policies, whereas governance refers to activities backed by shared goals that may or may not derive from legal and formally prescribed responsibilities and that do not necessarily rely on police powers to overcome defiance and attain compliance. Governance, in other words, is a more encompassing phenomenon than government. It embraces governmental institutions, but it also subsumes informal, non-governmental mechanisms whereby those persons and organizations within its purview move ahead, satisfy their needs, and fulfill their wants. Governance is thus a system of rule that is as dependent on intersubjective meanings as on formally sanctioned constitutions and charters.

---

115 Payne, Anthony (2000), 'Globalization and Modes of Regionalist Governance' in Jon Pierre (ed), *Debating Governance: Authority, Steering and Democracy*, Oxford: Oxford University Press, 203.

116 Keohane, Robert O. and Joseph S. Nye (2002), 'Governance in a Globalizing World' in Robert O. Keohane (ed), *Power and Governance in a Partially Globalized World*, London: Routledge, 202.

117 Anders, Gerhard (2004), 'Lawyers and Anthropologists: A Legal Pluralist Approach to Global Governance' in Ige F. Dekker and Wouter G. Werner (eds), *Governance and International Legal Theory*, Leiden: Martinus Nijhoff Publishers, 39.

118 Rosenau, James N. (1992), 'Governance, Order, and Change in World Politics' in James N. Rosenau and Ernst-Otto Czempiel (eds), *Governance without Government: Order and Change in World Politics*, Cambridge: Cambridge University Press, 4.

It is also worth noting Schuppert's[119] concise comparison between government and governance. The author explains that government focuses on the state; it is hierarchical and generally relies on majority rule in the context of democracy; it relates to competition between political parties for power and between interest groups for influence; it regulates conflicts by means of decisions of organs of state and the enforcement of these decisions; it makes rules (mostly of a legal nature) that prohibit and allow certain actions and behaviour; and it is concerned with the division of public power and service delivery. Governance is different in that it connects the institutional structures, the elements of a hierarchy, the negotiation systems and competition mechanisms of government; it is concerned with conflicts between the regulator and the regulated; steering and coordination occur in the context of institutional systems of rule; both state and non-state actors play a role; it employs compromises and trade-offs; it aims at the co-production of collective goods; it is based on network management; and it is often concerned with institutional politics.

When interpreted in the context of the various descriptions of governance surveyed earlier in this chapter, the distinction between government and governance suggests that governance could operate as a universal or generic concept (*Oberbegriff*) that describes all of the coordinating activities of the various actors involved; and/or as a contra-concept (*Gegenbegriff*) to hierarchical state-centred government. A definition of governance which synthesizes both its function as a universal generic concept (*Oberbegriff*) and as a contra-concept (*Gegenbegriff*) might be that it is the collection of all interconnected and related forms of regulation of a community's issues, problems or subject matters, and it could range from the institutionalization of private self-regulation to different forms of cooperation between public and private actors and to the sovereign actions of state (public) actors.[120] Governance in this sense is used as both a universal generic concept and a contra-concept to hierarchical public government which, admittedly, is a liberal way of loosely describing a very broad regulatory arrangement with a broad scope of application. Nevertheless, it is in this broad sense that governance is currently used in many areas including, for example, industrial governance, corporate governance and, as this book argues in later chapters, global governance and global environmental governance.[121]

---

119 Schuppert, Gunnar Folke (2007), 'Was ist und wozu Governance?', *Die Verwaltung: Zeitschrift für Verwaltungsrecht und Verwaltungswissenschaften*, **40**(1), 463–511 at 466.

120 Mayntz, Renate (2004), 'Governance im modernen Staat' in Arthur Benz (ed), *Governance- Regieren in komplexen Regelsystemen: Eine Einführung*, Wiesbaden: VS Verlag für Sozialwissenschaften, 66.

121 Mayntz, Renate (2004), 'Governance im modernen Staat' in Arthur Benz (ed),

7. GOVERNANCE AND BUREAUCRACY

As was shown earlier in this chapter, governance is concerned not only with addressing societal problems through the interventions of certain actors. It is equally concerned with the governance of the actors themselves in their efforts to govern;[122] a phenomenon which is called bureaucracy or administration. Max Weber famously sketched the principles of a modern bureaucracy, which still forms the administrative basis of modern conceptions of Western states and, more importantly, their governments.[123] Weber's theory concerns public bureaucracy, which is the instrument through which a sovereign state exercises political power in terms of its legislative, judicial and executive powers.[124] A bureaucracy has a distinct public character and a political flavour, and sits well in the Leviathan metaphor of the state. It administers the affairs of a national government, and thus has to do to a greater or lesser extent with sovereign actions; levels of government and interactions between them; specific actors (such as government departments and officials) in each of these levels and their interaction; interaction between organs of state situated on different levels; and a specific hierarchy with respect to all of these actors and their interaction. A bureaucracy could thus be understood as manifesting vertically and horizontally while the levels, actors and functions often overlap.[125]

Bureaucracy is of course not the sole domain and prerogative of states, but also an element of governance which increasingly occurs within the structures of the growing number of non-state inter-governmental organizations. As a result, Weber's administrative principles are now increasingly transplanted to apply also to international organizations which operate in global governance;[126] a development which is evidenced by the growing field of global

---

Governance- Regieren in komplexen Regelsystemen: Eine Einführung, Wiesbaden: VS Verlag für Sozialwissenschaften, 67. See Chapters 7 and 8.

122 This distinction is further explained by Kooiman, Jan and Kjell A. Eliassen (1987), 'Preface' in Jan Kooiman and Kjell A. Eliassen (eds), *Managing Public Organizations: Lessons from Contemporary European Experience*, London: SAGE Publications, 1.

123 Weber, Max (1922), *Wirtschaft und Gesellschaft*, J.C.B. Mohr, Paul Siebeck, Tübingen. For commentary on Weber's work see Rheinstein, Max (ed) (1954), *Max Weber on Law in Economy and Society*, Cambridge, Massachusetts: Harvard University Press, and Gephart, Werner and Siegfried Hermes (eds) (2010), *Max Weber Wirtschaft und Gesellschaft: Die Wirtschaft und die gesellschaftlichen Ordungen und die Mächte-Nachlaß*, Tübingen: ‚J.C.B. Mohr Paul Siebeck, amongst others.

124 Kjær Anne Mette (2004), *Governance*, Cambridge: Polity Press, 20.

125 Mayntz, Renate (2004), 'Governance im modernen Staat' in Arthur Benz (ed), *Governance- Regieren in komplexen Regelsystemen: Eine Einführung*, Wiesbaden, Germany: VS Verlag für Sozialwissenschaften, 69.

126 See Chapter 4.

administrative law, or international organizational or institutional law, which is centrally concerned with regulating, among others, the bureaucracy and administration of these intergovernmental organizations.[127]

8. GOVERNANCE AND MANAGEMENT

As with 'government' the concept 'management' is sometimes used interchangeably with governance, as a complementary term or as an alternative. Environmental management, ecosystem management and natural resources management are some clear examples in the environmental context. The reasons for this overlap could be threefold: governance and management are both terms which are used in new public management discourse;[128] in the private sector, the term management is often used to describe corporate governance activities that apply to a corporation's environmental issues; and both governance and management are concerned with directing or steering human activities with a view to achieving a common objective (i.e., they have the same objective and rationale).[129] Is there a difference between governance and management?

---

127 See, among others, Klabbers, Jan (2009), *An Introduction to International Institutional Law* 2nd edn, Cambridge: Cambridge University Press; Harlow, Carol (2006), 'Global Administrative Law: the Quest for Principles and Values', *European Journal of International Law*, **17**(1), 187–214; Kingsbury, Benedict (2005), 'Global Governance as Administration: National and Transnational Approaches to Global Administrative Law', *Law and Contemporary Problems*, **68**, 1–13; Kingsbury, Benedict (2009), 'The Concept of "Law" in Global Administrative Law', *European Journal of International Law*, **20**(1), 23–57; Kingsbury, Benedict and Lorenzo Casini (2009), 'Global Administrative Law Dimensions of International Organizational Law', *International Organizations Law Review*, **6**, 319–58; Von Bogdandy, Armin *et al.* (eds) (2010), *The Exercise of Public Authority by International Institutions: Advancing International Institutional Law*, Heidelberg: Springer Verlag.

128 New public management is crucial to the governance discourse because: '[N]ew public management ideas try to translate managerial ideas from the private sector, such as client orientation, better performance by contracting out and improving efficiency by the introduction of market mechanisms, to the public sector'. Klijn, Erik-Hans and Geert R. Teisman (2000), 'Managing Public-Private Partnerships: Influencing Processes and Institutional Context of Public-Private Partnerships' in Oscar Van Heffen, Walter J.M. Kickert and Jacques J.A. Thomassen (eds), *Governance in Modern Society: Effects, Change and Formation of Government Institutions*, Dordrecht: Kluwer Academic Publishers, 329.

129 As Rhodes puts it: 'NPM [New Public Management] is relevant to this discussion of governance because steering is central to the analysis of public management and steering is a synonym for governance.' Rhodes, Rod A.W. (2000), 'Governance and Public Administration' in Jon Pierre (ed), *Debating Governance: Authority, Steering and Democracy*, Oxford: Oxford University Press, 56.

While both management and governance are connected with regulation to the extent that they relate to influencing or changing behaviour, traditionally the difference between them is that management denotes a distinct private sector character (meaning that management generally takes place in private corporations, for example), and governance is more (but not exclusively) publicly oriented as it also focuses on government, the state, and sovereign and political power, as has been explained earlier in this chapter. Today, however, management is steadily penetrating the public governance realm, especially in the form of public management or, more recently, the phenomenon of new public management, and the public sector is increasingly concerned with management as a new strategy to address 'the difficulties governments face in coping with the scale and complexity of problems in society today'.[130] Compare, for example, the view of Kickert and Hakvoort[131] who explain that:

> Public governance has a broader meaning than the restricted business-like, market-oriented interpretation of the term 'management'. Public governance is related to legality and legitimacy and [entails] more than strict business values. In public governance the context of political democracy and Rechtsstaat plays a crucial role, as do the external orientation at the social-political context, the complexity of administrative relations, and the specific character of 'governance' in complex networks in social policy sectors.

This suggests that management, as opposed to governance, is a term which is primarily used in the private sector (specifically in the corporate sector). It is focused on market outcomes, transaction costs and ways to increase profitability. Like governance, management is also a value-laden concept, but it is based on business values as opposed to political values such as democracy, legality, the rule of law, and legitimacy. Yet public sector management cannot be entirely divorced from basic constitutional principles, especially those

[130] Kooiman, Jan and Kjell A. Eliassen (1987), 'Preface' in Jan Kooiman and Kjell A. Eliassen (eds), *Managing Public Organizations: Lessons from Contemporary European Experience*, London: SAGE Publications, 1. See also Pierre, Jon (2000), 'Introduction: Understanding Governance' in Jon Pierre (ed), *Debating Governance: Authority, Steering and Democracy*, Oxford: Oxford University Press, 1–2; Jann, Werner (2006), 'Governance als Reformstrategie- Vom Wandel und der Bedeutung verwaltungspolitischer Leitbilder' in Gunnar Folke Schuppert (ed), *Governance-Forschung*, Baden-Baden: Nomos Verlag, 31.

[131] Kickert, Walter J.M. and Jan L.M. Hakvoort (2000), 'Public Governance in Europe: A Historical-Institutional *Tour D'Horizon*' in Oscar Van Heffen, Walter J.M. Kickert and Jacques J.A. Thomassen (eds), *Governance in Modern Society: Effects, Change and Formation of Government Institutions*, Dordrecht: Kluwer Academic Publishers, 224.

relating to the rule of law. At a minimum, in the public sector context, public management 'must guarantee as a general normative prerequisite that administration is reliably bound to political objectives and rules'.[132] The concept of governance could be useful here to the extent that it might import principles of good governance such as transparency, legitimacy, democracy, and accountability into the private corporate realm. Conversely, private sector management that is based on business values and profitability, for instance, could be used in the public governance domain to improve the outcomes of public governance.

The nuanced differences between management and governance are also evident in Schuppert's[133] useful analysis. He finds that management is concerned with single organizations and units; it is focused on internal steering; it is result-driven; and often makes use of privatization and outsourcing. Management is also mostly decentralized and independent; its legal base is that of private contractual arrangements; and it is market-driven and motivated by the incentives of competition, profit, and money. Governance, on the other hand, does not focus on single (business) units, but rather on the coordination of public societal actors and interests; it combines various steering modes and is not only internally focused; it makes use of network management; it is based on self-regulation, and often consists of autonomous self-regulatory actor networks. Mostly, though, instead of the money and profit incentive, governance is based on trust and power.

Despite these differences it is increasingly difficult to separate management from governance because of extensive reforms of traditional forms of state-centred government bureaucracy that have taken place, especially in terms of the new public management movement, which aims to increase the efficiency of public service delivery through the introduction of the principles of governance. Kickert and Hakvoort[134] explain as follows:

> ... most Western public sectors are adopting a more 'managerial' and 'businesslike' approach to administration ... [including] ... the introduction of techniques of business

---

132 Kooiman, Jan and Kjell A. Eliassen (1987), 'Introduction' in Jan Kooiman and Kjell A. Eliassen (eds), *Managing Public Organizations: Lessons from Contemporary European Experience*, London: SAGE Publications, 8.

133 Schuppert, Gunnar Folke (2007), 'Was ist und wozu Governance?', *Die Verwaltung: Zeitschrift für Verwaltungsrecht und Verwaltungswissenschaften*, **40**(1), 463–511 at 465.

134 Kickert, Walter J.M. and Jan L.M. Hakvoort (2000), 'Public Governance in Europe: A Historical-Institutional *Tour D' Horizon*' in Oscar Van Heffen, Walter J.M. Kickert and Jacques J.A. Thomassen (eds), *Governance in Modern Society: Effects, Change and Formation of Government Institutions*, Dordrecht: Kluwer Academic Publishers, 223.

> management, a greater orientation to service and the client, [and] the introduction of market mechanisms and competition into public services. Indeed, there is no doubt that the severe fiscal crisis necessarily leaves no other option to the public sector than to reduce costs, increase effectiveness and efficiency, deliver 'more value for money', hence to become more 'businesslike', and to 'work better and cost less'.

New public management reforms include, among others: the transfer of private sector management principles to the public sector (or managerialism); privatization and the transfer of public sector interests and institutions to private ownership; the increased isolation of government agencies from political intervention and control; the introduction of competition as a means to enhance efficiency; decentralization; and the increased empowerment of citizens.[135] All of these factors are leading to a gradual convergence of management and governance, and indeed a conceptual blur which is currently permeating the regulatory discourse.

The foregoing suggests that while it would not be entirely incorrect to equate management with governance, there is a nuanced difference between the two concepts. Management has a distinctly private flavour, but its principles could also be applied in the public governance sector with a view to improving public sector governance. Governance is a wider concept which, as was shown earlier in this chapter, also increasingly encapsulates private forms of regulation and private or non-state actors. If management therefore means 'private' regulation, then it could be considered as an important component of public sector governance to the extent that public governance increasingly incorporates private governance (management) aspect. As Chapter 6 will argue, the concept 'environmental management' frequently surfaces in the literature, where it means either private corporate environmental governance or environmental governance in the public context.[136] This is so because environmental management is often used in a private corporate context, where it refers to the management of a company's environmental products, processes, services and issues.[137] The foregoing analysis would then suggest that environmental management as private corporate environmental governance, instead of being synonymous to, is rather a part of the broader concept of environmental governance because the latter usefully accommodates private and public aspects.

---

135 Kjær, Anne Mette (2004), *Governance*, Cambridge: Polity Press, 24–31.

136 See, for example, Blanco, Elena and Jona Razzaque (2011), *Globalisation and Natural Resources Law: Challenges, Key Issues and Perspectives*, Cheltenham: Edward Elgar Publishing, 65–6; 85–130, where the authors use environmental management in the context of natural resources management.

137 Nel, Johan and Louis J. Kotzé (2009), 'Environmental Management: An Introduction' in Hennie Strydom and Nick King (eds), *Fuggle and Rabie's Environmental Management in South Africa* 2nd edn, Cape Town: Juta, 1–33.

9. GOVERNANCE AND LAW

Law is important for governance and vice versa. It has been explained earlier that law, governance, politics, power, authority and regulation are all linked to a greater or lesser extent. More specifically, law also provides mechanisms by means of which governance is executed; it justifies governance, legitimizes it; creates and controls the systems of rule inherent in governance; and it provides the means to achieve the objectives of governance.[138] Governance, however, is also important for law and has an impact on law. While Chapter 5 surveys the relationship between law and governance in some detail, the following section briefly highlights the metamorphosis of law in the context of governance.

Governance is fundamentally changing the way that regulation, especially political steering and control, occurs and is conceived. Governance in a globalized world suggests regulation which is characterized by multiple actors, it occurs at multiple levels, it is both private and public, and it is increasingly non-hierarchical. As a result, the traditional, strict and clear delineation between the state and society is falling away because governance, its processes, and their effects are increasingly crossing the clear divide between the state and society. At the same time governance is responsible for muddling the hitherto distinct differentiation between the political and the non-political, and between state and non-state elements of regulation.[139] With the increased involvement of multiple non-state actors in governance, private or non-political elements and forms of authority[140] have been introduced into the regulatory mix and they now act in tandem with political processes and forms of sovereign, state-derived authority, most of which are premised on the idea of top-down regulation.[141] For them to successfully participate in governance,

---

138 These aspects are elaborated in Chapter 5.

139 Engi, Lorenz (2008), 'Governance: Umrisse und Problematik eines staatstheoretischen Leitbildes', *Der Staat: Zeitschrift für Staatslehre und Verfassungsgesichte, deutsches und europäisiches Öffentliches Recht*, **47**, 573–87 at 585.

140 Rosenau's spheres of authority described earlier are also relevant here. While government would clearly be a sphere of authority, so too would a non-governmental organization and any other actor where 'systems of rule' are observed that intend to pursue goals through the exercise of control. It is these spheres and the nature of the authority associated with each sphere that are being changed by governance. Rosenau, James N. (1997), *Along the Domestic-Foreign Frontier: Exploring Governance in a Turbulent World*, Cambridge: Cambridge University Press, 145.

141 Notably, the application of non-politically derived or private authority is often much narrower than the traditional forms of political authority in the sense that sovereign public authority exercised by a government, for example, applies to everyone in a given jurisdiction. This is not necessarily the case with private forms of authority, which would apply only to those people and issues that the private actors so decide (in

these private or non-state actors will also have to use some form of normative arrangements and mechanisms. They would do so through non-legal but law-like instruments which could be used to coordinate the activities of numerous actors and to steer and influence behaviour. In the environmental context an example of such a non-legal, often highly effective mechanism is the ISO 14001 EMS.[142] It is a private form of self-regulation which prioritizes legal compliance, but it is not a legal mechanism *per se*. Yet it succeeds in achieving a number of objectives traditionally reserved for normative legal rules and it contributes to environmental governance insofar as it is able to change corporate behaviour with respect to the environment.

The implications for authority and the role of law in the governance of the foregoing are profound because governance is slowly changing traditional concepts of the state, and more specifically the nature and traditional foundations of the state (*Staatlichkeit*) and the way that regulation and the exercise of political and non-political authority is perceived. It is quite conceivable that with these changes law as a main regulatory foundation of the state and source of authority is also changing, as the increasing popularity of 'softer' regulatory norms such as codes of conduct and guidelines suggests. While it is unrealistic to suggest that state-derived political authority and private forms of non-political authority are now the same and have the same impact,[143] the inevitable result of these transformations of the state and notions of authority is that the precise location and source of authority for regulation, steering and control, are increasingly blurring and becoming hybrid.

The gradual yet steady reconception of law in the broader governance paradigm does not by any means suggest that 'hard' forms of law will fall into disuse. That is as unrealistic a proposition as the suggestion that the state is becoming redundant in governance. It is rather to be expected that 'harder' forms of deterring and coercive laws, such as treaties, statutory directives, conventions, and criminal sanctions will increasingly have to function alongside 'softer' varieties of law that are created by non-state actors, for instance,

---

terms of a contract, perhaps). Engi, Lorenz (2008), 'Governance: Umrisse und Problematik eines staatstheoretischen Leitbildes', *Der Staat: Zeitschrift für Staatslehre und Verfassungsgesichte, deutsches und europäisiches Öffentliches Recht*, **47**, 573–87 at 584.

142 See Chapter 7.

143 The state will always be the state and society will remain distinct from the state; so too will authority exercised by the state remain sovereign and political, while authority emanating from private sources will retain its specific apolitical or less political and 'softer' private characteristics. These forms of authority are, however, increasingly becoming interwoven in a plural regulatory setting. If one accepts that, at a minimum, most traditional forms of regulatory authority are derived from law, then it could be argued that the role of law and the way it is currently being perceived will also have to change alongside contemporary regulatory pluralism.

and which have serving as guidelines as their primary function. The increasing reliance by states on a mixture of hard and soft law in international law is proof that this is already happening.

In parallel with the increasing popularity of the paradigms of governance and globalization, there has been a concomitant expansion of various subdisciplines in law in addition to the growth of private forms of law. As the number and type of governance actors increase and interaction among them becomes increasingly complex, one could reasonably expect that the nature, function, and ambit of laws regulating these interactions will change in an apt way and that new forms of law will emerge.[144] One example of such change is the growing body of global administrative law which applies to intergovernmental organizations, their internal governance matters, relations and dealings *inter se* and with states and other non-state actors.[145] If governance in a globalized world is thus understood to be the main impetus for a movement towards the steady creation of intergovernmental organizations and other insti-

---

[144] As Johnston argues:

> In the era of global institutionalization, when the international legal system became 'organizational' as well as 'transactional' in orientation, the operational life of the system became routinized through hundreds of international regulatory agencies. For over a century, the norms of international law have been applied, on a day-to-day basis, within a vast and constantly expanding network of cooperative regimes designed to regulate governmental, industrial and commercial activities over a broad spectrum of sectors.

Johnston, Douglas M. (2005), 'World Constitutionalism in the Theory of International Law' in Ronald St. John Macdonald and Douglas M. Johnston, *Towards World Constitutionalism: Issues in the Legal Ordering of the World Community*, Leiden: Martinus Nijhoff Publishers, 6.

[145] That there is a clear link between the growing number of global institutions that regulate matters beyond the state (global governance) on the one hand, and the accompanying growth of global administrative law on the other, is explained by Schwöbel as follows:

> Another form of global governance in international law, concerning regulation and administration, is found in the growing area of global administrative law. Global administrative law proponents regard the blurring of the domestic and the international, the performing of administrative functions of different officials and institutions at different levels, and the general increase of public power in the administrative realm as a 'growing trend towards administrative law type mechanisms' on the global scale.

Schwöbel, Christine E.J. (2011), *Global Constitutionalism in International Legal Perspective*, Leiden: Martinus Nijhoff Publishers, 28. See also the discussion above.

tutional arrangements, then it is also governance which is responsible for the steady growth in 'new' fields of law, such as global administrative law. In sum, then, it is clear that in addition to changing the regulatory landscape governance is simultaneously changing perceptions of law and the role of law and other normative rules as important elements of governance.

10. SUMMARY

Governance is an ancient concept which has historically been used to signify the function of steering the state. Over the years it has not lost this characteristic, and the term is still used to denote steering, regulation, and direction, albeit in the completely different contemporary setting of globalization. Because of globalization and the regulatory challenges resulting therefrom, governance has gradually metamorphosed from a strictly state-centred concept to one which today aims to describe a multi-level, multi-actor, hybrid and plural mass of regulatory arrangements. It is used in many disciplines either as an analytical perspective and a means to view the world and reality or as a normative concept, where it functions as a distinct political programme which aims to achieve specific objectives. Global environmental governance, although it could be employed as an analytic perspective, is mostly a specific manifestation of governance as a normative concept which aims to address global environmental problems.

Despite its plurality, vagueness and malleability, the governance concept includes numerous core commonalities. For example, it is centrally concerned with human agency in the institutional context; it focuses on steering or regulating human activities, interactions and behaviour to achieve common objectives; and it has to do with authority, politics and the law. Governance takes on many forms, as is evident from the earlier definitional analysis and it has many different characteristics depending on the context in which and the purpose for which it is used. In an abstract sense, it sets the goals and the means to achieve the ideal of human well-being, satisfaction and happiness. It could be entirely state-based, coercive and top-down in the Leviathan sense, or the direct opposite, in which case it would be hybrid and based on many different levels, and involving many different actors; it is mostly about steering behaviour for the achievement of common collective gains, and in this sense it describes 'how things get done'[146] in society; it could provide the means for cooperation,

[146] Hunt, Alan and Gary Wickham (1994), *Foucault and the Law: Towards a Sociology of Law as Governance*, London: Pluto Press, 25, use this description to indicate that governance is a very practical matter.

interaction and coordination; it has a distinct normative foundation including law and law-like rules; it could relate to spheres of authority; and it needs to legitimately derive from some form of authority. Notably, governance is focused on the broadly defined common interests of society where: '[C]ommon interest is not merely an aggregation of particular interests. It is formed at the intersection between the ideal and the real, as society responds to its current and potential situation ... It is an idea of society's enlightened self-interest formed in society's public mind.'[147]

There is a clear and important difference between governance and government. First, government is often employed to describe the institutional structure that is responsible for the action of governing. Second, as a result the concept of government has assumed a distinct (often negatively tinged) public character with an emphasis on the dominance of the state. Governance, on the other hand, describes a plural setting in which various state and non-state actors at various levels are significantly involved. In this sense, governance is both an umbrella-like term to describe all of the activities and actors of governing, and simultaneously a contra-concept which denotes that which the orthodox notion of state-centred governance implied by the term government is not.

This chapter has also argued that there is a connection between governance and bureaucracy and that bureaucracy, in the context of the state and its organizations, and also of supra-national organizations, is an element of governance. As with bureaucracy, management is another term often used in the same breath as governance. While management has a more distinct 'private' flavour, it is mostly used as meaning governance, and an expansive grasp of the nature of governance includes the concept of management. The reciprocal relationship between law and governance was also addressed. First, governance depends on law because law forms the normative foundation of governance. Second, governance is changing the face of law because governance is changing manifestations and perceptions of the state and shifting the location and exercise of authority from strictly state to non-state and hybrid manifestations. In doing so, governance increasingly invites perceptions of 'softer' forms of law and even non-legal mechanisms into the traditionally orthodox hard law-dominated governance terrain, and it is to be expected that law will have to change concomitantly if it is to keep up with governance in a globalized era.

---

147 Allot, Philip (2000), 'The Concept of International Law' in Michael Byers (ed), *The Role of Law in International Politics: Essays in International Relations and International Law*, Oxford: Oxford University Press, 73.

4. Global governance

> ... the idea of global governance has become almost all-inclusive. It comes close to an empty formula that can take virtually any meaning, covering a vast conceptual space to be filled with content by those involved in the theory and practice of world affairs.[1]
>
> (Jörg Friedrichs, 2004)

1. INTRODUCTION

Chapter 2 sketched the general outlines and meaning of the term globalization and it argued that globalization is changing the way society perceives and regulates problems arising from globalization itself. Global environmental problems are among these. It also showed that globalization is a consideration intricately linked with governance and that the prevalence of governance is largely an outcome of globalization. Chapter 3 investigated the concept of governance and attempted to provide an analysis of the nature, purpose and theoretical composition of governance. It also described and situated the concept in the context of globalization. Based on this analysis, this chapter focuses on global governance, which it suggests is the theoretical fulcrum around which global environmental governance revolves.

The environment is one of the global problems or issues which state and non-state actors are increasingly required to address by means of globally conceived governance arrangements. As a result, global governance in the context of the environment has of late become a popular subject of analysis for political scientists, with extensive work being done in this area by, among others, Haas, Hurrell, Kingsbury, and Young.[2] For a reasonably comprehen-

---

1 Friedrichs, Jörg (2004), 'The Neomedieval Renaissance: Global Governance and International Law in the New Middle Ages' in Ige F. Dekker and Wouter G. Werner (eds), *Governance and International Legal Theory*, Leiden: Martinus Nijhoff Publishers, 12.

2 See, for example, Young, Oran R. (1994), *International Governance: Protecting the Environment in a Stateless Society*, Ithaca, NY and London: Cornell University Press; Young, Oran R. (ed) (1997), *Global Governance: Drawing Insights from the Environmental Experience*, Cambridge, Massachusetts: MIT Press; Hurrell, Andrew and Benedict Kingsbury (eds), (1992), *The International Politics of the*

sive and informed view of global environmental governance, it thus seems unavoidable to explore, at least to some extent, the rich political science literature that deals with global governance.

The chapter commences with a brief reflection on international relations theory and institutionalism, which together provide the general context for global governance. It then distinguishes between state and non-state actors, which are key ingredients and determinants of the extent and nature of governance in the larger global governance paradigm. The chapter then briefly maps the theory of global governance by means of a literature review of this concept with a view to identifying and describing the general characteristics of global governance. The discussion then turns to more specific concepts which form the theoretical building blocks of global governance, or what Leonard[3] terms the 'means of global governance'. These include international regimes, international organizations, and networks which provide the means through which global governance happens, as it were. The chapter concludes with a discussion of regional governance, which it sees as an important and often neglected component of global governance. Taken as a whole, the analysis in this chapter seeks to identify and describe insights into the phenomenon of global governance that would usefully inform a comprehensive understanding and description of global environmental governance.

2. INTERNATIONAL RELATIONS AND GLOBAL GOVERNANCE

Global governance is neatly nestled in the context of international relations. The following sections investigate the multi-disciplinary setting of international relations, the relationship between international relations and global governance, and the *problématique* of anarchy.

2.1 A Multi-disciplinary Setting

Global governance must first be understood in the context of the theory of international relations, which is a sub-discipline of political science set against

---

Environment: Actors, Interests, and Institutions, Oxford: Clarendon Press; Kanie, Norichika and Peter M. Haas (eds) 2004, *Emerging Forces in Environmental Governance*, Tokyo: United Nations University Press.

3 Leonard also refers elsewhere to the means of global governance as consisting of 'material-structural forces' which are 'basic material capabilities, resources and actors that control these sources'. Leonard, Eric K. (2005), *The Onset of Global Governance: International Relations Theory and the International Criminal Court*, Aldershot: Ashgate, 170, 173.

the more general backdrop of globalization discussed in Chapter 2. It concerns international relations between sovereign states among themselves and increasingly, between states and non-state actors.[4] It thus seeks to understand and describe the conditions in which global state and non-state actor behaviour and interactions take place, the reasons for such behaviour, and the many ways in which relationships between these state and non-state actors play out globally.[5] The focus of international relations theory is mostly a political one[6] and it concentrates on 'an increasingly complex, interdependent, and dangerous world' with a view to 'organiz[ing] intellectually and understand[ing] international activity'.[7] The value of international relations theory for understanding global governance in the political science and legal context lies therein that it 'is as much a mode of thinking as a body of knowledge, a way of looking at both the world and the law'.[8]

There is a growing inter-disciplinary overlap between international relations theory and law, especially as far as it concerns the contribution of inter-

---

[4] The view that states are the only actors in international relations has been tempered by neoliberalism, which argues for the increased involvement of a wide range of private (or non-state) actors in global governance: '[G]overnments of nation-states are the prime official members of most international regimes, although international, transnational and sometimes subnational organizations may practically and legitimately participate.' Puchala, Donald J. and Raymond F. Hopkins (1983), 'International Regimes: Lessons from Inductive Analysis' in Stephen D. Krasner (ed), *International Regimes*, London: Cornell University Press, 63. Generally speaking, non-state actors contribute to global governance in two ways: a) states could create international institutions based on the practices and norms established by non-state actors; and b) non-state actors could very directly contribute to the state-controlled process of international institutional development. Haufler, Virginia (1993), 'Crossing the Boundary between Public and Private: International Regimes and Non-state Actors' in Volker Rittberger (ed), *Regime Theory and International Relations*, Oxford: Clarendon Press, 94–5.

[5] International relations theory is premised on the need for increased global cooperation as a result of globalization, not only between states, but also between states and other non-state global actors. It is therefore not surprising that the focus of international relations theory is on governance issues of a global nature.

[6] For an extensive discussion on the centrality of 'the political' to the international relations debate see Walker, Rob B.J. (1995), 'International Relations and the Concept of the Political' in Ken Booth and Steve Smith (eds), *International Relations Theory Today*, Cambridge: Polity Press, 306–27.

[7] Puchala, Donald J. and Raymond F. Hopkins (1983), 'International Regimes: Lessons from Inductive Analysis' in Stephen D. Krasner (ed), *International Regimes*, London: Cornell University Press, 61.

[8] Slaughter, Anne-Marie (2001), *Recueil des Cours, Collected Courses of the Hague Academy of International Law, 2000: International Law and International Relations*, The Hague: Martinus Nijhoff Publishers, 190.

national law to the discourse of public relations theory.[9] There is also a growing relationship and observable overlap between international relations theory and (international) environmental law, especially in the area of global environmental governance, as we shall see later on in this and subsequent chapters.[10] Most environmental issues are global in nature and require cooperative action between states as the main international actors, and increasingly with the involvement of non-state actors such as NGOs and networks. Whereas law provides the norms and standards, and instruments and mechanisms for enforcing compliance with norms and standards, international relations theory busies itself with the manner in which all of the foregoing plays out globally. In the environmental regulatory context, law therefore attempts to answer the 'what' and international relations theory the 'why' and 'how'. In this way, for environmental purposes, international relations theory is centrally occupied with the question of how global institutions and existing mechanisms for interstate co-operation facilitate (or hinder) the identification and governance of environmental problems. In many ways, in an environmental context, international relation is therefore (at least partly) international environmental law in action, and it provides the institutional means to understand anarchy in the global environmental context and to address problems in global environmental regulation.

2.2 Between World Anarchy and World Order

In simplified terms, international relations theory occupies itself with the problem of how to address world anarchy in a continuum where the one unlikely and undesirable extreme is total anarchy and disorder and the other is complete order (or hierarchy) enforced through an equally unlikely and undesirable centralized world government or 'higher supranational authority ... that can impose order through an international legal system ultimately backed by centralized use of force'.[11] 'Anarchy' has a very specific meaning in the context of international relations, which could be explained as follows:

> The Westphalian system put states at the center of the world stage, unconstrained by any higher political authority. If all states are masters of their own fates, if no

[9] Krasner, Stephen D. (2000), 'International Law and International Relations: Together, Apart, Together?', *Chicago Journal of International Law*, **1**(1), 93–9.

[10] See Chapters 6 and 7.

[11] Willetts, Peter (2011), *Non-governmental Organizations in World Politics: the Construction of Global Governance*, London: Routledge, 145.

> government exists above them, then the system lacks hierarchy. The absence of a higher authority is termed *anarchy*. Anarchy in this sense ... does not mean chaos. Rather, anarchy means that states have to protect and look out for themselves – that they must rely on themselves to insure order and obtain needed resources.[12]

Thus, in the absence of hierarchy or a centralized world government there is anarchy. The connection between anarchy, order, and governance lies in the fact that they are interactive phenomena and '[A]s intentional activities designed to regularize the arrangements which sustain world affairs, governance obviously shapes the nature of the prevailing global order.'[13] Governance is thus a way to understand and to achieve hierarchy or order, and global governance is a means to achieve some form of global hierarchy or order in the absence of a world (global) government.[14]

Anarchy in the environmental context exists insofar as environmental issues, directly or indirectly, form part of the focus of international relations; i.e., insofar as environmental issues are concerns which state and non-state actors are occupied with and in terms of which they need to protect their own interests, cooperate, achieve order, and obtain the requisite resources. Moreover, the world lacks a central hierarchical environmental governmental structure, a world environment organization, or a world environmental government.[15] Therefore, if anarchy means the lack of hierarchy or a global (environmental) government, anarchy presumably exists as far as the governance of global environmental issues is concerned. This does not suggest that a centralized world environment government or organization is the only

[12] Rosenau, James N. and Mary Durfee (1995), *Thinking Theory Through: Coherent Approaches to an Incoherent World*, Boulder: Westview Press, 14. Leonard describes anarchy as meaning a 'lack of government'. Leonard, Eric K. (2005), *The Onset of Global Governance: International Relations Theory and the International Criminal Court*, Aldershot: Ashgate, 79. Keohane, in similar vein, refers to anarchy as a lack of 'authoritative government that can enact and enforce rules of behaviour'. Keohane, Robert O. (1984), *After Hegemony: Cooperation and Discord in the World Political Economy*, Princeton: Princeton University Press, 7.

[13] Rosenau, James N. (1992), 'Governance, Order, and Change in World Politics' in James N. Rosenau and Ernst-Otto Czempiel (eds), *Governance without Government: Order and Change in World Politics*, Cambridge: Cambridge University Press, 8.

[14] There is no universal and uniform understanding of what order, or world order, entails. It is a value-laden and value-driven concept and as such will have different meanings to different people from varying cultures in different parts of the world. For example, world order to a manifestly Westernized country's citizens would differ markedly from the way a Middle-Eastern country's citizens would view world order.

[15] See also Chapter 3.

or preferable way to achieve hierarchy and order.[16] In the words of Habermas:[17]

> The institutionalization of procedures for global coordination and generalization of interests, and for the imaginative construction of common interests, will not work in the organizational form of a world state; a form that is itself not even desirable. The autonomy, particularity, and uniqueness of formerly sovereign states will have to be taken into account.

More importantly, it does not ignore the important role and contribution of the myriad of existing global institutional responses to address anarchy in the context of the environment. It rather illustrates that, despite the existence of various institutions such as organizations, regimes and other global arrangements, anarchy still exists insofar as 'order' lies somewhere in the middle of the continuum between having no world environmental government and having an all-powerful centralized world environmental government. More importantly, it highlights the fact that states and non-state actors will try to establish and maintain order (or address anarchy) by increasingly moving towards a more hierarchical, co-ordinated and co-operative global effort to tackle global environmental problems insofar as this would be in their best interests. One way in which global actors would try to do so is by means of global *governance*, which consists mainly of regimes, organizations and networks, as is further discussed below.

3. STATE AND NON-STATE ACTORS

The types of actors involved in global governance will largely determine the type of global governance performed, i.e., whether it is private or public or a mixture of these, and the type and extent of the institutional arrangement that is chosen. The actors in global governance can basically be divided into two broad categories, namely, state and non-state actors. While there is no universally accepted definition of 'the state', we intuitively know what we mean when we refer to a state. The term is most frequently used in the context of a nation state as referring to a country which has borders, a population and a government. In fact, the four requirements of statehood are stipulated by the

---

16 Various international institutions will often play the primary role in addressing anarchy, in the absence of a strong centralized world government. See the discussion elsewhere in this chapter and Haas, Peter M. and Ernst B. Haas (1995), 'Learning to Learn: Improving International Governance', *Global Governance*, **1**, 255–85 at 256.

17 Habermas, Jürgen (2001), *The Postnational Constellation: Political Essays*, Cambridge: Polity Press, 56.

Montevideo Convention on the Rights and Duties of States, 1933, as including: a permanent population; a defined territory; a government; and the capacity to enter into relations with other states.[18] States have been, they currently are, and in all likelihood will remain the primary actors in global governance unless some dramatic and unlikely paradigmatic and structural changes occur in the architecture of international politics, law, and the world order. While there have been numerous subtle changes to the role of the state and the extent of its functions, it is highly unlikely that another authoritative entity will replace the state in world affairs. If such an entity does surface, it will have to grapple with and overcome the complexities associated with statehood, territoriality and sovereignty, among others.[19] Nevertheless, it is especially with respect to its role as the author, addressee and guardian of (environmental) law that the state will continue to play the predominant role in carving out the contours of global (environmental) governance. It remains the only actor enjoying full legitimacy as a domestic and supra-national actor, and remains the sole entity to implement and sanction domestic and supra-national (environmental) rules.[20] It therefore plays both an internal and an external role in global governance. Internally, most usually through its government and government agencies, the state would enforce international and/or regional legal provisions through a domestic legal framework that it is responsible for creating, interpreting, and applying. Considering the reciprocity and interconnected nature of the global processes explained in Chapters 1 and 2, it is also possible that domestic laws could influence supra-national ones, thus providing the state with an avenue of exerting external global influence. The state would also seek to directly influence global relations, global law and policy making and global politics externally (i.e., beyond its borders). During this 'external' process, states would often not act in global governance *in persona propra*, but rather through institutions that they create for this purpose, mostly in the form of regimes and international organizations. These state actors act with considerable public authority because they are institutions through which states act outside their borders.[21] Strictly speaking they are not states in terms

[18] Article 1 of the *Montevideo Convention on the Rights and Duties of States*, 1933.

[19] Marauhn, Thilo (2007), 'Changing Role of the State' in Daniel Bodansky, Jutta Brunnée and Ellen Hey (eds), *The Oxford Handbook of International Environmental Law*, Oxford: Oxford University Press, 730. See more generally the definitive work on the creation of states and the matter of statehood, Crawford, James R. (2007), *The Creation of States in International Law*, Oxford: Oxford University Press.

[20] Beyerlin, Ulrich and Thilo Marauhn (2011), *International Environmental Law*, Oxford: Hart Publishers, 245–8.

[21] See generally, Von Bogdandy, Armin *et al.* (eds) (2010), *The Exercise of*

of the definition given above,[22] but they have nevertheless been created by states to enable them to govern global issues beyond their borders. They are thus in a way extensions of the state which allow the state to govern globally. Collectively, states and their international organizations are part of what one could call public global governance. Public global environmental governance would thus focus on the role, for example, of individual states and regional political and economic bodies such as the EU, and UNEP in the governance of global environmental issues.[23]

The fact that the state plays a primary role in global governance demonstrates that the national level of governance (domestic governance), is an important part of global governance. Because global governance cannot exist without the state, it would also depend on domestic governance. This realization reinforces the idea that global governance includes domestic governance. In fact, global governance encompasses all levels of governance, including regional governance, as is shown below. A broad and holistic view of 'the global', as explained elsewhere in this book,[24] by necessary implication demands the inclusion of all levels of governance which might contribute to addressing shared issues or problems such as the environment. Domestic environmental governance is thus a fundamental part of global environmental governance. This issue is further explored in Chapters 7 and 8. The opposite, however, is also true: supra-national governance cannot replace domestic governance. It can act only in tandem with domestic governance, and mainly to solve the problems created by domestic governance and governments in the first place. 'Crises of governance' and their causes are decidedly domestic. It is their effects, however, that are often felt globally (at all other levels including the regional and international). For example, the emissions of oil refineries in the Gulf States are contributing to *global* climate change. So too are energy inefficient buildings in South Africa doing their bit to eat away at the

---

Public Authority by International Institutions: Advancing International Institutional Law, Heidelberg: Springer Verlag. Hey, for example, postulates that international organizations exercise delegated powers which should be subject to limitations and the requirements of accountability. This is an indication of the increased extent of their public (state-derived) authority. Hey, Ellen (2007), 'International Institutions' in Daniel Bodansky, Jutta Brunnée and Ellen Hey (eds), *The Oxford Handbook of International Environmental Law*, Oxford: Oxford University Press, 750–69.

22 While international institutions such as international organizations clearly are not states, they are at the same time also not non-state actors, because they do not fit within the strict 'private' sphere of authority traditionally reserved for non-state actors such as NGOs. Because they are so intricately linked to the state, it would for all practical purposes be best to loosely gather them under the umbrella of state actors.

23 See also Chapter 6 for a discussion of public global environmental governance.

24 See Chapters 1 and 2.

country's renowned but dwindling coal supplies, which are still the major source of electricity generation. These have sub-national and supra-national environmental impacts and implications for environmental governance. This suggests that insufficient domestic regulation, a lack of political commitment, and poor strategic long-term vision are causing supra-national problems. Domestic governments are thus making their problems the problems of others as well. To put it differently, domestic problems truly become global. With reference to the current global financial crisis, Weiss and Thakur[25] explain that:

> The causes of the crises lie in domestic governance imperfections and the solutions entail domestic government and market responses. The role for global governance institutions is restricted to containing the contagion. Global governance can play a facilitative and constraining role, but rarely a determinant and predominant one. The authority and capacity for the latter is vested almost exclusively in domestic public authorities.

This reality must force one to carefully and realistically re-consider the contribution of global governance to addressing common global problems. It is no panacea for these, but it remains a crucially indispensable part of the many social constructions for regulating common issues. More importantly, it again underlines the causality and reciprocity between the different levels of global governance to the extent that domestic success in actually addressing governance issues such as the environment is contingent on supra-national success and vice versa.

While the continuation of state predominance in global governance should be clear, various non-state actors have become increasingly involved in the global governance effort because of globalization; a point which has been fully explored elsewhere in this book.[26] Non-state actors are all those actors which are not states or which do not act with public (state) authority, and could include a wide array of specific manifestations such as the media, NGOs, community-based organizations (CBOs), multinational corporations (MNCs), epistemic communities, and networks. For non-state actors to fully take part in global governance on an equal footing with state actors is of course difficult, because they do not act with authoritative, public, state-centred power. Yet non-state actors are increasingly playing an important role and are increasingly becoming influential in the practice and composition of global governance. It is, for example, possible that an epistemic community in a country

25 Weiss, Thomas G. and Ramesh Thakur (2011), 'Framing Global Governance, Five Gaps' in Thomas G. Weiss, *Thinking about Global Governance: Why People and Ideas Matter*, Abingdon: Routledge, 146.

26 See Chapter 2.

consisting of climate law experts, NGOs or even CBOs, could influence the policies of a national government to such an extent that this government takes an entirely different position during climate negotiations from what it would have taken if it had not consulted with or had not been influenced by these experts.[27] Private individuals and entities are thus able (however subtly and unlikely) to influence global decision-making and norm creation in this way.

Where non-state actors act without any form of public authority one can speak of private global governance, and with reference to the role of non-state actors in global environmental governance it is possible to speak of private global environmental governance. Collectively the latter actors are referred to as global civil society, a term that suggests that there is little or no public or state authority involved in these governance efforts. Global civil society usefully emphasizes the private character of global governance. It is described as:

> ... [the] general nomenclature encompassing all non-governmental, non-profit-making or voluntary organizations involved in international law-making, but it can also refer to a more expansive group of non-State civil actors that includes social movements and other forms of mass dissent.[28]

While this definition could be criticized for being too narrow by limiting the functions of global civil society only to international law-making instead of acknowledging global civil society's role in the broader global governance effort, it does make the point that global civil society is a generous term which is gaining in phenomenological and conceptual reach.

4. INSTITUTIONALISM AND GLOBAL GOVERNANCE

Institutionalism is a focus area of international relations which seeks to understand how institutions interact with one another and how they influence society. Institutionalism is particularly important for global governance because it considers to what extent institutions, including regimes, organizations, and networks contribute to ensure cooperation, order, and the collective achieve-

---

27 See, among others, Spiro, Peter J. (2007), 'Non-governmental Organizations and Civil Society' in Daniel Bodansky, Jutta Brunnée and Ellen Hey (eds), *The Oxford Handbook of International Environmental Law*, Oxford: Oxford University Press, 771–90; Haas, Peter M. (2007), 'Epistemic Communities' in Daniel Bodansky, Jutta Brunnée and Ellen Hey (eds), *The Oxford Handbook of International Environmental Law*, Oxford: Oxford University Press, 792–806.

28 Woodward, Barbara K. (2010), *Global Civil Society in International Lawmaking and Global Governance*, Leiden: Martinus Nijhoff Publishers, 9.

ment of the common good (or to address anarchy) in the global governance domain.[29] In Abbott's[30] view:

> Institutionalism is predominantly rationalist. States pursue many interests, not just power or security; goals such as prosperity, clean air and freedom from disease can only be achieved through cooperation. Scholars in this tradition [of institutionalism] identify conditions that impede beneficial cooperation, such as uncertainty and free-rider problems, and analyze how institutions can help overcome them, for example by disseminating information, assuring states that others are cooperating, and monitoring behaviour to reduce the incentive to cheat. Through mechanisms like these, institutions can affect behaviour independent of power.

The central *problématique* of international relations, and indeed global governance, that institutions must deal with is that of anarchy, as described above:

> The horizontally organized international system lacks an authority that is able to determine the community interest and enforce adequate behaviour of the individual actors. States as the main actors of the international system may determine their behaviour unilaterally and they are able to pursue primarily, if not exclusively, their own interests. The international system may, therefore, appear as 'anarchical', i.e. as regulated merely by constraints external to the actors, and not by man-made norms.[31]

States would therefore seek to promote community interests and enforce a standard of behaviour primarily by means of institutions which would establish norms, standards and procedures to ensure collective action for the benefit of mutual interests. The essence of institutionalism is further explained by its core assumptions, which include the following: the global system is characterized by anarchy; states are the primary actors in the global system, but non-state actors increasingly play an important role; states primarily act out of self-interest, but will cooperate where they share complementary interests with other states; this cooperation takes place by means of institutions in order to diminish cheating, create iterativeness, and reduce the costs of transactions; and in pursuit of interests, be they individual or collective interests, states seek absolute instead of relative gains.[32]

---

29 For a discussion see Young, Oran R. (2003), 'Environmental Governance: The Role of Institutions in Causing and Confronting Environmental Problems', *International Environmental Agreements*, **3**, 377–93, for instance.

30 Abbott, Kenneth W. (2004/2005), 'Toward a Richer Institutionalism for International Law and Policy', *Journal of International Law and International Relations*, **1**(1–2), 9–34 at 13.

31 Gehring, Thomas (1994), *Dynamic International Regimes: Institutions for International Environmental Governance*, Frankfurt am Main: Peter Lang, 481.

32 Leonard, Eric K. (2005), *The Onset of Global Governance: International*

Institutionalism is divided into a centralized and decentralized approach. While a centralized approach emphasizes the importance of a centralized world government, or at least a centralized institutional approach to address global regulatory problems (or anarchy), the decentralized approach instead focuses on international, regional, sub-regional, national and sub-national state and non-state actors that are involved in addressing global issues;[33] (the decentralized approach corresponds with the idea of 'the global' explained elsewhere).[34] Although some disagree on the extent of this,[35] decentralized institutionalism affords a significant role to non-state actors in international relations, while at the same time recognizing that the state plays an indispensable role in this respect.[36]

Relations Theory and the International Criminal Court, Aldershot: Ashgate, 9. Kysar's more pessimistic view on the motivation behind international relations and cooperation holds that:

> ... to the extent that internationally cooperative regulation has been acknowledged as necessary, it has been modeled as a strategic game in which each state cares only about maximizing its own citizens' aggregate well-being. From this perspective, international law and international relations are seen merely as spaces within which rationally motivated competition occurs, rather than as forums for discussion and mutual social influence.

Kysar, Douglas (2010), *Regulating From Nowhere: Environmental Law and the Search for Objectivity*, New Haven: Yale University Press, 127.

33 Pease, Kelly-Kate S. (2008), *International Organizations: Perspectives on Governance in the Twenty-First Century* 3rd edn, New Jersey: Pearson Prentice Hall, 241.

34 Chapters 1 and 2.

35 For two divergent views see Pease, Kelly-Kate S. (2008), *International Organizations: Perspectives on Governance in the Twenty-First Century* 3rd edn, New Jersey: Pearson Prentice Hall, 242; and Leonard, Eric K. (2005), *The Onset of Global Governance: International Relations Theory and the International Criminal Court*, Aldershot: Ashgate, 9.

36 This view corresponds with the Commission on Global Governance's assertion on the role of the state in global governance:

> Contemporary practice acknowledges that governments do not bear the whole burden of global governance. Yet states and governments remain primary public institutions for constructive responses to issues affecting peoples and the global community as a whole.

Commission on Global Governance (1995), *Our Global Neighbourhood*, Oxford: Oxford University Press, 4.

4.1 Institutions

Institutions are by definition central to institutionalism and therefore to global governance. To be sure:

> Complex institutional arrangements are now prominent in global governance. These involve a range of actors, from IOs [international organisations] to NSAs [non-state actors], often in combination; a range of actor motivations, from the material to the normative; and a range of causal and constitutive governance mechanisms, from material incentives to normative persuasion.[37]

Yet this does not tell us what institutions are. Definitions of 'institution' vary considerably and some of the reasons for this ambiguity are that:

> ... scholars who have written about institutions have often been rather casual about defining them; institutionalism has disparate meanings in different disciplines; and, even within organizational theory, 'institutionalists' vary in their relative emphasis on micro and macro features, in their weightings of cognitive and normative aspects of institutions, and in the importance they attribute to interests and relational networks in the creation and diffusion of institutions.[38]

'Institution' is therefore a highly fluid and variable term. Nevertheless, broadly described, it could signify one of two things. First, the term 'institution' intuitively suggests that it has to do with some sort of material, even physical, structure. According to the old-institutionalist model that prevailed in America in the 1960s and 1970s, institutions are material structures which include 'constitutions, cabinets, parliaments, bureaucracies, courts, armies, federal or autonomy arrangements, and in some instances, party systems. In other words, institutions referred to the state or, more exactly to "government".'[39] Institutions in this sense therefore relate to material and often formal organizational structures that have to do with governments or their agencies in the strict formal and material sense. The government of a state would be an institution. So too would its agencies be considered institutions. Supranational organizations such as the European Commission (EC), its subsidiary

---

[37] Abbott, Kenneth W. (2004/2005), 'Toward a Richer Institutionalism for International Law and Policy', *Journal of International Law and International Relations*, **1**(1 2), 9 34 at 21.

[38] DiMaggio, Paul J. and Walter W. Powell (1991), 'Introduction' in Walter W. Powell and Paul J. DiMaggio (eds), *The New Institutionalism in Organizational Analysis*, Chicago: University of Chicago Press, 1.

[39] Lecours, André (2005), 'New Institutionalism: Issues and Questions' in André Lecours (ed), *New Institutionalism: Theory and Analysis*, Toronto: University of Toronto Press, 6.

bodies, UNEP and other UN affiliated organizations would also be considered institutions. A NGO such as Greenpeace would similarly be regarded an institution, albeit one that is based on private instead of public authority as the former examples are. A further example of a strictly material take on institutions in the global environmental governance context is Bodansky's[40] following estimation:

> ... a patchwork of international institutions address environmental issues ... Some institutions are global, others regional or bilateral. Some relate to a particular issue area such as whaling or forestry, others have a broader environmental mandate, and still others, a mandate encompassing non-environmental as well as environmental issues. Some are scientific in orientation, others focus on capacity building or have a more policy-oriented role.

The second, broader and prevailing view of institutions sees them as comprehensive and all-encompassing sociological phenomena which include:

> ... persistent and connected sets of rules (formal and informal) that prescribe behavioural roles, constrain activity, and shape expectations ... International institutions include formal intergovernmental or transnational organizations, international regimes, and conventions. International organizations are purposive entities, with bureaucratic structures and leadership, permitting them to respond to events. International regimes are institutions with explicit rules, agreed upon by governments, that pertain to particular sets of issues in international relations. Conventions are informal institutions, with implicit rules and understandings, that shape the expectations of actors.[41]

In this context physical, material entities such as governments are institutions, but they are only part of a much larger global institutional mass which also includes rules (laws), regimes and networks, among other such phenomena. The second perspective thus suggests that an institution is an all-inclusive phenomenon which at its core consists of formal and informal rules designed by people to regulate behaviour through social constructs with a view to creating social order:[42]

---

40 Bodansky, Daniel (2010), *The Art and Craft of International Environmental Law*, Cambridge, Massachusetts: Harvard University Press, 117.

41 Keohane, Robert O. (1993), 'The Analysis of International Regimes: Towards a European-American Research Programme' in Volker Rittberger (ed), *Regime Theory and International Relations*, Oxford: Clarendon Press, 28–9. See also Keohane, Robert O., Peter M. Haas and Marc A. Levy (1994), 'The Effectiveness of International Environmental Institutions' in Peter M. Haas, Robert O. Keohane and Marc A. Levy, *Institutions for the Earth: Sources of Effective International Environmental Protection*, Cambridge, Massachusetts: MIT Press, 4–5, 8.

42 Breitmeier confirms that modern social order is based on institutions through

> ... in a general way, social institutions and their constituent behavioural conventions constitute a response to coordination problems or situations in which the pursuit of interests defined in narrow individual terms characteristically leads to socially undesirable outcomes.[43]

Generally speaking, governance and law are examples of institutional social constructs with more concrete examples being treaty regimes, international organizations and professional transnational networks which, as the discussion below shows, are meant to create and execute formal and informal rules. Because 'institutions shape action',[44] something could be an institution insofar as it aims to prescribe and proscribe behaviour and shape human activities. Institutions could thus be almost anything that aims to accomplish the foregoing because '[I]n principle, any socially relevant practice can be institutionalized.'[45] This broader view of institutions then also includes the orthodox old-institutionalist approach and it should be clear that institutions would include governments, regimes, organizations and normative arrangements such as laws:

> International regimes are multilateral agreements, at once resulting from and facilitating cooperative behavior, by means of which states regulate their relations with one another within a particular issue area. Some of these *international institutions* (e.g., the United Nations or the World Bank) are formal organizations; others, such as the international regime for money and trade (the GATT or General Agreement on Trade and Tariffs) are *complex sets of rules, standards, and agencies. Regimes are institutions* in that they build upon, homogenize, and reproduce standard expectations and, in doing so, stabilize the international order.[46]

---

which states achieve their objectives: '[M]oderne soziale Ordnungen sind auf Institutionen gegründet, durch welche modernes Regieren seine Ziele erreicht.' Breitmeier, Helmut (2006), 'Die Output-orientierte Legitimität des globalen Regierens: Empirische Befunde aus der quantitativen Erforschung internationaler Umweltregime', *Zeitschrift für Internationale Beziehungen*, **13**(1), 39–74 at 39–40.

43 Young, Oran R. (1983), 'Regime Dynamics: the Rise and Fall of International Regimes' in Stephen D. Krasner (ed), *International Regimes*, London: Cornell University Press, 97.

44 Lecours, André (2005), 'New Institutionalism: Issues and Questions' in André Lecours (ed), *New Institutionalism: Theory and Analysis*, Toronto: University of Toronto Press, 8.

45 Diggelmann, Oliver and Tilmann Altwicker (2008), 'Is there something like a Constitution of International Law: A Critical Analysis of the Debate on World Constitutionalism', *Zeitschrift für ausländisches öffentliches Recht und Völkerrecht*, **68**, 623–50 at 644.

46 Emphasis added. DiMaggio, Paul J. and Walter W. Powell (1991), 'Introduction' in Walter W. Powell and Paul J. DiMaggio (eds), *The New Institutionalism in Organizational Analysis*, Chicago: University of Chicago Press, 6.

Thus considered institutions relate to Young's[47] 'rules of the game', described earlier in the governance context, which are 'capable of resolving conflicts, facilitating cooperation, or, more generally, alleviating collective-action problems in a world of interdependent actors'. Institutions therefore aim to make collectively binding decisions about how to regulate common interests and provide ways to implement these decisions, to resolve disputes where they arise, and to enforce compliance.[48]

While there may be more views on institutions, the foregoing suggests at least two manifestations of this sociological phenomenon. On the one end of the spectrum institutions could be described very broadly as meaning the 'rules of the game' that aim to shape behaviour. At the other end of the spectrum, an old-institutionalist reading suggests institutions are formal organizations with headquarters, buildings and specialized staff, among others. While the narrow old-institutionalist definition accounts for the organizational structures in institutions (government), it evidently neglects the complex process and influence of governance in a globalized world, which, for present purposes, includes not only the physical structures of government, but also rule-creation, interpretation, application and enforcement in a strong social context. Indeed, '[E]xtending the notion of institutions beyond formal structures ... may serve to bridge the gap between institutionalist approaches (in the traditional materialist sense) and approaches emphasizing norms, values, culture and ideas.'[49] In sum then, viewed in the context of globalization and governance explained earlier in Chapters 2 and 3, institutions are social constructs created by people to achieve a certain outcome:

---

47 Young, Oran R. (1994), *International Governance: Protecting the Environment in a Stateless Society*, Ithaca, NY and London: Cornell University Press, 15. See also Chapter 3.

48 Rohstein, Bo (1996), 'Political Institutions: An Overview' in Robert E. Goodin and Hans Dieter Klingemann (eds), *A New Handbook of Political Science*, Oxford: Oxford University Press, 133–4; 145. Finger similarly posits that 'institutions' in a broad sense include:

> ... all relevant societal actors, in particular government, business, and civil society, as well as the rules and norms governing their relationships. Institutions are viewed as codified power structures that shape the behavior of the actors involved. Simultaneously, institutions are shaped by these actors as they compete to exert agency over institutional frameworks, ideologies, and practices.

Finger, Matthias (2005), 'The New Water Paradigm: The Privatization of Governance and the Instrumentalization of the State' in David L. Levy and Peter J. Newell, *The Business of Global Environmental Governance*, Cambridge, Massachusetts: MIT Press, 275.

49 Lecours, André (2005), 'New Institutionalism: Issues and Questions' in André Lecours (ed), *New Institutionalism: Theory and Analysis*, Toronto: University of Toronto Press, 7–8.

> Institutions ... are sets of rules of the game or codes of conduct that serve to define social practices, assign roles to the participants in these practices, and guide the interactions among occupants of these roles ... all institutions are social artefacts created by human beings – consciously or unconsciously – to cope with problems of coordination and cooperation that arise as a result of interdependencies among the activities of distinct individuals or social groups.[50]

In this sense law, governance and global governance are institutions. So too are regimes, organizations and networks which are used to achieve the objectives of law and global governance. If governance as an institution is a social human artefact which defines social practices, assigns roles to the participants in these practices and guides the interactions among occupants of these roles, among other functions, then governance applied to the environmental domain could be described as the institution of environmental governance. Where the institution of environmental governance focuses on the global environment, one could conceivably speak of the *institution of global environmental governance*.

5. DEFINITIONAL ASPECTS OF GLOBAL GOVERNANCE

Now that the general institutional context of global governance has been described, this chapter turns to an overview of the meaning of global governance. One of the central hypotheses of this book is that global governance constitutes the fulcrum around which global environmental governance revolves. Global governance is also part of the new 'globalized vocabulary', which is endemic to the 21st Century.[51] Because of its importance for global

---

[50] Young, Oran R. (1994), *International Governance: Protecting the Environment in a Stateless Society*, Ithaca, NY and London: Cornell University Press, 3.

[51] Like globalization, global governance provides a 'new vocabulary' and analytical concepts and frameworks to help us form a better understanding of an increasingly complex world. Dingwerth and Pattberg explain that the new global social realities and the variously different actors in a globalized world demand a new vocabulary that is presented by global governance. This new vocabulary would serve as a useful point of departure for understanding world politics in the 21st Century:

> Um die von vielen Autoren skizzierten Veränderungen begreifen zu können, ist das alte Vokabular nicht immer adäquat; es lässt sich nur schwerlich von den Zusammenhängen lösen, in denen es selbst entstanden ist. Insofern bietet das begriffliche Instrumentarium der Global-Governance-Literatur einen sinvollen Ausgangspunkt für die Beschäftigung mit der 'Weltpolitik im 21. Jahrhundert'.

environmental governance and because it is a notoriously vague concept and 'appear[s] to be virtually anything',[52] it necessarily invites some clarification and comprehensive description, if not exact definition. Notably, these definitional endeavours are complicated due to its not being a static concept. It is highly dynamic and its form and content will vary and will depend, for instance, on the issue area it focuses on, the geographic location of its focus (for example Southern Africa or Europe), and its objectives.[53] While some propose that global governance is 'governance in the age of globalization',[54] what follows suggests that this is only part of the answer.

5.1 Global Governance as an Analytical Perspective

As a point of departure, one must distinguish between global governance as an analytical perspective and as a normative programme.[55] Functioning as an analytical perspective, it is particularly popular in the political sciences where it is used as a lens through which to consider global realities. Thus viewed, global governance is a recent attempt to find an 'alternative to the anarchy-supranationalism dichotomy'[56] discussed above, and its origins can generally be traced to issues dealing with globalization and global change, international relations, and the impact of the UN and other international organizations on

---

Dingwerth, Klaus and Philipp Pattberg (2006), 'Was ist Global Governance?', *Leviathan*, **34**(3), 377–99 at 396.

52 Finkelstein, Lawrence S. (1995), 'What is Global Governance?', *Global Governance*, **1**, 367–72 at 368. See also, Leonard, Eric K. (2005), *The Onset of Global Governance: International Relations Theory and the International Criminal Court*, Aldershot: Ashgate, 161.

53 O'Brien, Robert (2005), 'Global Civil Society and Global Governance' in Alice D. Ba and Matthew J. Hoffmann (eds), *Contending Perspectives on Global Governance, Coherence, Contestation, and World Order*, London: Routledge, 219.

54 Overbeek, Henk (2005), 'Global Governance, Class, Hegemony' in Alice D. Ba and Matthew J. Hoffmann (eds), *Contending Perspectives on Global Governance, Coherence, Contestation, and World Order*, London: Routledge, 42.

55 Dingwerth and Pattberg even distinguish three uses of global governance in literature: an analytical perspective, a political programme or project, and a scientific discourse. Dingwerth, Klaus and Philipp Pattberg (2006), 'Was ist Global Governance?', *Leviathan*, **34**(3), 377–99 at 377. Biermann, on the other hand, finds that global governance manifests only in the phenomenological and normative sense. See further Biermann, Frank (2004), 'Global Environmental Governance: Conceptualization and Examples' (Global Governance Working Paper No 12 November 2004, Amsterdam, Berlin, Oldenburg, Potsdam: The Global Governance Project) available at www.Glogov.org [accessed 26 February 2011], 6–9.

56 Willetts, Peter (2011), *Non-governmental Organizations in World Politics: the Construction of Global Governance*, London: Routledge, 145.

global regulation.[57] For Leonard,[58] in his attempt to explain global governance's epistemological basis and the concept's contribution to society's ontological understanding of the world, one assumption is key: 'reality is always in flux' and one can better understand change (in terms of ontological shifts, change in the global order and the emergence of new governance structures) in the context of global governance if one accepts this truism.[59] He explains that under global governance, the traditional Westphalian focus on the state has made way for a new description of spheres of authority which are increasingly characterized by a 'mixture of state and non-state units, whose interactions entail working collectively to achieve solutions to the rising number of transnational problems'.[60] Notably, this explanation resonates well with the globalization rhetoric dealt with in Chapter 2.

As an analytical perspective, global governance seeks to understand this fluctuating reality and specifically 'entails an analysis of shifting ontology, global order change, and the material and ideational forces that helped shape that change'.[61] Global governance challenges traditional state-centred analytical approaches that seek to regulate the effects of globalization by discarding the dominant role of states as the supreme and only actors in international relations and instead replacing it with a hypothesis which holds that all actors collectively (state and non-state) play an equally important role in the regulation of global issues.[62] As an analytical perspective global governance is thus

---

57 Pattberg, Philipp (2005), 'What Role for Private Rule-making in Global Environmental Governance? Analysing the Forest Stewardship Council (FSC)', *International Environmental Agreements*, **5**, 175–89 at 177.

58 Leonard, Eric K. (2005), *The Onset of Global Governance: International Relations Theory and the International Criminal Court*, Aldershot: Ashgate, 163.

59 Rosenau speaks of the 'obvious but often ignored dynamics of change' and adds that:

> ... no matter how institutionalized rule systems may be, governance is not a constant in these turbulent and disaggregated times. It is, rather, a continuous process of evolution, a becoming that fluctuates between order and disorder as conditions change and emergent properties consolidate and solidify. To analyze governance by freezing it in time is to ensure failure in comprehending its nature and vagaries.

Rosenau, James N. (1995), 'Governance in the Twenty-first Century', *Global Governance*, **1**(1), 13–34 at 17.

60 Leonard, Eric K. (2005), *The Onset of Global Governance: International Relations Theory and the International Criminal Court*, Aldershot: Ashgate, 164.

61 Leonard, Eric K. (2005), *The Onset of Global Governance: International Relations Theory and the International Criminal Court*, Aldershot: Ashgate, 164.

62 Dingwerth, Klaus and Philipp Pattberg (2006), 'Was ist Global Governance?', *Leviathan*, **34**(3), 377–99 at 381–2. These actors may include, among others, nation

'generally believed to encompass different systems of rule on different levels of human activity as an organising principle beyond hierarchical steering and the sovereignty of states'.[63]

5.2 Global Governance as a Normative Programme

Global governance is also used as a political programme in the phenomenological and normative sense, and it is its manifestation as a normative programme that is especially important for present purposes. As a normative programme, global governance relates to all of the rules, principles, standards, practices, actors, regimes, organizations, networks, and their governance processes and mechanisms, that are used to govern global matters of common concern, and could be described as a 'reactionary condition to the material-structural changes of the past decades'.[64] It has been broadly defined as 'the sum of laws, norms, policies, and institutions that define, constitute, and mediate relations between citizens, societies, markets, and states in the international system – the wielders and objects of the exercise of international public power'.[65] There are of course many other definitions of this contentious and contemporary concept and the remainder of this chapter reflects on some of these.

5.2.1 The Commission on Global Governance

One of the most popular and arguably the most famous definitions of global governance as a normative programme is that of the Commission on Global Governance, which published an influential report on the issue in 1995

---

states, legislative and executive actors such as the European Commission (EC); judicial actors such as the International Criminal Court (ICC), the European Court of Justice (ECJ), the International Court of Justice (ICJ); dispute resolution bodies resorting under the WTO; international organizations such as the World Bank and treaty secretariats; hybrid organizations such as the International Organisation for Standardisation (ISO); private regulatory organizations such as the Internet Corporation for Assigned Names and Numbers (ICANN); and a further range of formal and informal actors, which cannot necessarily be grouped under any one of the former categories, including, for example, the media and global networks.

[63] Pattberg, Philipp (2005), 'What Role for Private Rule-making in Global Environmental Governance? Analysing the Forest Stewardship Council (FSC)', *International Environmental Agreements*, **5**, 175–89 at 177.

[64] Leonard, Eric K. (2005), *The Onset of Global Governance: International Relations Theory and the International Criminal Court*, Aldershot: Ashgate, 178.

[65] Weiss, Thomas G. and Ramesh Thakur (2011), 'Framing Global Governance, Five Gaps' in Thomas G. Weiss, *Thinking about Global Governance: Why People and Ideas Matter*, Abingdon: Routledge, 144.

entitled *Our Global Neighbourhood*.[66] The Commission[67] explains that governance is:

> ... the sum of the many ways individuals and institutions, public and private, manage their common affairs. It is a continuing process through which conflicting or diverse interests may be accommodated and co-operative action may be taken. It includes formal institutions and regimes empowered to enforce compliance, as well as informal arrangements that people and institutions either have agreed to or perceive to be in their interest.

Global governance is thus understood as referring to the ways of managing common affairs, including the procedures of cooperation, and those formal and informal institutions, regimes and organizations that manifest at intergovernmental and supra-national level. For the Commission, the principal actors in global governance are states, NGOs, citizens' movements, MNCs, the global capital market, and the global mass media.[68] It seems that it is the elements of commonality and shared problems or issues and the supra-national nature of the entire machinery that must respond to these common problems that make governance 'global'. Notably, the Commission's definition emphasizes that global governance is neither 'world government' in the sense of one centralized global power to which all states and people are subject, nor does it mean world federalism. It is, rather, an amorphous amalgamation of state and non-state actors, and their activities are undertaken by a whole range of institutions, regimes, and organizations to 'manage their common affairs'. Global governance is thus as fluid and indeterminate as those who engage with it wish it to be: '[T]here is no single model or form of global governance, nor is there a single structure or set of structures. It is a broad, dynamic, complex process of interactive decision-making that is constantly evolving and responding to changing circumstances.'[69]

5.2.2 Global governance and globalization

It can be deduced from the Commission's description of global governance that in an era of globalization it provides the global framework (*globalen*

---

[66] Commission on Global Governance (1995), *Our Global Neighbourhood*, Oxford: Oxford University Press. In many ways the report of the Commission did for global governance what the Brundtland Report (Our Common Future) did for sustainable development. See also Chapter 1.

[67] Commission on Global Governance (1995), *Our Global Neighbourhood*, Oxford: Oxford University Press, 2.

[68] Commission on Global Governance (1995), *Our Global Neighbourhood*, Oxford: Oxford University Press, 2–3.

[69] Commission on Global Governance (1995), *Our Global Neighbourhood*, Oxford: Oxford University Press, 4.

Ordnungsrahmens) and even the means to facilitate global cooperation and global regulation of issues that cannot be dealt with by states in isolation.[70] In this sense, global governance could arguably be described as a reaction to the regulatory challenges posed by globalization; it has an 'omnipresent',[71] multi-level regulatory character which fits well with the equally omnipresent and multi-level character of globalization described earlier in this book.[72] As Biermann[73] argues: 'global governance is seen here as a solution, as a tool that politicians need to develop and employ to solve the problems that globalization has brought about'. In similar vein Späth[74] points to the popular description of global governance as a counter-measure to globalization:

> ... the sovereign state is increasingly losing control over central aspects of governing ... global governance offers an analytical concept to subsume various efforts at the global level to come to terms with this loss of control and to balance the uncontrolled processes of globalization. In this perspective, the concept of global governance is used to describe certain developments and institutions beyond the state which try to regulate and control the new forces of globalization.

That global governance is both a result of globalization and a reaction or solution to what some perceive as the problems caused by globalization is a clear reiteration of a point made earlier in Chapter 2, namely that globalization is a paradox, and so is global governance. More importantly, the foregoing also suggests the inalienable relationship between globalization and global governance.

5.2.3 Trans-nationality, collective action and policy domains

Finkelstein[75] suggests that global governance is 'any purposeful activity

---

[70] Dingwerth, Klaus and Philipp Pattberg (2006), 'Was ist Global Governance?', *Leviathan*, **34**(3), 377–99 at 385.

[71] Dingwerth, Klaus and Philipp Pattberg (2006), 'Was ist Global Governance?', *Leviathan*, **34**(3), 377–99 at 392.

[72] See Chapter 2.

[73] Biermann, Frank (2004), 'Global Environmental Governance: Conceptualization and Examples' (Global Governance Working Paper No 12 November 2004, Amsterdam, Berlin, Oldenburg, Potsdam: The Global Governance Project) available at www.Glogov.org [accessed 26 February 2011], 7.

[74] Späth, Konrad, 'Inside Global Governance: New Borders of a Concept' available at http://www.cpogg.org/paper%20amerang/Konrad%20Spaeth.pdf [accessed 26 February 2011], 1/13.

[75] Finkelstein, Lawrence S. (1995), 'What is Global Governance?', *Global Governance*, **1**, 367–72 at 368, 369. Finkelstein's functionalist view of global governance is perhaps too simplistic and generalized since it is conceivable that various national government functions, for example the conclusion of marriages, would not have a significant global influence or repercussions. Elsewhere in the article he does,

intended to "control" or influence someone else that either occurs in the arena occupied by nations, or occurring at other levels, [by] project[ing] influence into that arena', which means that '[G]lobal governance is governing, without sovereign authority, relationships that transcend national frontiers ... [I]t is doing internationally what governments do at home.' In addition to its being an activity or process, it could also have an institutional character which often consists of regimes and various actors, organizations, or agencies that are 'doing something'.[76]

For Willetts,[77] global governance is a 'pluralist concept'; a 'political process of attempting to agree upon coherent and effective collective action'. He describes it as:

> ... a global political system that is more than the sum of the actions of the separate governments of the world. There is some degree of holism at the global level: systemic interactions produce coherent behavior rather than anarchy. Sovereignty is increasingly giving way to authoritative collective action. Patterns of expectations, desires for efficiency, and avoidance of costs can constrain behavior at the global level and promote order without government. Global governance designates relationships that maintain non-hierarchical, non-coercive processes of governed behavior, without the existence of government structures.[78]

Willetts[79] also emphasizes the central role that international organizations,

---

however, admit that global governance will mainly be concerned with 'international' functions which consist of the following categories:

> ... information creation and exchange; formulation and promulgation of principles and promotion of consensual knowledge affecting the general international order, regional orders, particular issues on the international agenda, and efforts to influence the domestic rules and behavior of states; good offices, conciliation, mediation, and compulsory resolution of disputes; regime formation, tending and execution; adoption of rules, codes, and regulations; allocation of material and program resources; provision of technical assistance and development programs; relief, humanitarian, emergency, and disaster activities; and maintenance of peace and order.

Finkelstein, Lawrence S. (1995), 'What is Global Governance?', *Global Governance*, **1**, 367–72 at 370–71.

[76] Finkelstein, Lawrence S. (1995), 'What is Global Governance?', *Global Governance*, **1**, 367–72 at 368.

[77] Willetts, Peter (2011), *Non-governmental Organizations in World Politics: the Construction of Global Governance*, London: Routledge, 148–9.

[78] Willetts, Peter (2011), *Non-governmental Organizations in World Politics: the Construction of Global Governance*, London: Routledge, 148.

[79] See for a similar view, among others, Stone, Randall W. (2011), *Controlling Institutions: International Organizations and the Global Economy*, Cambridge: Cambridge University Press.

both within and outside the UN system, play in global governance. He then explains that global governance is variously constructed around different 'policy domains' including, for example, the environment, human rights and world trade, which would dictate the design of each specific system of global governance. While there might be some overlap among the different systems (because of common concerns and objectives among them), each system will differ, depending on the nature of the problem or policy domain, the actors, and the objectives that must be achieved. While global governance concerns both rule-making in regimes as well as the process by means of which regimes are created, it also relates to creating mutual support for political values and norms in policy formulation and implementation.[80] In sum, global governance for Willetts:[81]

> ... refers to systemic processes of interactions between governments and global civil society, primarily focused on the policy outcomes of international organizations, each operating within their own distinct set of structured political relationships, to establish norms, formulate rules, promote the implementation of rules, allocate resources, or endorse the status of political actors, through the mobilization of support for political values.

5.2.4 Ambiguity and the objectives of social steering

For Rosenau,[82] in order to understand global governance one must be able to appreciate nuances and tolerate ambiguity. In a frequently cited definition of global governance, Rosenau[83] views it as including 'systems of rule at all levels of human activity – from the family to the international organization – in which the pursuit of goals through the exercise of control has transnational repercussions'. 'Control' does not imply a hierarchy of power and the issuing of commands; it rather points to governance as being a social process of steering and controlling society, with a view to modifying and directing behaviour in a global context. International organizations and other institutions such as networks, laws and regimes are considered 'control mechanisms', which implies that these goal-driven institutions, among others, are responsible for steering society and modifying behaviour. This view corresponds with the general description and objective of governance described in Chapter 3.

---

80 Willetts, Peter (2011), *Non-governmental Organizations in World Politics: the Construction of Global Governance*, London: Routledge, 149–50.

81 Willetts, Peter (2011), *Non-governmental Organizations in World Politics: the Construction of Global Governance*, London: Routledge, 150.

82 Rosenau, James N. (1995), 'Governance in the Twenty-first Century', *Global Governance*, **1**(1), 13–34 at 13.

83 Rosenau, James N. (1995), 'Governance in the Twenty-first Century', *Global Governance*, **1**(1), 13–34 at 13.

Rosenau[84] believes governance is 'global' to the extent that it 'knows no boundaries – geographical, social, cultural, economic or political'. Despite his attempts to define global governance, or perhaps as a caveat attached to these attempts, Rosenau[85] again highlights the ambiguity of global governance:

> There is no single organizing principle on which global governance rests, no emergent order around which communities and nations are likely to convert. Global governance is the sum of myriad – literally millions of – control mechanisms driven by different histories, goals, structures, and processes ... there are no characteristics or attributes common to all mechanisms. This means that any attempt to assess the dynamics of global governance will perforce have multiple dimensions, that any effort to trace a hierarchical structure of authority that loosely links disparate sources of governance to each other is bound to fail.

Dingwerth and Pattberg[86] explain that Rosenau's 'systems of rule' exist where numerous inter-connected social mechanisms, institutions, shared norms, expectations and behavioural patterns determine or influence a specific area. Neither political nor legal authority is a prerequisite for the operation of this regulatory framework. This would mean that global governance could easily accommodate non-state actors and the institutions through which they seek to contribute to global governance. Rosenau's definition, in their view, is sufficiently broad to include a virtually endless range of actors on all levels. They note, for example, his 'provocative' inclusion of the family as an actor in an area of international relations traditionally reserved for nation-states and state-created international organizations.

5.2.5 Global governance versus global government

Just as there is a distinction between governance and government,[87] global governance similarly does not imply global government, but could include aspects of what could be perceived to be a world government. Global government, as the name suggests, relates to a centralized world structure which is responsible for exercising public authority over all nations the globe over. This is unlikely to become a reality and one must agree with Keohane and Nye[88] who explain that:

---

84 Rosenau, James N. (1995), 'Governance in the Twenty-first Century', *Global Governance*, **1**(1), 13–34 at 14.

85 Rosenau, James N. (1995), 'Governance in the Twenty-first Century', *Global Governance*, **1**(1), 13–34 at 16.

86 Dingwerth, Klaus and Philipp Pattberg (2006), 'Was ist Global Governance?', *Leviathan*, **34**(3), 377–99 at 379–80.

87 See Chapter 3.

88 Keohane, Robert O. and Joseph S. Nye (2002), 'Governance in a Globalizing World' in Robert O. Keohane (ed), *Power and Governance in a Partially Globalized*

> ... world government during our lifetimes seems highly unlikely, at least in the absence of an overwhelming global threat that could only be dealt with in a unified way. In the absence of such a threat, it seems highly unlikely that peoples in some two hundred states will be willing to act on the domestic analogy for well into the new century. World government might or might not be desirable – we think it would have many adverse consequences – but in any event, it is hardly likely to be feasible.[89]

Moreover, for there to be a global government there would have to be some form of a world state, which would be highly problematic for many reasons: the problems of the South would automatically become the problems of the North, a situation which the North would be unlikely to accept; a global state would be too remote from its citizens; a world state could not easily protect and foster social and cultural diversity; and the process of becoming a world state would probably be fraught with conflict as states fought out issues primarily surrounding their sovereign interests.[90] To be sure, while it is true that '[T]he physiognomy of the world of states is changing irreversibly'[91] the sacredness of state sovereignty should not be underestimated, even in today's globalized world. It is unlikely that even the current and predicted ecological crisis (severe as it may be) would be sufficient to justify and move the world to a global environmental government in the light of state sovereignty. As Kennedy[92] states:

World, London: Routledge, 203. See also Rosenau, James N. (2009), 'Governing the Ungovernable: The Challenge of a Global Disaggregation of Authority' in Dries Lesage and Pierre Vercauteren (eds), *Contemporary Global Governance: Multipolarity vs New Discourses on Global Governance*, Brussels: P.I.E. Peter Lang, 259, where the author states that '[T]he world is too complex and diverse for global government that consists of a single global authority to evolve.'

89 Global governance is rather the aggregated result of the activities of a wide range of actors: '[D]em Begriff *Global Governance* ist sogar eingeschrieben, dass es eben nicht zwingend einer globalen Regierung bedarf, damit globales Regieren möglich wird. Vielmehr kann es auch das aggregierte Resultat der Tätigkeiten verschiedener Akteure sein.' Zürn, Michael (2006), 'Global Governance' in Gunnar Folke Schuppert (ed), *Governance Forschung: Vergewisserung über Stand und Entwicklungslinien*, Baden-Baden: Nomos Verlag, 126.

90 Messner, Dirk (2002), 'World Society: Structure and Trends' in Paul Kennedy, Dirk Messner and Franz Nuscheler (eds), *Global Trends and Global Governance*, London: Pluto Press, 41.

91 Messner, Dirk (2002), 'World Society: Structure and Trends' in Paul Kennedy, Dirk Messner and Franz Nuscheler (eds), *Global Trends and Global Governance*, London: Pluto Press, 37.

92 Kennedy, Paul (2002), 'Global Challenges at the Beginning of the Twenty-First Century' in Paul Kennedy, Dirk Messner and Franz Nuscheler (eds), *Global Trends and Global Governance*, London: Pluto Press, 13.

> Protecting the global commons is much harder to achieve politically, and it seems probable that neither North nor South, rich nor poor, will be willing to take all the steps necessary, to make all the sacrifices required, to reduce or even stabilize the overall trace gas emissions, short of some environmental disaster that sounds the tocsin for change.

The continued failure to establish a world environment organization, despite increased calls and support for the establishment of such an institution, is evidence of global reticence in creating a world environment government.[93] Conducting global governance through the aggregated mass of global regulatory measures therefore remains a more realistic approach, in which states and non-state actors seek to respond to many of the global problems they perceive as being sufficiently grave to merit intervention.

It is within this aggregated mass of regulatory measures that regimes, international organizations and networks fulfil important functions as some of the principal elements of global governance. All of these are examples of institutions (in the broader sense) that aim to change behaviour in the environmental context. The following sections reflect on the meaning and functions of these.

6. REGIMES

Regimes are among the institutional constructs that society has devised to respond to global regulatory problems. They play a fundamentally important role in global (environmental) governance. The following sections explain what regimes are and why they are important for global (environmental) governance.

6.1 Cooperation through Regimes

Regime theory,[94] despite its having been described as a fad, has stood the test

---

93 See, among others, Biermann, Frank and Steffen Bauer (eds) (2005), *A World Environment Organization: Solution or Threat for Effective International Environmental Governance?*, Aldershot: Ashgate.

94 Hurrell explains that the central question of regime theory is: 'how is co-operation possible between states claiming sovereignty but competing for power and influence in a situation of anarchy?' Regime theory thus focuses on the issue of cooperation between states within the broader context of institutionalism discussed earlier in this chapter. Hurrell, Andrew (1993), 'International Society and the Study of Regimes: A Reflective Approach' in Volker Rittberger (ed), *Regime Theory and International Relations*, Oxford: Clarendon Press, 50. For a general discussion on the role of regime theory in international relations context, also see Crawford, Robert M.A. (1996),

of time and scholarly criticism;[95] it has not 'vanished from the pages of global politics scholarship' as some have predicted and is even enjoying a 'sort of renaissance in the literature.'[96] Regime theory derives from institutionalism (discussed above) and it focuses on the role that regimes as institutions play in international relations and global governance.[97] Regimes are created by states for very specific reasons.[98] They primarily promote cooperation between states; they reduce uncertainty and transaction and information costs to states; they regularize state behaviour and promote transparency; and they establish common expectations:

> States form regimes as a method of gaining their exogenously given goals ... [they] ... believe that the benefits derived from cooperation far outweigh those of unilateral action. Therefore, states acting in a rational manner naturally form regimes to increase their personal gains.[99]

International relations theorists suggest that some predominant characteristics of international regimes include the following: regimes are governance arrangements designed to regulate behaviour; as their most important constitutive elements, regimes consist of formal and informal principles, norms, rules, procedures, organizations, and networks;[100] and regimes are aimed at

---

Regime Theory in the Post-Cold War World: Rethinking Neoliberal Approaches to International Relations, Aldershot: Dartmouth.

95 See, for example, Strange, Susan (1983), 'Cave! Hic Dragones: a Critique of Regime Analysis' in Stephen D. Krasner (ed), *International Regimes*, London: Cornell University Press, 337–54.

96 Leonard, Eric K. (2005), *The Onset of Global Governance: International Relations Theory and the International Criminal Court*, Aldershot: Ashgate, 107.

97 Beyerlin, Ulrich and Thilo Marauhn (2011), *International Environmental Law*, Oxford: Hart Publishers, 243. Oberthür and Gehring state that '[I]nternational environmental governance is already supported by intergovernmental organizations and regimes. Although the latter prevail, both forms are relevant.' Oberthür, Sebastian and Thomas Gehring (2005), 'Reforming International Environmental Governance: An Institutional Perspective on Proposals for a World Environment Organization' in Frank Biermann and Steffen Bauer (eds), *A World Environment Organization: Solution or Threat for Effective International Environmental Governance?*, Aldershot: Ashgate, 209.

98 It is also important to note that regime-creation is not the sole prerogative and domain of states. A 'knowledge based' or 'constructivist' approach to international regimes proposes that a wide array of non-state actors including, for example, intergovernmental organizations, NGOs, MNCs, and epistemic communities, could also be involved. Betsill, Michelle M. and Harriet Bulkeley (2006), 'Cities and the Multilevel Governance of Global Climate Change', *Global Governance*, **12**, 141–59 at 145.

99 Leonard, Eric K. (2005), *The Onset of Global Governance: International Relations Theory and the International Criminal Court*, Aldershot: Ashgate, 81.

100 Young, Oran R. (1983), 'Regime Dynamics: the Rise and Fall of International Regimes' in Stephen D. Krasner (ed), *International Regimes*, London: Cornell University Press, 93.

achieving regulatory objectives which could include 'adherence to rules by formulating, communicating, administering, enforcing, interpreting, legitimating and adapting them'.[101] Regimes also 'constrain and regularize the behavior of participants, affect which issues among protagonists move on and off agendas, determine which activities are legitimized or condemned and influence whether, when and how conflicts are resolved'.[102] Regimes therefore have strong social characteristics because they are created by people and as human artefacts (in the sense of being social institutions), they have 'no existence or meaning apart from the behavior of individuals or groups of human beings'.[103]

In short, regimes are valuable assets to states because they enable states to act authoritatively outside their borders with a view to promoting and protecting their interests, and as a result, states increasingly create and maintain these regimes.[104] Within this context, regimes were initially used by states only as instruments to transpose national power and interests to world politics, which meant that they had little or no reciprocal autonomous authority over and noteworthy influence on states. This is, however, gradually changing with the onset of global governance, which is resulting in regimes increasingly acquiring autonomous character and influence.[105] Currently, instead of acting only as an expression of state interests at the supra-national level, regimes increasingly also function more independently, and through their activities they are able to influence what happens in states.[106] In other words, regimes now increasingly affect state behaviour, instead of acting only as pure expressions of state interests at the supra-national level through which states would seek to determine what happens globally.

---

[101] Krasner, Stephen D. (1983), 'Structural Causes and Regime Consequences: Regimes as Intervening Variables' in Stephen D. Krasner (ed), *International Regimes*, London: Cornell University Press, 2.

[102] Puchala, Donald J. and Raymond F. Hopkins (1983), 'International Regimes: Lessons from Inductive Analysis' in Stephen D. Krasner (ed), *International Regimes*, London: Cornell University Press, 62.

[103] Young, Oran R. (1983), 'Regime Dynamics: the Rise and Fall of International Regimes' in Stephen D. Krasner (ed), *International Regimes*, London: Cornell University Press, 95.

[104] Pease, Kelly-Kate S. (2008), *International Organizations: Perspectives on Governance in the Twenty-First Century* 3rd edn, New Jersey: Pearson Prentice Hall, 65.

[105] It is still impossible, though, to suggest that regimes have become more influential or powerful than states.

[106] Breitmeier, Helmut (2006), 'Die Output-orientierte Legitimität des globalen Regierens: Empirische Befunde aus der quantitativen Erforschung internationaler Umweltregime', *Zeitschrift für Internationale Beziehungen*, **13**(1), 39–74 at 40.

While the central role of the state is obvious in the creation, maintenance, and expansion of regimes, it is arguably possible today also to speak of private global governance regimes which are created by non-state actors. These regimes could have aims broadly similar to those of state-based regimes, especially insofar as they aim to promote cooperation between specific non-state actors; reduce uncertainty and transaction and information costs; regularize behaviour; promote transparency; and establish common expectations among a range of non-state actors. An example of a private environmental regime could be those schemes and rules to which companies voluntarily subscribe to regulate and improve their environmental performance. Although these sets of (mostly voluntary) rules exist and act less coherently than public regimes, they often display common objectives and common characteristics. Examples of private regimes in an environmental context are the Ceres Principles and the ISO 14001 EMS, which could act in tandem to improve the in-house 'private' environmental governance practices and performance of a corporation. These issues are further discussed in Chapters 6–8.

6.2 Definitional Aspects

What are regimes? Krasner's[107] is the political science definition of choice, which suggests that regimes are 'principles, norms, rules, and decision-making procedures around which actor expectations converge in a given issue-area'. These issue areas would typically be determined by the loci or concentration of broader global regulatory issues or problems such as human rights, trade, and for present purposes, the environment. Within these broader issue areas it is also possible to identify sub-sets of problems or issue areas such as climate change, biodiversity conservation, and marine pollution in the environmental context. Thus, one could speak of the trade regime, the human rights regime and the environment regime. Nestled within the environment regime one finds the biodiversity protection regime, the climate change regime and the marine pollution regime. In this sense they are also referred to as environment sub-regimes.

With reference to the above definition, Krasner[108] further explains that:

---

107 Krasner, Stephen D. (1983), 'Structural Causes and Regime Consequences: Regimes as Intervening Variables' in Stephen D. Krasner (ed), *International Regimes*, London: Cornell University Press, 2.

108 Krasner, Stephen D. (1983), 'Structural Causes and Regime Consequences: Regimes as Intervening Variables' in Stephen D. Krasner (ed), *International Regimes*, London: Cornell University Press, 2.

> Principles are beliefs of fact, causation, and rectitude. Norms are standards of behaviour defined in terms of rights and obligations. Rules are specific prescriptions or proscriptions for action. Decision-making procedures are prevailing practices for making and implementing collective choice.

Norms therefore define entitlements and obligations, rules determine what is allowed and what is not, and decision-making procedures are used to operationalize the objectives of the regime and to give effect to the principles, norms and rules. While principles and norms 'provide the basic defining characteristics of a regime'[109] (any change of which would cause the regime itself to be changed), rules and procedures are designed and created around principles and norms and are much more specific. While this distinction is perhaps academic, more importantly, as elements of regimes:

> Principles, norms, rules, and procedures all contain injunctions about behaviour: they prescribe certain actions and proscribe others. They imply obligations, even though these obligations are not enforceable through a hierarchical legal system. It clarifies the definition of regime, therefore, to think of it in terms of injunctions of greater and lesser specificity.[110]

In other words, principles could form the foundation of cooperation among states, particularly as they do not provide strict prescriptions and proscriptions. Material prescriptions and proscriptions are provided by the norms and rules of regimes, which are based on the principles and which require parties to do or refrain from doing something.[111] Norms and rules could range from being very specific to being more general and vague. In addition to principles, rules and norms, regimes also contain procedural arrangements which could loosely be described as decision-making procedures which should facilitate interaction and cooperation in practical terms.[112] It is within this context that the role of law in global governance also becomes apparent: it provides the means to create international institutions such as regimes in terms of which the prescriptive and proscriptive norms and rules are created that would be binding on specific subjects such as states. In addition to providing the normative content to regimes, law also provides the principles which form the basis for coopera-

---

109 Krasner, Stephen D. (1983), 'Structural Causes and Regime Consequences: Regimes as Intervening Variables' in Stephen D. Krasner (ed), *International Regimes*, London: Cornell University Press, 3.

110 Keohane, Robert O. (1984), *After Hegemony: Cooperation and Discord in the World Political Economy*, Princeton: Princeton University Press, 59.

111 Gehring, Thomas (1994), *Dynamic International Regimes: Institutions for International Environmental Governance*, Frankfurt am Main: Peter Lang, 60.

112 Gehring, Thomas (1994), *Dynamic International Regimes: Institutions for International Environmental Governance*, Frankfurt am Main: Peter Lang, 60.

tion between states in terms of a specific issue area. For example, various principles such as sustainable development, the polluter pays principle, the preventive principle and the inter-generational equity principle have been developed around the specific issue area of the environment, and a burgeoning body of international environmental law has been developed to provide concrete norms and rules which aim to prescribe and to proscribe. The procedural aspects of regimes are mostly facilitated by means of international organizations and international organizational law (otherwise referred to as global administrative law), a matter to which this chapter returns to in the following section.[113]

Rittberger[114] describes regimes as 'rules of the game agreed upon by actors in the international arena (usually nation states) and delimiting, for these actors, the range of legitimate or admissible behaviour in a specific context of activity'. Haas[115] posits that regimes are 'man-made arrangements (social institutions) for managing conflict in a setting of interdependence' and thinks that these arrangements are 'peculiar to substantive issue-areas in international relations that are characterized by the condition of complex interdependence'. Another definition similarly holds that international regimes are 'international institutions for the governance of limited issue-areas',[116] such as the environment. It is possible to glean from these definitions that regimes are institutional responses to social issues or to problems which society perceives as giving rise to social externalities (such as infringements of human rights, obstacles to trade, and environmental pollution) and which would thus require regulatory intervention through the creation of common cooperative platforms for collective action.

Regimes are generally organized around a set of multilateral treaties, for example, the climate change instruments,[117] where they provide useful vehicles for actors to cooperate globally to address problems arising in these issue areas by fostering deliberative collaboration and cooperative action between parties who would not normally cooperate with one another if these regimes did not exist. Because regimes are mostly based on treaties, treaty bodies such as permanent conferences of parties (COPs) and secretariats play an important

---

113 See also Chapter 7.

114 Rittberger, Volker (1993), 'Editor's Introduction' in Volker Rittberger (ed), *Regime Theory and International Relations*, Oxford: Clarendon Press, xii.

115 Haas, Ernst B. (1983) 'Words can Hurt you; or Who Said What to Whom about Regimes' in Stephen D. Krasner (ed), *International Regimes*, London: Cornell University Press, 26, 27.

116 Gehring, Thomas (1994), *Dynamic International Regimes: Institutions for International Environmental Governance*, Frankfurt am Main: Peter Lang, 15.

117 These are the *United Nations Framework Convention on Climate Change*, 31 I.L.M. 849 (1992) and the *Kyoto Protocol to the United Nations Framework Convention on Climate Change*, 37 I.L.M. 22 (1998).

organizational role insofar as they function as the institutional apparatus that gives effect to treaties and contributes to the realization of the overall objectives of a broader treaty regime.[118] It is these entities that are responsible for devising decision-making procedures as part of the regime, and they would oversee rule-making, rule interpretation and rule enforcement, among other procedures. The continuous growth of treaty bodies has even been heralded as 'a key feature of the institutional development of international environmental law'.[119] Private regimes, on the other hand, are not based on treaties, but rather on non-state or private normative instruments that fulfil a guiding role fundamentally embedded in persuasion and voluntary subscription. As Chapter 8 will argue, while guiding rules such as the Ceres Principles, for example, lack the force of state authority, they play an increasingly important role in changing behaviour as far as the environment is concerned.

6.3 The Environment Regime

In the light of the foregoing, the environment regime can be described in the following terms:

> The international environmental regime consists of states, IGOs [inter-governmental organisations], nonprofit NGOs [non-governmental organisations], businesses, and the scientific community. These different actors represent both congruent and competing interests – interests that must be addressed openly and systematically in international forums. While all interests may not be equitably addressed and bargaining power may vary, the balance of all these interests will approximate an international public good. This dynamic brings about a consensus among a variety of groups and leads to the formation of knowledge-based groups known as epistemic communities.[120]

The international environmental regime is an all-encompassing system of governance which includes various actors and mechanisms involved in governing global environmental issues. In addition, numerous sub-regimes

---

118 Beyerlin, Ulrich and Thilo Marauhn (2011), *International Environmental Law*, Oxford: Hart Publishers, 253.

119 French, Duncan (2009), 'Finding Autonomy in International Environmental Law and Governance', *Journal of Environmental Law*, **21**(2), 255–89 at 260.

120 Pease, Kelly-Kate S. (2008), *International Organizations: Perspectives on Governance in the Twenty-First Century* 3rd edn, New Jersey: Pearson Prentice Hall, 240–41. Epistemic communities are networks of professional experts who provide information to decision-makers with a view to informing and guiding their actions to such an extent that global cooperation is more probable. Leonard, Eric K. (2005), *The Onset of Global Governance: International Relations Theory and the International Criminal Court*, Aldershot: Ashgate, 122.

which are based on international treaties are embedded in the broader environment regime. Breitmeier[121] provides evidence of at least 23 international environmental sub-regimes, which range from nature conservation, pollution control and desertification to ocean governance; all specific issue areas within the broader issue area of the environment.[122] Environmental sub-regimes aim to provide the regulatory milieu with the means to achieve extensive collective global action around specific environmental 'problems', especially in the light of the reality that because 'no single state can comprehensively regulate access or use, states must agree on mutual restraints in order to prevent a tragedy of the commons'.[123] These mutual restraints would be established through and given effect to by environmental sub-regimes. Moreover, international environmental lawyers are increasingly focusing on environmental sub-regimes as means to create international environmental law because:

> ... many lawyers have come to view international treaties and conventions over such matters as the environment, not as a definitive and unchanging set of rules, but

---

121 These include the Antarctic Regime; Baltic Sea Regime; Barents Sea Fisheries Regime; Biodiversity Regime; CITES-Regime; Climate Change Regime; Danube River Protection Regime; Desertification Regime; Great Lakes Management Regime; Hazardous Waste Regime; Inter-American Tropical Tuna Convention Regime; International Convention for the Conservation of Atlantic Tunas Regime; Regime for the International Regulation of Whaling; London Convention Regime; Economic Commission for Europe Regime on Long Range Transboundary Air Pollution; North Sea Regime; Oil Pollution Regime; Regime for Protection of the Rhine Against Pollution; Ramsar Regime on Wetlands; Regime for Protection of the Black Sea; South Pacific Fisheries Forum Agency Regime; Stratospheric Ozone Regime; and Tropical Timber Trade Regime. Breitmeier, Helmut (2006), 'Die Output-orientierte Legitimität des globalen Regierens: Empirische Befunde aus der quantitativen Erforschung internationaler Umweltregime', *Zeitschrift für Internationale Beziehungen*, **13**(1), 39–74 at 46–7.

122 The type of regime will depend chiefly on its purpose and focus which, in turn, will also affect its design. This varies and changes over time: '[T]he purposes of international regimes have not only changed over time; they vary across issue areas in the extent to which they are designed to support, supplement, or supplant a world market economy'. Keohane, Robert O. (1993), 'The Analysis of International Regimes: Towards a European-American Research Programme' in Volker Rittberger (ed), *Regime Theory and International Relations*, Oxford: Clarendon Press, 44. In theory, this would mean that the design, and ultimately the effect of the climate change regime, for example, would depend on the extent to which it has been designed in relation to supporting, supplementing or supplanting the world market economy. This might explain some of its failures to decrease green-house gas emissions.

123 Bodansky, Daniel, Jutta Brunnée and Ellen Hey (2007), 'International Environmental Law: Mapping the Field' in Daniel Bodansky, Jutta Brunnée and Ellen Hey (eds), *The Oxford Handbook of International Environmental Law*, Oxford: Oxford University Press, 11.

> rather as a means of creating law-making frameworks. Their purpose is to provide a framework for negotiation in which the techniques and general principles of international law can be employed, first to negotiate and formalize accepted but very general principles, and second to create a means of facilitating ongoing negotiations from which more specific, 'harder' rules may subsequently emerge.[124]

An environmental regime in this sense is also a supra-national law-making mechanism that allows for the creation of softer principles and harder enforceable norms. This functional description clearly focuses on environmental sub-regimes as law-making vehicles. In sum, then, the broader environment regime and its sub-regimes provide the opportunity and means for collective global action and a concerted regulatory response to environmental issues through various state and non-state actors and by means of a multitude of normative arrangements including many laws.

Regimes in global environmental governance have various benefits. Birnie, Boyle and Redgwell,[125] for example, point out that:

> The strength of the regime model of governance is the opportunity it offers for multilateral solutions to environmental problems and the negotiated application and development of international legal standards. It enables states to exercise a fiduciary or trusteeship role in the protection of the environment ... No other model of governance offers adequate solutions to the problem of controlling phenomena of global character, such as global warming or ozone depletion, where no single state's acts are responsible and where the interests of all are at stake.

Moreover, environmental regimes 'help determine the degree to which homeostasis or ecological balance will be legally recognized and protected across states of the commons they share'; they help to determine the 'economic "trophic" levels that competing states, as natural resource consumers, will be allowed to occupy'; and 'they help to determine how asymmetries in political interdependence and in environmental relations between states will be redressed'.[126] The environmental regime and its sub-regimes form crucial building blocks of the broader global governance construct. They are essential components of global environmental governance.

---

124 Hurrell, Andrew (1993), 'International Society and the Study of Regimes: A Reflective Approach' in Volker Rittberger (ed), *Regime Theory and International Relations*, Oxford: Clarendon Press, 54.

125 Birnie, Patricia, Alan Boyle and Catherine Redgwell (2009), *International Law and the Environment* 3rd edn, Oxford: Oxford University Press, 84.

126 Hempel, Lamont C. (1996), *Environmental Governance: The Global Challenge*, Washington: Island Press, 175.

7. INTERNATIONAL ORGANIZATIONS

In a generic sense, organizations 'provide decision points through which the steering mechanisms of governance can be carried forward',[127] and because they facilitate cooperative and organized action they are well-placed to act as vehicles by means of which people (and in this context state and non-state actors) can express their wants and needs on various different levels ranging from the local to the supra-national. Organizations have become popular institutions through which society seeks to respond to societal regulatory problems. Rosenau,[128] for example, does not find it surprising that 'the organizational explosion of our time is no less consequential than the population explosion'. While domestic organizations also play an important part in global governance to the extent that they influence what happens at the supra-national level, it is especially in the supra-national sphere that international organizations are playing a crucial role and are mushrooming at a rate hitherto unseen.[129] International organizations operating in the supra-national sphere are most usually situated in the regimes described above and, together with the regimes, it is through international organizations as institutions of deliberate cooperation that state and non-state actors would seek to establish a collective approach to governing global issues such as the environment.

7.1 Distinguishing Regimes and International Organizations

Like regimes, international organizations derive from the institutionalism paradigm, where they play an important part in global governance. As Pease[130] suggests: '[T]he world has been tied together through economic,

---

[127] Rosenau, James N. (1995), 'Governance in the Twenty-first Century', *Global Governance*, **1**(1), 13–34 at 16. For a discussion on the role of international organizations in global governance, generally, also see Heere, Wybo P. (ed) (2004), *From Government to Governance: The Growing Impact of Non-state Actors on the International and European Legal System*, The Hague: T.M.C. Asser Press, 31–172.

[128] Rosenau, James N. (1995), 'Governance in the Twenty-first Century', *Global Governance*, **1**(1), 13–34 at 16.

[129] Rosenau reiterates elsewhere that: '[I]ndeed, political agendas grow at a rate comparable to the ever greater complexity of modern life, with the result that there are new organizations in literally every realm of human activity, with some that encompass large concerns and others that are limited to particularistic issues in particular locales.' Rosenau, James N. (2009), 'Governing the Ungovernable: The Challenge of a Global Disaggregation of Authority' in Dries Lesage and Pierre Vercauteren (eds), *Contemporary Global Governance: Multipolarity vs New Discourses on Global Governance*, Brussels: P.I.E. Peter Lang, 258.

[130] Pease, Kelly-Kate S. (2008), *International Organizations: Perspectives on Governance in the Twenty-First Century* 3rd edn, New Jersey: Pearson Prentice Hall, 73.

political, social, and moral interdependence, making effective international governance a necessity for nation-states. International organizations play an important role in international governance.' While it is clear that both regimes and organizations are institutions (in the context of institutionalism as discussed above), Leonard[131] explains the distinction between them as follows:

> An international regime can exist without the presence of an international organization (although it may eventually become embodied in an international organization). This is due to the fact that international regimes do not always possess the capacity to act on the norms and principles that form them. International organizations, on the other hand, can. International organizations have the ability to respond to world events because of the formal institutionalization that exists within these entities. Thus, one can think of regimes as the underlying foundation of many international organizations, but they are not co-constitutive terms.

Thus considered, international organizations are institutionally more formalized than regimes and display the characteristics of institutions in the formal, material sense described above. They could nevertheless be based on regimes and usually arise from regimes. They also give effect to the objectives that regimes aim to accomplish, and could be considered concrete vehicles that give effect to the objectives of global governance more generally and regimes more specifically.

7.2 Definitional Aspects and Objectives of International Organizations

Pease[132] states that international organizations could manifest variously, including, as inter-governmental organizations (within and outside the UN system), NGOs, and MNCs. Biermann, Davies and Van der Grijp[133] define international organizations as 'actors that have physical qualities, such as staff, headquarters, resources, and formalized leadership, and that effectively pursue a policy ... organizations can apply to all kinds of entities, scales, and objectives and may range from public to private and from global to local'. These descriptions suggest that international organizations are physical (literally *organizational* in the administrative sense) entities tasked with the practicali-

---

131 Leonard, Eric K. (2005), *The Onset of Global Governance: International Relations Theory and the International Criminal Court*, Aldershot: Ashgate, 109.

132 Pease, Kelly-Kate S. (2008), *International Organizations: Perspectives on Governance in the Twenty-First Century* 3rd edn, New Jersey: Pearson Prentice Hall, 4.

133 Biermann, Frank, Olwen Davies and Nicolien Van der Grijp (2009), 'Environmental Policy Integration and the Architecture of Global Environmental Governance', *International Environmental Agreements*, **9**, 351–69 at 354.

ties of pursuing policy objectives determined by those who have established the organizations. They have a material character consisting, for example, of a secretariat, a head office, and personnel working for the organization. International organizations could be private or public depending on whether they are state or non-state driven. Greenpeace would be an example of a non-state (private) international environmental organization, whereas UNEP is clearly a state (public) international organization.

International organizations are particularly well suited to facilitate scientific and policy-making cooperation and to achieve new norm creation and compliance monitoring and enforcement.[134] They also provide a 'permanent forum where states and other participants can engage in dialogue and negotiations, [by] facilitating the compromises necessary for lawmaking by states at very different stages of economic and social development'.[135] International organizations further play an important role in identifying shared global problems which must be addressed; they often host secretariats that administer multilateral global agreements;[136] they are tools for collective action; they are forums for the formulation of global governance and actors in those forums; they act as convenors of multiple actors; they provide an engagement platform or 'safe space' for these actors; they can be multi-level network managers in a multi-stakeholder network setting; and they can even act, albeit to a limited extent, as financiers and sponsors to implement or operationalize policy programmes.[137] Other commentators explain that international organizations

---

[134] Kiss, Alexandre and Dinah Shelton (2007), *Guide to International Environmental Law*, Leiden: Martinus Nijhoff Publishers, 49.

[135] Birnie, Patricia, Alan Boyle and Catherine Redgwell (2009), *International Law and the Environment* 3rd edn, Oxford: Oxford University Press, 45.

[136] Bodansky, Daniel, Jutta Brunnée and Ellen Hey (2007), 'International Environmental Law: Mapping the Field' in Daniel Bodansky, Jutta Brunnée and Ellen Hey (eds), *The Oxford Handbook of International Environmental Law*, Oxford: Oxford University Press, 18–19.

[137] Ivanova, Maria H., 'Partnerships, International Organizations, and Global Environmental Governance' at 20–21 available at http://www.gppi.net/fileadmin/gppi/Ivanova_Article.pdf [accessed 11 March 2011]. Unlike domestic environmental organizations, international organizations play a 'softer' and more nuanced role of facilitating, guiding and assisting; they do not rely on extensive regulation, coercion and enforcement:

> Outside the circumscribed administrative roles, no agency has been endowed with the supranational authority to devise rules binding either on states or on individuals addressing environmental problems. Therefore, unlike its domestic counterparts, treaty norms outline explicit duties for contracting states to regulate, supervise, monitor and legislate ... but in most instances, implementation and enforcement remain the responsibility of each state concerned.

provide support for state interactions and negotiations; they manage substantive operations (for example, the World Bank); they act as vehicles for pooling activities, assets or risks; they act as vehicles for joint state production (for example, the European Organization for Nuclear Research (CERN)); they elaborate and coordinate norms; they act as relatively neutral information and knowledge providers; they could act as arbitrators (for example, the International Atomic Energy Agency (IAEA)); they facilitate international intervention; they act as community representatives in global governance matters; and they manage enforcement and compliance.[138] In short, as Volgy *et al.*[139] suggest, international organizations are 'entities created with sufficient organizational structure and autonomy to provide formal, ongoing, multilateral processes of decision making between states, along with the capacity to execute the collective will of their members (states)'. The same could be said for private international organizations, and it is especially in the environmental context that NGOs such as Greenpeace, for example, aim to achieve objectives similar to those of public international organizations, albeit with the backing of private as opposed to public authority.

Often, international organizations are themselves not a product of global governance, but act as instigators or creators of governance. In other words, organizations are sometimes not created only because of or by the need for global governance; they often themselves give rise to new forms of governance and even norm creation.[140] In this sense, intergovernmental organization can probably never be divorced from nation states, but then neither can states from organizations or regimes for that matter. As Rosenau and Durfee[141] explain '[S]tates may well set up international organizations, but once in place,

---

Hierlmeier, Jodie (2002), 'UNEP: Retrospect and Prospect – Options for Reforming the Global Environmental Governance Regime', *Georgetown International Environmental Law Review*, **14**, 767–805 at 784.

[138] Abbot, Kenneth W. and Duncan Snidal (2010), 'Why States Act through Formal International Organizations' in Paul F. Diehl and B. Frederking (eds), *The Politics of Global Governance: International Organizations in an Interdependent World*, Boulder: Lynne Rienner Publishers, 34–58.

[139] Volgy Thomas J. *et al.* (2010), 'Identifying Formal Intergovernmental Organizations' in Paul F. Diehl and B. Frederking (eds), *The Politics of Global Governance: International Organizations in an Interdependent World*, Boulder: Lynne Rienner Publishers, 15.

[140] Rosenau confirms that '[T]he proliferation of organizations and their ever greater interdependence may stimulate felt needs for new forms of governance.' Rosenau, James N. (1995), 'Governance in the Twenty-first Century', *Global Governance*, **1**(1), 13–34 at 17.

[141] Rosenau, James N. and Mary Durfee (1995), *Thinking Theory Through: Coherent Approaches to an Incoherent World*, Boulder: Westview Press, 66.

these organizations often set the rules for states.'[142] Ivanova[143] explains this complex duality as follows:

> Conceived as tools for collective action among states, international organizations exemplify the inherent tensions in the global governance system ... they are influential in their own right yet also subservient to member state interests; they shape negotiations but their own mandate is shaped by these discussions; they are supranational entities, yet expected to deliver practical results at subnational levels.

In sum, the foregoing suggests that international organizations are crucial elements of the cumulative institutional character of global governance; they are part of the general social construct of global governance and play an important part in addressing world anarchy.[144]

Today, there are many international organizations that operate in the global milieu. One study estimates there to be around 3000, which include 'programme organizations' such as the Council of Europe or the United Nations Commission on Sustainable Development (UNCSD); 'forum organizations' such as the UN General Assembly; 'service organizations' such as the World Health Organization (WHO); and 'control organizations' such as the International Monetary Fund (IMF).[145] This classification is arguably not

---

142 Strand supports this view:

> ... international organizations can be viewed as relatively organic entities that exist within a larger global society. The national interests of their members impact on international organizations, yet international organizations also affect the policy goals and negotiations strategies their members employ. Put differently, there is a reflexive relationship between states and global social structures.

Strand, Jonathan R. (2004), 'The Case for Regional Environmental Organizations' in Norichika Kanie and Peter M. Haas (eds), *Emerging Forces in Environmental Governance*, Tokyo: United Nations University Press, 80.

143 Ivanova, Maria H., 'Partnerships, International Organizations, and Global Environmental Governance' at 20 available at http://www.gppi.net/fileadmin/gppi/Ivanova_Article.pdf [accessed 11 March 2011].

144 For Birnie, Boyle and Redgwell '[I]nternational organizations have become an important part of the lawmaking process, even if they are not in themselves the process.' In this sense, organizations are closer to 'governance' than to 'government'. Birnie, Patricia, Alan Boyle and Catherine Redgwell (2009), *International Law and the Environment* 3rd edn, Oxford: Oxford University Press, 45.

145 Messner, Dirk (2002), 'World Society: Structure and Trends' in Paul Kennedy, Dirk Messner and Franz Nuscheler (eds), *Global Trends and Global Governance*, London: Pluto Press, 44. Another account puts this figure at 36 486, which includes public and private organizations. Amerashinghe, Chittharanjan F. (2008), 'International Institutional Law: A Point of View', *International Organizations Law*, **5**, 143–50 at 147.

meant to be too strict. It is possible that some organizations may be classified as having the characteristics of more than one of these and that there would be one organization which performs functions relevant for various issue areas such as trade, investment, environment, and agriculture. In the environmental context, Strand[146] estimates that there are at least 27 international organizations with some or other environmental function. These include, among others, development banks, the Food and Agricultural Organization (FAO), the Global Environment Facility (GEF), the International Labour Organization (ILO), the International Maritime Organization (IMO), the World Bank, the WTO, the various UN bodies, and regional environmental organizations. The most prominent international environmental organization is arguably UNEP. As one of the primary environmental organizations, it plays an important role to energize 'the institutional bargaining processes that produce constitutional contracts giving rise to environmental regimes',[147] and it oversees the governance systems and provisions of regimes that were created under its auspices.

7.3 International Organizations, Bureaucracy and Administration

It was shown above that international organizations are central components of global governance to the extent that they assist in establishing global governance systems and regimes and then in *administering* these. The administration of regimes and organizations occurs principally through decision-making procedures inherent in institutions, as is evident in Krasner's definition of institutions above. The procedural (bureaucratic/administrative) aspects of an organization as an institution are thus important components of that institution.

It is in this context that one further important distinction must be drawn, namely that between the objectives of organizations on the one hand and their internal administration or bureaucracy on the other. For example, the primary objective of an international environmental organization such as UNEP is to pursue the policy objectives of the parties that created it, but it can do so only by means of its own internal administrative procedures and bureaucracy (the day-to-day operation of the organization) for which a secretariat is usually

---

[146] Strand, Jonathan R., 'The Case for Regional Environmental Organizations: Regional Integration and Multilateral Environmental Governance' (United Nations University, Institute of Advanced Studies Working Paper) available at http://www.ieg.earthsystemgovernance.org/sites/default/files/files/publications/Strand_The%20Case%20for%20REOs_2002.pdf [accessed 4 October 2011], 3.

[147] Young, Oran R. (1994), *International Governance: Protecting the Environment in a Stateless Society*, Ithaca, NY and London: Cornell University Press, 164.

responsible.[148] In addition to performing its internal administrative processes it will also regularly interact with other organizations and institutions. It is thus possible to observe numerous administrative relationships that exist within and between organizations. Global administrative or international organizations law, among others, govern these administrative relationships. This issue is further addressed elsewhere in this book.[149] While this insight may seem unremarkable, it is significant as far as governance is concerned, because inter- and intra-organizational administration and bureaucracy could arguably be considered a form of governance insofar as governance is understood to mean collective action to achieve collective goals. In short, bureaucracy enables international organizations to accomplish their objectives and gives effect to their principal rationales through routine institutionalized interactions which occur by means of administrative or bureaucratic actions.[150] The internal and external bureaucracy and administrative arrangements, together with the procedural rules that enable an organization to function, are therefore important parts of global governance. This would also apply in the environmental context, where the bureaucratic and administrative procedures and functions of an environmental organization could be considered elements of global environmental governance.[151] One could therefore conceivably speak of 'global environmental administration as global environmental governance'.[152]

---

148 Biermann, Davies and Van der Grijp see international organizations as: 'the complex of three elements (a) a normative framework of principles and rules governing the organization; (b) state members of the organization; and (c) a bureaucracy and its leader at the center of the organization'. Biermann, Frank, Olwen Davies and Nicolien Van der Grijp (2009), 'Environmental Policy Integration and the Architecture of Global Environmental Governance', *International Environmental Agreements*, **9**, 351–69 at 354.

149 See Chapter 7.

150 Vogly Thomas J. *et al.* (2010), 'Identifying Formal Intergovernmental Organizations' in Paul F. Diehl and B. Frederking (eds), *The Politics of Global Governance: International Organizations in an Interdependent World*, Boulder: Lynne Rienner Publishers, 16.

151 See further Chapters 6 and 7.

152 See also Kingsbury Benedict (2007), 'Global Environmental Governance as Administration: Implications for International Law' in Daniel Bodansky, Jutta Brunnée and Ellen Hey (eds), *The Oxford Handbook of International Environmental Law*, Oxford: Oxford University Press, 63.

8. NETWORKS

Like regimes and international organizations, networks[153] are important components of global governance.[154] The distinction between international organizations and regimes on the one hand and networks on the other, however, is that while states play a prominent role in the former, they play a lesser role in networks. In fact, non-state actors are the principal role players in networks, because they provide non-state actors functioning as 'members of domestic society' (usually groups of individuals in the form of NGOs) with the opportunity to take part in global governance with the traditional (state) members of global society.[155] Moreover, the focus on non-state actors in networks must be considered in the context of globalization, and more specifically the concomitant increase in the participation of non-state actors and their influence in governing global issues alongside nation states:

> The intensification of the globalization process has perpetuated a change in the material-structural forces that make up the global system, and as a result, it is also perpetuating a change in the global order. Thus, one could assert that the globalization process is causing a fundamental shift in the spatial construction of the world and transforming whom is considered an international actor and what their interactions look like. This transformation is also causing an alteration in the governance pattern and the location of authority.[156]

Networks represent a new pattern of governance and they manifest in the 'joined-up' or 'network governance' paradigm.[157] Networks have developed

---

153 Detomasi, David Antony (2007), 'The Multinational Corporation and Global Governance: Modelling Global Public Policy Networks', *Journal of Business Ethics*, **71**, 321–34 at 321; Slaughter, Anne-Marie and Thomas Hale (2010), 'Transnational Networks and Emerging Powers' in Alan S. Alexandroff and Andrew F. Cooper (eds), *Rising States, Rising Institutions: Challenges for Global Governance*, Washington: Brookings Institution Press, 48–62.

154 For a comprehensive discussion see Slaughter, Anne-Marie and Thomas Hale (2010), 'Transnational Networks and Emerging Powers' in Alan S. Alexandroff and Andrew F. Cooper (eds), *Rising States, Rising Institutions: Challenges for Global Governance*, Washington: Brookings Institution Press, 48–62.

155 Young, Oran R. (1994), *International Governance: Protecting the Environment in a Stateless Society*, Ithaca, NY and London: Cornell University Press, 185.

156 Leonard, Eric K. (2005), *The Onset of Global Governance: International Relations Theory and the International Criminal Court*, Aldershot: Ashgate, 184.

157 For a discussion of network governance, see for example, Jones, Candace, William S. Hesterly and Stephen P. Borgatti (1997), 'A General Theory of Network Governance: Exchange Conditions and Social Mechanisms', *Academy of Management Review*, **22**(4), 911–45. See also Chapter 3.

as a response to the many perceived failures of global governance with specific reference to operational and participative governance asymmetries or deficits. Some of these include the discontinuity between the locus of the nation state and the extent of global problems (geographical asymmetry); the discontinuity between decisions taken today and the effects that they will have for future generations (temporal asymmetry); the increased complexity and extent of global problems which require the input of a widely diverse range of experts in addition to the nation state; and the need to optimize the protection and distribution of global public goods in the wake of increased monopolization.[158] The formation of networks is also a response to the participatory deficits of global governance, where non-state actors are demanding their say and asserting their roles as increasingly influential actors.[159] A wide range of non-state actors, and to lesser extent state actors,[160] will then form networks with a view to asserting themselves more fully in global governance, providing representation for the interests of future generations, providing expertise on complex global problems, and ensuring a more just allocation of global public goods. Another goal of networks could also be to provide mutual support with a view to overcoming collective substantive and procedural governance difficulties where 'the strengths of state, market, and civil society actors combine to create an effective international governance system that overcomes the weaknesses afflicting each individually'.[161] Ultimately, networks aim to increase the capacity of governance because they have 'the ability to use networking as the flexible, interactive, borderless form of structuration of whatever activity in

158 These are also expressed as 'political crises' that affect the institutions of governance and include the crisis of efficiency, the crisis of legitimacy, the crisis of identity, and the crisis of equity. Castells, Manuel (2008), 'The New Public Sphere: Global Civil Society, Communication Networks, and Global Governance', *The Annals of the American Academy*, March, 78–93 at 82.

159 Benner, Thorsten, Wolfgang H. Reinicke and Jan Martin Witte (2004), 'Multisectoral Networks in Global Governance: Towards a Pluralistic System of Accountability', *Government and Opposition*, **39**(2), 191–210 at 194.

160 This section argues that non-state actors are the primary role-players in networks. This, however, does not exclude states as important means of providing legitimacy to networked governance, or their having the ability to form their own interstate networks. An easy example of states forming networks is the G-20 Group of Finance Ministers. See Kirton, John (2010), 'The G-20 Finance Ministers: Network Governance' in Alan S. Alexandroff and Andrew F. Cooper (eds), *Rising States, Rising Institutions: Challenges for Global Governance*, Washington: Brookings Institution Press, 196–217.

161 Detomasi, David Antony (2007), 'The Multinational Corporation and Global Governance: Modelling Global Public Policy Networks', *Journal of Business Ethics*, **71**, 321–34.

whatever domain';[162] and they are able to expand the capacity of state and non-state actors to address global regulatory issues.[163]

Generally speaking, networks are pluralistic multi-sectoral arrangements that traverse orthodox political and sectoral boundaries. They are created and exist in the sphere which lies between the state and society.[164] Networks are organized around specific issues of common global concern and commentators have explained them as follows:

> Multisectoral networks create bridges on a transnational scale among the public sector ... the private sector and civil society. Networks seek to complement rather than replace traditional governance mechanisms – they are not legislating but help to develop standards and norms, provide global public goods and implement international agreements. They co-exist and co-evolve with other modes of governance: state-centred unilateralism, purely intergovernmental multilateralism, regional integration, [and] private self-regulation.[165]

Networks are evidently particularly adept at linking the public, private and civil society spheres of authority; they are highly flexible and open; and they focus on the transfer of global knowledge. As Detomasi[166] states:

---

162 Castells, Manuel (2008), 'The New Public Sphere: Global Civil Society, Communication Networks, and Global Governance', *The Annals of the American Academy*, March, 78–93 at 81.

163 Slaughter, Anne-Marie and Thomas Hale (2010), 'Transnational Networks and Emerging Powers' in Alan S. Alexandroff and Andrew F. Cooper (eds), *Rising States, Rising Institutions: Challenges for Global Governance*, Washington: Brookings Institution Press, 49.

164 Castells describes the 'public sphere' as 'an essential component of socio-political organization because it is the space where people come together as citizens and articulate their autonomous views to influence the political institutions of society.' Castells, Manuel (2008), 'The New Public Sphere: Global Civil Society, Communication Networks, and Global Governance', *The Annals of the American Academy*, March, 78–93 at 78. In this public sphere, networks fit in between states, international organizations and regimes on the one hand, and *ad hoc* forms of governance on the other. Slaughter, Anne-Marie and Thomas Hale (2010), 'Transnational Networks and Emerging Powers' in Alan S. Alexandroff and Andrew F. Cooper (eds), *Rising States, Rising Institutions: Challenges for Global Governance*, Washington: Brookings Institution Press, 48.

165 Benner, Thorsten, Wolfgang H. Reinicke and Jan Martin Witte (2004), 'Multisectoral Networks in Global Governance: Towards a Pluralistic System of Accountability', *Government and Opposition*, **39**(2), 191–210 at 196.

166 Detomasi, David Antony (2007), 'The Multinational Corporation and Global Governance: Modelling Global Public Policy Networks', *Journal of Business Ethics*, **71**, 321–34 at 328.

> Their particular strengths lie in their ability to integrate public, private, and non-governmental efforts in managing the governance challenges posed by particular policy areas ... Their particular strength is inclusiveness: they operate by bridging the technical and administrative expertize possessed by industry actors, and the legitimacy garnered by state regulatory endorsement. They occupy the indeterminate zone between formal institutions of domestic and interstate law and the realm of anarchy. They are symptomatic of an associated concept of 'governance through networks' in which interested parties, both state and non-state, combine their specific strengths to establish procedural and expected norms that condition their mutual activity.

Networks can therefore be formal or informal and often include commissions or specialist bodies created by organizations within the greater rubric of specific regimes. Networks are also distinctly non-hierarchical and are horizontally structured. This means that they are a result of and 'have contributed to the disaggregation of authority as well as the formation of new collectivities not founded on hierarchical principles'.[167]

While there is no generally accepted typology of networks, most agree that they could include, among others, epistemic communities functioning as global knowledge networks, transnational social movement organizations,[168] transnational advocacy networks, and global civil society.[169] Some concrete examples in the environmental context include the International Council for Local Environmental Initiatives (ICLEI), the International Network for Environmental Compliance and Enforcement (INECE), and the IUCN Academy of Environmental Law (IUCN AEL).

---

167 Rosenau, James N. (2005), 'Global Governance as Disaggregated Complexity' in Alice D. Ba and Matthew J. Hoffmann (eds), *Contending Perspectives on Global Governance, Coherence, Contestation, and World Order*, London: Routledge, 140; Betsill, Michelle M. and Harriet Bulkeley (2006), 'Cities and the Multilevel Governance of Global Climate Change', *Global Governance*, **12**, 141–59 at 148.

168 See on the relatively new concept of transnational social movement organizations, Benford, Robert D. (2011), 'Framing Global Governance from Below: Discursive Opportunities and Challenges in the Transnational Social Movement Arena' in Cerneliu Bjola and Markus Kornprobst (eds), *Arguing Global Governance*, London: Routledge, 67–84.

169 Betsill, Michelle M. and Harriet Bulkeley (2006), 'Cities and the Multilevel Governance of Global Climate Change', *Global Governance*, **12**, 141–59 at 147.

9. REGIONAL GOVERNANCE AS AN ELEMENT OF GLOBAL GOVERNANCE

Regional governance is considered to be a part of global governance in the same way as domestic governance is. It is thus one of the levels inherent in global governance and it is equally important for global environmental governance. It is an aspect of global governance which has received considerable attention as a separate issue but less attention as an integral component of global governance.

Regional governance is a result of fundamental changes *within* the realm of global governance. These changes mostly involve a shift of the locus of power from the nation state and state governments and a gradual (re)concentration and reallocation of power in regional governance foci.[170] Examples are the EU, the African Union (AU), and the Southern African Development Community (SADC). These regional structures have, and continue to develop, comprehensive and far-reaching regional norms and other institutional arrangements related to many issues including trade, a common market, the movement of people, and the environment, among others.

Generally speaking, regional structures create regional governance spaces that aim to facilitate governance with respect to common matters, concerns and interests that individual country Member States share, and they form what Benz[171] calls an intermediate-level between national and international interests. Regional governance bodies provide the opportunity to further facilitate the governance of common issues at a supra-national but nevertheless uniform level. They are usually responses to the need for increased cultural, economic and social integration by various countries situated in the same region and in the same environmental context, and they could be highly effective in advancing the common regional environmental interests of states through common institutions, actors, processes and governance mechanisms. The allure of these regional governance arrangements also lies partly in the fact that they provide some degree of authoritative rule-making and rule execution for common and trans-boundary environmental matters (often more than the truly international dispensation), more than for the truly international dispensation, while remaining subject to the dictates of state sovereignty and state independence. The degree and extent of regional normative arrangements such as laws, organiza-

---

170 Lee, Robert and Elen Stokes (2009), 'Environmental Governance: Reconnecting the Global and Local', *Journal of Law and Society*, **36**(1), 1–10 at 4.

171 Benz, Arthur (2004), 'Einleitung: Governance-Modebegriff oder nützliches sozialwissenschaftliches Konzept?' in Arthur Benz (ed), *Governance- Regieren in komplexen Regelsystemen: Eine Einführung*, Wiesbaden, Germany: VS Verlag für Sozialwissenschaften, 23.

tions and regimes; governance mechanisms, the variety and composition of state and non-state actors; and the relationship between countries and their regional governance bodies vary considerably, and the plurality in regional governance approaches contributes further to global disaggregation and the plurality of global governance. The geographic locale of the specific regions would also have a distinct influence on the design, objectives and composition of regional governance responses. It could be expected that the regional arrangements in the 'North' would differ markedly from those in the 'South', both in terms of objectives, content, scope and effectiveness.

Notably, regional governance does not operate in isolation from global governance and its institutions. Just as domestic governance is part of global governance, regional governance is an important part of global governance and it is not uncommon to find networks, regimes and organizations in these regional arrangements. In fact, some commentators view governance in the EU as an example of network governance.[172] Regional governance is also a part of global governance organizations, regimes and its other institutions, especially insofar as regional bodies act as representatives of their Member States' interests in creating, enforcing and administering these global regimes and institutions. The collective representation of the EU Member States in the climate change regime is one example. Conversely, regional governance developments could also influence global governance, as they often do. Examples are article 24 of the *African Charter on Human and Peoples' Rights*, 1981, OAU Doc. CAB/LEG/67/3 rev. 5, 21 I.L.M. 58 (1982), which has been influential in steering the debate on the recognition of an international environmental right;[173] and the United Nations Economic Commission for Europe (UNECE) *Convention on Access to Information, Public Participation in Decision-Making and Access to Justice in Environmental Matters* (Aarhus Convention), June 25, 1998, 38 I.L.M. 517 (1999), which, although regional, is open to international accession by states and is considered to set the international standard in procedural environmental governance matters.[174]

As far as the exercise of public political power is concerned, regional governance in this context is much weaker than at the national level, although

---

[172] Börzel, Tanja A. (2006), 'European Governance: nicht neu, aber anders' in Gunnar Folke Schuppert (ed), *Governance-Forschung: Vergewisserung über Stand und Entwicklungslinien*, Baden-Baden: Nomos Verlaggesellschaft, 80–86.

[173] According to article 24: '[A]ll peoples shall have the right to a general satisfactory environment favorable to their development.' It is still considered the only explicit recognition of an international environmental right in 'broadly qualitative terms'. Birnie, Patricia, Alan Boyle and Catherine Redgwell (2009), *International Law and the Environment* 3rd edn, Oxford: Oxford University Press, 273–5.

[174] Beyerlin, Ulrich and Thilo Marauhn (2011), *International Environmental Law*, Oxford: Hart Publishers, 236–8.

the EU especially is increasingly asserting itself as an independent and autonomous body in world affairs. Some regional structures such as the EU have in fact become such influential role players that they act as a single entity in various global governance processes and forums while remaining representative of their members' interests. This gradual regional emancipation is also evident from the development and recognition of concepts such as 'European governance'[175] and European environmental governance.

10. SUMMARY

The preceding sections described global governance as a social institutional response to global regulatory problems. It was shown that global governance is an attempt mainly by states to regulate issues beyond their borders and their sovereign sphere of influence, in other words, in that particular space which the sovereign nation state traditionally cannot reach. These issues are commonly referred to as global governance issues and could include, for example, the environment, human rights, world trade and so forth. The need to regulate these global issues stems from globalization, which has been extensively canvassed in Chapter 2. In fact, it is globalized processes that have led to intensified economic, political and social interactions world-wide and therefore in many instances have caused or contributed to these issues of regulatory concern.

In addition to state actors, non-state actors are increasingly asserting themselves in the governance of global issues, and together with state actors, in the absence of a world government, they endeavour to steer behaviour with the view to achieving a common good, collective gains or promoting majority interests. Globally this occurs by means of institutions consisting of laws, regimes, organizations and networks such as those to be found in the environmental context:

> ... the globalization of environmental problems has contributed to the creation and development of new global regimes, institutions, and organizations dedicated to environmental governance. More efficient use and transfer of technology, freer flow of information, and novel institutional arrangements based on public-private partnerships have the potential to contribute positively to environmental governance.[176]

The entire disaggregated mass of global regulatory arrangements could collectively be described as global governance. While the breadth and depth of

---

175 Börzel, Tanja A. (2006), 'European Governance: nicht neu, aber anders' in Gunnar Folke Schuppert (ed), *Governance-Forschung: Vergewisserung über Stand und Entwicklungslinien*, Baden-Baden: Nomos Verlaggesellschaft, 79.

176 Lemos, Maria Carmen and Arun Agrawal (2006), 'Environmental Governance', *Annual Review of Environment and Resources*, **31**, 297–325 at 300.

global governance is incredibly wide, in its simplest form it is best understood as a dynamic phenomenon that 'encompasses all aspects of steering or guidance in world politics'.[177] This process of steering also occurs at regional and national levels in the global dispensation. In this way global governance seeks to drive and maintain global order. It manifests in a reality where there is no authoritative means of central decision-making and enforcement (in the space between order and anarchy). In other words 'global governance can be understood as the outcome of a process of global ordering steered by two opposing forces: growing demand for collective action and accelerating political fragmentation of collective agency'.[178]

Global governance either functions as an analytical perspective or as a normative programme. While it is most often invoked in the latter guise, global governance as an analytical perspective has considerable value insofar as it provides one with the analytical means to understand international relations in an increasingly disaggregated world. It is a 'heuristic device to capture and describe the confusing and seemingly ever-accelerating transformation of the international system'.[179] As a normative programme, in the absence of a world government, global governance focuses on common problems or issues that state and non-state actors seek to regulate beyond their national borders by means of a range of socially constructed institutions such as laws, regimes, organizations and networks. The foregoing analysis suggests that the following working definition of global governance may serve: In the absence of a centralized world government, global governance is a regulatory response in a globalized world that ranges from the local to the international, through which state and non-state actors make use of institutions such as laws and other rules, regimes, organizations and networks to prescribe and proscribe behaviour, constrain activity, and shape expectations with a view to collectively addressing global regulatory issues and to ensuring collective action, collective problem solving and the achievement of mutual benefits. Insofar as this regulatory response applies to environmental issues, one could speak of global environmental governance. The remaining chapters of this book reflect in greater detail on the nature of global environmental governance.

---

[177] Leonard, Eric K. (2005), *The Onset of Global Governance: International Relations Theory and the International Criminal Court*, Aldershot: Ashgate, 162.

[178] Bjola, Corneliu and Markus Kornprobst (2011), 'Introduction: the Argumentative Deontology of Global Governance' in Cerneliu Bjola and Markus Kornprobst (eds), *Arguing Global Governance*, London: Routledge, 3.

[179] Weiss, Thomas G. (2011), 'Governance, Good Governance, and Global Governance' in Thomas G. Weiss, *Thinking about Global Governance: Why People and Ideas Matter*, Abingdon: Routledge, 182.

5. Law and governance

> ... to govern is to engage in attempts to act upon the actions or conduct of others. Hence, law is one of the forms of governance, a distinctive set of techniques that impact on the conduct of others.[1]
>
> (Alan Hunt, 2002)

1. INTRODUCTION

Chapter 3 indicated that law presupposes governance and *vice versa*; the two are interdependent and inseparably intertwined. This chapter further elaborates on the relationship between law and governance with specific reference to the broader social function of law as the predominant but not the only social institution in society (others are, for example, politics, economics and religion).[2] The latter discussion specifically focuses on the constitutive, regulative, steering and legitimizing functions of law in society. While Chapter 2 has briefly referred to the changing face of law as a result of globalization, this chapter also more comprehensively discusses the increased plurality or hybridization of law in the global governance paradigm. This part of the discussion emphasizes that law (in tandem with governance) is increasingly assuming a more diverse or plural character and that, like governance, law is no longer exclusively connected to the state and the formal, 'hard'[3] forms of law generated by

---

1 Hunt, Alan (2002), 'Legal Governance and Social Relations: Empowering Agents and the Limits of Law' in Michael MacNeil, Neil Sargent and Peter Swan (eds), *Law, Regulation and Governance*, Oxford: Oxford University Press, 63.

2 This is also true in the environmental context:

> Law aims to influence behavior in order to promote environmental quality. It works in parallel with other institutions. It also works according to dynamics that some theorists would not classify as institutional. Law interacts – sometimes effectively, sometimes awkwardly, sometimes counter productively – with other systems that seek to order behavior and achieve social control.

DiMento, Joseph F.C. (2003), *The Global Environment and International Law*, Austin: University of Texas Press, 7.

3 Heyvaert explains 'hard law' in the international law context as 'norms which

state actors.[4] Notably, as a consequence of globalization, many 'softer', informal and private rules, guidelines and principles are generated and used by a wide range of non-state actors to form a global body of law that collectively serves as the legal base of the global governance effort. To the extent that it is influenced by globalization, governance itself necessitates a manifestly different approach to law:

> The concept of 'governance' thus points to a turn from a normative substantive conception of government exclusively tied to the national state based on constitutional and international law towards a functional characterization of governing activities. It embraces the possibility of a multiplicity of governance agents, who engage in new modes of exercising power, often guided and legitimized by 'alternative' legalities.[5]

The collective body of law that consists of 'alternative legalities' could best be described as an enmeshed mass of hard and soft, public, private and/or hybrid law and law-like rules. In being a catalyst involved in this change in the nature of regulation, globalization has had a profound impact on law and governance, between which there is a reciprocal cause and effect relationship in which each may be considered to be the source of the other. In other words, the straightforward implementation of top-down governance by means of laws promulgated, enforced and sanctioned by nation states has changed and continues to change alongside the inevitable changes brought about by globalization and the prevalence of the governance paradigm. This gives rise to many complexities and questions regarding the manner in which society views and uses law as one of its means to address common global problems through governance,

---

states recognize as binding. To be binding, norms require precision, or at least the potential of precision, and delegation of authority for interpretation and implementation. The binding nature of the norm justifies its enforceability, if necessary through coercion.' Hard law is thus binding, enforceable, and precise. It relies on delegated authority for its implementation which could be coercive in nature. In this way, domestic statutes could also be considered 'hard' law. Heyvaert, Veerle (2009), 'Levelling Down, Levelling Up, and Governing Across: Three Responses to Hybridization in International Law', *European Journal of International Law*, **20**(1), 647–74 at 648–9.

4 Von Benda-Beckmann, Franz, Keebet Von Benda-Beckmann and Julia Eckert (2009), 'Rules of Law and Laws of Ruling: Law and Governance between Past and Future' in Franz Von Benda-Beckmann, Keebet Von Benda-Beckmann and Julia Eckert (eds), *Rules of Law and Laws of Ruling: on the Governance of Law*, Farnham: Ashgate, 4.

5 Von Benda-Beckmann, Franz, Keebet Von Benda-Beckmann and Julia Eckert (2009), 'Rules of Law and Laws of Ruling: Law and Governance between Past and Future' in Franz Von Benda-Beckmann, Keebet Von Benda-Beckmann and Julia Eckert (eds), *Rules of Law and Laws of Ruling: on the Governance of Law*, Farnham: Ashgate, 1–2.

in the environmental context as in any other. The continuously changing role of law in global governance would presumably have an equally significant impact on global environmental governance. The relationship between law and governance therefore inevitably requires deeper analysis with a view to explaining the manner in and extent to which law is currently used in the governance and the global governance paradigm.

2. LAW, SOCIETY AND REGULATION

Ubi societas ibi ius: where there is a society there (is) will be law; or put differently, society presupposes law and law presupposes the existence of a society. While this is undisputed, there are many views on what law is and what its purpose in society is or should be.[6] Black[7] indicates that:

> Lawyers' (and others') view of law is complex and contested. Legal and other scholars remain deeply divided as to law's relationship to society ... Law is for some an instrument for governing complex social and economic relations and serving social and economic interests ('law as order'). For others, it is an expression of society's morality ('law as glue'). For others, it is a reflection of society's customs and usages ('law as mirror'). For yet others, it is a mechanism of state power and of capitalist, male, or white domination ('law as a selective mirror').

Allot[8] chooses to describe the social functions of law very generally and rather abstractly as being three-fold: '(1) Law carries the structures and systems of society through time. (2) Law inserts the common interest of society into the behaviour of society-members. (3) Law establishes possible futures for society, in accordance with society's theories, values and purposes.' In terms of this description, law is the architecture of society; it ensures that society protects its common interests and realizes its goals by influencing behaviour; and through the foregoing interventions, based on its temporal forward-looking view, law acts now to make possible a certain kind of world and society for the present and for the future. In this sense, if one accepts that a primary

---

6 Writers such as Hart, Kelsen and Fuller, among others, have devoted extensive scholarship to these issues. See, for example, Hart, H.L.A. (1994), *The Concept of Law* 2nd edn, Oxford: Clarendon Press; Fuller, Lon L. (1968), *Anatomy of the Law*, New York: Frederick Praeger; Kelsen, Hans (1945), *General Theory of Law and State*, Cambridge, Massachusetts: Harvard University Press.

7 Black, Julia (2004), 'Law and Regulation: The Case of Finance' in Christine Parker *et al.* (eds), *Regulating Law*, Oxford: Oxford University Press, 37–8.

8 Allot, Philip (2000), 'The Concept of International Law' in Michael Byers (ed), *The Role of Law in International Politics: Essays in International Relations and International Law*, Oxford: Oxford University Press, 69.

societal function of law is to stabilize normative expectations, as Calliess and Renner argue,[9] then law stabilizes present expectations and society itself through the creation of a specifically desired societal order which, in turn, creates the possibility for future generations to stabilize their own expectations and societal order:

> The legal order depends not on the power of coercion but on the co-ordination of interests and on patterned expectations. On this classical view, law codifies the basic rules of social coexistence and establishes a society of States as the basic organizing principle of world politics; it regulates international co-operation and places constraints on international conflict; and it helps to promote a co-operative international political culture and develop a shared normative discourse.[10]

If 'order' is broadly interpreted as also embodying some notion of global common good and the preservation thereof, as some argue it does,[11] then law could be used to safeguard the present environment for the sake of future generations insofar as an environment (as a global common good) of an acceptable quality is conducive to 'stabilizing' a society and its normative expectations.

In this respect it is also worth noting Kelsen's[12] view that while the object of law is human behaviour, law is not exclusively concerned *only* with human behaviour; it is also concerned with the objects of human behaviour and the results or effects of human behaviour on animate and inanimate objects. In other words, law could be seen as mediating the interactions within society and between society and non-human objects.[13] It is therefore not true that 'nothing but human behaviour enters into the contents of legal rules';[14] law also concerns the effects of human behaviour on other animate and inanimate

---

9 Calliess, Gralf-Peter and Moritz Renner (2009), 'Between Law and Social Norms: the Evolution of Global Governance', *Ratio Iuris*, **22**(2), 260 80 at 267.

10 Hurrell, Andrew (2000), 'International Law and the Changing Constitution of International Society' in Michael Byers (ed), *The Role of Law in International Politics: Essays in International Relations and International Law*, Oxford: Oxford University Press, 328–9.

11 Hurrell, Andrew (2000), 'International Law and the Changing Constitution of International Society' in Michael Byers (ed), *The Role of Law in International Politics: Essays in International Relations and International Law*, Oxford: Oxford University Press, 337.

12 Kelsen, Hans (1945), *General Theory of Law and State*, Cambridge, Massachusetts: Harvard University Press, 3.

13 Pelletier, Nathan (2010), 'Of Laws and Limits: An Ecological Economic Perspective on Redressing the Failure of Contemporary Global Environmental Governance', *Global Environmental Change*, **20**, 220–28 at 221.

14 Kelsen, Hans (1945), *General Theory of Law and State*, Cambridge, Massachusetts: Harvard University Press, 3.

objects and the manner in which people behave towards and interact with these objects. Law is thus used as part of governance by humans who themselves 'stand out in relief against a world which is conceived as comprising a collection of mechanistic, causal and systematic processes, and discrete elements which are amenable by means of rational thought to human control and direction'.[15] For present purposes, in regulating human behaviour law is therefore concerned with the effects of human behaviour on the environment, and it would seek to change, steer or influence human behaviour to such an extent that the impacts of this behaviour on the environment conform to a standard that is acceptable to society. 'Acceptable' could mean that human behaviour conforms to universally agreed standards or rules of behaviour set by society itself and it implies that the extent of the impact on the environment does not exceed the thresholds of what society deems to be acceptable. If the standards and rules of regulating behaviour and impact thresholds are provided in laws, so too are the means to achieve these standards. For example, in its efforts to ensure that people have clean drinking water, law will allow and prohibit certain human actions that might affect water. Most usually by means of a statute (or a treaty at the supra-national level), law will provide rules of behaviour and it will contain minimum thresholds or requirements that are scientifically determined in terms of the carrying capacity of the environment. These thresholds or minimum requirements are usually set out in an authorization (in this example the authorization is an administrative-legal mechanism which has its basis in and derives its authority from law) and they cannot be exceeded, otherwise this will result in the environment's being damaged or unsustainably depleted. If the authorized limits are exceeded or if a person does not have an authorization at all, that person is acting *illegally* and the state will deploy measures to enforce compliance which could be, for example, by means of imposing fines.[16] Through fines, law will thus attempt to influence human behaviour to such an extent that people will not do what they would have done in the absence of punishment. In this way human behaviour and the effects of human behaviour on the environment (or rather on the quality of the environment) are the regulatory focus and the objectives of law in the environmental regulatory domain.

Regardless of how one chooses to view law and its relationship to and function in society, one characteristic of law is generally undisputed: it is normative to the extent that law provides the rules (or norms) that guide or steer

---

15 Godden, Lee and Jacqueline Peel (2010), *Environmental Law: Scientific, Policy and Regulatory Dimensions*, Melbourne: Oxford University Press, 58.

16 Law can of course also reward behaviour which does not harm the environment. Instead of punishing it can encourage behaviour which complies with legal requirements and which is not harmful to the environment.

human behaviour in society according to a generally accepted ideology that prescribes what is acceptable and not acceptable, what type of behaviour must be rewarded, and what type of behaviour must be punished to avoid future repetition. 'Law as norms' therefore suggests a distinct behaviourist understanding of interaction where norms (couched in terms of law) are used to shape interaction and to determine behaviour in society: 'interaction is both regulated and constituted by norms; norms are conceptualised as "social facts" which structure behaviour ... and the concept of a norm is used "to describe collective expectations for the proper behavior of actors with a given identity."'[17] In other words, law provides a required standard of social behaviour and sets a minimum level that must at least be adhered to by people in society. This would mean that law primarily performs a valuable social regulatory function with a view to achieving social (and other) objectives.

Like law, governance is also a social phenomenon because, as Chapter 3 has argued, governance has a predominant social foundation. To be sure, '[G]overnance is always social and always works to bind societies together.'[18] Law fulfils an important social function in the governance paradigm, especially insofar as it shapes and steers human (social) behaviour to achieve a common objective and helps to 'bind societies together'. This objective could be to achieve and maintain peace, to ensure unhindered global trade between nations, or to achieve and maintain an environment that is acceptable to people. In other words, law is a means to an end and provides people with the opportunity and mechanisms to regulate, to order, to steer and to change behaviour. This simplistic (functionalist) view of law admittedly ignores its many intricacies and complexities (including, for example, issues of values, legitimacy, morality and justice).[19] It is also oblivious to the many perceived deficiencies of law in a regulatory context. For example, even though regulatory law is 'the most ambitious, modern, goal-oriented, sociologically informed type of law representing a political mechanism of social guidance',[20]

---

17 Wiener, Antje (2008), *The Invisible Constitution of Politics: Contested Norms and International Encounters*, Cambridge: Cambridge University Press, 38.

18 Hunt, Alan and Gary Wickham (1994), *Foucault and the Law: Towards a Sociology of Law as Governance*, London: Pluto Press, 92.

19 For example, it ignores the fact that '[L]aw is a purposive human activity, a particular species of willing and acting, so that it is necessarily action of moral significance, action which is subject to moral duty and gives rise to moral responsibility.' Allot, Philip (2000), 'The Concept of International Law' in Michael Byers (ed), *The Role of Law in International Politics: Essays in International Relations and International Law*, Oxford: Oxford University Press, 71.

20 Teubner, Gunther (1984), *After Legal Instrumentalism? Strategic Models of Post-regulatory Law* (EUI Working Paper No. 100, European University Institute, Florence), 16.

some perceive it to be failing at an institutional level. Yet describing law in these functionalist/instrumentalist/regulatory terms remains useful for the social governance/regulatory context within which global environmental governance, as the primary focus of this book, is situated.

3. A REGULATIVE/FUNCTIONALIST READING OF LAW

Clearly, the role of law in society can be described in terms of the objectives of law, or its functions. Generally speaking, law fulfils a steering objective in society. Law provides the authority to regulate and thus the authority for governance; it provides legitimacy to govern; it designates governance actors and endows them with authority; it prescribes the parameters within which these actors must govern and how they must govern; it provides these actors with coercive and other types of rules and mechanisms to govern, and it provides the means to create additional law.[21] The steering objective of law in the social context of the governance paradigm is evident from Taekema's[22] approach, which relies on Llewellyn's[23] 'law-jobs theory' in terms of which law has certain functions (or jobs) that need to be done in a social group to ensure that group's survival. These functions include the resolution of disputes; the channelling and reorientation of conduct; the allocation of authority; and the provision of direction and incentives to society by 'coordinating diverging perspectives into one focused vision'.[24] Law thus fulfils very

---

[21] Or as others put it:

> Law is a source for constituting and legitimating power. It defines and validates positions and relations of power of persons or organizations over other persons, organizations and resources. It lays down in general terms which exercises of power are permissible or prohibited. It can be actualized in social interaction when the exercise of power is rationalized and justified with reference to law.

Franz Von Benda-Beckmann, Keebet Von Benda-Beckmann and Anne Griffiths (2009), 'The Power of Law' in Franz Von Benda-Beckmann, Keebet Von Benda-Beckmann and Anne Griffiths (eds), *The Power of Law in a Transnational World: Anthropological Enquiries*, New York: Berghahn Books, 1.

[22] Taekema, Sanne (2008), 'The Point of Law: the Interdependent Functionality of State and Non-state Regulation' in Hanneke Van Schooten and Jonathan Verschuuren (eds), *International Governance and Law: State Regulation and Non-state Law*, Cheltenham: Edward Elgar Publishing, 57–69.

[23] Llewellyn, Karl N. (1940), 'The Normative, the Legal, and the Law-Jobs: The Problem of Juristic Method', *Yale Law Journal*, **49**(8), 1355–1400.

[24] Taekema, Sanne (2008), 'The Point of Law: the Interdependent Functionality of State and Non-state Regulation' in Hanneke Van Schooten and Jonathan

specific regulative functions in society; it resolves conflicts which arise in law as a result of normative clashes; it resolves conflicts in society as a result of human interaction with other animate and inanimate objects and conflicts that arise in the day-to-day practice of governance; and it provides direction for human behaviour by either forcefully coercing people or by amicably promoting a specific standard and/or way of behaviour. In so doing, for the purpose of governance, it provides the carrot and the stick to punish or reward people for their actions. Law also authorizes and enables specific people (the governors) to use the rules and mechanisms (such as environmental authorizations, for example) provided by law itself to change the behaviour of the governed while simultaneously legitimizing the authority, the decisions, and the actions of the governors. In fact, law is a social system that plays an important role in creating generally accepted notions of legitimacy and legality because: '[I]n any social relationship whatsoever, it is difficult to take a stance that is legally indefensible.'[25] In other words, law makes human behaviour (including that of the governor and the governed) legal or acceptable; law is a 'source of legitimation that ensures respect for institutional authority',[26] and law is a source of legitimacy because it assigns responsibility to an entity to govern. In summary, law is one of the social institutions that provide the authority, legitimacy, and foundations of governance as well as the means to govern.

Notably, law also institutionalizes the values of a society and carries these over to and embeds them in governance systems. An example is environmental care, which is a value that expresses aspects of the shared morality of a community, and which has been 'institutionalized' by honouring the principles of sustainable development and environmental rights in a number of legal instruments ranging from national constitutions and statutes to international law instruments. While a comprehensive evaluative critique of law and its effects on the environment falls outside the scope of this book, it is worth noting that this latter function of law is frequently criticized by environmentalists as contributing to the prevailing environmentally deleterious social culture of consumption without limits:

Verschuuren (eds), *International Governance and Law: State Regulation and Non-state Law*, Cheltenham: Edward Elgar Publishing, 58.

25 Friedrichs, Jörg (2004), 'The Neomedieval Renaissance: Global Governance and International Law in the New Middle Ages' in Ige F. Dekker and Wouter G. Werner (eds), *Governance and International Legal Theory*, Leiden: Martinus Nijhoff Publishers, 25.

26 Hunt, Alan (2002), 'Legal Governance and Social Relations: Empowering Agents and the Limits of Law' in Michael MacNeil, Neil Sargent and Peter Swan (eds), *Law, Regulation and Governance*, Oxford: Oxford University Press, 55.

> ... the legal tradition that we have inherited very much concerns itself with the protection of private property and the right to accumulation. Similarly, if we consider the kind of economic system that western law legitimizes and maintains we see that it is above all an expansionary system premised on an instrumental conception of non-human nature, technological optimism, and a belief in the possibility of unlimited economic growth. It is further a system which reduces the calculus of well-being to individualist, instrumental rationality in place of societal, values-based discourse. Our environmental laws similarly reflect these assumptions ... [for example] in the contemporary conception of sustainable development, which constitutes an uneasy (if rarely challenged) marriage of the promotion of environmental integrity and greener yet similarly unconstrained economic growth.[27]

Clearly then, in addition to its instrumental/facilitative/functionalist/regulative role, which it expresses mainly through policing, coercion, sanction and deterrence, law also plays an expressive role in terms of which it institutionalizes with a view to expressing certain values which a society considers important.[28] However, whether law has been successful in improving environmental quality through the institutionalization of sustainable development remains an open question.

4. LAW IN A GLOBALIZED CONTEXT

The societal setting within which law seeks to achieve the objectives of governance has changed and continues to change. This has far-reaching implications for the manner in which we view the role of law in a regulatory context and specifically in the governance paradigm:

> ... it is widely agreed that fundamental changes taking place in the regulatory terrain require us to re-evaluate the roles of both the state and the law itself. These changes necessitate a reformulation of the concept of regulation not only to take account of the use of law to prescribe behaviour but also to consider a range of self-governing practices by non-state organizations that also have a regulatory effect.[29]

One could add that these changes also require a re-evaluation of the role of law in a changing social reality where these fundamental societal changes have been

27 Pelletier, Nathan (2010), 'Of Laws and Limits: An Ecological Economic Perspective on Redressing the Failure of Contemporary Global Environmental Governance', *Global Environmental Change*, **20**, 220–28 at 221.

28 Morgan, Bronwen and Karen Yeung (2007), *An Introduction to Law and Regulation: Text and Materials*, Cambridge: Cambridge University Press, 6.

29 Swan, Peter (2002), 'Governing at a Distance: An Introduction to Law, Regulation, and Governance' in Michael MacNeil, Neil Sargent and Peter Swan (eds), *Law, Regulation and Governance*, Oxford: Oxford University Press, 3.

brought about by globalization which, as was illustrated in Chapter 2, has had and continues to have a profound impact on society, law and governance. The following sections reflect on the changing face of law in a globalized context.

4.1 Law and Globalization

Previous parts of this book have already devoted some attention to the impact of globalization on law and governance.[30] In short, in a regulatory context globalization is contributing to the phenomenological rise of global governance, and with it comes a rearrangement of the world order, as well as the creation of new actor constellations that create and implement a widely diverse set of rules ranging from strict or orthodox 'hard', state-made rules to softer, non-state yet law-like rules. While it would have been much easier to explain the role of law in a pre-globalization era, today it is not entirely clear who governs the globalized world and with what law,[31] or as Wiener[32] asks more pertinently in an environmental context: '[W]hat law shall govern the deep blue sky?'[33] Efforts to answer these questions must first accept that globalization is having a profound impact on law in a global regulatory context to the extent that it requires us to fundamentally revisit orthodox conceptions of the role of law in society, the contribution of law to governance, and the role of law in global environmental governance:[34]

> When the frame of rule hierarchy, with constitutional legitimated political legislation at its top breaks under the pressures of globalization, then the new frame which replaces it can only be heterarchical. It decentres political law-making, moves it away from its privileged place at the top of the norm-hierarchy and puts it on an equal footing with other types of social law-making. The replacement of frames from hierarchy to heterarchy, allows for the recognition of other types of social rule production, such as that of 'law', but only under the condition that they are produced in the periphery of the legal system in close contact with the external social processes of rule formation.[35]

---

[30] See Chapters 2 and 3.

[31] Rittberger, Volker (ed) (2009), *Wer regiert die Welt und mit welchem Recht? Beiträge zur Global Governance-Forschung*, Baden-Baden: Nomos Verlag.

[32] Wiener, Jonathan B. (2000/2001), 'Something Borrowed for Something Blue: Legal Transplants and the Evolution of Global Environmental Law', *Ecology Law Quarterly*, **27**, 1295–1372 at 1296.

[33] See more generally Snyder, F.G. (2002), 'Governing Globalisation' in Michael Likosky (ed), *Transnational Legal Processes: Globalisation and Power Disparities*, London: Butterworths LexisNexis, 65–97.

[34] For a thorough discussion on the globalization of law generally, see Shapiro, Martin (1993/1994), 'The Globalization of Law', *Global Legal Studies Journal*, **1**(37), 37–64.

[35] Teubner, Gunther (1997), 'Foreword: Legal Regimes of Global Non-state

While globalization has a definitive impact on law, law conversely influences globalization by increasingly facilitating globalized processes and by providing the foundation of numerous institutional arrangements that seek to respond to the realities of globalization. As Dekker and Werner[36] state: '[I]t is a truism that international law shapes and is being shaped by globalization and international [or global] governance.' More pertinently, Friedrichs[37] points out that: '[I]f there really is a transformation of the world system underway, it will have its repercussions *on*, and sooner or later finds its expression *in*, the legal superstructure.' It is in this globalized context that law (including state and non-state law) could be considered a means to an end in the broader governance paradigm, since it intends to regulate in the sense that it 'emerges as an instrument of governance of societies that are large and no longer closely knit or that face an external environment that changes too rapidly for social custom to adapt to these changes'.[38]

4.2 Global Legal Pluralism

In addition to what has already been said on globalization and law, another way to understand the nexus between the two, and more importantly the role of law in governance, is by means of the familiar phenomenological concept of legal pluralism. Law is increasingly becoming plural because of globalization in ways that transcend restricted views of traditional anthropological legal

---

Actors' in Gunther Teubner (ed), *Global Law without a State*, Aldershot: Dartmouth, xiv. Kingsbury adds the following:

> No doubt there is much sloppy thinking in the practice and especially the legal theorization of global governance. But it is also highly possible that the limitation is not simply (if at all) in the phenomena, but rather in the state-based concepts of law. Taking this possibility seriously calls for the primary focus to be on concepts of law that do not begin and end with the state.

Kingsbury, Benedict (2009), 'The Concept of "Law" in Global Administrative Law', *European Journal of International Law*, **20**(1), 23–57 at 27.

36 Dekker, Ige F. and Wouter G. Werner (2004), 'Introduction' in Ige F. Dekker and Wouter G. Werner (eds), *Governance and International Legal Theory*, Leiden: Martinus Nijhoff Publishers, xiii.

37 Friedrichs, Jörg (2004), 'The Neomedieval Renaissance: Global Governance and International Law in the New Middle Ages' in Ige F. Dekker and Wouter G. Werner (eds), *Governance and International Legal Theory*, Leiden: Martinus Nijhoff Publishers, 5.

38 Kornhauser, Lewis A. (2004), 'Governance Structures, Legal Systems, and the Concept of Law', *Chicago-Kent Law Review*, **79**(2), 355–81 at 358.

pluralism (i.e., the existence of multiple legal systems in a country). Anders[39] proposes an extended view of legal pluralism that embraces the diverse and plural social realities of globalization in the context of governance (in addition to the traditional view that considers legal pluralism merely as the co-existence of various legal systems):

> First, state law is not the only form of regulating human interaction; other forms of ordering exist side by side with state law and should be treated equally ... Second, this interaction of different normative orders can be observed in a specific social space that forms the unit of analysis. Third, state law and the institutions of the state do not form a coherent system but are rather a patchwork of different elements thus resulting in internal legal pluralism within the state.

This expanded view suggests that one might talk of 'global legal pluralism', one of the causes of which is globalization in the context of global governance. The result of global legal pluralism for global governance may be profound since it explains the extent to which an expanded concept of the role of law is 'one of a plurality of ways of providing the mechanisms through which processes of governance are practiced'.[40] In other words, in accord with the plurality of global governance, global legal pluralism provides an opportunity to focus on the plurality of law itself and on alternatives to orthodox forms of law with a view to examining the simultaneous disaggregation of and compatibility between law and global governance. Global legal pluralism is both necessary and inevitable because, as Keohane and Nye[41] state: '[R]ulemaking as rule interpretation in global governance have become pluralized. Rules are no longer a matter simply for states or intergovernmental organizations. Private firms, NGOs, subunits of governments, and the transnational and transgovernmental networks that result, all play a role.' This means that the traditional role of the state and state-law as constituting the primary sources of rules of and for global governance must also be revisited. An expansive view of law as including many different types of rules is therefore required, which takes into account that the state and traditional law will always provide the primary foundation for rules in a governance setting, most predominantly in

---

39 Anders, Gerhard (2004), 'Lawyers and Anthropologists: A Legal Pluralist Approach to Global Governance' in Ige F. Dekker and Wouter G. Werner (eds), *Governance and International Legal Theory*, Leiden: Martinus Nijhoff Publishers, 40.

40 Swan, Peter (2002), 'Governing at a Distance: An Introduction to Law, Regulation, and Governance' in Michael MacNeil, Neil Sargent and Peter Swan (eds), *Law, Regulation and Governance*, Oxford: Oxford University Press, 11.

41 Keohane, Robert O. and Joseph S. Nye (2002), 'Governance in a Globalizing World' in Robert O. Keohane (ed), *Power and Governance in a Partially Globalized World*, London: Routledge, 214.

the public state-centred context, but increasingly also in the private non-state sphere. This is a view that:

> ... rejects any idea of a single site of legal sovereignty embodied in the state ... [and it] ... challenges conventional, doctrinal approaches to law that present it as a concept, universal across time and space, that can only derive its legitimacy and validity from the state and that represents a system of law that is coherent and uniform.[42]

In this way global legal pluralism and its proponents 'undermine stereotypical depictions of the global, the state and the local, and their relationships with one another that are founded on a bounded, hierarchical and stratified notion of law'.[43] To what extent and in which ways has law become globally pluralized as a result of globalization?

4.2.1 Going beyond the state

Law is increasingly becoming global in that it 'goes beyond the state' geographically; and it is increasingly becoming global and 'going beyond the state' in that it is made, interpreted and enforced by non-state actors. These phenomena can be explained as follows.

Reliance on state-centred law as the only or predominant legal type of regulatory rules is slowly yet steadily diminishing in the wake of the emergence of governance in the global context.[44] Today global governance is a plural, multi-stakeholder enterprise. It is also multi-level, and while states continue to play dominant roles, a myriad of non-state actors is involved in a disaggregated form of public-private or hybrid global governance.[45] As Koppen[46] states:

---

42 Von Benda-Beckmann, Franz, Keeber Von Benda-Beckmann and Anne Griffiths (2009), 'The Power of Law' in Franz Von Benda-Beckmann, Keebet Von Benda-Beckmann and Anne Griffiths (eds), *The Power of Law in a Transnational World: Anthropological Enquiries*, New York: Berghahn Books, 3.

43 Von Benda-Beckmann, Franz, Keeber Von Benda-Beckmann and Anne Griffiths (2009), 'The Power of Law' in Franz Von Benda-Beckmann, Keebet Von Benda-Beckmann and Anne Griffiths (eds), *The Power of Law in a Transnational World: Anthropological Enquiries*, New York: Berghahn Books, 3.

44 As Gunningham points out: '[W]hile law ... was dominant in the 1970s and the early-1980s, it gradually had to share the "regulatory space" with other forms of social control.' Gunningham, Neil (2009), 'Environmental Law, Regulation and Governance: Shifting Architectures', *Journal of Environmental Law*, **21**(2), 179–212 at 206.

45 See Chapter 4.

46 Koppen, Ida (1994), 'Ecological Covenants: Regulatory Informality in Dutch Waste Reduction Policy' in Gunther Teubner, Lindsay Farmer and Declan Murphy (eds), *Environmental Law and Ecological Responsibility: The Concept and Practice of Ecological Self-Organization*, Chichester: John Wiley and Sons, 185.

> The unilateral imposition of norms is no longer the prevalent model for state intervention in societal processes ... a model is evolving that is characterized by complex multilateral interactions between the various social actors involved. Interactive network-like relationships emerge around social issues that facilitate the informal exchange of information and typically include some form of negotiated decision-making ... In this model the state is no longer superimposed on society, but functions as an horizontally juxtaposed entity, a partner, although primus inter pares.

This inevitably results in the emergence of new constellations of rules authorizing, legitimizing and organizing global governance due to multifarious forms of secondary rule-making authority vested in a whole range of non-state actors.[47] The steady growth of these forms of non-state law means that the pure doctrinal approach to law is steadily being diluted.[48]

Globalization thus gives rise to two separate but not disconnected bodies of law, namely state and non-state law, and in some instances legal rules with the characteristics of both state and non-state law.[49] While the notion of state law is straightforward, non-state law is fuzzier. Non-state law is made by global non-state actors, and today it is possible to discern various forms of non-state law:

> Technical standardization, professional rule production, human rights, intra-organizational regulation in multinational enterprises, contracting, arbitration and other institutions of *lex mercatoria* are forms of rule-making by 'private governments' which have appeared on a massive global scale. They claim worldwide validity independently of the law of the nation-states and in relative distance to the rules of international public law. They have come into existence not by formal acts of nation-states but by strange paradoxical acts of self-validation.[50]

In a contemporary globalized setting and for the purpose of global governance, the 'non-state' in non-state law is therefore usually meant to denote '*beyond* the national state' in a geographical sense, and it also implies increased private

---

47 Von Benda-Beckmann, Franz, Keebet Von Benda-Beckmann and Julia Eckert (2009), 'Rules of Law and Laws of Ruling: Law and Governance between Past and Future' in Franz Von Benda-Beckmann, Keebet Von Benda-Beckmann and Julia Eckert (eds), *Rules of Law and Laws of Ruling: on the Governance of Law*, Farnham: Ashgate, 1–2.

48 Bodansky, Daniel (2010), *The Art and Craft of International Environmental Law*, Cambridge, Massachusetts: Harvard University Press, 5.

49 Heyvaert cites as an example in the latter respect instances where voluntary codes of practice are used as benchmarks for compliance with the prescriptions of a hard law. Heyvaert, Veerle (2009), 'Levelling Down, Levelling Up, and Governing Across: Three Responses to Hybridization in International Law', *European Journal of International Law*, **20**(1), 647–74 at 649.

50 Teubner, Gunther (1997), 'Foreword: Legal Regimes of Global Non-state Actors' in Gunther Teubner (ed), *Global Law without a State*, Aldershot: Dartmouth, xiii.

and even self-regulation where state authority is less pronounced.[51] With respect to the latter, non-state law is:

> ... not made of the familiar sources of public international law, such as treaties and state-practice, but, rather, ... [is] ... the result of (private) norm-production by trade associations, professional/technical organisations, commercial arbitrators, Multinational Enterprises (sic) and other civic players.[52]

The 'privatization' or hybridization (and thus pluralization) of law is a result of many globalized social processes including, among others, the expansion of international trade; the growth and increased global activities of MNCs; universal standardization; increased codes of conduct or standards for especially industrial or corporate behaviour (for example, company codes on labour rights and environmental practices);[53] an increase in the number of international corporate disputes and the mushrooming of dispute settlement bodies; and the expansion of modern communication technology.[54] These examples also illustrate the rise of law 'beyond the geographical borders' of the state, where one observes the emergence of global law or the phenomenological rise of the transnationalization of law. (At the other end of the spectrum is what Richardson[55] calls the sub-nationalization of law.) While there may be others, the following serve as examples of these forms of transnational (or global) law: the new *lex mercatoria* (including, for example, international construction law, world trade law, international financial law, and international standard setting), internet law, and human rights law.[56]

---

51 Hertogh, Marc (2008), 'What is Non-state Law? Mapping the other Hemisphere of the Legal World' in Hanneke Van Schooten and Jonathan Verschuuren (eds), *International Governance and Law: State Regulation and Non-state Law*, Cheltenham: Edward Elgar Publishing, 21.

52 Perez, Oren (2004), *Ecological Sensitivity and Global Legal Pluralism: Rethinking the Trade and Environment Conflict*, Oregon: Hart Publishing, 8.

53 Blackett, Adelle (2001), 'Global Governance, Legal Pluralism and the Decentered State: A Labor Law Critique of Codes of Corporate Conduct', *Indiana Journal of Global Legal Studies*, **8**(2), 401–47.

54 Perez, Oren (2004), *Ecological Sensitivity and Global Legal Pluralism: Rethinking the Trade and Environment Conflict*, Oregon: Hart Publishing, 8–9.

55 Richardson, Benjamin J. (2000), 'Environmental Law in Postcolonial Societies: Straddling the Local-Global Institutional Spectrum', *Colorado Journal of International Environmental Law and Policy*, **11**, 1–82 at 13.

56 Hertogh, Marc (2008), 'What is Non-state Law? Mapping the other Hemisphere of the Legal World' in Hanneke Van Schooten and Jonathan Verschuuren (eds), *International Governance and Law: State Regulation and Non-state Law*, Cheltenham: Edward Elgar Publishing, 23–5; Perez, Oren (2004), *Ecological Sensitivity and Global Legal Pluralism: Rethinking the Trade and Environment Conflict*, Oregon: Hart Publishing, 10.

Some parts of environmental law also 'go beyond the state'. These include, for example, traditional international and regional environmental law; global codes of conduct and best practices; and, as some argue, the rules and principles of global (or transnational) environmental law.[57] Environmental law is also 'going beyond the state' to the extent that it is increasingly privatized. Examples include the ISO 14001 voluntary EMS, ecolabels, the UN Global Compact, the Global Reporting Initiative (GRI), the UN Principles for Responsible Investment, and the Equator Principles.[58] Chapter 8 further investigates the phenomenological rise of global environmental law.

4.2.2 Variable legalization

The variability of legalization is another way to understand global legal pluralism and to explain the hybridization or pluralization of law globally. Global legal pluralism is evident in terms of the variability of the legalization of laws, which is understood as a 'particular form of institutionalization'[59] consisting of three components, namely, obligation, precision and delegation. Highly legalized institutions are those with obligatory binding rules instead of mere guiding rules. They are characterized by precise and highly elaborated rules instead of vague principles, and the authority to interpret and apply these rules has been delegated to third parties which themselves are subject to specific rules of conduct.[60] For example, a multilateral environmental agreement (which is a typical example of 'hard', state-made law) such as the *United Nations Framework Convention on Climate Change*, 31 I.L.M. 849 (1992) would thus be a highly legalized institution because it provides various obligations which are spelt out in more precise terms in the *Kyoto Protocol to the United Nations Framework Convention on Climate Change*, 37 I.L.M. 22 (1998). The interpretation of the rules of these agreements and their enforcement (including dispute resolution) are in the hands of third parties created in terms of the agreements. On the other hand, international guidelines and principles of law (to the extent that they are *not* recognized as *ius cogens* with *erga omnes* application)

---

[57] See the discussion in Chapter 8.

[58] For a detailed discussion of the Equator Principles as an example of global environmental law, see Ong, David M. (2010), 'From "International" to "Transnational" Environmental Law? A Legal Assessment of the Contribution of the "Equator Principles" to International Environmental Law', *Nordic Journal of International Law*, **79**(1), 35–74.

[59] Abbott, Kenneth W. *et al.* (2002), 'The Concept of Legalization' in Robert O. Keohane (ed), *Power and Governance in a Partially Globalized World*, London: Routledge, 132.

[60] Abbott, Kenneth W. *et al.* (2002), 'The Concept of Legalization' in Robert O. Keohane (ed), *Power and Governance in a Partially Globalized World*, London: Routledge, 135, 148.

could typically be characterized as non-highly legalized rules or principles. These rules, principles or guidelines do not usually create binding obligations. They are often vague and there is no or few arrangements for delegated enforcement. In the environmental context, the principle of sustainable development is an example of a non-highly legalized principle. So too are voluntary environmental standards and corporate codes of conduct.

The variable legalization of law is also evident in the different sources of international law. Young[61] emphatically states in this respect that:

> Life would be simpler ... if the entire body of international law were set forth in a collection of treaties or conventions. Those who devote themselves to the codification of international law seem to be motivated in part by a vision of this sort. But a moment's thought will remind us that much of international law takes the form of customary law and, increasingly, of what has come to be known as 'soft law'.

Notably, the 'type' of international law source (soft law, custom or treaty law) is largely determined by the degree of legalization of that source. For example, soft law is not legally binding in any formal sense, but it is generally considered to play 'a regulative role in international society'.[62] Soft law is therefore informal because it is not binding, often vague and unenforceable. Treaty law (hard law), on the other hand, is formal law made by state actors and plays a predominantly regulatory role. It is obligatory, often detailed, and enforceable. Nevertheless, although it is limited, treaty law can also acquire informal characteristics, especially insofar as it concerns procedural aspects related to the implementation and enforcement of treaty law or the way that concepts such as 'sustainable development' are translated into practice from the treaty laws that provide for them. This is in fact a common character trait of all social institutions which have a 'propensity to acquire informal dimensions or elements with the passage of time ... [as] a result of the development of common understandings of what formal, but often imprecise, formulas are taken to mean in practice'.[63] Treaty law could thus be used to devise softer and more informal means to achieve the objectives of the original treaty law instrument, or it could at least act as the rationale behind the development of voluntary and more informal guidelines and opportunities to achieve the objectives originally set out in the hard law instrument. The Carbon Disclosure Project (CDP) is an example of a non-state and more informal arrangement

---

61 Young, Oran R. (1994), *International Governance: Protecting the Environment in a Stateless Society*, Ithaca, NY and London: Cornell University Press, 190.

62 Young, Oran R. (1994), *International Governance: Protecting the Environment in a Stateless Society*, Ithaca, NY and London: Cornell University Press, 190.

63 Young, Oran R. (1994), *International Governance: Protecting the Environment in a Stateless Society*, Ithaca, NY and London: Cornell University Press, 190–91.

which uses non-state legal means to achieve better compliance with international, regional and national climate laws. It holds the largest collection globally of self-reported climate change data, and through its 'global system companies and cities are better able to mitigate risk, capitalise on opportunities and make investment decisions that drive action towards a more sustainable world'.[64]

The foregoing clearly illustrates that the global legal order provides predominantly formal state-based law, but also increasingly softer forms of legal rules which emanate from non-state actors. These different types of legal rules, ranging from hard to soft, state to non-state, coercive to voluntary and so forth, do not exist independently of one another or act alone in achieving the regulatory objectives in and of society. The nature of global governance and the real effects of disaggregated multi-actor and multi-level global governance in the regulatory context suggest, rather, that it is not a question of 'either or' but instead of the extent to which traditional, hard forms of law can be married to and co-exist with non-traditional and unorthodox softer or non-state forms of law.

4.2.3 Repressive and regulatory versus reflexive law

The opposite poles of legalization (as expressing global legal pluralism) are also evident in terms of the differences between repressive law, regulatory law, and the more recent conception of reflexive law. Repressive and regulatory law represent earlier orthodox manifestations of law which focus on the rule-oriented resolution of disputes. It is purpose oriented, state-centred and 'aggressively instrumental in order to determine outcomes'.[65] Reflexive law is instead based on reflexive rationality and self-regulation as the ideal, and is thus situated at the other end of the legalization spectrum. It is less coercive, prescriptive, and 'regulatory' than repressive and regulatory law:

> The legal control of society under a regime of reflexive rationality becomes indirect as the legal system attempts only to set out the organizational and procedural basis of future action rather than to dictate or plan the outcome of future action. The role of law, therefore, is no longer the aggressively instrumental one typified by command-and-control regulation; rather, law is limited to providing forms of organization, procedures and competencies for relationships within and between organizations.[66]

---

64 Carbon Disclosure Project, https://www.cdproject.net/en-US/Pages/About-Us.aspx [accessed 24 January 2012].

65 Schneider, David J. (2002), 'Radical or Rational? Reflexive Law as *Res Novo* in the Canadian Environmental Regulatory Regime' in Michael MacNeil, Neil Sargent and Peter Swan (eds), *Law, Regulation and Governance*, Oxford: Oxford University Press, 100–101.

66 Schneider, David J. (2002), 'Radical or Rational? Reflexive Law as *Res Novo*

Reflexive law focuses less on the achievement of the substantive content of law, thereby discarding direct regulation in favour of 'proceduralization', in that it seeks to establish the parameters for future action.[67] In doing so, '[R]eflexive law is premised on the idea that regulatory interventions are most likely to be successful if normativity is developed with the participation of those who are to be subjected to the norms.'[68] It is thus highly participative and provides the basis for self organization without predetermining the outcome of any regulatory intervention. The implication of reflexive law for governance is that 'law should stand further back and specify the procedures to allow interested participants to work out the content of rules and policies';[69] consequently, law assumes a less prominent coercive or direct regulatory role in governance. Reflexive law only 'aims at using legal procedures to establish a communicative strategy for the disclosure of information and for the provision of greater accountability'[70] to the extent that one might be able to speak of 'deliberative ... governance'.[71] Examples of reflexive law in the context of the global environment are voluntary EMSs such as ISO 14001, and its European equivalent, Eco-management and Audit Scheme (EMAS), which seek to improve private sector environmental performance and environmental legal compliance:

> Such systems seek by law to stimulate modes of self-organization within the firm in such a way as to encourage internal self-critical reflection about its environmental performance. They establish processes and procedures that encourage self-reflexive learning and thinking about reducing environmental impact rather than seeking to influence behaviour directly by proscribing certain activities.[72]

---

in the Canadian Environmental Regulatory Regime' in Michael MacNeil, Neil Sargent and Peter Swan (eds), *Law, Regulation and Governance*, Oxford: Oxford University Press, 101.

[67] S chneider, David J. (2002), 'Radical or Rational? Reflexive Law as *Res Novo* in the Canadian Environmental Regulatory Regime' in Michael MacNeil, Neil Sargent and Peter Swan (eds), *Law, Regulation and Governance*, Oxford: Oxford University Press, 107.

[68] Buhmann, Karin (2009), 'Regulating Corporate Social and Human Rights Responsibilities at the UN Plane: Institutionalising New Forms of Law and Law-making Approaches?', *Nordic Journal of International Law*, **78**, 1–52 at 17.

[69] Swan, Peter (2002), 'Democratic Environmental Governance and Environmental Justice' in Michael MacNeil, Neil Sargent and Peter Swan (eds), *Law, Regulation and Governance*, Oxford: Oxford University Press, 122.

[70] Swan, Peter (2002), 'Democratic Environmental Governance and Environmental Justice' in Michael MacNeil, Neil Sargent and Peter Swan (eds), *Law, Regulation and Governance*, Oxford: Oxford University Press, 124.

[71] Swan, Peter (2002), 'Democratic Environmental Governance and Environmental Justice' in Michael MacNeil, Neil Sargent and Peter Swan (eds), *Law, Regulation and Governance*, Oxford: Oxford University Press, 129.

[72] Gunningham, Neil (2008), 'Environmental Regulation and Non-state Law:

Other examples are the Responsible Care Programme, which is a voluntary regulatory scheme developed by the chemical sector,[73] ecolabels which aim to reward goods and services that are environmentally superior,[74] and the Equator Principles, which is a set of social and environmental principles that should guide the lending practices of banks.[75] These forms of non-state environment-related law, manifesting as reflexive law, are complementary to repressive, coercive, regulatory law, because these different 'types' of law can achieve their desired outcomes (for example, the improvement of environmental quality) only if they act in tandem. They should be considered co-existing and complementary parts of the greater rubric of different regulatory legal and non-legal (such as economic) institutional means; and regulatory, reflexive and coercive forms of law available to achieve specific outcomes. As Selznick[76] argues, while there clearly is a *prima facie* case to be made for more reflexivity in law and regulation (for example, by means of self-regulation), reflexivity must remain feasible and 'the quest for appropriate external regulation [should not be] abandoned. On the contrary, the question is what form it should take and what its limits should be.'

The Future Public Policy Agenda' in Hanneke Van Schooten and Jonathan Verschuuren (eds), *International Governance and Law: State Regulation and Non-state Law*, Cheltenham: Edward Elgar Publishing, 113. See also Roht-Arriaza, Naomi (1995), 'Private Voluntary Standard-Setting, the International Organization for Standardization, and International Environmental Lawmaking', *Yearbook of International Environmental Law*, **6**, 107–63. While these EMSs are leading to the hybridization of global law through the private processes of non-state law making and enforcement, they also contribute to the standardization, harmonization, or convergence of some of the rules governing the corporate world. Yang, Tseming and Robert V. Percival (2009), 'The Emergence of Global Environmental Law', *Ecology Law Quarterly*, **36**, 615–64 at 640.

73 Perez, Oren (2004), *Ecological Sensitivity and Global Legal Pluralism: Rethinking the Trade and Environment Conflict*, Oregon: Hart Publishing, 11.

74 Roht-Arriaza, Naomi (1995), 'Private Voluntary Standard-Setting, the International Organization for Standardization, and International Environmental Lawmaking', *Yearbook of International Environmental Law*, **6**, 107–63 at 111. For a comprehensive treatment of reflexive law and self-regulation in the environmental context, see Teubner, Gunther, Lindsay Farmer and Declan Murphy (eds) (1994), *Environmental Law and Ecological Responsibility: The Concept and Practice of Ecological Self-Organization*, Chichester: John Wiley and Sons.

75 Ong, David M. (2010), 'From "International" to "Transnational" Environmental Law? A Legal Assessment of the Contribution of the "Equator Principles" to International Environmental Law', *Nordic Journal of International Law*, **79**(1), 35–74 at 36 *et seq.*

76 Selznick, Philip (1994), 'Self-regulation and the Theory of Institutions' in Gunther Teubner, Lindsay Farmer and Declan Murphy (eds), *Environmental Law and Ecological Responsibility: The Concept and Practice of Ecological Self-Organization*, Chichester: John Wiley and Sons, 395.

4.2.4 Multi-level law

In addition to the pluralistic effect of multiple state and non-state actors on law described above, law is also becoming globally plural because it is increasingly becoming multi-level in a vertical sense. It has been shown elsewhere in this book that 'global' is sufficiently expansive to encapsulate domestic and regional laws in addition to international law.[77] This would imply that the laws of specific countries related to environmental matters would be important for the global regulatory effort insofar as these laws translate the obligations of supra-national laws into a domestic context. As this chapter further illustrates below, so too does infra-national law have the ability to influence law situated at the supra-national level. The argument applies similarly to regional law. The laws of the EU and SADC would, for example, coexist with domestic and international law to form a plural global body of law that is truly multi-level.

Law is also disaggregating horizontally to the extent that various different issue areas are developing within each level (national, regional and international), and each has its own set of legal rules. One observes, for example, distinct bodies of trade law, humanitarian law, security law and, for present purposes, environmental law, on all of these levels. Because of the greater interconnectivity and trans-nationality of social processes, these issue areas often overlap and influence one another. Various different legal rules dealing with different, but often interrelated issue areas are therefore developing and are further contributing to the global pluralization of law.

4.2.5 The fragmentation of law

The final way that law could be considered to be pluralistic in a global setting is through the process of the fragmentation of law. The phenomenon of fragmentation is especially prevalent in the context of international environmental law. Wolfrum and Matz[78] explain fragmentation in this context as follows:

> In the absence of a universal legislature or an administration with a comprehensive mandate, most international treaties exist parallel to one another and are further developed without the benefit of consideration being given to potential conflicts with other agreements either during their negotiation or at a later stage of their existence. Insofar as these agreements overlap, this overlap can either take the form of a doubling of efforts concerning a particular problem or as a contradiction or conflict between the objectives, programs or means of the respective agreements.

---

[77] Chapters 1 and 2.

[78] Wolfrum, Rüdiger and Nele Matz (2003), *Conflicts in International Environmental Law*, Heidelberg: Springer-Verlag, 2–3. For a more comprehensive supplement to the foregoing, generally, see also Matz, Nele (2005), *Wege zur Koordinierung völkerrechtlicher Verträge: Völkervertragrechtliche und institutionelle Ansätze*, Heidelberg: Springer-Verlag.

> The phenomenon of a multitude of parallel, substantially or partial overlapping and colliding agreements in international environmental law, exacerbated by the practice of negotiating ever more binding instruments, has been labelled 'treaty congestion'.

If one accepts that law has a constitutive function in addition to its regulative function, in terms of this description it follows that the fragmentation of law leads to the fragmentation of governance (or polycentric global environmental governance, as some term it),[79] because the multiplicity of the laws creates a multitude of organizations, processes and other governance mechanisms that must administer and enforce these laws and endeavour to achieve their objectives. The numerous types of law and legal arrangements that global actors use to achieve their collective goals give rise to the establishment of a multitude of global governance institutions such as treaty regimes, treaty bodies, and international organizations, among others. These institutions, in turn, further contribute to fragmentation by creating supplementary legal rules. The result is a mass of parallel, often conflicting and multifarious legal rules and institutional arrangements that are responsible for specific issue areas in global governance. As this takes place law is changing the global governance landscape through a process of normative and institutional expansion, differentiation and hybridization. Yet it is these same pluralistic global governance institutional arrangements that are conversely contributing to pluralizing and further disaggregating global law. This is another clear example of the manifestly intertwined causality between law and governance, where the composition of the legal structure determines the composition and functioning of the governance response and vice versa.

4.3 The Merits of Non-traditional Non-state Law

Many lawyers will probably be uncomfortable with the phenomenological rise of non-state and other forms of non-traditional law:

> For a lawyer who is used to think of law or 'the legal system' in the terms of court rulings, legislation, statutes and opinions of other lawyers it is difficult to accept the idea that there might exist other ways of regulating human interaction within a given social field, which deserve the label law. Lawyers tend to equate social order with 'rule of law' ignoring the existing non-state regimes of order.[80]

---

79 Dunoff, Jeffrey L. (2007), 'Levels of Environmental Governance' in Daniel Bodansky, Jutta Brunnée and Ellen Hey (eds), *The Oxford Handbook of International Environmental Law*, Oxford: Oxford University Press, 98–100.

80 Anders, Gerhard (2004), 'Lawyers and Anthropologists: A Legal Pluralist Approach to Global Governance' in Ige F. Dekker and Wouter G. Werner (eds), *Governance and International Legal Theory*, Leiden: Martinus Nijhoff Publishers, 48.

With the emergence of non-state and non-traditional forms of law comes the concomitant need to (re)construct legal concepts and to develop new ones such as reflexive law. This is an exercise which does not sit well with diehard doctrinal legal theorists. As Teubner[81] (a controversial 'reconstructive' theorist) points out:

> To construct 'Rechtsbegriffe' (concepts of law) raises suspicion in the scientific community of today. When legal theorists dealing with the function of law in the welfare state present ambitious intellectual constructs, such as instrumental versus expressive law ..., autonomous versus responsive law ..., substantive versus reflexive law ..., purposive versus procedural law ..., they have to face the accusations of violating the basic norms of scientific discourse.

Nevertheless, these changes occur regardless of lawyers' reluctance to accept the inevitable global pluralization of law, and they are set to continue and even to intensify as the global governance and legal order further expands, disaggregates, and hybridizes.

Of particular concern to hard-line doctrinal lawyers is the question of whether or not these softer, non-state forms of regulation could in fact be considered law (a debate that is occurring in the context of the broader question: what is law?).[82] One view posits that:

> The distinction between law and non-law is based on a hierarchy of legal rules where the higher rules legitimate the lower rules. Normative phenomena outside of this hierarchy are not law, just facts. The highest rule in our time is, after the decline of natural law, the constitution of the nation-state which refers to democratic political legislation as the ultimate legitimation of legal validity.[83]

The distinction between law and non-law is a raging debate that makes for topical analyses resulting in divergent views.[84] Yet this distinction is arguably

---

81 Teubner, Gunther (1984), *After Legal Instrumentalism? Strategic Models of Post-regulatory Law* (EUI Working Paper No. 100, European University Institute, Florence), 2.

82 See generally, among others, Hart, H.L.A. (1994), *The Concept of Law* 2nd edn, Oxford: Clarendon Press.

83 Teubner, Gunther (1997), 'Foreword: Legal Regimes of Global Non-state Actors' in Gunther Teubner (ed), *Global Law without a State*, Aldershot: Dartmouth, xiii.

84 For some examples of these views see Anders, Gerhard (2004), 'Lawyers and Anthropologists: A Legal Pluralist Approach to Global Governance' in Ige F. Dekker and Wouter G. Werner (eds), *Governance and International Legal Theory*, Leiden: Martinus Nijhoff Publishers, 49–50; Hertogh, Marc (2008), 'What is Non-state Law? Mapping the other Hemisphere of the Legal World' in Hanneke Van Schooten and Jonathan Verschuuren (eds), *International Governance and Law: State Regulation and Non-state Law*, Cheltenham: Edward Elgar Publishing, 11–30.

redundant for the purpose of governance because the very notion of governance considered in a globalized context postulates the existence and need for hybridity, plurality and the proliferation of heterogeneous forms of normative regulatory arrangements beyond the strict conventionalities of orthodox conceptions of law. Non-state law (whether it is law or not) is an inevitable reality that is part of the prevailing globalized world order, and the fact that laws exist that are variously legalized is a reality that must be accepted even by sceptic hard-line doctrinal lawyers. When viewed in the context of the governance paradigm, law and non-traditional forms of law are equally important to the extent that they provide the means to direct human behaviour with a view to addressing regulatory problems. As Ong[85] states 'even international law, and especially international relations, has arguably long accepted both the existence and normative implications of different categories of instruments established to regulate, or otherwise guide, the behaviour of their target entities'. The general recognition and continued growth of soft law instruments, among others, are evidence of this.

Another argument in favour of discarding the law/non-law distinction is that strict state-law cannot alone achieve the objectives of governance. To be sure, state law does not have a good record of accomplishment in adequately realizing global regulatory objectives and many bemoan the ineffectiveness of international law, especially treaty law, in this respect.[86] Thus:

> ... we cannot and should not look for the principal location for regulatory impulses in the state alone. Increasingly, we must also locate such impulses in the codes of conduct of corporations or industrial associations, in the activities of domestic and transnational non-governmental organizations, and in the rules and practices of supranational organizations such as the European Union and international organizations.[87]

---

85 Ong, David M. (2010), 'From "International" to "Transnational" Environmental Law? A Legal Assessment of the Contribution of the "Equator Principles" to International Environmental Law', *Nordic Journal of International Law*, **79**(1), 35–74 at 45.

86 Macrory, for example, states that 'there is a crisis of confidence in the ability of conventional environmental regulation to deliver. We look at the worst examples of environmental legalism in the States and like not what we see.' Macrory, Richard (2008), *Regulation, Enforcement and Governance in Environmental Law*, London: Cameron May, 369. In arguing what he terms the 'globalization of international environmental law', Dunoff makes the point that '[G]lobalization is necessary to address one of the most serious shortcomings of international environmental lawmaking: the ability of a small minority of nations to set the international environmental agenda and effectively to determine the success or failure of multilateral environmental initiatives.' Dunoff, Jeffrey L. (1995), 'From Green to Global: Toward the Transformation of International Environmental Law', *Harvard Environmental Law Review*, **19**(2), 241–301 at 242.

87 Swan, Peter (2002), 'Governing at a Distance: An Introduction to Law,

In other words, the law versus non-law debate in relation to non-state forms of law becomes less important if one accepts that non-state law (while different from state law) is a set of important rules or normative arrangements with 'regulatory impulses' that aim to change behaviour, and they should be used as such. While the legitimacy (and hence the authority) of these non-state laws are necessarily different from state laws, and while they are voluntary, reflexive and persuasive as opposed to being obligatory and coercive, they nevertheless fulfil at least one of the principal objectives of law in society, namely that they influence, change and/or direct human behaviour with a view to achieving some form of societal outcome which, for present purposes, includes environmental protection.

Non-state laws have many disadvantages, including the fact that they are non-enforceable, often vague, sometimes non-codified and mostly voluntary. Yet these shortcomings are simultaneously non-state law's greatest strengths and advantages, a fact which strongly supports the need to discard the law/non-law debate. According to Verschuuren[88] 'non-state law' has several advantages over state-law:

> ... since the people who develop, apply and enforce the [non-state] rules are the same as those bound by them, these people are probably more committed to them than to state rules ... [Non-state rules] are better known to the regulated, easier to understand, more flexible ... and so, in general are more effective ... non-state law could also be better suited to address problems connected to globalization, as non-state law is not necessarily restrained by national borders.

With specific reference to voluntary EMSs such as the ISO 14001 series, Roht-Arriaza[89] highlights other advantages of non-state environmental law, including the fact that non-state forms of law predominantly rely on market forces or private capital to achieve compliance and enforcement, thus resulting in less pressure on the public purse, and that they allow for a more direct and immediate focus on environmental problems instead of relying on the cumbersome and generalist efforts of states to transfer international law obligations into national law and governance structures. Moreover, as Ong[90] indicates in the

---

Regulation, and Governance' in Michael MacNeil, Neil Sargent and Peter Swan (eds), *Law, Regulation and Governance*, Oxford: Oxford University Press, 23.

88 Verschuuren, Jonathan (2008), 'Introduction' in Hanneke Van Schooten and Jonathan Verschuuren (eds), *International Governance and Law: State Regulation and Non-state Law*, Cheltenham: Edward Elgar Publishing, 2.

89 Roht-Arriaza, Naomi (1995), 'Private Voluntary Standard-Setting, the International Organization for Standardization, and International Environmental Lawmaking', *Yearbook of International Environmental Law*, **6**, 107–63 at 108.

90 Ong, David M. (2010), 'From "International" to "Transnational" Environmental Law? A Legal Assessment of the Contribution of the "Equator Principles" to International Environmental Law', *Nordic Journal of International Law*, **79**(1), 35–74 at 74.

context of the Equator Principles, non-state law also has the potential to enhance and even expand the normative reach of international soft law. It could therefore supplement and strengthen the effect of state law by achieving regulatory objectives where state law is inadequate and/or inappropriate.

Yet, despite the surge in the number of non-state actors and the amount of non-state law and the numerous advantages associated with these forms of law, states and state-made law will continue to play the dominant role in global governance, especially insofar as states provide the architecture to enforce non-state law. The point has been made elsewhere in this book that non-state actors are far from being the primary actors in global governance,[91] and despite its many flaws the state continues to provide the only stable architecture for world society and world order. No arrangement has yet emerged as an alternative to the state's function in establishing and maintaining the architecture of global society and global order. The influence of non-state actors in global law-making, law-interpretation and law enforcement should therefore not be overdrawn: '[S]tates remain the *unique vectors of law creation and enforcement*. This is true for the creation and enforcement of national law, for the enforcement of all other non-State systems of regulation, and even for the creation and enforcement of international law.'[92]

5. LAW AND GOVERNANCE

It is possible to derive from the foregoing that 'law, regulation and governance are inherently relational activities'.[93] In a more abstract sense, the theoretical link between law and governance lies in the interconnectivity between law and politics (specifically from an institutionalist point of view): '[I]t is a truism, though sadly one that both political scientists and lawyers sometimes seem to forget, that law and politics – in both their theoretical and their practical aspects – are very closely interconnected.'[94] In fact, as Wiener[95] points out: '[L]aw and politics are intertwined by a concept of law that links positive law

---

[91] See Chapters 3 and 4.

[92] Stern, Brigitte (2000), 'How to Regulate Globalization?' in Michael Byers (ed), *The Role of Law in International Politics: Essays in International Relations and International Law*, Oxford: Oxford University Press, 267.

[93] Swan, Peter (2002), 'Governing at a Distance: An Introduction to Law, Regulation, and Governance' in Michael MacNeil, Neil Sargent and Peter Swan (eds), *Law, Regulation and Governance*, Oxford: Oxford University Press, 23.

[94] Drewry, Gavin (1996), 'Political Institutions: Legal Perspectives' in Robert E. Goodin and Hans Dieter Klingemann (eds), *A New Handbook of Political Science*, Oxford: Oxford University Press, 191.

[95] Wiener, Antje (2008), *The Invisible Constitution of Politics: Contested Norms and International Encounters*, Cambridge: Cambridge University Press, 13.

with a legitimating mode of law-making.' Likewise, governance is the primary domain of politics because politics and the exercise of authority are central features of governance. Governance is also concerned with power and the collective steering of society: '[T]here is a direct connection between law and politics in so far as legal actions and decisions contribute to collective practice ... law is an expression of power, its instrument and issue ... [and] law is the source of, or prerequisite for, or limit on power.'[96] Or, as Hurrell[97] puts it:

> Legal rules and relations are important, then, in so far as they constitute the game of power politics. But they are also important more directly in stabilizing and legitimizing the power of particular actors. To a much greater extent that realists acknowledge, States need international law and institutions both to share the material and political costs of protecting their interests and to gain the authority and legitimacy that the possession of crude power can never on its own secure. Law and legal institutions do indeed reflect power, but there is much more to this than the idea of 'mere reflection' might suggest. It is therefore a mistake to view 'law' as something that is, or can be, wholly separated from 'power' or 'power-political interest'.

If one now considers Keohane's[98] suggestion that 'rules structure politics', it follows that law (as rules) plays a fundamentally important role in governance. This logical connection is also evident in the dialectical complexity of the interrelationship between law and politics: '[P]olitics is included in the process of law creation, and the use of law or, at least, the reference to law is one of the elements of politics.'[99]

An equally broad interpretation of law sees it as an institution (like governance) which, as was suggested earlier in this book,[100] can be described very generally as a comprehensive and all-encompassing sociological phenomenon or as the 'rules of the game' that aim to shape human behaviour. To repeat Young's[101] definition of institutions (first quoted in Chapter 4 of this book):

---

96 La Torre, Massimo (2010), *Law as Institution*, Heidelberg: Springer, 3.

97 Hurrell, Andrew (2000), 'International Law and the Changing Constitution of International Society' in Michael Byers (ed), *The Role of Law in International Politics: Essays in International Relations and International Law*, Oxford: Oxford University Press, 330–31.

98 Keohane, Robert O. (2002), *Power and Governance in a Partially Globalized World*, London: Routledge, 118.

99 Stern, Brigitte (2000), 'How to Regulate Globalization?' in Michael Byers (ed), *The Role of Law in International Politics: Essays in International Relations and International Law*, Oxford: Oxford University Press, 252.

100 See Chapter 4.

101 Young, Oran R. (1994), *International Governance: Protecting the Environment in a Stateless Society*, Ithaca, NY and London: Cornell University Press, 3.

> Institutions ... are sets of rules of the game or codes of conduct that serve to define social practices, assign roles to the participants in these practices, and guide the interactions among occupants of these roles ... all institutions are social artefacts created by human beings – consciously or unconsciously – to cope with problems of coordination and cooperation that arise as a result of interdependencies among the activities of distinct individuals or social groups.

In fact, this definition of institutions would be a suitably useful substitute for any other definition of law. While law and governance are not the same, law, like governance, is an institution created by people. It is a social artefact and it has a distinct normative character that regulates human behaviour with a view to creating order and achieving desired collective outcomes and/or addressing collective issues that society perceives to be problematic. In this sense, the objectives of law and governance are the same, and an instrumentalist approach suggests that law could be used as a vehicle to achieve the objectives of governance or, put differently, that law facilitates governance.

Another approach to the consideration of the relationship between law and governance is Köck's.[102] He presents three (rather abstract) perspectives on the relationship between law and governance. First, law could be an objective and element of governance research (*Recht als Gegenstand der Governanceforschung*). This is so because governance research occupies itself with the regulation of public (often shared) goods, subject matters and interests, and it seeks to analyse regulatory structures and the structures of rules in interaction and in an institutional context, and the effect of these on the activities of actors. Law is an important part of this regulatory structure of rules and specifically aims to prescribe and regulate the forms of interaction in society. Law also establishes and underpins new constellations of actors, and it directs the focus to the central role that various actors play in governance, especially those actors that take part in juridical discourse and processes.

Second, law is a standard for the evaluation of regulatory structures. The growing change in the modes of the regulation of common goods, subject matters and interests from strictly public, state-centred approaches to hybrid, private-public forms of governance raises several fundamental questions in the democratic *Rechtsstaat* context related for instance to legitimacy, the rule of law and constitutionality. Where democratic deficits arise in these new forms of hybrid regulatory structures, it is law that will form the standard to measure these against, and it is usually law that will be used to compensate for democratic deficits where they arise. In other words, whereas legal rules and regulatory structures that conform to the rule of law and *rechtsstaatlichkeit* would

---

102 Köck, Wolfgang (2006), 'Governance in der Umweltpolitik' in Gunnar Folke Schuppert (ed), *Governance-Forschung*, Baden-Baden: Nomos Verlag, 339–40.

raise little concern as far as their democratic legitimacy is concerned, private, non-state rules, actors and structures which have not been constituted in terms of a legitimate constitution in a democratic manner might have various democratic deficits.[103] Law will then play an important role as a measurable standard to determine if there is a democratic deficit, and law could be used to correct situations of illegitimacy.

Köck's third and more concrete approach to the link between law and governance is to view it as an instrument for the improvement of the capability and capacity of governance to actually solve those problems governance was designed to solve in the first place. This view emphasizes the functional role of law as an important steering (regulatory) instrument, arguably *the* most important steering instrument in the regulatory context, to improve the capacity and ability of regulatory structures to achieve their outcomes. As regulatory needs change, so too will it be possible to adapt law to provide more adequate legal structures that are in tune with the nature, scope and depth of regulatory problems (including environmental problems). Law could also be used, itself, to change social reality and to respond to social changes. Law therefore is a crucial element in a changing regulatory or governance milieu, especially insofar as it improves the capacity of governance actors to address changing regulatory problems and insofar as it contributes to legalizing steering and regulatory processes. An example of law improving governance, the capacity to govern and/or the outcomes of governance is the rules it sets for good governance. Through the institutionalization of values and constitutional standards such as democracy, transparency, rationality, administrative justice, the rule of law and participation, law would seek to achieve what people perceive as good governance. These legal rules already exist in some domestic jurisdictions, and even internationally.[104]

A more concrete interpretation of the nexus between law and governance sees 'law as governance'.[105] This is a distinct sociological and functionalist view of law and governance which considers that 'the law is what the law does'.[106] In terms of this perspective, law contains elements of an 'attempt to

---

103 On the legitimacy crisis in international environmental law, see among others Bodansky, Daniel (1999), 'The Legitimacy of International Governance: A Coming Challenge for International Environmental Law?', *American Journal of International Law*, **93**(3), 596–624.

104 See, for example, sections 32 and 33 of the *Constitution of the Republic of South Africa*, 1996, which deal with access to information and administrative justice; and the *Convention on Access to Information, Public Participation in Decision-Making and Access to Justice in Environmental Matters*, June 25, 1998, 38 I.L.M. 517 (1999).

105 Hunt, Alan and Gary Wickham (1994), *Foucault and the Law: Towards a Sociology of Law as Governance*, London: Pluto Press, 99.

106 Hunt, Alan and Gary Wickham (1994), *Foucault and the Law: Towards a Sociology of Law as Governance*, London: Pluto Press, 99.

achieve conformity with an historically received norm or an attempt to achieve the avengement of a violation of an historically received norm'; law involves power to the extent that it 'helps [to] drive society' and it helps 'power [to] produce all aspects of social life'.[107] Because law cannot exist without people, law is always social. It has to do with social coherence and has been invented by society as an integral part of that society: '[W]hat is important is that the law helps guide/coerce/encourage/induce individuals towards certain ways of doing right and away from certain ways of doing wrong.'[108] Clearly, law enables governance in and of a society because it has certain regulatory dimensions.[109] In other words, 'law as governance' (or the 'regulatory process', as some term it in this context)[110] is that part of social life where laws are applied to society and its members through the process of governance and its institutions.

In addition to its constraining and regulative roles, law 'constitutes' through its constitutive function to the extent that it enables people to 'pursue their own plans',[111] i.e., to act in society in a particular (acceptable) way. It constitutes the architecture through which society will act and interact. In so doing, law is also the institutional architecture of governance. If one accepts that governance aims to change or shape behaviour, then it is law that provides the norms that set out the standards of behaviour which have been agreed by actors globally. Through a formal process of codification or less formal processes of private rule making, these policy standards are translated into law and expressed as rules of behaviour.[112] In other words, law provides the architecture for governance to the

---

[107] Hunt, Alan and Gary Wickham (1994), *Foucault and the Law: Towards a Sociology of Law as Governance*, London: Pluto Press, 111–12.

[108] Hunt, Alan and Gary Wickham (1994), *Foucault and the Law: Towards a Sociology of Law as Governance*, London: Pluto Press, 114.

[109] Weiler, J.H.H. (2004), 'The Geology of International Law: Governance, Democracy and Legitimacy', *Zeitschrift für Ausländisches Öffentliches Recht und Völkerrecht*, **64**, 547–62 at 559.

[110] Percival, Robert V. *et al.* (2009), *Environmental Regulation: Law, Science, and Policy* 6th edn, New York: Aspen Publishers, 159.

[111] Kratochwil, Friedrich V. (2000), 'How do Norms Matter?' in Michael Byers (ed), *The Role of Law in International Politics: Essays in International Relations and International Law*, Oxford: Oxford University Press, 47.

[112] Weiss, Thomas G. and Ramesh Thakur (2011), 'Framing Global Governance, Five Gaps' in Thomas G. Weiss (ed), *Thinking about Global Governance: Why People and Ideas Matter*, Abingdon: Routledge, 150. Global policies and laws are not the same. While laws are codified norms, policies could be regarded as the basis of these codified norms. They include articulated and linked governing principles and goals and programmes of action agreed to by the international community. Weiss, Thomas G. and Ramesh Thakur (2011), 'Framing Global Governance, Five Gaps' in Thomas G. Weiss, *Thinking about Global Governance: Why People and Ideas Matter*, Abingdon: Routledge, 151.

extent that it creates the rules that proscribe and prescribe behaviour, as well as the institutions that must interpret and enforce these laws. Viewed from this pragmatic-functionalist point of view, this suggests that law establishes or constitutes governance: '[I]t constitutes, organizes, and legitimizes positions of authority of governance agents and governance activities.'[113] According to Walker and De Búrca:[114] '[L]aw is perceived as a tool of the top-down approach to regulation, an instrument for stabilizing expectations, improving clarity by articulating and maintaining specific goals, and delivering predictable outcomes.' In this sense law is a 'purposive project [that is] part of a general strategy of governance directed at sustaining political stability by ensuring the social conditions for individual well-being'.[115] Law also provides governance actors with legal personality by recognizing the ability of state and increasingly non-state actors to participate in the creation and execution of governance.[116] In other words, law provides for governance and it provides the rules along which governance should be performed; law truly becomes a vehicle for and a source of governance to the extent that it is even possible to speak of 'governance by law'.[117] Conversely, while law creates the sources of governance, these governance sources are also responsible for the creation of law. For example, from a normative point of view the climate change regime, including the whole range of its institutional arrangements, has primarily been created by and is based on the *United Nations Framework Convention on Climate Change*, 31 I.L.M. 849 (1992) and the *Kyoto Protocol to the United Nations Framework Convention on Climate Change*, 37 I.L.M. 22 (1998), which function alongside numerous soft law arrangements. These instruments provide the actors in the regime with the authority and the means to fulfil the objectives of the regime, i.e., to change human behaviour with a view to reducing greenhouse gas emissions. Within this framework, state and non-state actors are contin-

---

113 Von Benda-Beckmann, Franz, Keebet Von Benda-Beckmann and Julia Eckert (2009), 'Rules of Law and Laws of Ruling: Law and Governance between Past and Future' in Franz Von Benda-Beckmann, Keebet Von Benda-Beckmann and Julia Eckert (eds), *Rules of Law and Laws of Ruling: on the Governance of Law*, Farnham: Ashgate, 4.

114 Walker, Neil and Gráinne De Búrca (2007), 'Reconceiving Law and New Governance', *Columbia Journal of European Law*, **13**(3), 519–37 at 521–2.

115 Hunt, Alan (2002), 'Legal Governance and Social Relations: Empowering Agents and the Limits of Law' in Michael MacNeil, Neil Sargent and Peter Swan (eds), *Law, Regulation and Governance*, Oxford: Oxford University Press, 58.

116 Young, Oran R. (1994), *International Governance: Protecting the Environment in a Stateless Society*, Ithaca, NY and London: Cornell University Press, 186.

117 Hunt, Alan (2002), 'Legal Governance and Social Relations: Empowering Agents and the Limits of Law' in Michael MacNeil, Neil Sargent and Peter Swan (eds), *Law, Regulation and Governance*, Oxford: Oxford University Press, 57.

uously engaged, mostly through regimes, international organizations and networks, in a process of negotiating and creating new legal arrangements through which they must set new targets and establish a range of enforcement mechanisms. Law therefore constitutes, legitimizes and enables governance, and governance creates and implements law. Insofar as it is possible to equate the regulative objectives of law and governance, legal processes, including the creation of law, could themselves be regarded as governance processes.

In addition to providing the means and architecture of governance, law also regulates governance actors, both private and public. In other words, law provides the rules with which to govern, it applies to a regulator and a regulated entity, and it determines how to govern. In the domestic context, these functions are easily discernible in terms of the regulator-regulated distinction between governance actors. Where, for example, a local authority (a municipality) creates, implements, administers and enforces local environmental bylaws, it fulfils the function of the regulator. However, a municipality can also cause pollution because of its own activities, processes and regulatory services, for example where the waste management division of a municipality accidentally dumps hazardous waste in a public river. In this instance the municipality is subject to the same pollution control laws that regulate private entities and it would thus be considered a regulated entity. The regulator-regulated distinction is less clear in the supra-national context since there are no designated central authorities in this sphere. Nevertheless, legal entities or entities with legal personality such as states and international organizations are subject to the rules for example of international environmental law to the extent that they must abide by the prescriptions and proscriptions of international environmental law (at least of treaty and customary international law). In this sense, they (the regulators) are also regulated entities and could be held accountable for their acts where these contravene the rules of international environmental law. These entities, however, must also ensure the implementation and enforcement of international environmental law as regulators (generally through domestic authorities and international organizations such as the UN and treaty bodies). In terms of governance, law will therefore dictate the manner in which a local authority or a country abides by the prescriptions of the applicable legal order and law will simultaneously provide the means in terms of which standards and prescriptions are enforced and implemented by this very same local authority or country. Another related consideration in the regulator-regulated distinction is where the municipality is regulated by various other (non-environmental) laws relating to *how* it governs (as opposed to *what* it governs) including, for example, procedural rules on access to information, transparent and participative governance, administrative justice, and judicial review (collectively referred to as good governance). These laws could be provided for in statutes (which have ironically been described as 'disagreement[s] reduced to writing'),[118] or more popularly in constitutions.[119] There are considerably fewer formal, enforceable laws regulating how global actors govern beyond the nation-state at the supra-national level, or that at least afford states, individuals or other entities the protection and the right to claim a standard of good governance that is acceptable to them. One example is the United Nations Economic Commission for Europe (UNECE) *Convention on Access to Information, Public Participation in Decision-making, and Access to Justice in Environmental Context*, June 25, 1998, 38 I.L.M. 517 (1999). Another legal source determining how governance takes place in the global domain is global administrative (or institutional or international organizational) law. To the extent that global administrative law provides the procedures for the implementation of substantive law, it resembles domestic administrative law and it provides the legal means to ensure a 'good' standard of governance. Global administrative law therefore dictates how global governance must occur and, more specifically, the manner in which the substantive objectives of global laws should be realized by means of and in compliance with certain procedural rules.

Law is also related to governance because it plays an important part in resolving disputes that arise during governance:

> A critical function of law in human societies is to provide a means for solving problems that arise when efforts of individual actors to pursue their own interests come into conflict ... legal systems can [also] be treated as procedural devices for arriving at authoritative judgments regarding the merits of two or more conflicting interpretations of the same fact pattern.[120]

---

118 Allot, Philip (2000), 'The Concept of International Law' in Michael Byers (ed), *The Role of Law in International Politics: Essays in International Relations and International Law*, Oxford: Oxford University Press, 81.

119 See, for example, sections 32 and 33 of the *Constitution of the Republic of South Africa*, 1996, which provide for the rights of access to information and administrative justice as justiciable fundamental rights respectively. Section 195 further sets out the principles governing public administration and provides, among other things, that public administration must be governed by the democratic values and principles enshrined in the Constitution, including the following principles: a high standard of professional ethics must be promoted and maintained; efficient, economic and effective use of resources must be promoted; public administration must be development-oriented; services must be provided impartially, fairly, equitably and without bias; people's needs must be responded to, and the public must be encouraged to participate in policy-making; public administration must be accountable; transparency must be fostered by providing the public with timely, accessible and accurate information; and good human-resource management and career-development practices which maximize human potential must be cultivated.

120 Young, Oran R. (1994), *International Governance: Protecting the Environment in a Stateless Society*, Ithaca, NY and London: Cornell University Press, 196.

Law creates the institutions (for example courts or tribunals) that must resolve conflicts that arise during governance processes, and it sets the procedural rules that determine how conflicts of governance are resolved, such as the internal rules of court or tribunals. In other words, law provides the means to interpret other laws and to resolve disputes where they arise, including normative legal disputes and societal disputes. While there are abundant legal rules on interpretation and dispute resolution in domestic jurisdictions, the same cannot be said of the supra-national scene where, apart from the ICJ, treaty regime adjudication bodies and other similar institutions, very few institutional arrangements exist to fulfil the interpretative and adjudicative function of law in global governance. The *Vienna Convention on the Law of Treaties*, May 23, 1969, 1155 U.N.T.S. 331; 8 I.L.M. 679 (1969), is perhaps the most evident example of a supra-national law (a treaty) that provides the rules for conflict resolution and the interpretation of other laws (treaties). The absence of authoritative institutions for the interpretation and adjudication of disputes that arise in the global environmental law and governance domain is especially remarkable.[121]

6. SUMMARY

Law, like governance, is a social phenomenon. It is an institution and normative social intervention which seeks to change human behaviour and is considered a 'solution to diverse social problems'.[122] It is the dominant mode of or vehicle for social regulation,[123] especially to the extent that it shapes social behaviour.[124] In doing so it primarily fulfils preventive and reactive social ordering (regulative) functions.[125] To fulfil its regulative functions, law is

---

[121] See generally, on this matter, Stephens, Tim (2009), *International Courts and Environmental Protection*, Cambridge: Cambridge University Press.

[122] Hunt, Alan (2002), 'Legal Governance and Social Relations: Empowering Agents and the Limits of Law' in Michael MacNeil, Neil Sargent and Peter Swan (eds), *Law, Regulation and Governance*, Oxford: Oxford University Press, 56.

[123] Walker, Neil and Gráinne De Búrca (2007), 'Reconceiving Law and New Governance', *Columbia Journal of European Law*, 13(3), 519–37 at 522.

[124] Morgan, Bronwen and Karen Yeung (2007), *An Introduction to Law and Regulation: Text and Materials*, Cambridge: Cambridge University Press, 5. On the interface between law, regulation and governance, see more generally MacNeil, Michael, Neil Sargent and Peter Swan (eds), *Law, Regulation and Governance*, Oxford: Oxford University Press.

[125] Von Benda-Beckmann, Franz, Keebet Von Benda-Beckmann and Anne Griffiths (2009), 'The Power of Law' in Franz Von Benda-Beckmann, Keebet Von Benda-Beckmann and Anne Griffiths (eds), *The Power of Law in a Transnational World: Anthropological Enquiries*, New York: Berghahn Books, 1.

based on an ideology that prescribes what is acceptable and not acceptable, what type of behaviour must be rewarded, and what type of behaviour must be punished to avoid future repetition.

These characteristics of law mirror those of governance, which also seek to change human behaviour. In this respect law is governance, or at the very least, law is a (if not *the* most) critical component of governance. It plays a constitutive, legitimizing, regulative and steering role in, of and through governance. It resolves conflicts in, of and through governance, and provides the architecture of governance and the rules that determine who must govern, what to govern, and how to govern. Through governance and its institutions, law also creates new law.

Globalization is changing the nature of law and its manifestation and role in governance, especially to the extent that it is requiring and introducing a wide variety of non-state or hybrid forms of law or law-like rules into governance. Law is thus becoming less regulatory and more reflexive, less obligatory and more voluntary, less formal ('hard') and more informal ('soft'). In reaction to globalization, law is also becoming globally pluralized in that it is 'going beyond the state' and it is increasingly fragmented and becoming multilevelled to the point that one might speak of the emergence of a form of global or transnational law.

Following an investigation of the concept of global environmental governance in Chapters 6 and 7, Chapter 8 takes up the current chapter's discussion on the role of law in governance by viewing it in the global environmental regulatory context.

6. In search of (global) environmental governance

> Environmental governance is varied in form, critical in importance, and near ubiquitous in spread.[1]
>
> (Maria Carmen Lemos and Arun Agrawal, 2006)

1. INTRODUCTION

Chapter 1 showed that environmental governance has found its way into and across multiple disciplines and has now become a popular topic in political, legal, policy, and regulatory domains. Chapter 2 explained the phenomenon of globalization, which it argued is both the context for and the instigator of contemporary concepts of governance and global governance. The latter two issues were extensively canvassed in Chapters 3 and 4 respectively. The focus of this chapter is on the multi-dimensional aspects of environmental governance as it manifests generically and in the global context.

The environment is a specific issue area in the global governance milieu that increasingly requires a global regulatory response. This is so because environmental degradation and resource depletion, for example, lead to externalities which 'may persist within a single jurisdiction, across political jurisdictions, or intertemporally'.[2] Global governance, as we have seen, typically deals with these externalities to the extent that it seeks to solve collective global problems, reduce costs, and protect and increase common benefits and interests. It is a regulatory response through which the world endeavours to create and apply institutional arrangements that make regulatory action possible in the global context. This would apply equally to global environmental issues. It is through global environmental governance that state and non-state actors at various levels would seek to prescribe and proscribe behaviour, constrain activity, and shape expectations with a view to collectively addressing global environmental issues

1 Lemos, Maria Carmen and Arun Agrawal (2006), 'Environmental Governance', *Annual Review of Environment and Resources*, **31**, 297–325 at 299.

2 Esty, Daniel C. (1999), 'Toward Optimal Environmental Governance', *New York University Law Review*, **74**(6), 1495–1574 at 1511.

and to ensuring collective action, collective problem solving and the achievement of mutual benefits as far as the environment is concerned.

Building on the general theory of governance and global governance developed earlier, the discussion commences with a section dedicated to indicating and clarifying terminological inconsistencies and anomalies that often arise in the global environmental governance discourse. These include the *global* dimension of environmental governance and the concept of environmental *management* vis-à-vis environmental *governance*. The chapter then offers a generic description of environmental governance, whereafter it investigates the legal doctrinal aspects of global environmental governance with a view to highlighting the important role that norms generally and laws specifically play in global environmental governance. The chapter concludes with an analysis of the multi-actor and multi-level aspects of global environmental governance.

2. WHAT IS IN A WORD?

When engaging with global environmental governance literature, one often stumbles across terms such as 'international environmental governance', 'transnational environmental governance', 'supra-national environmental governance', and 'interstate environmental governance'.[3] The varied use of terms to denote some or other supra-national form of environmental governance, which differs from domestic environmental governance, is leading to significant terminological inconsistency and therefore to interpretative anomalies. Terminological consistency is more muddled when 'management' is thrown into the mix to replace 'governance'. 'Environmental management', 'global environmental management' or 'global resources management' are examples of the way in which the management concept has infiltrated the terminological framework of environmental governance.[4] The inter-

3 For some examples see Esty, Daniel C. (1999), 'Toward Optimal Environmental Governance', *New York University Law Review*, **74**(6), 1495–1574 at 1569; Young, Oran R. (1994), *International Governance: Protecting the Environment in a Stateless Society*, Ithaca, NY and London: Cornell University Press, 12–32; Levy, David L. and Peter J. Newell (eds) (2005), *The Business of Global Environmental Governance*, Cambridge, Massachusetts: MIT Press; Etzioni, Amitai (2001), 'Beyond Transnational Governance', *International Journal*, 595–610; Roch, Philippe and Franz Xaver Perrez (2005), 'International Environmental Governance: The Strive Towards a Comprehensive, Coherent, Effective and Efficient International Environmental Regime', *Colorado Journal of International Environmental Law and Policy*, **16**(1), 1–25.

4 See among the many examples, Hansen, Michael W. (2003), 'Managing the Environment across Borders: A Survey of Environmental Management in

changeability with which these terms are used could be a cause for concern,[5] and a subsequent effort to establish some conceptual uniformity and terminological consistency raises the following questions: a) are international, transnational, supra-national and interstate the same as *global*; and b) are environmental management and environmental governance similar terms?

2.1 The Global

The answer to the first question naturally seems to lie in what one considers to be 'global' in the environmental context. Chapters 1 and 2 argued that 'global' is an all-inclusive term, which refers to governance occurring at various levels by means of multiple actors. Such a broadened perspective allows one to consider general trends in an interconnected globalized world where there is considerable causality in their occurring on one level and their having repercussions on the other levels. Global is therefore used in terms of its spatial characteristics and as a causal category which applies in the globalization context.

'Global' could also be understood in terms of what Hempel[6] calls the 'political ecosystem':

> Organized within this political ecosystem can be found more than 180 nation-states, approximately two thousand inter-governmental organizations, the United Nations system, and nearly eighteen thousand transnational NGOs operating at the intersections of state power.

As an outcome of globalization, these institutional arrangements are all gradually transforming toward 'glocal [global and local] forms of governance that portend greater interdependence between local, national, and supranational forms of authority' to the extent that 'the earth's political geography bears no resemblance to its appearance from space'.[7] In other words, as the world is increasingly becoming a single place because of globalization (for lack of a better description), environmental regulation now occurs in and over the

---

Transnational Corporations in Asia', *Transnational Corporations*, **12**(1), 27–52; Peel, Jacqueline and Lee Godden (2005), 'Australian Environmental Management: A "Dams" Story', *University of New South Wales Law Journal*, **28**(3), 668–95.

5 Mayntz, for example, seems to use transnational, global and international governance all simultaneously in one publication to denote one meaning. Mayntz, Renate (2010), *Legitimacy and Compliance in Transnational Governance: MPIfG Working Paper 10/5* (Max-Planck-Institut für Gesellschaftforschung, Cologne).

6 Hempel, Lamont C. (1996), *Environmental Governance: The Global Challenge*, Washington: Island Press, 154.

7 Hempel, Lamont C. (1996), *Environmental Governance: The Global Challenge*, Washington: Island Press, 154–5.

globe, and regulation is metamorphosing from single, mostly state-based foci that are constrained by national borders, to a complex mass of intertwined and causally linked reciprocal institutional arrangements that collectively seek to address the *problématique* of global environmental problems.

Speth and Haas[8] explain this *problématique* in more concrete terms by identifying several types of environmental problems that give rise to collective actions among nations.[9] The first type concerns the use and devastation of the global commons which fall outside the jurisdictional area and authority of nation states, such as the oceans. The second is transboundary environmental impacts and cross-jurisdictional environmental harm, while the third related type refers to the common interests that people have in environmental impacts that occur outside the borders of their nations but which nevertheless affect the entire global environment. The tropical rainforest in Brazil is an example of such a concern, in which the entire world has an interest even though it falls in a specific country's jurisdiction. Another type of environmental problem is the set of those that are local, but which lend themselves well to supra-national solutions, information sharing and cooperation because they occur simultaneously in almost all countries in the world. They are thus environmental problems which many countries share. Examples are the dumping and recycling of hazardous waste and soil erosion. A fifth type of environmental problem, which the authors do not specifically mention, but which contains elements of all of the foregoing, is the set of those that are truly supra-national in nature, such as climate change or ozone layer depletion. These are environmental problems of a planetary magnitude that are the result of complex infra-national and supra-national 'causation chains [which] have multiplied to the extent that the complex biophysical-chemical mechanics of the biosphere as a whole are put under strain'.[10]

---

8 Speth, Gustave James and Peter M. Haas (2006), *Global Environmental Governance*, Washington: Island Press, 15–16.

9 For Habermas, the nature of transnational environmental problems is indicative of the increasingly porous borders of states and their inability to address environmental problems in their territories unilaterally:

> Door de verstoring van ecologische kringlopen en de storingsgevoeligheid van grote technische complexen zijn echter nieuwe risico's van grensoverschrijdende aard ontstaan. 'Tsjernobyl', 'ozongat' of 'zure regen' vestigen de aandacht op ongevallen of ecologische veranderingen die gezien hun intensiteit en reijkwijdte binnen een nationaal kader niet meer zijn te beheersen en die dus het regelend vermogen van de enkele staat te boven gaan.

Habermas, Jürgen (2009), *Geloven en Weten en andere Politieke Essays*, Amsterdam: Boom, 43.

10 Winter, Gerd (2006), 'Introduction' in Gerd Winter (ed), *Multilevel*

Yet the logic of the foregoing should not divert attention away from the fact that the governance of environmental issues in the global domain is a very complex endeavour. Addressing environmental externalities within a jurisdiction or country, on the other hand, should be a less complicated endeavour because there is less loci of authority and a particular government exists which could exercise direct control. While environmental impacts that occur within a country conceivably could reach beyond its borders to affect other states and their citizens also, as they often do, within a specific country the government would need only to immediately attend to the country's and its own citizens' interests. Country-specific environmental problems therefore allow states to practise a certain degree of selfishness. Where these externalities, however, reach beyond the borders of a state the matter becomes a whole lot more complex, because the locus of authority that must enable states to address environmental externalities does not exist any longer. As a result, questions about legitimacy arise, there are many different complex relationships and interests at stake, and numerous state and non-state actors are suddenly involved. The global domain therefore does not permit the luxury of unilateralism and selfishness as far as the governance of global environmental issues is concerned.

Esty[11] understands the global environmental *problématique* in terms of 'regular intra-jurisdictional externalities' and 'super inter-jurisdictional externalities'. The difference between these is that intra-jurisdictional externalities arise as a result of technical or political failures, and not from a structural failure in the regulatory architecture, as is the case with supra-environmental externalities. It is these structural failures and inabilities that cause difficulties for states which seek to address inter-jurisdictional environmental externalities, and it is in this context that *global* environmental governance becomes relevant:

> The problem of managing externalities is particularly glaring when it comes to the environment. It exists in all areas of social life. Hence the appeal to the notion of governance, which encourages interest not only in traditional institutions, in forms of democracy, in power and its instruments, but in the new social co-ordination mechanisms that make political action possible.[12]

The broad view of the 'global' that the foregoing approach suggests, coupled with the equally expansive view of the 'global' that this book takes, suggests

---

Governance of Global Environmental Change: Perspectives from Science, Sociology, and the Law, Cambridge: Cambridge University Press, 1.

11 Esty, Daniel C. (1999), 'Toward Optimal Environmental Governance', *New York University Law Review*, **74**(6), 1495–1574 at 1511.

12 Smouts, Marie-Claude (1998), 'The Proper Use of Governance in International Relations', *International Social Science Journal*, **50**(155), 81–9 at 84.

that it is a heavily loaded term with spatial, temporal and causal characteristics.[13] It is simultaneously national, regional and international, but rarely only one of these. While global environmental governance is thus more than international environmental governance, the latter is nevertheless an important component of global environmental governance. So too are local, national and regional environmental governance.[14] Supra-national environmental governance is also a feature of global environmental governance insofar as it relates to environmental governance that occurs beyond the borders of states. But it cannot be equated to global environmental governance because if the focus of global environmental governance is also on the national and sub-national, as it is, supra-national environmental governance would automatically exclude these levels. Global environmental governance is also not only interstate environmental governance, since global governance, as was argued in Chapter 4, occurs not only between states but also involves non-state actors. Thus considered, interstate governance is also a component of global environmental governance. Transnational environmental governance perhaps comes closest to mirroring global environmental governance, because it 'goes beyond' traditional concepts of state-based and domestically-focused governance. Transnational environmental governance is therefore more loosely connected to a specific level and specific actors and more sensitive to the context of globalization.[15] Pattberg and

---

[13] As with intra-jurisdictional environmental problems and externalities, inter-jurisdictional environmental problems and externalities could also have temporal dimensions insofar as an environmental event occurs now but its effects are perceived only many years later. The now well-established concepts of 'future generations' and 'inter-generational equity' embody the temporal aspects of the global environmental governance effort. See the standard work in this respect, Brown Weiss, Edith (1989), *In Fairness to Future Generations: International Law, Common Patrimony, and Intergenerational Equity*, New York: Transnational Publishers, and more recently, Collins, Lynda M. (2007), 'Revisiting the Doctrine of Intergenerational Equity in Global Environmental Governance', *Dalhousie Law Journal*, **30**(2), 79–140.

[14] Indeed, 'environmental protection is at once a global and a national task, and competencies in this field are not merely shared by global and national bodies; rather, areas of jurisdiction overlap and compete with each other. The line between the national and the international is becoming increasingly blurred.' Cassese, Sabino (2009), 'Is There a Global Administrative Law?' in Armin Von Bogdandy *et al.* (eds), *The Exercise of Public Authority by International Institutions: Advancing International Institutional Law*, Heidelberg: Springer Verlag, 767–8.

[15] In focusing on the possible interactions by many administrative agencies in different countries with one another, Gehring explains transnationalism as follows:

> States cannot any more be considered as 'unitary actors' ... it must be assumed that different administrative units conduct their own external relations [disconnected from the state]. If administrative units from different countries active in the same

Stripple,[16] for example, indicate that the 'transnationalization' of global governance refers to a proliferation of policies; the prevalence of a multitude of state and non-state governance actors; an increase in the divergent polities and principles on how the overall architecture of global governance should be structured; an increasingly fragmented global governance dispensation which retains some interconnections; and a multiplication of functional inter-linkages and communication channels. The transnationalization of environmental governance in this sense is equally a reality in a globalized world, which demands a holistic view of the truly intertwined global setting in which environmental governance occurs today.

What is important then is to realize that global environmental governance describes governance that addresses environmental regulatory problems that could occur everywhere and that have an impact everywhere in a global space where regulatory authority is diversified, interlinked, complex and multidimensional:

> The global order can be illustrated by the well-known metaphor of the marble cake, as there are no clear dividing lines between layers (national and global) and (global) sectoral regimes; rather, the two worlds are linked both vertically and horizontally through a complex array of relations and networks.[17]

Where any one of international, supra-national, transnational or interstate environmental governance is used to denote the foregoing, it is highly likely that these terms are intended to mean global environmental governance. Yet some form of terminological consistency would be in order and, for all of the foregoing reasons, the use of global environmental governance as a universal term that means a holistic form of environmental governance in the global domain is probably the best candidate to fulfil this role.

2.2 Environmental Management versus Environmental Governance

The term 'environmental management' is often used interchangeably with

---

> issue-area cooperate, international relations may be transformed into transnational relations.

Gehring, Thomas (1994), *Dynamic International Regimes: Institutions for International Environmental Governance*, Frankfurt am Main: Peter Lang, 27.

16 Pattberg, Philipp and Johannes Stripple (2008), 'Beyond the Public and Private Divide: Remapping Transnational Climate Governance in the 21st Century', *International Environmental Agreements*, **8**, 367–88 at 368–9.

17 Cassese, Sabino (2009), 'Is There a Global Administrative Law?' in Armin Von Bogdandy *et al.* (eds), *The Exercise of Public Authority by International Institutions: Advancing International Institutional Law*, Heidelberg: Springer Verlag, 768.

environmental governance, and while some commentators rely on the term management, they actually imply governance.[18] This confusion is not surprising when one considers that the historical roots of governance also lie in the management paradigm, as was explained in Chapter 3, and that environmental management was the term of choice in the 1970s. For example, in 1973 Strong[19] described the central tenet of global environmental governance as follows:

> ... if man is to realize his fundamental right to 'an environment of a quality that permits a life of dignity and well-being,' something more than enlightened awareness is needed. Somehow such an environment must be created through some form of management which will involve, on both national and international levels, new kinds of institutional arrangements and novel procedures for decision-making.

He defines management in this context as:

> ... arrangement of the decision-making process – to organizing the necessary research and analysis and monitoring functions, formulating alternative courses of action and evolving procedures through which conscious choices can be made in the fullest possible knowledge of their consequences. These are essential ... functions for decision-making at the highest political level.[20]

The 'arrangement of the decision-making process' is closely related to the essence of governance, as meaning the institutional arrangements to change behaviour.

In an environmental context the term management is also used in private, and more specifically, corporate environmental governance practices through voluntary codes and standards of practice such as the ISO 14000 EMS and its European equivalent, the EMAS, for example.[21] Environmental management

---

18 See, for example, Stephens, Tim (2009), *International Courts and Environmental Protection*, Cambridge: Cambridge University Press, 7; Cordonier Segger, Marie-Claire and Ashfaq Khalfan (2004), *Sustainable Development Law: Principles, Practices and Prospects*, Oxford: Oxford University Press, 89–90. Also see Chapter 3.

19 Strong, Maurice (1973), 'One Year after Stockholm: An Ecological Approach to Management', *Foreign Affairs*, **51**(4), 690–707 at 696.

20 Strong, Maurice (1973), 'One Year after Stockholm: An Ecological Approach to Management', *Foreign Affairs*, **51**(4), 690–707 at 702.

21 Among the many examples see Pratt, Lawrence, Richard P. Wells and Foster C. Knight (1995), 'Environmental Management: Helping Industry Worldwide Advance toward Sustainable Development', *Review of European Community and International Environmental Law*, **4**(2), 106–12; Carr, Donald A. and William L. Thomas (1997), 'Devising a Compliance Strategy under the ISO 14000 International Environmental Management Standards', *Pace Environmental Law Review*, **15**(1), 85–231.

originated in the private sector and is now also sometimes applied to state actors' governance activities in the public domain where, for example, an environmental government department could itself subscribe to the foregoing environmental standards to better regulate the environmental impacts of its own activities. Environmental management is therefore, strictly speaking, more private than it is public, and it is conceptually more 'limited' than governance.

Yet one cannot ignore the fact that management is steadily penetrating the public governance realm, especially in the form of new public management, and more than ever before the public sector is concerned with management in the narrow private sense as a new strategy to overcome governance deficiencies.[22] In the environmental context new public management could refer to public sector endeavours and ways to improve service delivery by state actors through the transfer of private sector management principles to the public sector (or managerialism), privatization, and the transfer of public sector interests and institutions to private ownership, for instance. Here, one could then conceivably speak of environmental management in the public sector. On the other hand, one could also argue that new public management is a strategy to improve environmental governance and as such is a part of environmental governance. The implication of that argument would be that environmental management would be subsumed in the broader phenomenon of environmental governance. This leads to the logical conclusion that environmental governance and environmental management are not wholly synonymous and that the broader notion of environmental governance includes environmental management if it is the former's intention to provide for a private, 'managerial' type of regulation. To avoid any terminological confusion and inconsistencies, it would probably be best to use the term environmental governance consistently, instead of environmental management.

3. A GENERIC DESCRIPTION OF ENVIRONMENTAL GOVERNANCE

Until this stage the analysis in this book has focused on generic descriptions of governance and global governance that collectively serve as the greater context and as parts of the theoretical foundation for global environmental governance. While governance and global governance are two crucial central considerations in global environmental governance, so too is the concept of environmental governance as it manifests generically. In continuing this interpretive exercise, this section therefore canvasses some of the generic

22 See Chapter 3.

descriptions of environmental governance that would be relevant and useful to informing the broader construct of global environmental governance.

Hempel's[23] description of environmental governance in general terms serves as an informative point of departure. In his view environmental governance is about 'policy responses and political processes needed to reverse ... [environmental] destruction':

> How members of a society organize power and authority over their lives is intimately connected with how they organize power over nature. By tying environmental improvement to the art of governing, the challenge of ecological sustainability can be seen for what it really is – a challenge to traditional notions of national security, national sovereignty, and individual freedom.[24]

This description suggests that it is possible to improve the environment and achieve ecological sustainability through policy and political processes, or through governance that aims to re-connect and resituate power and authority over the environment. Environmental governance is thus a social process that aims to answer to the challenge of ecological sustainability through a fundamental reorganization of institutional arrangements that influence how people perceive and interact with the environment.

Levy and Newell[25] also provide a useful generic description of environmental governance, a term which they describe as implying a broad, general system of order and structure. This system is 'always present' and it can include a varying range of state and/or non-state actors playing more or sometimes less prominent roles. In their view, environmental governance is:

> ... the broad range of political, economic, and social structures and processes that shape and constrain actors' behavior towards the environment. Environmental governance thus refers to the multiple channels through which human impacts on the natural environment are ordered and regulated. It implies rule creation, institution-building, and monitoring and enforcement. But it also implies a soft infrastructure of norms, expectations, and social understandings of acceptable behavior towards the environment, in processes that engage the participation of a broad range of stakeholders.[26]

---

23 Hempel, Lamont C. (1996), *Environmental Governance: The Global Challenge*, Washington: Island Press, xiii.

24 Hempel, Lamont C. (1996), *Environmental Governance: The Global Challenge*, Washington: Island Press, xiii.

25 Levy, David L. and Peter J. Newell (2005), 'Introduction' in David L. Levy and Peter J. Newell (eds), *The Business of Global Environmental Governance*, Cambridge, Massachusetts: MIT Press, 2.

26 Levy, David L. and Peter J. Newell (2005), 'Introduction' in David L. Levy and Peter J. Newell (eds), *The Business of Global Environmental Governance*, Cambridge, Massachusetts: MIT Press, 2–3.

This definition suggests that environmental governance is an institutionalized social construct which provides for formal (presumably meaning 'state') and informal (presumably meaning 'non-state') means that influence and direct human behaviour vis-à-vis the environment. It is an institutional response (juridical, political, economic and social) that orders and regulates human impacts to the extent that human behaviour and impacts conform to what society perceives to be acceptable in this respect. The main functions of environmental governance are rule creation (mostly in the form of laws), which presumably include the revision, improvement and/or repeal of rules; the interpretation of these rules; and the establishment of institutions that must oversee and conduct rule creation and ensure monitoring and enforcement of these rules. Environmental governance, however, does not only employ 'hard' legal rules. A 'softer' collection of non-coercive, participative and flexible arrangements also play an ancillary role in shaping behaviour towards the environment.

Lemos and Agrawal[27] proffer an almost identically broad definition of environmental governance. They see it as being:

> ... synonymous with interventions aiming at changes in environment-related incentives, knowledge, institutions, decision making and behaviors [including] the set of regulatory processes, mechanisms and organizations through which political actors influence environmental actions and outcomes ... It includes the actions of the state and, in addition, encompasses actors such as communities, businesses, and NGOs ... International accords, national policies and legislation, local decision-making structures, transnational institutions, and environmental NGOs are all examples of the forms through which environmental governance takes place.[28]

Their definition suggests that environmental governance is a procedural intervention consisting of mechanisms and organizations that aims to influence those aspects (incentives, knowledge, institutions, decision-making and behaviour) which might have an impact on the environment; it has a strong institutional character; and state and non-state actors are part of the institutional response. Strangely, despite their broad inclusion of state and non-state actors in environmental governance, they nevertheless limit these to political actors (which they do not define), thereby presumably excluding non-political

---

27 Lemos, Maria Carmen and Arun Agrawal (2006), 'Environmental Governance', *Annual Review of Environment and Resources*, **31**, 297–325 at 298.

28 They stress that the locus of environmental governance will determine whether it is public, private or both, and further make a strong case for new hybrid forms of governance with a greater emphasis on 'soft', multi-level and cross-sectoral private governance strategies and co-governance (bottom-up approaches), as opposed to traditional modes of top-down and state-centred approaches.

actors.[29] While it is not clear what a 'political actor' is, one possible suggestion could be that for an actor to be 'political' it must have some impact on political processes, or it must have some politically derived legitimacy and authority that justifies its existence and that enables it to act. In addition, for activities to have a political dimension, it seems that an important criterion is for them to be able to 'shape widespread behavior in matters of public concern and involvement'.[30] The disaggregated nature of governance in a globalized world suggests that 'political actors' and their actions should be broadly construed as including the decisions and actions of those actors who intervene with some form of authority, be it public or private, with a view to influencing environmental actions and outcomes, regardless whether they are 'political' in the strict sense or not. The term political is used in this context arguably to denote a broader meaning of authority, which could include any type of actor that acts with some form of authority in its endeavours to influence behaviour towards the environment.

Bosselmann[31] highlights the centrality of the state in environmental governance, but simultaneously points to the important role that international organizations and NGOs could play in addition to states. He uses the term environmental governance loosely (by his own admission) to 'include the various institutions and structures of authority engaged in the protection of the natural environment', and posits that this manifestation of environmental governance in modern societies 'has been a minor concern, an add-on, or a minimalist, shallow programme, designed to stay at the periphery of public governance'. Environmental governance thus conceived is the 'poor cousin of economic governance'.[32] Bosselmann then proposes a theory of 'governance for sustainability'[33] which is a value-based approach that heeds and incorpo-

---

29 The limitation that actors must be political could be intended to impose a realistic limit on the range of actors involved in environmental governance; if not, everyone could be actors in environmental governance. If this is the case their argument is questionable, since it militates against everything that inclusive, participative, transparent and representative governance in a globalized age represents.

30 Wapner, Paul (1997), 'Governance in Global Civil Society' in Oran R. Young (ed), *Global Governance: Drawing Insights from the Environmental Experience*. Cambridge, Massachusetts: MIT Press, 66.

31 Bosselmann, Klaus (2008), *The Principle of Sustainability: Transforming Law and Governance*, Aldershot: Ashgate, 175.

32 Bosselmann, Klaus (2008), *The Principle of Sustainability: Transforming Law and Governance*, Aldershot: Ashgate, 175–6.

33 Other commentators such as Chambers, Green, Kanie and Haas similarly speak of 'sustainable development governance'. While they do not define it, the authors seem to use the term as a synonym for more orthodox conceptions of environmental law and governance. Their concept cannot therefore be said to be similar to Bosselmann's 'governance for sustainability', with the latter's strong ecocentric focus on ecological integrity. See, Chambers, Bradnee W. and Jessica F. Green (2005),

rates the need to protect ecological integrity, as opposed to the economic and developmental focus of what he perceives to be inherent in environmental governance. He proposes that governance for sustainability has its origins in holistic awareness and responsible values and it broadens the concept of governance to apply not only to people and social relationships but also to ecological relationships. Governance for sustainability, in addition to recognizing ecological integrity, also proposes a fundamental shift away from state-centred or public environmental governance to an approach which involves a whole range of non-state actors, including global civil society. In short, governance for sustainability implies a radical shift from the current anthropocentric approach to environmental governance to one in which ecocentrism is paramount.[34] This ecocentric take on environmental governance suggests that ecological sustainable development should play a central role in widening the governance construct to include the entire Earth system and all of its (ecological) relationships. For Bosselmann, then, environmental governance is mostly state-centred, it applies only to societal relationships between people, and it is dominated by the desire to promote socio-economic development. Governance for sustainability, on the other hand, is the ethically grounded, value-based and ecocentrist version of environmental governance and arguably sets the standard to which environmental governance should aspire. Governance for sustainability is also predicated on the notion of ecological integrity, which would significantly extend the application of the governance construct to include ecological relationships. Despite Bosselmann's well-founded justification of governance for sustainability, the reality is that global institutional responses, clothed in his version of people-centred environmental governance, currently remain the most viable approach to facilitate, at least to the extent that it is possible, a concerted global response to address shared problems in the shadow of state sovereignty and economic and developmental realities. It is in this context that some argue that 'sustainability, although a useful conceptual guide and rhetorical device, has proven too ambiguous and fluid a concept to anchor serious institution building'.[35] In my view, a more

---

'Introduction: Toward an Effective Framework for Sustainable Development' in Bradnee W. Chambers and Jessica F. Green (eds), *Reforming International Environmental Governance: From Institutional Limits to Innovative Reforms*, Tokyo: United Nations University Press, 1–11; Kanie, Norichika and Peter M. Haas (2004), 'Introduction' in Norichika Kanie and Peter M. Haas (eds), *Emerging Forces in Environmental Governance*, Tokyo: United Nations University Press, 6.

[34] Bosselmann, Klaus (2008), *The Principle of Sustainability: Transforming Law and Governance*, Aldershot: Ashgate, 176–7.

[35] Conca, Ken (2004/2005), 'Environmental Governance after Johannesburg: From Stalled Legalization to Environmental Human Rights?', *Journal of International Law and International Relations*, **1**(1)/**1**(2), 121–66 at 128.

pragmatic and perhaps a more useful approach to the inclusion of sustainability in the environmental governance paradigm is that which is proposed by Haas and Haas:[36]

> Introducing global institutions to turn SD [sustainable development] into more than a value-laden slogan, to turn it into an ongoing activity, implies upgrading environmental management [or governance in this context] by adding new issue areas and new connecting tissue among them. Such upgrading calls for the augmentation of environmental management with development economics, planned technology transfers, resource allocation, and resource planning that takes the future needs of all of humankind into account.

Despite the differences in opinion, the foregoing suggests the important conclusion that sustainability (whether it is ecocentric or anthropocentric) is an objective or probably the central overarching objective, desirable consequence or ideal of environmental governance.

In Köck's[37] view, environmental governance is centrally concerned with environmental politics, which he describes as the politics that aim to protect natural, living (environmental) and life-supporting foundations against damage, pollution and other adverse impacts. The principal objective of environmental governance is to harmonize increased wealth, well-being and human satisfaction on the one hand with resource use, exploitation and environmental degradation on the other, with the ultimate view to sustainably prolonging and securing the foundations and conditions of life, increasing and improving the utility of environmental resources, and rehabilitating the environment where damage and deterioration have occurred.[38] This explanation reiterates the centrality of sustainability as the primary objective or ideal of environmental governance. Notably, as a new regulatory or steering approach environmental governance should not be thought to be a replacement for governmental, supra-governmental and inter-governmental environmental politics. It is rather a complementary addition to a repeatedly changing regulatory milieu where the constellation of actors (*Akteurskonstellationen*), the many forms of interaction between these, the institutional structures and political addressees are constantly changing and growing.[39] In sum, environmental governance is fundamentally embedded in politics. It is an expression of envi-

---

[36] Haas, Peter M. and Ernst B. Haas (1995), 'Learning to Learn: Improving International Governance', *Global Governance*, **1**, 255–85 at 274.

[37] Köck, Wolfgang (2006), 'Governance in der Umweltpolitik' in Gunnar Folke Schuppert (ed), *Governance-Forschung*, Baden-Baden: Nomos Verlag, 326.

[38] Köck, Wolfgang (2006), 'Governance in der Umweltpolitik' in Gunnar Folke Schuppert (ed), *Governance-Forschung*, Baden-Baden: Nomos Verlag, 325.

[39] Köck, Wolfgang (2006), 'Governance in der Umweltpolitik' in Gunnar Folke Schuppert (ed), *Governance-Forschung*, Baden-Baden: Nomos Verlag, 326, 338.

ronmental politics and a strategy to deal with environmental politics. It is also a dynamic process of change which aims to sustainably optimize environmental benefits and use, while at the same time aiming to protect environmental capital.

My own earlier attempt to define environmental governance suggested that it is primarily a management process to formulate and implement strategies for regulating human impacts on the environment. I described environmental governance as:

> A management process executed by institutions and individuals in the public and private sector to holistically regulate human activities and the effects of human activities on the total environment (including all environmental media, and biological, chemical, aesthetic and socio-economic processes and conditions) at international, regional, national and local levels; by means of formal and informal institutions, processes and mechanisms embedded in and mandated by law, so as to promote the common present and future interests human beings hold in the environment.[40]

This definition suggests that law is the foundation for environmental governance and that environmental governance would be illegitimate if it were not provided for and mandated by law. It is anthropocentric with its emphasis on human interests, and it views environmental governance as a management process with an institutional character in which state and non-state actors aim to regulate human activities and their effects on the environment by means of a myriad of mechanisms. Environmental governance in these terms is also multi-level. It could be formal, informal or both, and it aims to address common environmental interests and issues of this and future generations. It therefore has a distinctly temporal element in addition to spatial characteristics. The definition also takes a broad view of the environment as including everything that people perceive to be the environment. The definition stresses that environmental governance is not so much aimed at governing (or managing, as I understood it then) the environment as an object *per se*. Environmental governance focuses rather on governing human behaviour (*inter se*) that might have environmental impacts, and human behaviour that affects the environment. It therefore departs from the 'environment as object of environmental governance' approach which is based on the ideas of those

---

[40] Kotzé, Louis J. (2009), 'Environmental Governance' in Alexander Paterson and Louis J. Kotzé (eds), *Environmental Compliance and Enforcement in South Africa: Legal Perspectives*, Cape Town: Juta, 107–108. See also, Kotzé, Louis J. (2010), 'Towards a Tentative Legal Formulation of Environmental Governance' in Tuula Honkonen and Ed Couzens (eds), *International Environmental Law-making and Diplomacy Review 2009*, UNEP Course series 9, Joensuu, Finland: University of Eastern Finland, 3–20.

who understand governance to be 'any attempt to control or manage any known object', where a '"known object" is an event, a relationship, an animate object, an inanimate object, [or] any phenomenon which human beings try to control or manage'.[41] My earlier definition is based instead on the 'human beings and human behaviour as objects of environmental governance' approach.

Collectively considered, the foregoing descriptions suggest that environmental governance is a normative institutional regulatory intervention and social construct that is predominantly based on law and that aims to influence how people interact with the environment. It entails a pluralistic, dynamic, multi-level, multi-actor response and process of change which pragmatically aims to change human behaviour vis-à-vis the environment, and idealistically to optimize environmental benefits and use, while at the same time seeking to protect and preserve sufficient environmental capital for present and future generations.

4. LEGAL DOCTRINAL ASPECTS OF GLOBAL ENVIRONMENTAL GOVERNANCE

Law plays a decidedly important, even manifestly predominant role in global environmental governance. This is not to say, however, that other types of law-like rules and institutions such as economics and religion do not also contribute to this effort. On the contrary, '[F]acing the challenges of global environmental change is more than a political and legal problem.'[42] The perspective of this enquiry, however, is a legal one, and mindful of the non-exclusive role of law and the increased prominence of 'softer' law-like norms in global environmental governance (which are further investigated in Chapter 8) this section provides some views on the legal doctrinal aspects of environmental governance.

Godden and Peel[43] describe environmental governance from a domestic point of view as 'the complex of legislation, legal rules and principles derived from statutes and case law sitting within a framework of policy, institutional

---

41 Hunt, Alan and Gary Wickham (1994), *Foucault and the Law: Towards a Sociology of Law as Governance*, London: Pluto Press, 78.

42 Brand, Karl-Werner and Fritz Reusswig (2006), 'The Social Embeddedness of Global Environmental Governance' in Gerd Winter (ed), *Multilevel Governance of Global Environmental Change: Perspectives from Science, Sociology, and the Law*, Cambridge: Cambridge University Press, 79.

43 Godden, Lee and Jacqueline Peel (2010), *Environmental Law: Scientific, Policy and Regulatory Dimensions*, Melbourne: Oxford University Press, 61.

and social structures that together have a major influence upon the directions of change in environmental law'. They add that '[I]n essence, governance is concerned with the interface between people and the state institutions and structures (including legal rules) that govern those people within defined ambits' and 'environmental governance, and indeed environmental law, is concerned with influencing environmental behaviour and decision making'.[44] They situate law and policy in the governance paradigm as follows:

> As our conception of the environment has evolved, this has created momentum for transformations in the broader frameworks of law, policy and social structures that for convenience, rather than more precise articulation, we have designated as governance. Different models of governance thus provide a significant framework affecting the manner in which the human-environment interrelationship is conceived.[45]

They see environmental governance thus as consisting of a legal framework (including harder and softer forms of law) contained in a broader policy, institutional and social setting. Environmental governance is the sum of this legal and socio-institutional framework, which cumulatively aims to influence the manner in which people approach and respond to the human-environment interface and relationship on the one hand and on the other, the behaviour and decision-making processes which might affect the environment. Their description further suggests that law performs a specific function in the broader socio-institutional setting, namely that 'it provides the legal means for managing and regulating the environment'.[46]

An equally legalistic view is proffered by Stephens,[47] who states that:

---

44 Godden, Lee and Jacqueline Peel (2010), *Environmental Law: Scientific, Policy and Regulatory Dimensions*, Melbourne: Oxford University Press, 62.

45 Godden, Lee and Jacqueline Peel (2010), *Environmental Law: Scientific, Policy and Regulatory Dimensions*, Melbourne: Oxford University Press, 83.

46 Godden, Lee and Jacqueline Peel (2010), *Environmental Law: Scientific, Policy and Regulatory Dimensions*, Melbourne: Oxford University Press, 15. The notion that law provides part of the foundation of environmental governance and that law acts in tandem with institutions in addressing environmental problems, is supported by the Global Ministerial Environment Forum, which states in the Malmö Ministerial Declaration that: '[T]he evolving framework of international environmental law and the development of national law provide a sound basis for addressing the major environmental threats of the day. It must be underpinned by a more coherent and coordinated approach among international environmental instruments.' Global Ministerial Environment Forum, *Malmö Ministerial Declaration 2000* available at http://www.unep.org/malmo/malmo_ministerial.htm [accessed 16 March 2011].

47 Stephens, Tim (2009), *International Courts and Environmental Protection*, Cambridge: Cambridge University Press, 7.

> International environmental governance may be described as the way in which rules of environmental law are developed, applied, and enforced. It is an ongoing process in which norms and structures are transformed over time in response to the changing needs of international society.

International environmental governance in his view is thus a dynamic process that is centrally concerned with law creation, interpretation, application, and enforcement.

Scanlon and Burhenne-Guilmin[48] state that the primary purpose of international environmental law is 'to provide international governance for environmental and natural resources conservation'. They even speak of 'international environmental law governance'. In their view it is the different sources of international environmental law and international environmental law itself 'which each generate elements of international governance'. Because these sources differ (ranging from hard to soft law), the mandatory nature of the elements of international governance will also vary accordingly. Soft law instruments thus provide guiding elements of governance, while treaties and international customary law provide more powerful, binding and mandatory obligations. While it is unclear what the authors mean by 'international governance elements', considering the strong legal doctrinal context in which they use the term, they presumably intend it to refer to treaty regimes, subsequent organizations, and all actors, processes and mechanisms in terms of these regimes on the one hand and on the other, all 'softer' regulatory arrangements (such as guidelines), which would also include the involvement of non-state actors. In other words, the elements of international environmental governance arguably are those institutions resulting from law and legal processes. In this sense, environmental governance, and indeed global environmental governance is a product of (environmental) law.

While law today by no means exclusively constitutes the normative foundation of environmental governance, as part of the greater normative rubric in the globalized context, it does remain the primary normative and rule-providing basis for environmental governance. A more hardcore, doctrinal legal approach to environmental governance is thus neither incorrect nor undesirable. It is an approach that one would typically expect to find in the company of lawyers, but it can be valid only insofar as it also acknowledges the important functions that other normative arrangements play in global environmental governance including, for example, 'softer' law-like rules, information shar-

48 Scanlon, John and Francoise Burhenne-Guilmin (2004), 'Executive Summary' in John Scanlon and Francoise Burhenne-Guilmin (eds), *International Environmental Governance: An International Regime for Protected Areas*, Gland, Switzerland and Cambridge: IUCN, 3.

ing, capacity building, politics, economics, communication and ethics. In fact, while multilateral environmental agreements arguably play the most important normative role in global environmental governance, '[T]he concern of international environmental governance is broader than MEAs [multilateral environmental agreements]. It seeks to maximize environmental improvements from all the organizations and processes established by the international community.'[49] In its search to do so it will employ law and a range of other types of rules to influence human behaviour with respect to the environment. Chapter 8 further elaborates on the role of law and its increasing plurality in global environmental governance.

5. MULTI-ACTOR ASPECTS OF GLOBAL ENVIRONMENTAL GOVERNANCE

Globalization has given rise to a widely diversified array of state and non-state actors that are involved in global governance.[50] These include states and domestic state actors, supra-national state actors such as intergovernmental organizations, and domestic and supra-national non-state actors such as networks and NGOs, among others. The authority through which these actors act in the global domain is either public (state) or private (non-state). Where state and non-state actors act together in global environmental governance, as they generally do, one could speak of a hybrid form of authority which is both public and private. It is thus possible to typify environmental governance as being either public, private or both. The public-private distinction is traditionally used in international relations theory to conceptualize authority in world politics. It denotes the involvement of state and non-state actors in governance respectively. Although some argue that the divide has become obsolete in the light of the disaggregation of global governance, the divide still provides a useful way of distinguishing between the types of actors involved in global (environmental) governance.[51] The following sections explore the public, private and hybrid aspects of global environmental governance with a view to understanding the multi-actor dimensions thereof.

---

49 Steiner, Achim, Lee A. Kimball and John Scanlon (2003), 'Global Governance for the Environment and the Role of Multilateral Environmental Agreements in Conservation', *Oryx*, **37**(2), 227–37 at 228.

50 See Chapter 4 for a detailed discussion.

51 See, for example, Pattberg, Philipp and Johannes Stripple (2008), 'Beyond the Public and Private Divide: Remapping Transnational Climate Governance in the 21st Century', *International Environmental Agreements*, **8**, 367–88 at 371–2.

5.1 Public Global Environmental Governance

States, through their 'representatives of governments who claim the legal authority to take authoritative decisions in international institutions',[52] are the principal actors in global environmental governance. The reason for this lies in the nature of the state and the manner in which the state is perceived in society:

> ... the modern state is a product of territorial thinking. It is by definition an autonomous part of the earth wherein citizens openly declare their independence from other parts and from the planetary whole. Although it is ecologically untenable to conceive of sovereign parts in an interdependent world, the concept has managed to flourish in its secular form since at least the Treaty of Westphalia in 1648. The need to manage and coordinate large populations, economic trade, and technological innovation has seemingly cemented the nation-state as the ultimate successor to tribal, feudal, and city-state forms of political organization. Because of its amazing capacity for organized power and geopolitical differentiation, the state has become the most widely accepted instrument of group identity outside of the family.[53]

Yet, despite its central importance, today it is increasingly difficult to find proponents who advocate outright that states (should) play the only role in global environmental governance.[54] Most authors have instead noted the changing role of the state and the increasing move towards decentralized and 'plural' or hybrid global environmental governance, the steady and increased inclusion of a whole range of non-state actors, and the creation of new participative global civil society environmental governance, or private environmen-

---

52 Haas, Peter M. (1995), 'Global Environmental Governance' in Commission on Global Governance, *Issues in Global Governance*, London: Kluwer Law International, 340.

53 Hempel, Lamont C. (1996), *Environmental Governance: The Global Challenge*, Washington: Island Press, 156.

54 Strand's view probably comes closest to a pure, public environmental governance approach in which the state plays the primary role in global environmental governance:

> ... we can think of international organizations as manifestations of legal accords among states. The agreements entered into by governments lay the foundation for governance as well as broad policy mandates such as development. By 'governance' is meant how institutions comprised of sovereign states arrive at decisions concerning what actions will be taken and the means to implement such actions.

Strand, Jonathan R. (2004), 'The Case for Regional Environmental Organizations' in Norichika Kanie and Peter M. Haas (eds), *Emerging Forces in Environmental Governance*, Tokyo: United Nations University Press, 80.

tal governance.[55] This might mean that if the concept public environmental governance primarily entails 'environmental governance by the state and its institutions', then the concept of public environmental governance has become obsolete, and that the Westphalian emphasis on the state in global environmental governance is an orthodox construct which belongs to the past. Considering the considerable appeal of hybrid private-public forms of global environmental governance, where the state is only one among many other actors, one could conceivably be moved to accept the legitimacy of this argument. Yet, as Marauhn[56] (justifiably in my view) points out:

> ... doubts regarding the role of the state should not be overdrawn. On the one hand, as a descriptive matter, the state is much less in decline than is often claimed. On the other hand, from a normative perspective, it must be asked whether an early demise of the state would not destabilize the international legal order and entail more problems than benefits. In the environmental and in other contexts when states have indeed 'failed' they have not been replaced by meaningful and effective local, regional, or supranational actors.

While Marauhn[57] does not advocate state-centred public environmental governance, he does remind us that the state has a central yet increasingly difficult role to fulfil in tackling environmental issues beyond its borders and spheres of direct influence:

---

55 Mori, for example, pleads as follows: '[N]o matter what new framework for global environmental governance is designed, it should not be another organization mandated solely by states.' Mori, Satoko (2004), 'Institutionalization of NGO Involvement in Policy Functions for Global Environmental Governance' in Norichika Kanie and Peter M. Haas (eds), *Emerging Forces in Environmental Governance*, Tokyo: United Nations University Press, 157. Ellis and Wood assert:

> The role of the state in international society has changed dramatically, with some commentators arguing that the state is becoming increasingly irrelevant in the face of international economic forces. One of the implications of this from the point of view of the environment is that states may be losing their ability to establish and implement environmental policies.

Ellis, Jaye and Stepan Wood (2006), 'International Environmental Law' in Benjamin J. Richardson and Stepan Wood (eds), *Environmental Law for Sustainability: A Reader*, Portland: Hart Publishing, 344–5.

56 Marauhn, Thilo (2007), 'Changing Role of the State' in Daniel Bodansky, Jutta Brunnée and Ellen Hey (eds), *The Oxford Handbook of International Environmental Law*, Oxford: Oxford University Press, 728.

57 Marauhn, Thilo (2007), 'Changing Role of the State' in Daniel Bodansky, Jutta Brunnée and Ellen Hey (eds), *The Oxford Handbook of International Environmental Law*, Oxford: Oxford University Press, 728–9.

> ... the state remains a truly important actor in international relations. It forms part of international governance, which has become multilevel governance ... Today, states have to find their place within a complex environmental governance structure, which is based on a multitude of international environmental agreements, integrates a broad variety of actors, and extends across multiple and differing layers of governance, depending on the environmental problem at hand.

This explanation is instructive because it illustrates the point that in tandem with a variety of non-state actors, the state continues to play a dominant role in global environmental governance. Marauhn's perspective also suggests a progressive terminological development and a move from 'international governance' to 'multilevel governance'. Thus, whereas the state in the past was the sole actor in international environmental governance, today the state is only one among many such actors in a multi-level and multi-actor setting.

It is in this context that we must ask if 'pure' public environmental governance still has a legitimate place in modern global environmental governance discourse. The assertion that the state will continue to play the predominant role in global environmental governance means that it has, but only to the extent that public environmental governance, as a concept, is used to describe the role of the state in the greater framework of global environmental governance which, as a cumulative and all-encompassing phenomenon, cannot exclusively focus on the role of the state in a globalized reality. The important role of the state in global environmental governance cannot be ignored and the state will not diminish (by all realistic accounts, at least not soon). The state remains the steering force in global environmental governance, if not through the intervention and predominant role of states themselves very directly, then at least indirectly through the range of institutional arrangements which serve as vehicles by means of which states can exert influence, power and authority in global environmental matters. Nevertheless, the realities of globalization mean that public environmental governance in the global context cannot continue in a manner that pronounces the predominant role of the state in a Leviathan sense:

> Clearly, a new relationship is emerging between the regulatory state and the objects of its social-regulatory efforts, but the state remains importantly implicated in the outcomes of these transformations. The techniques and practices deployed in pursuit of particular regulatory objectives are shifting, but the state frequently remains implicated in the broader regulatory scheme of things, now, however, 'governing from a distance' through a dispersion of expertise.[58]

---

[58] Purvis, Trevor (2002), 'Regulation, Governance, and the State: Reflections on the Transformation of Regulatory Practices in Late-Modern Liberal Democracies' in Michael MacNeil, Neil Sargent and Peter Swan (eds), *Law, Regulation and Governance*, Oxford: Oxford University Press, 31.

Thus, in a post-Westphalian world globalization refocuses our attention on the important yet gradually changing role that the state, in addition to a wide range of other actors, is playing in global environmental governance.

5.2 Private Global Environmental Governance

It is now generally accepted that a broader concept of global environmental governance allows for it to be private, meaning that global environmental governance has not only a public, state-centred character, as was shown in the previous section, but also a very distinct private character, where a wide variety of non-state actors play an increasingly significant role alongside the state. It is the involvement of non-state actors in global environmental governance which makes it 'private', and this manifestation of global environmental governance is popularly referred to as private environmental governance.[59]

More specifically, private environmental governance is a form of environmental governance where there is no or little state authority, or the state is not the dominant form of political authority.[60] It instead envisages a more pronounced or dominant role for non-state actors including, for example, NGOs, corporate actors such as MNCs,[61] the scientific community, epistemic communities, the media, and entities nestled in the global civil society paradigm. These non-state actors are increasingly playing a significant role in a

---

[59] Levy, David L. and Peter J. Newell (2005), 'Introduction' in David L. Levy and Peter J. Newell (eds), *The Business of Global Environmental Governance*, Cambridge, Massachusetts: MIT Press, 7. The authors cite the ISO 14000 EMSs as an example of private environmental governance arrangements. Falkner sees private environmental governance as an 'important instrument in the political toolbox of global civil society in its efforts to promote environmental sustainability'. Falkner, Robert (2003), 'Private Environmental Governance and International Relations: Exploring the Links', *Global Environmental Politics*, **3**(2), 72–87 at 74.

[60] Newell, Peter J. (2005), 'Business and International Environmental Governance: The State of the Art' in David L. Levy and Peter J. Newell (eds), *The Business of Global Environmental Governance*, Cambridge, Massachusetts: MIT Press, 29. For a discussion on the role of non-state actors in global environmental governance from an international relations perspective, see also Auer, M.R. (2000), 'Who Participates in Global Environmental Governance? Partial Answers from International Relations Theory', *Policy Sciences*, **33**, 155–80.

[61] Bernstein sees the involvement of non-state actors in global environmental governance, and specifically corporations, as part of the world-wide response to globalization and the perpetuation of a development-oriented policy based on liberal environmentalism where the promotion of economic growth is paramount and the environment only a secondary consideration. Bernstein, Steven (2005), 'Globalization and the Requirements of "Good" Environmental Governance', *Perspectives on Global Development and Technology*, **4**(3/4), 645–79 at 660.

globalized era where the state is thought to have lost some of its absolute authority and direct control over various functions.[62] The move towards private governance has been motivated *inter alia* by the devolution of tasks to private organizations; formal decentralization; the establishment of independent, parallel and autonomous centres of governance authority; greater social and economic interdependence between formerly detached spheres of government; and the expansion of the mandates and roles of international organizations.[63] Non-state actors' increased roles and influence specifically relate to the non-official implementation of official policy, the non-official participation in official policy-making, and the non-official formulation of regulatory instruments, for instance.[64]

The foregoing does not imply that because private environmental governance is usually exercised by private parties it has no authority at all. It is simply a different form of authority when compared with the coercive nature of state authority, and private actors are still able to 'produce deep social changes across national boundaries instead of being limited to negotiations with governments within a nation state'.[65] As Pattberg[66] explains:

---

[62] Clapp, Jennifer (2005), 'The Privatization of Global Environmental Governance: ISO 14000 and the Developing World' in David L. Levy and Peter J. Newell (eds), *The Business of Global Environmental Governance*, Cambridge, Massachusetts: MIT Press, 227. Rhodes calls this the 'hollowing out of the state' which includes, *inter alia*, increased privatization and the limitation of the scope and forms of public intervention; the loss of state-centred governance functions to other non-state agencies; and the imposition of increased limits on public officials by new public management. Rhodes, Rod A.W. (1996), 'The New Governance: Governance without Government', *Political Studies*, **XLIV**, 652–67 at 661. See also Chapter 2 on the 'hollowed-out state'.

[63] Von Benda-Beckmann, Franz, Keebet Von Benda-Beckmann and Julia Eckert (2009), 'Rules of Law and Laws of Ruling: Law and Governance between Past and Future' in Franz Von Benda-Beckmann, Keebet Von Benda-Beckmann and Julia Eckert (eds), *Rules of Law and Laws of Ruling: on the Governance of Law*, Farnham: Ashgate, 5–6; Liverman, Diana (2004), 'Who Governs, at What Scale and at What Price? Geography, Environmental Governance, and the Commodification of Nature', *Annals of the Association of American Geographers*, **94**(4), 734–8 at 735.

[64] Scholte, Jan Aart (2000), *Globalization: A Critical Introduction*, London: Macmillan Press, 151–6. In addition to being activists, private actors can, for example, also join governments to enforce normative provisions and negotiate their own standards. Biermann, Frank *et al.* (2010), 'Earth System Governance: A Research Framework', *International Environmental Agreements: Politics, Law and Economics*, **10**(4), 277–98 at 282–3.

[65] Lemos, Maria Carmen and Arun Agrawal (2006), 'Environmental Governance', *Annual Review of Environment and Resources*, **31**, 297–325 at 300.

[66] Pattberg, Philipp (2005), 'What Role for Private Rule-making in Global Environmental Governance? Analysing the Forest Stewardship Council (FSC)', *International Environmental Agreements*, **5**, 175–89 at 176.

> They [private actors] have gone from being an intervening variable of the international system to establishing rules [such as codes of conduct, management standards, and certified product labels] that exist mainly outside it. Consequently, private authority is considered to be different from public authority, because the latter derives mainly from the possibility of coercion, whereas the former is based on persuasion.

The authority that arises from private actors in global environmental governance is therefore best described as moral authority of a persuasive nature.

Private environmental governance exudes a definite vertical character because it 'interacts with other processes such as economic globalization to produce simultaneous shifts of authority from the state to other arenas'.[67] Private environmental governance could therefore be described as having multi-level governance characteristics; an issue to which the chapter returns below.[68] Global environmental governance is also sometimes described in this private, multi-level context as being 'deterritorialized' and non-hierarchical:

> Deterritorialised governance tends to be based on transnational networks of actors, reflecting a general conception that contemporary global social change is best understood in terms of the emergent dominance of network forms of social organization. Both private business actors and social movements organize themselves in terms of networks rather than hierarchies, with such networks able to bypass hierarchical forms of organization like states and traditional business hierarchies.[69]

Deterritorialized, multi-level environmental governance is obviously a complex phenomenon which must be understood in the context of increased global governance complexity, or what Haas and Haas[70] call the global *problématique*,

---

[67] Paterson, Matthew, David Humphreys and Lloyd Pettiford (2003), 'Conceptualizing Global Environmental Governance: From Interstate Regimes to Counter-hegemonic Struggles', *Global Environmental Politics*, **3**(2), 1–10 at 5.

[68] Beyerlin, Ulrich and Thilo Marauhn (2011), *International Environmental Law*, Oxford: Hart Publishers, 261–2; Paterson, Matthew, David Humphreys and Lloyd Pettiford (2003), 'Conceptualizing Global Environmental Governance: From Interstate Regimes to Counter-hegemonic Struggles', *Global Environmental Politics*, **3**(2), 1–10 at 6.

[69] Paterson, Matthew, David Humphreys and Lloyd Pettiford (2003), 'Conceptualizing Global Environmental Governance: From Interstate Regimes to Counter-hegemonic Struggles', *Global Environmental Politics*, **3**(2), 1–10 at 6.

[70] Haas, Peter M. and Ernst B. Haas (1995), 'Learning to Learn: Improving International Governance', *Global Governance*, **1**, 255–85 at 255. The authors state elsewhere that '[W]e live in the presence of the global *problematique*. Whoever is concerned with the interplay of resource use, population growth, processes of democratization, the desire for higher living standards and a better quality of life for all, and the management of civil and interstate conflict is engulfed by it.' Haas, Peter M. and Ernst B. Haas (1995), 'Learning to Learn: Improving International Governance', *Global Governance*, **1**, 255–85 at 258.

which refers to the complex, dynamic and deepening 'intertwined and interdependent dimension of contemporary international existence'. Private global environmental governance is thus, at least in part, a result of and a response to increased global complexity, an increase in the scope and depth of environmental problems, and a multiplication of the appropriate levels and actors attempting to address these problems.

Private global environmental governance is determined not only by the type of actors and levels involved, but also by the type of environmental governance mechanism that is used.[71] In addition to the traditional state-centred environmental governance mechanisms of laws, policies and judicial dispute resolution, a host of self-regulatory or non-state environmental governance mechanisms have evolved and are themselves becoming drivers of private environmental governance.[72] Perez[73] states:

> Over the last years the field of transnational environmental governance has changed its face. The field, which was once dominated by treaty-based mechanisms, is now populated by numerous private schemes with significant transnational reach. These new instruments, which include voluntary corporate codes, environmental management systems, 'green label' schemes, environmental reporting standards, green financing schemes and green indexes, have taken an increasingly important role in the project of transnational environmental regulation.

Perez[74] views private environmental governance as an important emerging 'transnational phenomenon', a 'new form of global authority', and a 'new universe' which 'constitutes an intensely inter-connected network of governance' which, together with its private actor-centred environmental governance mechanisms, is changing the way transnational environmental regulation (presumably meaning global environmental governance) is occurring.

---

71 For a generic discussion of governance mechanisms see Kooiman, Jan (2003), *Governing as Governance*, London: Sage Publications Limited, 45–61.

72 See also Chapter 5.

73 Perez, Oren (2010), *Private Environmental Governance as Ensemble Regulation: A Critical Exploration of Sustainable Business Indexes and the New Ensemble Politics* (Theoretical Inquiries in Law, Forthcoming; Bar Ilan Univ. Pub Law Working Paper November 2010) at 3 [available at http://papers.ssrn.com/sol3/papers.cfm?abstract_id=1710639] [accessed 14 March 2011].

74 Perez, Oren (2010), *Private Environmental Governance as Ensemble Regulation: A Critical Exploration of Sustainable Business Indexes and the New Ensemble Politics* (Theoretical Inquiries in Law, Forthcoming; Bar Ilan Univ. Pub Law Working Paper November 2010) at 3; 33 [available at http://papers.ssrn.com/sol3/papers.cfm?abstract_id=1710639] [accessed 14 March 2011].

'Global civil society' is a frequently recurring theme in recent global governance literature and one which often surfaces in the private environmental governance context.[75] It seems to be used as a collective term to include all non-state actors that could be involved with private global environmental governance. In the environmental context, the involvement of global civil society in global environmental governance is resulting in an asserted justification and grounding of private environmental governance, because it is fundamentally changing traditional Westphalian conceptions of state-centred global governance in an era of globalization. Global civil society is described as a rising 'amorphous yet analytically distinct sphere ... in which people can collectively express their aspirations and pursue joint enterprises independent of their association with a particular state and outside the direct purview of the state system'.[76] Global civil society's contribution to private environmental governance therefore lies therein that most environmental problems transcend national borders, and where nation-states are ill-equipped, unwilling or unable to address these, global civil society can step in to regulate global environmental issues insofar as this is possible.[77] Global civil society would endeavour to achieve its objectives and participate in global environmental governance mainly through institutional constructs such as networks and private international organizations such as NGOs. Wapner[78] defines global civil society as 'that domain of associational life situated above the individual and below the state [which] is made up of complex networks based on interest, ideology, family, and cultural affinity through which people pursue various aims'. It is these networks created by global civil society actors which are

---

75 For a more general discussion of the concept civil society, and specifically the relationship between civil society and the state, see among others Branna, Tessa (2007), 'From "Antipolitics" to "Anti-politics": What Became of East European "Civil Society"?', *East European Human Rights Review*, **13**(2), 225–370; Blanco, Elena and Jona Razzaque (2011), *Globalisation and Natural Resources Law: Challenges, Key Issues and Perspectives*, Cheltenham: Edward Elgar Publishing, 235–50.

76 Wapner, Paul (1997), 'Governance in Global Civil Society' in Oran R. Young (ed), *Global Governance: Drawing Insights from the Environmental Experience*, Cambridge, Massachusetts: MIT Press, 66.

77 Wapner, Paul (1997), 'Governance in Global Civil Society' in Oran R. Young (ed), *Global Governance: Drawing Insights from the Environmental Experience*, Cambridge, Massachusetts: MIT Press, 65.

78 Wapner, Paul (1997), 'Governance in Global Civil Society' in Oran R. Young (ed), *Global Governance: Drawing Insights from the Environmental Experience*, Cambridge, Massachusetts: MIT Press, 65. See also Guruswamy, Lakshman D. (2002), 'Cartography of Governance: an Introduction', *Colorado Journal of International Environmental Law and Policy*, **13**(1), 1–13 at 3.

their most striking and defining architectural feature.[79] It may be worth remembering that Chapter 4 demonstrated that networks are an integral institutional arrangement and part of the greater global governance rubric because they provide the means for global civil society to exercise influence well beyond the traditional confines of the nation-state and to govern where the state is unable or unwilling to govern.

Allowing global civil society to actively take part in global environmental governance increases the legitimacy of the entire environmental governance effort and addresses apathy, thereby raising general political support.[80] It could also foster greater legitimacy of civil society and non-state actors themselves in global environmental governance. In fact, one of the most contentious issues regarding the participation of non-state actors in global environmental governance is that of their legitimacy, and the rise of non-state actors in global environmental governance is leading to a resurgence of the debate about legitimacy in global environmental law and governance.[81] The increasingly popular field of global administrative and institutional law attests to this increased focus.[82] Concerns about legitimacy will arguably only deepen as the global environmental governance regime further disaggregates into a plural multi-actor and multi-layered mass of institutional arrangements. As Perez[83] states: 'as more and more powers are transferred from state level to transnational level, the detachment between these global legal networks and

---

[79] Auer, M.R. (2000), 'Who Participates in Global Environmental Governance? Partial Answers from International Relations Theory', *Policy Sciences*, **33**, 155–80 at 163.

[80] Hierlmeier, Jodie (2002), 'UNEP: Retrospect and Prospect – Options for Reforming the Global Environmental Governance Regime', *Georgetown International Environmental Law Review*, **14**, 767–805 at 802. For an extensive discussion on the issue of legitimacy in global environmental governance, see among others Bodansky, Daniel (1999), 'The Legitimacy of International Governance: A Coming Challenge for International Environmental Law?', *American Journal of International Law*, **93**(3), 596–624.

[81] Alkoby, Asher (2003), 'Non-state Actors and the Legitimacy of International Environmental Law', *Non-state Actors and International Law*, **3**. 23–98.

[82] Harlow, Carol (2006), 'Global Administrative Law: the Quest for Principles and Values', *European Journal of International Law*, **17**(1), 187–214; Kingsbury, Benedict (2005), 'Global Governance as Administration: National and Transnational Approaches to Global Administrative Law', *Law and Contemporary Problems*, **68**, 1–13; Von Bogdandy, Armin *et al.* (eds) (2010), *The Exercise of Public Authority by International Institutions: Advancing International Institutional Law*, Heidelberg: Springer Verlag.

[83] Perez, Oren (2004), 'The Many Faces of the Trade-Environment Conflict: Some Lessons for the Constitutionalisation Project' in Christian Joerges, Inger-Johanne Sand and Gunther Teubner (eds), *Transnational Governance and Constitutionalism*, Oregon: Hart Publishing, 241.

the traditional sources of legitimacy – the nation, the cultural unit – is becoming more problematical. The result is a deepening legitimacy crisis.' Commentators have proposed some solutions to this legitimacy crisis including, among others, democratization, the integration of fragmented regimes, and the creation of a world environment organization. These proposed solutions, however, are not without their own difficulties, and they seem to have garnered little general appeal to date.[84]

Nevertheless, the foregoing analysis suggests that those who shun non-state actors and their increasingly important contribution to global environmental governance will do so at their peril. While the state remains the primary actor, the pluralistic transformation of state-centred global environmental governance resonates well with contemporary notions of governance in a globalized age. The involvement of non-state actors is arguably set to increase as global environmental problems become more complex and increasingly require a more diversified and comprehensive response from a hybrid of state and non-state actors.

5.3 Hybrid Global Environmental Governance

With respect to the type of actors involved, Levy and Newell[85] see global environmental governance as a continuum, which ranges between two extremes:

> ... on one extreme, overly rigid structural accounts that adduce overarching power to multinational capital or dominant states, and on the other side, pluralist approaches that presume a rough equivalence among actors and neglect the systematic asymmetries that flow from wider political economic structures.

These two extremes (public versus private) suggest that there must be some middle ground between them where a mixture of private and public is made possible through the equal involvement of state and non-state actors in global environmental governance. It was shown above that the notion of private

---

[84] See, among others, Swart, Lydia and Estelle Perry (eds) (2007), *Global Environmental Governance: Perspectives on the Current Debate*, New York: Centre for UN Reform Education; Chambers, Bradnee W. and Jessica F. Green (eds) (2005), *Reforming International Environmental Governance: From Institutional Limits to Innovative Reforms*, Tokyo: United Nations University Press; and Bodansky, Daniel (1999), 'The Legitimacy of International Governance: A Coming Challenge for International Environmental Law?', *American Journal of International Law*, **93**(3), 596–624.

[85] Levy, David L. and Peter J. Newell (2005), 'Introduction' in David L. Levy and Peter J. Newell (eds), *The Business of Global Environmental Governance*, Cambridge, Massachusetts: MIT Press, 9.

environmental governance is tempered by the inevitable role of the state in global environmental governance; so too is the notion of 'pure' public environmental governance considerably diluted by the involvement of non-state actors. In other words, contemporary notions of global environmental governance cannot realistically exclude either one of these types of actors:

> The development of a governance perspective involves recognizing the roles of supra-national and subnational state and nonstate actors, and the complex interactions between them, in the process of governing. Such an approach is particularly relevant in the context of global environmental issues, where modes of governing are multiple and include processes and institutions that traverse scales as well as networks of actors that cannot be easily characterized by the state/nonstate dichotomy.[86]

The arguments in the previous sections for the continued focus on the involvement of the state as the principal actor in governance affairs justifiably leads to a more balanced construction of global environmental governance, where the elements of private environmental governance will play a crucial role alongside those strongly cemented and traditional elements of public environmental governance. As far as the locus of authority and type of actors are concerned, hybrid public-private environmental governance is emerging as the current approach in global environmental governance. While it primarily relies on cooperation between state and non-state actors, it does not necessarily entail only direct cooperation between these actors with respect to governance issues. While direct cooperation is certainly not excluded, hybrid public-private governance also points to the many ways in which state and non-state actors co-exist, cooperate and combine functions to solve common issues.[87]

---

[86] Betsill, Michelle M. and Harriet Bulkeley (2006), 'Cities and the Multilevel Governance of Global Climate Change', *Global Governance*, **12**, 141–59 at 144.

[87] Mayntz notes that such cooperation (*Zusammenwirken*) entails much more than mere direct cooperation between state and non-state actors. Cooperation in the governance context rather presupposes co-existing regulatory arrangements that range from the purely state-oriented to the non-state oriented:

> 'Zusammenwirken' heißt aber nicht, dass kollektive Sachverhalte nur in direkter Kooperation von staatlichen und nicht-staatlichen Akteuren stattfänden ... Governance im modernen Staat besteht vielmehr aus dem Neben-und Miteinander von Regelungsformen, die von rein staatlichen bis hin zu rein zivilgesellschaftlichen reichen.

Mayntz, Renate (2004), 'Governance im modernen Staat' in Arthur Benz (ed), *Governance- Regieren in komplexen Regelsystemen: Eine Einführung*, Wiesbaden, Germany: VS Verlag für Sozialwissenschaften, 68.

The rise in the number of public-private partnerships in global environmental governance is an example of this trend, which could ultimately prove to be beneficial to the collective hybrid global environmental governance effort as it establishes reciprocal and mutually reinforcing partnerships between state and non-state parties that work towards a shared goal.[88] Bernstein,[89] for example, states that '[P]artnerships work under the assumption that combining the resources, skills, and commitment of non-state actors with the authority of states will succeed where state action has not.' Another example of hybrid environmental governance is the existence of global environmental organizations which are themselves to some extent hybrid. The World Conservation Union (IUCN) is an example of a hybrid environmental governance organization which consists of state and non-state actors.

Hybrid governance in the foregoing sense constitutes what Kooiman[90] calls 'co-governance' or 'co-management':

> Co-management, by definition, means that government agencies and [private] users share responsibility for the well-being of the [natural] resource, such as preventing depletion or illness. Co-management tries to steer a middle course between government regulation and community-initiated regulation, as it requires users to organise themselves formally. Organisation is participatory rather than hierarchical, it is decentralised rather than centralised ... typical interplay forms of interaction take place among the actors.

Hybrid global environmental governance is a trend manifestly embedded in the globalization rhetoric, and its prevalence is evidence of the need to transcend or to 'move beyond the state' and to succeed in achieving the goals of global environmental governance where the state alone is unable or unwilling to act. As some commentators remark:

> Many of these [contemporary social] changes affect the normative and empirical boundaries between private and public authority and responsibility that were previously taken for granted, at least according to the social-democratic European canon of state tasks of the twentieth century ... All over the world, under the recent conditions of globalization, we seem to face a proliferation of fully privatized and hybrid

---

88 Klijn, Erik-Hans and Geert R. Teisman (2000), 'Managing Public-Private Partnerships: Influencing Processes and Institutional Context of Public-Private Partnerships' in Oscar Van Heffen, Walter J.M. Kickert and Jacques J.A. Thomassen (eds), *Governance in Modern Society: Effects, Change and Formation of Government Institutions*, Dordrecht: Kluwer Academic Publishers, 329–48.

89 Bernstein, Steven (2005), 'Globalization and the Requirements of "Good" Environmental Governance', *Perspectives on Global Development and Technology*, **4**(3/4), 645–79 at 669.

90 Kooiman, Jan (2003), *Governing as Governance*, London: Sage Publications Limited, 102–103.

> governance practices ... in which a variety of agents co-operate and which give rise to the emergence of new constellations of rules authorizing and organizing governance.[91]

In this context, it is not surprising that hybrid public-private governance is also sometimes called multi-actor and multi-level governance.[92] Because the character of hybrid environmental governance is usually determined by the type of actors involved in this effort, one could conceivably also speak of multi-actor or plural global environmental governance. In sum, then, public-private partnerships, networks and modes of co-governance are some examples of governance reforms which 'are aimed at dealing with complex interdependencies and complexity of interorganizational decision making'[93] in a global setting where state and non-state actors are involved in an enmeshed and overlapping global environmental governance effort. Viewed as a whole, global environmental governance has become such a major, diverse and pluralistic enterprise that it would be rare to identify any one instance where state or non-state actors act on their own, or at least are *not* influenced by one another. In this sense, global environmental governance would arguably always be hybrid private-public or multi-actor environmental governance.

6. MULTI-LEVEL ASPECTS OF GLOBAL ENVIRONMENTAL GOVERNANCE

The term 'multi-level governance' is used in literature to describe the diffusion of authority and the creation of new political forms in the globalized era.[94] It

---

91 Von Benda-Beckmann, Franz, Keebet Von Benda-Beckmann and Julia Eckert (2009), 'Rules of Law and Laws of Ruling: Law and Governance between Past and Future' in Franz Von Benda-Beckmann, Keebet Von Benda-Beckmann and Julia Eckert (eds), *Rules of Law and Laws of Ruling: on the Governance of Law*, Farnham: Ashgate, 9.

92 Van Heffen, Oscar, Walter J.M. Kickert and Jacques J.A. Thomassen (2000), 'Introduction: Multi-level and Multi-actor Governance' in Oscar Van Heffen, Walter J.M. Kickert and Jacques J.A. Thomassen (eds), *Governance in Modern Society: Effects, Change and Formation of Government Institutions*, Dordrecht: Kluwer Academic Publishers, 5.

93 Klijn, Erik-Hans and Geert R. Teisman (2000), 'Managing Public-Private Partnerships: Influencing Processes and Institutional Context of Public-Private Partnerships' in Oscar Van Heffen, Walter J.M. Kickert and Jacques J.A. Thomassen (eds), *Governance in Modern Society: Effects, Change and Formation of Government Institutions*, Dordrecht: Kluwer Academic Publishers, 329.

94 For a general discussion of the multi-level governance phenomenon, including its application in the environmental realm, see Bache, Ian and Matthew Flinders

is a term closely related to multi-actor governance and it is often used interchangeably or associated with terms such as multi-tiered governance; multipolar governance; polycentric governance; multi-perspectival governance; functional, overlapping, and competing jurisdictions; 'fragmegration'; and spheres of authority, among others.[95] The central argument behind, justification for, and benefit of multi-level governance is that:

> ... the dispersion of governance across multiple jurisdictions is both more efficient than, and normatively superior to, central state monopoly ... governance must operate at multiple scales in order to capture variations in the territorial reach of policy externalities. Because externalities arising from the provision of public goods vary immensely ... so should the scale of governance. To internalize externalities, governance must be multi-level.[96]

Multi-level governance is also applied in the environmental context in various ways. Its first and most frequent application is to describe sub-national, national, regional and international environmental governance; i.e., environmental governance which occurs at various governance levels.[97] Collectively, these levels all form part of the global domain and manifest as global environmental governance. Global environmental governance is thus necessarily multi-levelled and it denotes a mutually reinforcing and reciprocal multi-level governance arrangement: '[E]ffective national governance underpins sound regional, multilateral, and global governance, and vice-versa. If the capacity for governance is weak at any level, positive results are far less likely.'[98] This manifestation of multi-level governance could also be termed vertical multi-level global environmental governance.

(eds) (2004), *Multi-level Governance*, Oxford: Oxford University Press. Some are critical of the term multi-level governance because it denotes some form of hierarchical structure and thus a certain spread of authority which changes according to the level at which it is exercised. Ladeur, for example, suggests that one should rather speak of multi-polar governance, a term which is less hierarchical and therefore more adequately fits within the primary purport and nature of private governance. Ladeur, Karl-Heinz (2004), 'Globalization and Public Governance: A Contradiction?' in Karl-Heinz Ladeur (ed), *Public Governance in the Age of Globalization*, Aldershot: Ashgate, 15.

95 Marks, Gary and Liesbet Hooge (2004), 'Contrasting Visions of Multi-level Governance' in Ian Bache and Matthew Flinders (eds), *Multi-level Governance*, Oxford: Oxford University Press, 15.

96 Marks, Gary and Liesbet Hooge (2004), 'Contrasting Visions of Multi-level Governance' in Ian Bache and Matthew Flinders (eds), *Multi-level Governance*, Oxford: Oxford University Press, 16.

97 Beyerlin, Ulrich and Thilo Marauhn (2011), *International Environmental Law*, Oxford: Hart Publishing, 244.

98 Steiner, Achim, Lee A. Kimball and John Scanlon (2003), 'Global Governance for the Environment and the Role of Multilateral Environmental Agreements in Conservation', *Oryx*, **37**(2), 227–37 at 227.

Multi-level governance is also used to denote the broad array of varied private and public actors that could be involved in global environmental governance, as was discussed in the previous section.[99] The idea is that specific actors usually operate on specific levels and that one could thus speak of multi-level governance to indicate multiple parties acting on these various levels. While it would probably not be incorrect to speak of multi-level governance in this context, it might be more appropriate to speak of multi-actor or hybrid public-private environmental governance.

Third, multi-level governance could be governance on one level, for instance the international level, but which addresses multiple issues on this level through various institutions which are sector-based:

> Its aim is to design governance mechanisms across levels of social and institutional aggregation. Multilevel governance is intended to counteract the fragmentation that is characteristic of sectorally based decision making or, indeed, of decision making that is organized by territorial, social, and political divisions.[100]

The multi-level character of global environmental governance manifests horizontally here. For example, natural resources are divided into various sectors for the purpose of their regulation, including fauna and flora, biodiversity, migratory species, habitat protection, genetic resources, biosafety, forests and soil. These issue areas or sectors have their own institutional arrangements, including laws and organizations that are most usually embedded in environmental sub-regimes. While these sectoral institutional arrangements exist alongside each other, they could also overlap, but they are nevertheless distinctly identifiable in terms of their different sectors or issue areas. Clearly global governance of natural resources then occurs in a multi-level, 'horizontal' way to the extent that each 'level' addresses several aspects of natural resource protection.

Fourth, multi-level governance is used to describe governance that is connected vertically *and* organized horizontally; it 'draws attention to the importance of considering how political authority and processes of policy-making cross traditional divides between state and nonstate actors, domestic and international spheres' and it is thus concerned with the various tiers of

---

[99] Van Heffen, Oscar, Walter J.M. Kickert and Jacques J.A. Thomassen (2000), 'Introduction: Multi-level and Multi-actor Governance' in Oscar Van Heffen, Walter J.M. Kickert and Jacques J.A. Thomassen (eds), *Governance in Modern Society: Effects, Change and Formation of Government Institutions*, Dordrecht: Kluwer Academic Publishers, 3–5.

[100] Lemos, Maria Carmen and Arun Agrawal (2006), 'Environmental Governance', *Annual Review of Environment and Resources*, **31**, 297–325 at 308.

authority and the different public and private spheres of authority.[101] Some argue that this broader, all-inclusive view of horizontal/vertical multi-level governance has its historical roots in the EU and in the debates on regional integration and governance. Regional environmental governance is thus a perfect example of governance that is simultaneously horizontal and vertical.[102] In the environmental context it manifests as regional environmental governance including, for example, European environmental governance, Southern African environmental governance and North American environmental governance, among others. Vertical/horizontal multi-level governance as regional environmental governance:

> ... posits that decision-making authority is not monopolized by the governments of the member states but is diffused to different levels of decision-making, the sub-national, national and supranational levels ... *Multi-level* thus signifies the interdependence of actors operating at different territorial levels ... while *governance* refers to the growing importance of non-hierarchical forms of policy-making, such as dynamic networks which involve public authorities as well as private actors.[103]

Today the importance of regional environmental governance for global environmental governance is so stark that:

> [N]ew global institutions are unlikely to produce sustainable environmental futures to the extent that they fail to account for regional differences and transformations that affect the drivers and impacts of environmental change and the local political support for national and transnational agreements.[104]

Others have argued that most supra-national environmental problems that global governance typically seeks to regulate first appear regionally.[105]

---

101 Betsill, Michelle M. and Harriet Bulkeley (2006), 'Cities and the Multilevel Governance of Global Climate Change', *Global Governance*, **12**, 141–59 at 149.

102 Fairbrass, Jenny and Andrew Jordan (2004), 'Multi-level Governance and Environmental Policy' in Ian Bache and Matthew Flinders (eds), *Multi-level Governance*, Oxford: Oxford University Press, 147–64.

103 Kohler-Koch, Beate and Berthold Rittberger (2009), 'A Futile Quest for Coherence: The Many Frames of EU Governance' in Beate Kohler-Koch and Fabrice Larat (eds), *European Multi-Level Governance: Contrasting Images in National Research*, Cheltenham: Edward Elgar Publishing, 7–8.

104 Liverman, Diana (2004), 'Who Governs, at What Scale and at What Price? Geography, Environmental Governance, and the Commodification of Nature', *Annals of the Association of American Geographers*, **94**(4), 734–8 at 737.

105 Koh, Kheng-Lian and Nicholas A. Robinson (2002), 'Strengthening Sustainable Development in Regional Inter-governmental Governance Lessons from the "ASEAN Way"', *Singapore Journal of International and Comparative Law*, **6**, 640–82 at 641.

Regional environmental governance is thus a logical midpoint between the national and international levels and could be the theoretical and pragmatic connection between local and global environmental governance insofar as it 'translates' national environmental problems and governance concerns into supra-national terms (and vice versa) and allows states to better govern environmental issues within and beyond their borders. In other words, regional environmental governance could connect 'the scope of the regulatory jurisdiction and the physical footprint of the public good or problem at hand'.[106] Other advantages of regional environmental governance include that it could accommodate specific regional environmental problems or issues and, apart from the obvious advantages in this respect, its successful operation would not be inhibited by a burgeoning group of state actors, which often have conflicting interests. It could also be easier to negotiate regional legal instruments and to enforce these.[107] Regional environmental governance is also often considered to be more effective than other international arrangements such as the (what some perceive to be 'inadequate' and 'dysfunctional')[108] UN-driven effort.[109] Although regional environmental governance itself is far from being optimally effective, it could nevertheless improve environmental outcomes in a specific and immediate region and bolster the entire global environmental governance effort:

> Stronger regional governance mechanisms are needed to address sustainability goals and trade-offs, using ecosystems as a framework for decision-making. The process of regional collaboration can build shared knowledge and improve communications and networks within each region. This may enhance prospects for harmonized approaches ... Regional agreement on goals and strategies can promote coordination and efficient use of resources on the part of international agencies active in the region ... [and they] offer an opportunity to integrate environmental and economic policies based on conditions in each region.[110]

---

106 Esty, Daniel C. (1999), 'Toward Optimal Environmental Governance', *New York University Law Review*, **74**(6), 1495–1574 at 1554.

107 Richardson, Benjamin J. (2000), 'Environmental Law in Postcolonial Societies: Straddling the Local-Global Institutional Spectrum', *Colorado Journal of International Environmental Law and Policy*, **11**, 1–82 at 73.

108 Esty, Daniel C. (1999), 'Toward Optimal Environmental Governance', *New York University Law Review*, **74**(6), 1495–1574 at 1553.

109 Krämer reiterates these sentiments: '[S]ince a global policy which leads to an improvement of the present environmental situation ... is not possible at present, it is suggested that some consideration be given to regionalisation of environmental issues.' Krämer, Ludwig (2006), 'The EU: A Regional Model?' in Gerd Winter (ed), *Multilevel Governance of Global Environmental Change: Perspectives from Science, Sociology, and the Law*, Cambridge: Cambridge University Press, 356.

110 Steiner, Achim, Lee A. Kimball and John Scanlon (2003), 'Global Governance for the Environment and the Role of Multilateral Environmental Agreements in Conservation', *Oryx*, **37**(2), 227–37 at 233.

In this sense, regional environmental governance is much more 'connected' to and in touch with nation states, local environmental conditions and the priorities, needs and interests of states and people. As Blanco and Razzaque[111] explain:

> ... regional institutions ... are closer to the local level and to the people they represent. The localisation of issues can mean that member countries are likely to share the same or very similar concerns, and it would be easier to make decisions and take action in respect of shared natural resources or about activities one of the consequences of which will be felt quite homogenously within a region. Regional organisations also have the advantage of grouping states and peoples with a shared history, culture and in many cases ethnicity, making the possibility of transfer of powers to the organisation easier.

Regional environmental governance initiatives could furthermore serve as effective ways to integrate and consolidate various national environmental governance actions through the harmonization of standards, norms and laws; they allow for joint implementation and collective enforcement; and could facilitate shared capacity building.[112] In his assessment of the possibility of establishing regional environment organizations, as opposed to a world environment organization, Strand[113] discusses various benefits that a regional environmental organization may offer. States that are situated in the same region with similar geographic attributes often share similar environmental concerns and a regional organization could be ideally suited to advance this homogeneous interest. States that are grouped in a regional organization usually already cooperate with respect to trade and the movement of goods, services and people, and they might therefore be better situated to cooperate in other regulatory domains such as the environment, which after all is often closely intertwined with these other areas that states already regulate together: '[R]egional integration in one area may lead to integration, or at least cooperation, in

---

[111] Blanco, Elena and Jona Razzaque (2011), *Globalisation and Natural Resources Law: Challenges, Key Issues and Perspectives*, Cheltenham: Edward Elgar Publishing, 203.

[112] Koh, Kheng-Lian and Nicholas A. Robinson (2002), 'Strengthening Sustainable Development in Regional Inter-governmental Governance Lessons from the "ASEAN Way"', *Singapore Journal of International and Comparative Law*, **6**, 640–82 at 641.

[113] Strand, Jonathan R., *The Case for Regional Environmental Organizations: Regional Integration and Multilateral Environmental Governance* (United Nations University, Institute of Advanced Studies Working Paper) available at http://www.ieg.earthsystemgovernance.org/sites/default/files/files/publications/Strand_The%20Case%20for%20REOs_2002.pdf [accessed 4 October 2011], 5–6.

another.'[114] Moreover, because fewer Member States would be involved with a regional organization, as opposed to a world environment organization, regional arrangements may be much more effective as the bureaucracy could be limited, decision-making could be simplified as a result, and it would be easier to reach political consensus among actors.

While we are far from establishing either one of these centralized supranational organizations, various regional environmental governance arrangements already exist, and they are playing an important role in the greater global environmental governance construct. For example, European environmental governance is now well established[115] and it provides for a multitude of normative arrangements such as regimes, directives and flexible framework legislation, various actors, institutions, networks, and organizations, among other such arrangements, to govern the common environmental affairs of EU Member States.[116] To be sure, as far as regional and global environmental governance are concerned, 'the EU is an actor in its own right: that is to say, it exhibits volition, is distinguishable from its constituent ... member states and is capable of taking action at the international level'.[117] The SADC has also developed various regional environmental norms in the form of protocols and some institutional arrangements exist to facilitate further norm creation, norm refinement, enforcement and dispute settlement, although these arrangements are far less comprehensive and effective than their European equivalents.[118] Another example is the Association of

---

114 Strand, Jonathan R., *The Case for Regional Environmental Organizations: Regional Integration and Multilateral Environmental Governance* (United Nations University, Institute of Advanced Studies Working Paper) available at http://www.ieg.earthsystemgovernance.org/sites/default/files/files/publications/Strand_The%20Case%20for%20REOs_2002.pdf [accessed 4 October 2011], 6.

115 See, for example, Giljum, Stefan *et al.* (2005), 'Environmental Governance in the European Union: Strategies and Instruments for Absolute Decoupling', *International Journal of Sustainable Development*, **8**(1/2), 31–46; Lenschow, Andrea (1997), *Transformation in European Environmental Governance: RSC No. 97/61 EUI Working Papers*, Florence, Italy: European University Institute; Scott, Joanne (ed) (2009), *Environmental Protection: European Law and Governance*, Oxford: Oxford University Press; Vogler, John and Hannes R. Stephan (2007), 'The European Union in Global Environmental Governance: Leadership in the Making?', *International Environmental Agreements*, **7**, 389–413.

116 Hofmeyer, Ingmar (2009), 'The Evolution of EU Environmental Governance' in Joanne Scott (ed), *Environmental Protection: European Law and Governance*, Oxford: Oxford University Press, 1–26.

117 Vogler, John (2005), 'The European Contribution to Global Environmental Governance', *International Affairs*, **81**(4), 835–50 at 837.

118 There is a dearth of literature on the SADC environmental governance effort. On aspects of biodiversity conservation in the SADC see Lubbe, Willem D. (2007),

Southeast Asian Nations (ASEAN), which is much more decentralized and less prominent than its European counterpart, but which nevertheless has considerable experience in regional environmental governance.[119] The concept of regional environmental governance is further populated and pluralized by the existence of numerous regional treaty regimes which often exist independently from official regional governance organizations such as SADC, the EU and ASEAN.[120] These examples illustrate that no one regional environmental effort is the same and that they will vary in terms of size, objectives, design and so forth. They are therefore themselves part of a pluralistic and disaggregated mass of global governance arrangements and further contribute to the plurality and vertical and horizontal disaggregation of multi-level global environmental governance.

7. SUMMARY

Generic descriptions of environmental governance suggest that it is an institutional response and societal construct which could be formal, informal, or both, and that it consists of many state and non-state actors that operate on various levels. Environmental governance aims to influence human behaviour with respect to the environment and has sustainability as a central guiding motive or overarching goal. It could be defined as a normative institutional regulatory intervention and social construct that is predominantly based on law and that aims to influence how people interact with the environment. It entails a pluralistic, dynamic, multi-level, multi-actor response and process of

---

'Straddling Borders and Legal Regimes: The Case for Cooperative Transfrontier Biodiversity Conservation in the Southern African Development Community', *Yearbook of International Environmental Law*, **18**, 126–52.

119 Koh, Kheng-Lian and Nicholas A. Robinson (2002), 'Strengthening Sustainable Development in Regional Inter-governmental Governance: Lessons from the "ASEAN Way"', *Singapore Journal of International and Comparative Law*, 6, 640–82. For perspectives on the Asia-Pacific Economic Cooperation Forum (APEC), see Zarsky, Lyuba (1997), 'The Asia-Pacific Economic Cooperation Forum and the Environment: Regional Environmental Governance in the Age of Economic Globalization', *Colorado Journal of International Environmental Law and Policy*, **8**(2), 323–57.

120 Examples are the *Convention for the Protection and Development of the Marine Environment of the Wider Caribbean Region*, 24 March 1983, in force 11 October 1986, 22 I.L.M. 221 (1983) and the *Convention for the Protection, Management and Development of the Marine and Coastal Environment of the Eastern African Region*, 1985. See further Richardson, Benjamin J. (2000), 'Environmental Law in Postcolonial Societies: Straddling the Local-Global Institutional Spectrum', *Colorado Journal of International Environmental Law and Policy*, 11, 1–82 at 72–6.

change which pragmatically aims to change human behaviour vis-à-vis the environment, and idealistically to optimize environmental benefits and use, while at the same time seeking to protect and preserve sufficient environmental capital for present and future generations.

Global environmental governance is a specific application of governance, which seeks to address environmental externalities that occur within and beyond the traditional confines of state borders, authority and influence. It is global in a spatial sense because it could be sub-national, national, regional and international, and it is global in a causal sense to the extent that governance on all of these levels is interlinked and acts in a cumulative way to address intra- and inter-jurisdictional environmental externalities. Due to its focus on sustainability and the interests of future generations, environmental governance is also temporally global.

While the phrase environmental management is often used interchangeably with environmental governance, the governance construct is broader than management. Environmental governance therefore also includes the mostly private and/or corporate aspects of environmental management. Law (both hard and soft) plays a decidedly important grounding, legitimizing and normative role in global environmental governance. It would nevertheless be insufficiently narrow to view global environmental governance as a purely legal institution that consists only of laws which are used primarily to produce additional laws, and as providing the means to interpret and enforce these legal rules, a point which is elaborated on in Chapter 8.

Global environmental governance consists of state and non-state actors, which means that it could be characterized as being public and private; it is therefore multi-actor governance. These state and non-state actors, however, rarely act separately from one another and it is preferable to speak of hybrid global environmental governance, which denotes a private-public mix of authority with decidedly multi-actor characteristics. Global environmental governance is also multi-levelled, which means that it is characterized by a diffusion of authority across levels, actors, and environmental sectors (simultaneously vertically and horizontally). All of these characteristics of global environmental governance cumulatively suggest that it is non-exact and that attempts to concretely delineate its exact contours would probably be futile. By mapping the field of global environmental governance, Chapter 7 investigates if it is at least possible to establish the broad conceptual contours, elements, and central tenets of global environmental governance in greater detail.

7. Mapping the definitional field of global environmental governance

> The argument for expanded global environmental governance is analytically powerful in a world where some harms span the planet, and thus only a world-scale response will be structurally adequate.[1]
>
> (Daniel Esty, 1999)

1. INTRODUCTION

Anyone who wishes to make sense of global environmental governance must consider that it is a multi-dimensional and highly complex phenomenon which aims to address a diverse array of plural issues: '[T]he search for simple solutions in a complex world can be distracting and even destructive. The pluralism of human values and the diversity of the environmental challenge – indeed, *challenges* – must be accepted and embraced.'[2] Because the issues that global environmental governance deals with are themselves complex, multi-dimensional, and far from clear, the inevitable complexity of the environment-governance-sustainability paradigm gives rise to pragmatic and conceptual challenges and further contributes to muddle conceptual clarity.[3]

---

[1] Esty, Daniel C. (1999), 'Toward Optimal Environmental Governance', *New York University Law Review*, **74**(6), 1495–1574 at 1569.

[2] Esty, Daniel C. (1999), 'Toward Optimal Environmental Governance', *New York University Law Review*, **74**(6), 1495–1574 at 1520–1521.

[3] Sustainability is arguably the objective of governance to the extent that it is a norm and reform agenda or programme for economics, politics and society. It must guide governance with a view to balancing socio-economic interests with ecological interests:

> Das gesellschaftliche Leitbild Nachhaltige Entwicklung ist also nach Verständnis ein mehr oder weniger anspruchvolles Reformprogramm für Wirtschaft, Politik und Gesellschaft, das darauf ausgerichtet ist, sozio-ökonomische Entwicklung mit ökologieschen Rahmenbedingunen in Einklang zu bringen.

Steurer, Reinhard and Rita Trattnigg (2010), 'Nachhaltigkeit regieren: Eine Einleitung

It would self-evidently be difficult to cast global environmental governance in clear and simple terms; its conceptual contours remain vague and unclear and there are probably as many views on global environmental governance as there are commentators on this issue, most of them with their own conceptual approaches to and interpretation of the concept and its elements. Indeed:

> The different conceptualizations of GEG [global environmental governance] ... cannot be explained simply as alternative interpretations or explanations of a generally agreed phenomena. Rather, the different approaches to the triad of concepts ('global', 'environmental', 'governance') understand the meaning of these terms in fundamentally different ways.[4]

The conceptual indeterminability of global environmental governance is also attributable to global governance. It was shown in Chapter 4 that global governance is a vague and amorphous concept which 'comprehends a whole range of diverging, if not opposing views' and '[A]nalytically, there is no agreement about what the term ... refers to and which phenomena are described by it.'[5] Yet global governance is part of an emerging vocabulary in the globalized age and fulfils a prominent 'discursive role ... in the political context'; it is a 'new social script' which redefines state sovereignty and defines issues that need to be governed in the global context.[6] The environment is one of these global issues, as was argued earlier, and global environmental governance has emerged as a manifestation of global governance that focuses specifically on the environment. In crudely simplified terms: '*[G]lobal environmental governance* is the intersection of global governance with environmental affairs.'[7]

---

im Wissenschaft-Praxis Dialog' in Reinhard Steurer and Rita Trattnigg (eds), *Nachhaltigkeit regieren: Eine Bilanz zu Governance-Prinzipien und -Praktiken*, Munich: Oekom Verlag, 21. See also Chambers, Bradnee W. and Jessica F. Green (2005), 'Introduction: Toward an Effective Framework for Sustainable Development' in Bradnee W. Chambers and Jessica F. Green (eds), *Reforming International Environmental Governance: From Institutional Limits to Innovative Reforms*, Tokyo: United Nations University Press, 4–5, and the discussion further below.

4 Paterson, Matthew, David Humphreys and Lloyd Pettiford (2003), 'Conceptualizing Global Environmental Governance: From Interstate Regimes to Counter-hegemonic Struggles', *Global Environmental Politics*, **3**(2), 1–10 at 2.

5 Späth, Konrad, *Inside Global Governance: New Borders of a Concept* available at http://www.cpogg.org/paper%20amerang/Konrad%20Spaeth.pdf [accessed 26 February 2011], 4/13.

6 Späth, Konrad, *Inside Global Governance: New Borders of a Concept* available at http://www.cpogg.org/paper%20amerang/Konrad%20Spaeth.pdf [accessed 26 February 2011], 6/13, 9/13, 10/13.

7 Speth, Gustave James and Peter M. Haas (2006), *Global Environmental Governance*, Washington: Island Press, 3.

While previous chapters have sought to analyse various aspects of global environmental governance, this chapter provides an overview of some of the existing descriptions of global environmental governance. In so doing it aims to map the definitional field of global environmental governance. By performing this general survey this chapter seeks first to establish the current, general, broad terminological trends and then to garner insights from the current use of the construct in the literature, with a view to ultimately informing this book's own reconstructive description of global environmental governance in Chapter 9.

There are no clear-cut divisions or categories of contexts, perspectives, and definitions of global environmental governance in the literature. They sometimes overlap, with the only distinguishing feature being a more pertinent focus on a particular aspect of global environmental governance by particular commentators. For the sake of systematization, however, this chapter identifies broad categories of perspectives or divisions in terms of which global environmental governance is described and could be understood. These are equally susceptible to overlap, and their division is not clear-cut. These categories and divisions include general institutionalist perspectives, reformative perspectives, cooperative perspectives, infra-national and supra-national reciprocity; UN-centred perspectives, law-centred perspectives, sustainability perspectives, political perspectives, pluralist perspectives, administrative perspectives, and perspectives on emerging forms of the next generation of global environmental governance.

2. GENERAL INSTITUTIONALIST PERSPECTIVES

Most descriptions of global environmental governance centre on institutions, organizations, regimes and/or networks; in other words, they derive from institutionalism as elaborated upon in Chapter 4. Paterson, Humphreys and Pettiford[8] state that this expression of global environmental governance is the most conventional, and it 'refers principally, if not exclusively, to the sum of the overlapping networks of inter-state regimes on environmental issues'. For these authors, because the focus of global environmental governance is interstate, it mostly assumes a strong public character, but it could also be described as having private environmental governance elements, as was shown in the previous chapter.

[8] Paterson, Matthew, David Humphreys and Lloyd Pettiford (2003), 'Conceptualizing Global Environmental Governance: From Interstate Regimes to Counter-hegemonic Struggles', *Global Environmental Politics*, **3**(2), 1–10 at 4.

In similar vein, Young[9] explains that:

> Governance arises as a social concern whenever the members of a group find that they are interdependent in the sense that the actions of each impinge on the welfare of the others ... At the most general level, governance involves the establishment and operation of social institutions (in the sense of rules of the game that serve to define social practices, assign roles, and guide interactions among the occupants of these roles) capable of resolving conflicts, facilitating cooperation, or, more generally, alleviating collective-action problems in a world of inter-dependent actors.

He shows later that global environmental governance (or international environmental governance, as he terms it) arises when the social institutions described here are applied to environmental 'problem sets' or 'clusters of interactive situations in which groups of interdependent actors are likely to suffer mutual losses or fail to reap joint gains in the absence of effective governance systems'.[10] In the context of global environmental problem sets, he identifies the following four clusters: the international commons (for example, Antarctica), shared natural resources (for example, shared river basins), transboundary externalities (such as transboundary air pollution), and linked issues (including, for example, trade and the environment).[11] These clusters are arguably situated in Rosenau's[12] 'pockets of coherence' that manifest in the midst of the amorphous mass of global governance arrangements. Where there is observable coherence around a specific area or issue, it would be possible to discern the existence of a more independent mass of governance arrangements (or pockets of coherence). These pockets of coherence are themselves imprecisely defined and by implication do not have to set precise parameters that determine the inclusion or exclusion of any level, issue, process, characteristic, actor, or governance mechanism. For example, where global governance forms a discernible pocket of coherence around the environmental issue

---

9 Young, Oran R. (1994), *International Governance: Protecting the Environment in a Stateless Society*, Ithaca, NY and London: Cornell University Press, 15.

10 Young, Oran R. (1994), *International Governance: Protecting the Environment in a Stateless Society*, Ithaca, NY and London: Cornell University Press, 19.

11 Young, Oran R. (1994), *International Governance: Protecting the Environment in a Stateless Society*, Ithaca, NY and London: Cornell University Press, 19–26. Ivanova follows another fairly similar approach by classifying global environmental issues into three categories, including: management of the global commons or the provision of global public goods; transboundary pollution or externalities; and ubiquitous environmental problems with a world-wide impact. Ivanova, Maria H., *Partnerships, International Organizations, and Global Environmental Governance* available at http://www.gppi.net/fileadmin/gppi/Ivanova_Article.pdf [accessed 11 March 2011], 11.

12 Rosenau, James N. (1995), 'Governance in the Twenty-first Century', *Global Governance*, **1**(1), 13–34 at 18.

area one could speak of global environmental governance. In addition to this more general pocket of coherence, it is also possible to identify sub-pockets which converge upon a specific issue area within the pocket of the broader issue area. These could include, for example, oceans governance, natural resources governance, and climate governance. Young[13] also makes a strong case for 'governance without government', a phrase which refers to 'the role that social institutions or governance systems, in contrast to organizations or material entities, play in solving the collective-action problems that pervade social relations under conditions of interdependence'. 'Governance without government' proposes that governance is possible without any formal involvement of the material entity of government, be it private or public.[14] In summary, Young's view posits that global environmental governance arises where members of a group realize they are interdependent and that their actions could affect one another. Global environmental governance could be considered to be a governance system to the extent that it is 'an institution that specializes in making collective choices on matters of common concern to the members of a distinct social group';[15] it establishes and operates institutions consisting of rules that apply to the 'game' of governing global environmental matters; it is global to the extent that it applies to the four global environmental problems sets or clusters; and while it often occurs through formal (generally state-based) organizations, a strong case can be made in favour of governance without formal state organizations or other material entities.

Esty[16] also follows a predominantly institutionalist approach to global environmental governance. He considers that global environmental governance includes 'governance structures' that 'manage international environmental relations', and it aims to address supra-national environmental challenges by facilitating international cooperation, which is needed in response to ecological interdependence. In his view, global environmental governance consists mainly of the UN and other specialized institutions.

---

13 Young, Oran R. (1994), *International Governance: Protecting the Environment in a Stateless Society*, Ithaca, NY and London: Cornell University Press, 16.

14 See the definitive work on 'governance without government': Rosenau, James N. and Ernst-Otto Czempiel (eds) (1992), *Governance without Government: Order and Change in World Politics*, Cambridge: Cambridge University Press.

15 Young, Oran R. (1994), *International Governance: Protecting the Environment in a Stateless Society*, Ithaca, NY and London: Cornell University Press, 26.

16 Esty, Daniel C. (2007), 'Global Environmental Governance' in Colin I. Bradford and Johannes F. Linn (eds), *Global Governance Reform: Breaking the Stalemate*, Washington: Brookings Institution Press, 108.

3. GLOBAL ENVIRONMENTAL GOVERNANCE AS A REFORM STRATEGY

The predominant institutional character of global environmental governance finds vivid expression in arguments for the creation of a world environment organization, which some commentators consider part of a broader initiative to make global environmental governance more effective.[17] Global environmental governance is ineffective to the extent that it does not answer to the dictates of what is perceived to be an effective governance system: '[A]n effective governance system is one that channels behavior in such a way as to eliminate or substantially to ameliorate the problem that led to its creation. A governance system that has little behavioral impact, by contrast, is ineffective.'[18] In this context, Bauer and Biermann[19] think that global

---

17 See among the many publications in this respect, Gehring, Thomas and Sebastian Oberthür (2000), 'Was bringt eine Weltumweltorganisation? Kooperationstheoretische Anmerkungen zur institutionellen Neuordnung der internationalen Umweltpolitik', *Zeitschrift für Internationale Beziehungen*, **7**(1), 185–211; Haas, Peter M. (2002), 'UN Conferences and Constructivist Governance of the Environment', *Global Governance*, **8**, 73–91 at 87–8; Hierlmeier, Jodie (2002), 'UNEP: Retrospect and Prospect – Options for Reforming the Global Environmental Governance Regime', *Georgetown International Environmental Law Review*, **14**, 767–805 at 792–6. Other commentators stand highly critical towards global institutional integration and centralization. Najam, for example, finds that:

> If one lived in a perfect world one might well have thought about investing resources and time into constructing the perfect environmental organization – but only after the multitude of the far more pressing problems of global environmental governance had been taken care of ... the current debate about global environmental governance with its dominant focus on establishing a super-organization for the environment, represents a serious misdiagnosis of the issues.

Najam, Adil (2005), 'Neither Necessary, nor Sufficient: Why Organizational Tinkering will not Improve Environmental Governance' in Frank Biermann and Steffen Bauer (eds), *A World Environment Organization: Solution or Threat for Effective International Environmental Governance?*, Aldershot: Ashgate, 235–6. Roch and Perrez explain that '[T]he purely institutional proposal for a WEO [World Environment Organization] does not in itself ensure the coherence, comprehensiveness, efficiency, and effectiveness of the international environmental regime.' Roch, Philippe and Franz Xaver Perrez (2005), 'International Environmental Governance: The Strive Towards a Comprehensive, Coherent, Effective and Efficient International Environmental Regime', *Colorado Journal of International Environmental Law and Policy*, **16**(1), 1–25 at 23.

18 Young, Oran R. (1994), *International Governance: Protecting the Environment in a Stateless Society*, Ithaca, NY and London: Cornell University Press, 30.

19 Bauer, Steffen and Frank Biermann (2005), 'The Debate on a World

environmental institutions play the primary role in global environmental governance:

> Global governance, as opposed to traditional interstate politics, has been most pronounced in trade, finance and economic policy, but also environmental policy ... Yet despite recent achievements in institutionalizing international environmental cooperation, the overall governance architecture, impressive as it may be in some respects, still fails to manage and halt global ecological degradation ... Creating a new world environment organization is but one proposal to address these shortcomings.

Their discussion suggests that global environmental governance is much more than traditional interstate politics. Global environmental governance is about the institutionalization of supra-national environmental cooperation,[20] or more particularly, the architecture of global environmental governance consists of institutions (in the material sense) which have as their primary aim the regulation of global ecological degradation by enabling and facilitating international cooperation among states.[21] A more centralized institutional response, as opposed to the current fragmented, uncoordinated and rudimentary effort, could, at least theoretically, be a possible way to improve the effectiveness of global environmental governance. Global governance is therefore considered part of a strategy to reform the material institutional architecture of global environmental governance, thus allowing it to have greater behavioural impact.

Environment Organization: An Introduction' in Frank Biermann and Steffen Bauer (eds), *A World Environment Organization: Solution or Threat for Effective International Environmental Governance?*, Aldershot: Ashgate, 2.

[20] Oberthür and Gehring also find that '[T]oday, international environmental governance takes place predominantly within numerous independent institutional arrangements.' Oberthür, Sebastian and Thomas Gehring (2005), 'Reforming International Environmental Governance: An Institutional Perspective on Proposals for a World Environment Organization' in Frank Biermann and Steffen Bauer (eds), *A World Environment Organization: Solution or Threat for Effective International Environmental Governance?*, Aldershot: Ashgate, 206.

[21] Other commentators have defined 'architecture' as 'the generic governance principles, the institutional design and the institutional interlinkages of different modes of governance within and across issue areas'. See Pattberg, Philipp and Johannes Stripple (2008), 'Beyond the Public and Private Divide: Remapping Transnational Climate Governance in the 21st Century', *International Environmental Agreements*, **8**, 367–88 at 373.

4. GLOBAL ENVIRONMENTAL GOVERNANCE AS INSTITUTIONAL COOPERATION

It has been illustrated in earlier chapters that institutionalism concerns itself, among other things, with the manner in and extent to which global actors cooperate to solve problems in connection with the taking of collective action, because the actors are deeply interdependent in a globalized world.[22] Institutionalism stresses that cooperation between states themselves (as the primary actors in international relations) and non-state actors is a way to ensure absolute gains in the pursuit of collective and/or individual interests, and that cooperation is primarily to be achieved by means of institutions.[23] Regimes, international organizations and networks are used by global actors as part of the institutional response to regulate global environmental matters. Because environmental problems threaten the very fabric of human existence, it would be in the interest of global actors to create order by means of a global regulatory institutional response. The global complexity and reach of environmental problems suggest that these regulatory endeavours should be collective and cooperative rather than individual.

---

[22] Strong states that:

> The changes which have so drastically re-cast the economic and political landscape of our planet are underlain by a phenomenon of a fundamental nature which will be pervasive in shaping the future of ... the world community. This is the global system of interacting cause-and-effect relationships which we call 'interdependence'. Interdependence is no longer a mere rhetorical concept, but the dominant reality if our times.

Strong, Maurice F. (1990), 'What Place will the Environment have in the Next Century – and at what Price?', *International Environmental Affairs*, **2**, 208–16 at 209–10.

[23] In underscoring the need for increased international co-operation by means of institutional responses, Caldwell explains that:

> The paradox then is that international cooperation is impossible without national concurrence, but mere concurrence as a formality is insufficient to insure that effective cooperation will occur. Something more than national governments is needed to attain the objectives of international environmental cooperation. The need has been answered in various ways through institutional structures capable of operating with limited autonomy apart from the governments that created them.

Caldwell, Lynton K. (1988), 'Beyond Environmental Diplomacy: the Changing Institutional Structure of International Cooperation' in John E. Carroll (ed), *International Environmental Diplomacy*, Cambridge: Cambridge University Press, 16.

It is no surprise then that some commentators have described global environmental governance as being primarily concerned with facilitating global cooperation with respect to global environmental issues. Hurrell,[24] for example, views global environmental governance as a matter of inter-state cooperation with a view to addressing global environmental issues by means of regime formation. These international regimes in turn consist of international environmental agreements, negotiations and organizations. He speaks of the 'emergence of a complex structure of global environmental governance with new sets of institutions and an array of new legal concepts', a 'dense set of international institutional arrangements designed to manage environmental problems', and a 'dense and wide-ranging juridical and institutional structure of environmental agreements', the success of which will depend on the ability of this cumulative mass or 'enmeshment' to 'tie states into a continuing and institutionalized process of negotiation'.[25]

The foregoing views are mirrored by Vogler,[26] who sees global environmental governance as an 'extensive network of international environmental institutions' and various multilateral environmental agreements with the UN playing the primary role in facilitating global coordination and cooperation. Global environmental governance at a formal level is 'virtually a synonym for international environmental cooperation; for the network of international environmental organizations and conventions and the spaces between them'.[27]

5. INFRA- AND SUPRA-NATIONAL RECIPROCITY

There is a direct connection and reciprocal relationship between supra-national environmental norms and governance efforts on the one hand, and infra-national environmental norms and governance on the other. This is because the main addressees of global environmental governance are states and the specific governance agencies in a state (a top-down relationship), and

---

24 Hurrell, Andrew (1995), 'International Political Theory and the Global Environment' in Ken Booth and Steve Smith (eds), *International Relations Theory Today*, Cambridge: Polity Press, 134.

25 Hurrell, Andrew (1995), 'International Political Theory and the Global Environment' in Ken Booth and Steve Smith (eds), *International Relations Theory Today*, Cambridge: Polity Press, 133–4, 136.

26 Vogler, John (2005), 'The European Contribution to Global Environmental Governance', *International Affairs*, **81**(4), 835–50 at 835–6.

27 Vogler, John (2005), 'The European Contribution to Global Environmental Governance', *International Affairs*, **81**(4), 835–50 at 835.

because states explicitly influence supra-national governance arrangements (a bottom-up relationship).[28]

This reciprocity between the supra-national level and the infra-national level of global environmental governance is a popular theme among commentators. Keohane, Haas and Levy,[29] for example, describe global environmental governance in the following terms:

> ... organized international responses to shared environmental problems will occur through cooperation among states, not through the imposition of government over them ... The international community's ability to preserve the quality of the planet for future generations depends upon international cooperation. Successful cooperation, in turn, requires effective international institutions to guide international behavior along a path of sustainable development.

They consider institutions to be 'persistent and connected sets of rules and practices that prescribe behavioral roles, constrain activity, and shape expectations', which in turn include bureaucratic organizations, formal regimes and informal practices which one finds at a supra-national level. However, even though global environmental governance is most frequently focused at the supra-national level, it aims to change the domestic behaviour of states. In fact, the effectiveness of global environmental governance will ultimately depend on the ability of international institutions to 'promote change in national behavior that is substantial enough to have a positive impact, eventually, on the quality of the natural environment'.[30] Notably then, global environmental governance is not only about governing shared supra-national

---

28 Focusing on international environmental regimes, Raustiala states that:

> International regime rules are commonly transformed into binding domestic rules or standards; regulatory cooperation in particular is marked by the degree to which this process of implementation relies upon and is shaped by existing domestic institutions and political structures ... regulatory regimes at the international level are nearly always administered through regulatory regimes at the domestic level.

Raustiala, Kal (1997), 'Domestic Institutions and International Regulatory Cooperation: Comparative Responses to the Convention on Biological Diversity', *World Politics*, **49**(4), 482–509 at 482.

29 Keohane, Robert O., Peter M. Haas and Marc A. Levy (1994), 'The Effectiveness of International Environmental Institutions' in Peter M. Haas, Robert O. Keohane and Marc A. Levy, *Institutions for the Earth: Sources of Effective International Environmental Protection*, Cambridge, Massachusetts: MIT Press, 4.

30 Keohane, Robert O., Peter M. Haas and Marc A. Levy (1994), 'The Effectiveness of International Environmental Institutions' in Peter M. Haas, Robert O. Keohane and Marc A. Levy, *Institutions for the Earth: Sources of Effective International Environmental Protection*, Cambridge, Massachusetts: MIT Press, 5.

environmental problems in those areas where the nation state cannot govern. It is also about the extent to which the global community (consisting of state and non-state actors) is able to influence *domestic* environmental governance through global institutional means.[31] This is a clear expression of the reciprocal and causal interconnectivity of *global* environmental governance, and it illustrates the contention that global environmental governance also has a decidedly local impact and domestic dimension. In other words, in the global environmental context 'the boundary between what is national and what is international quickly becomes blurred',[32] especially insofar as 'national actions are guided by international institutional pressures'.[33]

As was argued earlier, by definition the 'global' domain includes all of the various levels at which governance occurs. (Global environmental governance as multi-level governance.) Today relations among and within states are such that they impact on one another for the reason that they do not stand isolated from reciprocal influences in light of their interconnectivity. It is therefore possible that what happens at a sub-national and national level in terms of environmental governance will influence environmental governance at the regional and international levels. This effect is more pronounced with certain environmental phenomena (or issue areas) than with others. For example, in most instances supra-national rules are developed within specific issue areas to influence national environmental governance efforts. Biermann[34] cites global carbon governance as an example. He defines it as 'the development of global rules and rule-making systems to coordinate national responses to

---

[31] This reciprocity is further illustrated by the dualism of norm creation and norm transplantation:

> The origins of many international norms have been located in national understandings of what constitutes appropriate behaviour in a given issue area. The reverse, however, is also held to be true. Many national-level norms have been adopted after first finding their articulation in international institutions.

Cortell, Andrew P. and James W. Davis (2005), 'When Norms Clash: International Norms, Domestic Practices, and Japan's Internalisation of the GAT/WTO', *Review of International Studies*, **31**, 3–25 at 3.

[32] Strong, Maurice F. (1973), 'One Year after Stockholm: An Ecological Approach to Management', *Foreign Affairs*, **51**(4), 690–707 at 699–700.

[33] Keohane, Robert O., Peter M. Haas and Marc A. Levy (1994), 'The Effectiveness of International Environmental Institutions' in Peter M. Haas, Robert O. Keohane and Marc A. Levy, *Institutions for the Earth: Sources of Effective International Environmental Protection*, Cambridge, Massachusetts: MIT Press, 7.

[34] Biermann, Frank (2010), 'Beyond the Intergovernmental Regime: Recent Trends in Global Carbon Governance', *Current Opinion in Environmental Sustainability*, **2**, 284–8 at 284.

climate change'. These global rules refer to a specific common environmental problem (climate change), and it is the purpose of the global governance order to set rules and to ensure that these rules are imposed by the countries to which they apply, primarily by means of suitable coordination arrangements. What happens therefore at the supra-national level in global environmental governance very directly affects what happens at the national level:

> ... the increasing global institutionalization of carbon governance does not occur, and is indeed not conceivable, without continuing policy-making at national and sub-national levels. Global standards need to be implemented and put into practice locally, and global norm setting requires local decision-making and implementation. This results in the coexistence of policy-making at the subnational, national, regional and global levels, with the potential of both conflicts and synergies between different levels of regulatory authority.[35]

Hempel[36] defines global environmental governance as a form of global governance consisting of people, institutions, regimes and state and non-state actors which 'are collectively responsible for managing world affairs'. It focuses specifically on environmental concerns which have recently become threats to international security and development and which are perceived to need 'laws and institutions that operate beyond the zones of sovereignty'.[37] In this context environmental governance is a 'deliberative mechanism or process for making authoritative political choices about the future health of our planet', and the degree of environmental protection it offers will be determined by institutional structures and values.[38] He stresses that the success of global environmental governance will depend on national and sub-national governance (or 'political arrangements' as he terms it), but he points out that:

> ... the design [of global environmental governance] itself is likely to relegate nation states to a position of declining influence in world affairs ... political institutions will have to become increasingly 'glocal' in design if they are to cope successfully with growing biospheric crises. Both global and local ends of the political spectrum must be strengthened in order to achieve effective environmental governance. This means that some of the environmental authority currently reserved by sovereign states may have to be redistributed to supranational entities and to local communi-

---

35 Biermann, Frank (2010), 'Beyond the Intergovernmental Regime: Recent Trends in Global Carbon Governance', *Current Opinion in Environmental Sustainability*, **2**, 284–8 at 286.

36 Hempel, Lamont C. (1996), *Environmental Governance: The Global Challenge*, Washington: Island Press, 5.

37 Hempel, Lamont C. (1996), *Environmental Governance: The Global Challenge*, Washington: Island Press, 5.

38 Hempel, Lamont C. (1996), *Environmental Governance: The Global Challenge*, Washington: Island Press, 10.

> ties, simultaneously. The process through which this redistribution takes place is likely to involve some form of world or regional federalism.[39]

This approach highlights the global and local (or 'glocal') aspects of global environmental governance and the need for a balanced and proportional spread of shared responsibilities between all of the different loci of power in the political spectrum. In contrast to the dominant view, he believes that global environmental governance should be bottom-up instead of top-down: '[G]lobal environmental protection begins at the community and bioregional level – the level where complex living systems are most interdependent and vulnerable.'[40]

6. UN-CENTRED PERSPECTIVES

As global environmental governance would arguably lie somewhere between an unlikely central world environment government and an equally unlikely purely devolved and decentralized form of federal global environmental governance, the existence of arguments in favour of the UN as the principal facilitator of global environmental governance and thus a sort of compromise between the two extremes is not surprising. This proposition has garnered widespread support:

> ... the U.N. system has become, almost by default, the last, best hope of many green globalists. Many have regarded its fragile institutions as potential stepping stones to world federalism or some other kind of constitutional world order ... the U.N. represents the promise of world governance without the risk of world government ... [it] is capable ... of becoming a strong and effective confederation – one that can live with the continuing paradox of state sovereignty in an era of interdependence.[41]

It is especially the UN's function as an agent of legitimation and norm transmission that is important in the current era when 'the rules of the game are in flux, that is, when there is a transition from one order to another or when there are significant challenges to the established order'[42] brought about by

---

39 Hempel, Lamont C. (1996), *Environmental Governance: The Global Challenge*, Washington: Island Press, 5–6.

40 Hempel, Lamont C. (1996), *Environmental Governance: The Global Challenge*, Washington: Island Press, 6.

41 Hempel, Lamont C. (1996), *Environmental Governance: The Global Challenge*, Washington: Island Press, 165.

42 Barnett, Michael N. (1997), 'Bringing in the New World Order: Liberalism, Legitimacy and the United Nations', *World Politics*, **49**(4), 526–51 at 548.

globalization. In fact, as Barnett[43] reminds us: '[N]o other international organization or body has the capacity to legitimate the underlying principles and norms of the international order, so it is to the UN that states turn for legitimation and sanction.'

In her work entitled *Global Environmental Institutions*, DeSombre[44] opts not to provide a specific definition of global environmental governance. She instead describes global environmental governance broadly as an institutional response to global environmental problems and issues including species protection and conservation, the ocean commons, atmospheric commons, and the transboundary movement of hazardous substances. Global environmental institutions embedded in the UN framework and those stemming from international environmental treaty regimes are mostly responsible for addressing this range of global environmental problems and issues.[45] Despite her focus on public institutions, she admits that '[E]xamining institutions ... of necessity leaves out some important action on international environmental issues ... much of what happens of relevance to environmental protection happens alongside, and sometimes completely apart from, institutions.'[46] Nevertheless,

---

43 Barnett, Michael N. (1997), 'Bringing in the New World Order: Liberalism, Legitimacy and the United Nations', *World Politics*, **49**(4), 526–51 at 548.

44 DeSombre, Elizabeth R. (2006), *Global Environmental Institutions*, New York: Routledge, 1–6 *et seq*.

45 The view of the dominant role of the UN, and especially UNEP in global environmental governance, is a popular one supported by many authors; some of which are quoted in this chapter. It is also a view held by UNEP itself:

> ... the United Nations Environment Programme is confirmed as the leading global environmental authority that sets the global environmental agenda, that promotes the coherent implementation of the environmental dimension of sustainable development within the United Nations system and that serves as an authoritative advocate for the global environment.

UNEP Governing Council *Decision 21/21: International Environmental Governance 2001* available at http://www.un.org/documents/ga/docs/56/a5625.pdf [accessed 16 March 2011]. See also Hierlmeier who states that: '[T]he United Nations represents a global experiment which, by default, has become the best hope for environmentalism ... the web of governance built over the past three decades owes a great deal to UNEP, and other U.N. bodies, as advocates for greater global environmental responsibility and awareness.' Hierlmeier, Jodie (2002), 'UNEP: Retrospect and Prospect – Options for Reforming the Global Environmental Governance Regime', *Georgetown International Environmental Law Review*, **14**, 767–805 at 787. See also Sand, Peter H. (1991), 'Lessons Learned in Global Environmental Governance', *Boston College Environmental Affairs Law Review*, **18**, 213–77 at 217.

46 DeSombre, Elizabeth R. (2006), *Global Environmental Institutions*, New York: Routledge, 3.

while non-state actors and a range of actors other than international institutions play an important role in global environmental governance, the primary drivers of global environmental governance remain states and the organizations they create in terms of environmental regimes. In addition, fully fledged international institutions such as the UN, its subsidiary bodies and other entities, play an important role in the global environmental governance effort. This view is grounded in the public environmental governance paradigm which advocates that the primary actors in global environmental governance will be states, either acting on their own or through the UN and its institutions, or through those treaty regimes negotiated by states mostly within the UN framework. In terms of DeSombre's approach, global environmental governance is therefore a supra-national, institutional response centred on the UN and has a predominantly public environmental governance character.

Birnie, Boyle and Redgwell[47] highlight the significant role that institutions of global governance play in 'formulating and implementing international environmental policy and law'. These global environmental institutions consist of various specialized UN agencies and other international bodies with some environmental competence and influence. They rely on the definition of global governance proffered by the Commission on Global Governance discussed elsewhere in this book,[48] and estimate that:

> ... the term 'governance' when applied to the UN and its agencies implies rather less than global government, but more than the power to determine policy or initiate the process of international lawmaking. At the very least it captures the idea of a community of states with responsibility for addressing common problems through a variety of political processes which are inclusive in character, and which to some degree 'embody a limited sense of a collective interest, distinct in specific cases from the particular interests of individual states'.

Global environmental institutions thus explained cannot be considered as constituting a global or world environmental government. Their specific contribution lies in their ability to address common, global environmental concerns specifically through a process of international environmental law creation and their ability to influence global environmental politics. The foregoing processes occur in tandem with the work of various other international organizations including, *inter alia*, supervisory bodies, COPs, and other commissions and bodies established by environmental treaties.[49] It is possible

---

47 Birnie, Patricia, Alan Boyle and Catherine Redgwell (2009), *International Law and the Environment* 3rd edn, Oxford: Oxford University Press, 43.

48 See Chapter 4.

49 Birnie, Patricia, Alan Boyle and Catherine Redgwell (2009), *International Law and the Environment* 3rd edn, Oxford: Oxford University Press, 44–5.

to deduce from the foregoing that the UN-based global environmental institutions arise from and operate primarily within the scope of treaty regimes; and global environmental institutions are mainly responsible for making international environmental law and concomitantly influence international environmental politics through their activities. While the authors highlight the role of UN institutions, they also acknowledge elsewhere in their text that non-state parties such as NGOs and the scientific community play an important ancillary role in global environmental governance.

Elliott[50] admits that a precise definition of global governance remains elusive. While neoliberal institutionalism proffers the thought that global governance is a 'more effective form of multilateral management', the assumptions that institutional design is a panacea to improving the effectiveness of global environmental governance and that the establishment of more institutions will necessarily improve global environmental governance are doubtful. Elliot therefore takes a broad view of institutions in global environmental governance. Her approach suggests instead that '[A] more cosmopolitan or globalist [environmental governance] approach emphasizes the importance of obligations that transcend borders, social justice and equity, and the relations of power and powerlessness, which condition the practices and outcomes of global governance.'[51] She further suggests that global environmental governance has three dimensions, namely, institutional competence, multilateral cooperation and participatory diplomacy, and normative reform. These components remain institutional matters and Elliott expresses the opinion that the UN and its institutions should play the predominant role in the 'multilateral management' of environmental problems through increased institutional competence, improved multilateral cooperation and participatory diplomacy, and increased and improved norm creation. The responsibility for efficient, participative and cooperative multilateral governance of global environmental problems therefore rests primarily on the shoulders of UN institutions, which must discharge their responsibility chiefly through norm creation and cooperative diplomacy.

The centrality of the UN and its agencies in facilitating global environmental cooperation and regulating interdependencies around environmental

---

50 Elliott, Lorraine (2005), 'The United Nations' Record on Environmental Governance: An Assessment' in Frank Biermann and Steffen Bauer (eds), *A World Environment Organization: Solution or Threat for Effective International Environmental Governance?*, Aldershot: Ashgate, 29.

51 Elliott, Lorraine (2005), 'The United Nations' Record on Environmental Governance: An Assessment' in Frank Biermann and Steffen Bauer (eds), *A World Environment Organization: Solution or Threat for Effective International Environmental Governance?*, Aldershot: Ashgate, 29.

matters is further highlighted by Strong,[52] who states that: '[T]here is clearly no substitute for the United Nations. It is the only multilateral organization which is universal in its membership and global in its mandate.' He acknowledges that the need for supra-national cooperation has refocused attention on the principal means through which cooperation must be accomplished, namely through the UN and its system of agencies consisting, for example, of regional organizations, the World Bank and the International Monetary Fund (IMF). Collectively, these 'provide the indispensable structure and fora on which international cooperation depends' and '[T]hey represent not the precursors of a world government but the basic framework for a world system of governance which is imperative to the effective functioning of our global society.'[53]

7. THE CENTRALITY OF LAW

Beyerlin and Marauhn[54] use the term international environmental governance to also describe 'the purpose of addressing the making of and compliance with international environmental law'. They suggest that global environmental governance has a distinct functional role (it is 'action-oriented', in the words of the authors) in that it provides the institutions, organizations and regimes which are responsible for making laws or norms and enforcing these laws or norms related to global environmental matters. The normative framework of global environmental governance is provided by regimes that are mostly treaty-based, and these norms are enforced at various levels by a multitude of state and non-state actors in a non-hierarchical setting.[55] Global environmental governance also fulfils a prominent coordinating role with respect to the framework of international environmental law.[56]

That international environmental law and global environmental governance institutions are inherently intertwined is also explained by French,[57] who

---

52 Strong, Maurice F. (1990), 'What Place will the Environment have in the Next Century – and at what Price?', *International Environmental Affairs*, **2**, 208–16 at 212.

53 Strong, Maurice F. (1990), 'What Place will the Environment have in the Next Century – and at what Price?', *International Environmental Affairs*, **2**, 208–16 at 212.

54 Beyerlin, Ulrich and Thilo Marauhn (2011), *International Environmental Law*, Oxford: Hart Publishers, 243.

55 Beyerlin, Ulrich and Thilo Marauhn (2011), *International Environmental Law*, Oxford: Hart Publishers, 244–5.

56 Cordonier Segger, Marie-Claire and Ashfaq Khalfan (2004), *Sustainable Development Law: Principles, Practices and Prospects*, Oxford: Oxford University Press, 79.

57 French, Duncan (2009), 'Finding Autonomy in International Environmental Law and Governance', *Journal of Environmental Law*, **21**(2), 255–89 at 260.

loosely characterizes global environmental governance as a 'fragmented and disparate' institutional framework comprising of UN institutions, UNEP, treaty bodies, and other related institutions. International environmental law, as an autonomous legal sub-discipline, is distinguished from other legal sub-disciplines by the fact that its institutional framework is fragmented and disparate. International environmental law and the institutions of global environmental governance are thus reciprocally connected and causally intertwined to the extent that fragmentation in the one will cause fragmentation in the other. These perspectives suggest that international (environmental) law provides the normative foundation for the governance of global environmental problems, or what some term the 'institutionalization of international legal processes'.[58] Conversely, the physical institutions of global environmental governance provide the sources of international (environmental) law. Global environmental governance and law are thus manifestly interrelated and law plays an important foundational and steering role in global environmental governance.

Conca[59] understands environmental governance in a global setting to mean:

> ... a set of bargained rules about behaviour, with the character of the bargaining generating institutionalized cooperation to a greater or lesser extent. Non-state actors may wield knowledge-power, set agendas, and create political pressures, but ultimately it is the explicit efforts of states to bargain their way to cooperation on collective problems such as climate change, biodiversity loss, and ozone layer damage that are the source of institutionalization.

---

[58] Kimball, for example, finds that:

> The institutionalization of international legal processes derives from both legal and practical concerns. On the one hand, institutional support provides the means for ongoing review to ensure that commitments are met and to take stock of the need for new measures. On the other, the substantial scientific and technical content of problem diagnosis and response in the environment/development field raises the need for information and analysis to a new level. Institutional means are necessary to facilitate access by individual states and private actors to this information and, increasingly, to undertake collective assessments that foster common understanding so as to pave the way toward agreed response actions. In the final stage of implementation, international technical and financial cooperation has spawned new and dedicated institutional arrangements to assist nations in meeting their international obligations.

Kimball, Lee A. (2001), *International Ocean Governance: Using International Law and Organizations to Manage Marine Resources Sustainably*, Gland, Switzerland and Cambridge, United Kingdom: IUCN, 6.

[59] Conca, Ken (2004/2005), 'Environmental Governance after Johannesburg: From Stalled Legalization to Environmental Human Rights?', *Journal of International Law and International Relations*, **1**(1)/**1**(2), 121–66 at 130.

Conca[60] finds elsewhere that progressive legalization and norm inscription are two essential prerequisites for more effective global environmental governance. While progressive legalization refers to 'bargaining processes that yield greater obligation, precision, and delegation of environmental commitments', norm inscription entails 'more contentious politicking that promotes the construction, dissemination, and embedding of prescriptive and proscriptive rules and roles related to environmental protection'. Global environmental governance could therefore be described as a political bargaining process which results in the creation of rules (presumably including laws and law-like instruments) that have as their objective to influence behaviour with a view to solving collective environmental problems. It is the bargaining process, or rather the need for state and non-state actors alike to create rules and institutionalized cooperation with respect to collective environmental problems, that results in institutionalized cooperation and an institutionalized response to collective environmental problems. In less abstract terms, state and non-state actors will presumably first identify a collective environmental problem. They will then come together to bargain on a set of rules (or construct these rules) which must influence behaviour to such an extent that the problem is solved. The rules are then 'disseminated' and 'embedded' (or enforced) by means of cooperative institutionalized arrangements.

8. THE CENTRALITY OF SUSTAINABILITY

Najam, Papa and Tayiab[61] define global environmental governance as:

> ... the sum of organizations, policy instruments, financing mechanisms, rules, procedures and norms that regulate global environmental protection. Within the context of the evolution of global environmental politics and policy, the end goal of global environmental governance is to improve the state of the environment and to eventually lead to the broader goal of sustainable development.

---

60 Conca, Ken (2004/2005), 'Environmental Governance after Johannesburg: From Stalled Legalization to Environmental Human Rights?', *Journal of International Law and International Relations*, **1**(1)/**1**(2), 121–66 at 123.

61 Najam, Adil, Mihaela Papa, Nadaa Tayiab (2007), 'Global Environmental Governance: A Reform Agenda (e-book)' in Cutler J. Cleveland (ed), *Encyclopedia of Earth*, Washington, D.C. Environmental Information Coalition, National Council for Science and the Environment, available at http://www.eoearth.org/article/Global_Environmental_Governance:_A_Reform_Agenda_(e-book) [accessed 18 March 2011].

In an effort to set global environmental governance against the broader rubric of sustainability, the authors find that 'global environmental governance is a key component of sustainable development governance, but the latter is larger than the former'. They thus recognize the existence of a broader manifestation of environmental governance, one which, in their view, overshadows global environmental governance. The authors do not clarify what they mean by 'sustainable development governance' but presumably wish to imply that global *environmental* governance focuses only on environmental aspects and that sustainable development governance includes ecological, economic and social aspects (the orthodox three-pillar approach to sustainable development).[62] In other words, sustainable development governance (otherwise expressed as 'governance for sustainability') seems to be more comprehensive, integrated and multi-dimensional than global *environmental* governance.

The Commission on Global Governance sees the 'universal application' of sustainable development as 'a priority among the tasks of global governance'.[63] In the Commission's understanding, global environmental governance is seemingly global governance executed in accord with the dictates of sustainable development:

> Population, consumption, technology, development, and the environment, are linked in complex relationships that bear closely on human welfare in the global neighbourhood. Their effective and equitable management calls for a systemic,

---

[62] See also, for example, Cordonier Segger and Khalfan, who state that:

> Sustainable development is a global goal rather than just one project. From formulation to implementation and monitoring, in law and in policy, three interrelated international spheres of action-economic, environmental and social-are shaped by the sustainable development goal. This conceptual dilemma has one very practical result. Systems of governance and international cooperation for sustainable development are incredibly complex, and not very coherent.

Cordonier Segger, Marie-Claire and Ashfaq Khalfan (2004), *Sustainable Development Law: Principles, Practices and Prospects*, Oxford: Oxford University Press, 229. They also speak of 'global systems of sustainable development governance', which seem to refer to global environmental governance in its traditional guise. The Johannesburg Plan of Implementation of the World Summit on Sustainable Development also speaks of the 'institutional framework for sustainable development' which primarily relates to the UN framework which has been designed to achieve sustainable development. Johannesburg Plan of Implementation of the World Summit on Sustainable Development at sections 137–70 available at http://www.un.org/esa/sustdev/documents/WSSD_POI_PD/English/WSSD_PlanImpl.pdf [accessed 20 October 2012].

[63] Commission on Global Governance (1995), *Our Global Neighbourhood*, Oxford: Oxford University Press, 30.

> long-term, global approach guided by the principle of sustainable development, which has been the central lesson from the mounting ecological dangers of recent times.[64]

The Commission's treatment of global environmental issues in *Our Global Neighbourhood* under the heading 'Protecting the Environment' suggests the following regarding its view of global environmental governance: the 'system' of international environmental governance (the Commission's term) aims to achieve global sustainable development through the 'management' of cross-border environmental disputes and the protection of the global commons; as the 'most direct challenge to global governance in the environmental field', international environmental governance must focus on the global commons; the primary norms of international environmental governance are derived from environmental treaties; various UN and non-UN institutions play a valuable role in international environmental governance; and governance instruments, such as fiscal instruments, are useful to change the behaviour of consumers.[65] In terms of this definition, sustainability clearly is an important element of global environmental governance, both as a guiding measure and as an objective or ideal thereof.

A similar approach to that of the Commission is that of Vogler and Stephan:[66]

> Although [global environmental governance] has been variously defined – and can be drawn extremely broadly – it is normally seen by the policy community to involve efforts to reform and re-integrate those activities and organisations bearing upon questions of environmental degradation and sustainable development, that come under the very broad umbrella of the United Nations. Thus we might include the various environmental conventions and their autonomous conferences of the parties, the World Trade Organisation (WTO), the World Bank, the Global Environment Facility (GEF) and numerous other development-related organisations.

Global environmental governance is thus centred on the UN, and it consists of normative provisions and organizational apparatus which have as a collective goal to achieve a more integrated approach focused on solving problems of environmental degradation and achieving sustainability. In this sense it is also

---

64 Commission on Global Governance (1995), *Our Global Neighbourhood*, Oxford: Oxford University Press, 30.

65 Commission on Global Governance (1995), *Our Global Neighbourhood*, Oxford: Oxford University Press, 208–17.

66 Vogler, John and Hannes R. Stephan (2007), 'The European Union in Global Environmental Governance: Leadership in the Making?', *International Environmental Agreements*, **7**, 389–413 at 391.

considered a strategy to reform the foregoing institutional responses to the extent that these are better enabled to more fully integrate the three pillars of sustainability, namely economic, social and environmental concerns. In other words, global environmental governance is an institutional response to improve the ability of global institutions to better respond to and solve global environmental problems through a process of integration of sustainability considerations.

Chambers and Green[67] also highlight the centrality of sustainable development in the global environmental governance effort. They speak of a 'system of international sustainable development governance' and the 'international architecture for sustainable development', which they see as consisting mainly of international institutions that have been developed as a response to the Brundtland Report's challenge of achieving sustainable development. 'International sustainable development governance' is also a procedural approach that consists of international laws and policies and institutions for sustainable development that aim to achieve sustainable development.[68] In other words, the central objective of global environmental governance is not *environmental* governance, but *sustainable development* governance, the achievement of which depends on the extent to which international environmental institutions would be able to integrate the economic, social and environmental concerns into their governance activities.[69] The achievement of sustainable development is therefore as much an 'internal' process as it is an objective that should be achieved 'externally' by means of a more integrated approach. Their use of terminology is, however, strangely inconsistent, because while they seem to prefer the term 'sustainable development governance', at other times the authors speak of 'international environmental governance' without making an attempt to juxtapose these terms:

---

[67] Chambers, Bradnee W. and Jessica F. Green (2005), 'Introduction: Toward an Effective Framework for Sustainable Development' in Bradnee W. Chambers and Jessica F. Green (eds), *Reforming International Environmental Governance: From Institutional Limits to Innovative Reforms*, Tokyo: United Nations University Press, 2.

[68] Chambers, Bradnee W. and Jessica F. Green (2005), 'Introduction: Toward an Effective Framework for Sustainable Development' in Bradnee W. Chambers and Jessica F. Green (eds), *Reforming International Environmental Governance: From Institutional Limits to Innovative Reforms*, Tokyo: United Nations University Press, 4.

[69] They do not clarify their distinction between the environment and sustainable development as two seemingly separate issues in global environmental governance. See, for example, Chambers, Bradnee W. and Jessica F. Green (2005), 'Introduction: Toward an Effective Framework for Sustainable Development' in Bradnee W. Chambers and Jessica F. Green (eds), *Reforming International Environmental Governance: From Institutional Limits to Innovative Reforms*, Tokyo: United Nations University Press, 34.

> Although reducing fragmentation within IEG [international environmental governance] is the first step toward increased effectiveness of sustainable development governance, proposals for reform must look for ways to increase coordination, centralization and compliance across international governance structures beyond the scope of the environment.[70]

The foregoing arguably implies that sustainable development governance describes the broader framework in terms of which international environmental governance must function and be achieved. This view corresponds with Najam, Papa and Tayiab's above.

An even broader approach to describing the connection between sustainability and global environmental governance is that of Haas and Haas[71] who reflect on the *problématique* or the nature of the challenge of global environmental governance:

> The functional dimension for characterizing problems overlaps with both space and time. For instance, when we seek to specify the 'problems' of peace, economic growth, sustainable development or intergenerational equity we must show how such diverse 'places' as water, atmosphere, and terrestrial ecosystems interact with such human 'acts' as agriculture and industrial production, armaments, and the arms trade, and demographic trends, and how these in turn look in various 'social time frames'. 'Policy spaces', such as public health measures, macro-economic choices, and military operations, now demand to be studied in terms of these complications.

The authors later describe the global *problématique* as follows:

> … whoever is concerned with the interplay of resource use, population growth, democracy, the desire for higher living standards and a better quality of life for all, and the management of civil and interstate conflict is engulfed by the global *problematique*. Any multilateral effort to cope with even a subset of these problems cannot escape its logic.[72]

---

70 Chambers, Bradnee W. and Jessica F. Green (2005), 'Introduction: Toward an Effective Framework for Sustainable Development' in Bradnee W. Chambers and Jessica F. Green (eds), *Reforming International Environmental Governance: From Institutional Limits to Innovative Reforms*, Tokyo: United Nations University Press, 8.

71 Haas, Peter M. and Ernst B. Haas (1995), 'Learning to Learn: Some Thoughts on Improving International Governance of the Global Problematique' in Commission on Global Governance, *Issues in Global Governance*, London: Kluwer Law International, 297–8.

72 Haas, Peter M. and Ernst B. Haas (1995), 'Learning to Learn: Some Thoughts on Improving International Governance of the Global Problematique' in Commission on Global Governance, *Issues in Global Governance*, London: Kluwer Law International, 299.

This *problématique* of global environmental governance, in essence, is the challenge of sustainability which asks the question: how do state and non-state actors address social, economic and environmental 'problems' through a global institutional response and what does the response look like? This illustrates that sustainability in the global governance context is centrally concerned with the many intricate and complex causal links and ties between ecological 'problem sets', the broader economic *problématique*, and various other social practices, needs and human activities.[73]

9. GLOBAL ENVIRONMENTAL GOVERNANCE AS A POLITICAL PROCESS

The majority of the descriptions in this chapter thus far have focused on the functional element of global environmental governance; global environmental governance as a means to an end, namely, to facilitate global cooperation, and/or to change/direct or regulate human behaviour with a view to (positively) influencing environmental quality, or to achieving sustainability. This is the most conventional view of global environmental governance. It is interesting, then, to note Paterson, Humphreys and Pettiford's[74] caveat to the functionalist role of global environmental governance:

> GEG [global environmental governance] should not therefore be thought of as a management practice assuming a harmony of interests between different social actors. Rather it is a fundamentally political process involving struggles over who has the authority and legitimacy to propose rules guiding the practices of states, TNCs (transnational corporations), social movements and individuals, and who will benefit and lose out through the adoption of particular rules and their implementation.

Their description strongly reflects the tensions inherent in global environmental politics, and they see environmental governance as playing a fundamental role in this global political process. In fact, they consider environmental

---

[73] Haas, Peter M. and Ernst B. Haas (1995), 'Learning to Learn: Some Thoughts on Improving International Governance of the Global Problematique' in Commission on Global Governance, *Issues in Global Governance*, London: Kluwer Law International, 318.

[74] Paterson, Matthew, David Humphreys and Lloyd Pettiford (2003), 'Conceptualizing Global Environmental Governance: From Interstate Regimes to Counter-hegemonic Struggles', *Global Environmental Politics*, **3**(2), 1–10 at 8. See also Paterson, Matthew (1999), 'Interpreting Trends in Global Environmental Governance', *International Affairs*, **75**(4), 793–802.

governance itself to be fraught with conflicts, discord and power struggles. Their non-functionalist, political view emphasizes that environmental governance is an area of political power struggle rather than a method of creating a harmony of interests. Thus described, global environmental governance is a global political process where state and non-state actors at multiple levels act in their own interest to gain as much advantage and control as possible. It is thus not necessarily a global regulatory approach which aims to improve environmental quality *per se*; the latter seems to be an ancillary objective, one which is incidental to the principal objective of facilitating hegemony in the environmental context.

10. PLURALISTIC PERSPECTIVES

Biermann and Pattberg[75] consider global environmental governance against the broader backdrop of global governance, which in their view is increasingly leading to the emergence of new non-state actors in addition to traditional state actors; the notable emergence of new governance institutions and mechanisms outside the usual boundaries of treaty regimes; and in the wake of the increase in the number of actors, institutions and mechanisms, also the inevitable rise and spread of fragmentation in the entire global governance system. Like Paterson, Humphreys and Pettiford, global environmental governance for the authors thus describes world politics, which is characterized by the increased number of actors, new institutions and mechanisms, as well as the increased fragmentation of the system.[76] They define the fragmentation of the global environmental governance regime as follows:

> The emerging global environmental governance system is characterized by an increasing segmentation of different layers and clusters of rule making and rule implementing, fragmented both vertically between supranational, international, national and subnational layers of authority (multilevel governance) and horizontally between different parallel rule-making systems maintained by different groups of actors (multipolar governance).[77]

---

75 Biermann, Frank and Philipp Pattberg (2008), 'Global Environmental Governance: Taking Stock, Moving Forward', *Annual Review of Environment and Resources*, **33**, 277–94 at 280.

76 Biermann, Frank and Philipp Pattberg (2008), 'Global Environmental Governance: Taking Stock, Moving Forward', *Annual Review of Environment and Resources*, **33**, 277–94 at 280.

77 Biermann, Frank and Philipp Pattberg (2008), 'Global Environmental Governance: Taking Stock, Moving Forward', *Annual Review of Environment and Resources*, **33**, 277–94 at 284.

Because of vertical fragmentation, global environmental governance consists of multiple layers which in global context could include the sub-national, national, sub-regional, regional and international levels. In Biermann and Pattberg's view, in addition to being multi-levelled, global environmental governance is also multi-polar. This suggests that a whole range of actors is involved in global environmental governance, ranging from state actors clothed with pure public power to non-state actors exercising private power outside of the state authority realm. Multi-polar governance therefore describes what has been termed in Chapter 6 'hybrid environmental governance', to the extent that it involves a mixture of private and public sources of authority and state and non-state actors on different governance levels. In this sense, fragmentation is both a cause and consequence of global environmental governance and it would be possible to argue first that fragmentation is a phenomenon which arises because of multi-level and multi-actor governance, and conversely that fragmentary growth is responsible for multi-levelled and multi-actor global environmental governance.[78]

Rechkemmer[79] describes global environmental governance as a 'systematic approach ... on a rather phenomenological basis'. He considers it an institutionalized and multi-stakeholder process in which international organizations, networks and non-state actors play a crucial role in collective action problem identification, global agenda setting and the implementation of decisions, the generation and collection of knowledge, discussion and the setting of standards, and ongoing negotiations on various levels. The author nevertheless stresses the point that formal negotiation processes under the auspices of the UN and the principal role that states play in this respect remain paramount. Rechkemmer clearly follows a diversified approach in the inclusion of a wide variety of actors in global environmental governance and the

---

[78] One must also acknowledge fragmentation's significant impediments to effective global environmental governance. Biermann, for example, states that the 'fragmentation of global governance architectures appears on balance to bring more harm than positive effects and can generally be seen as a burden on the overall performance of the system'. Biermann, Frank (2010), 'Beyond the Intergovernmental Regime: Recent Trends in Global Carbon Governance', *Current Opinion in Environmental Sustainability*, **2**, 284–8 at 286. The issue of fragmentation is linked with the debate on a world environment organization, which was presented earlier in this book. On the issue of integration, generally as a reaction to fragmentation, see among others Biermann, Frank, Olwen Davies and Nicolien Van der Grijp (2009), 'Environmental Policy Integration and the Architecture of Global Environmental Governance', *International Environmental Agreements*, **9**, 351–69.

[79] Rechkemmer, Andreas (2006), *International Environmental Governance: Issues, Achievements, and Perspectives – Publication Series of UNU-EHS No. 3/2006*, Bonn: UNU Institute for Environment and Human Security, 13.

range of tasks these actors undertake, a view which is somewhat tempered by the restatement of the UN's predominant role in global environmental governance: '[F]ocusing on the UN system, global environmental governance has meanwhile become a widely-stretched, dense and diversified institutional framework consisting of a multitude of agencies, structures and bodies – not mentioning the less formalized ongoing negotiation processes and conference series.' It seems thus that the author considers global environmental governance simultaneously to be a phenomenon, a system and an institutional framework in which the UN, together with a host of other actors, plays the primary role.

Roch and Perrez[80] describe global environmental governance as a complex and multi-layered structure which has been developed as a response to 'the recognition that threats to the global environment undermine the resource base of human development and well-being'. This structure consists of numerous environmental institutions, processes and mechanisms which the authors do not specify, but which seem to include the UN machinery, and treaty regimes and 'mini-institutional machinery' established by each regime, including COPs, secretariats, advisory bodies and incidental actors such as technical experts.[81] Global environmental governance is described as an 'institutional and political framework' with a 'multi-faceted institutional architecture'. In their view, international environmental governance is distinct from global environmental governance: '[T]he international environmental regime must have a concrete and tangible positive impact on the global environmental regime.'[82] While they offer no further clarification as to what they consider this distinction to be, 'international' in this context is arguably seen as being subjugated by the bigger global scheme and is considered to be part of the *global*. One can derive from their description that global environmental governance is simultaneously a politicized institutional framework, a regime and an architecture (terms which are used interchangeably). The purpose of global environmental governance is distinctly anthropocentric, with its emphasis on

[80] Roch, Philippe and Franz Xaver Perrez (2005), 'International Environmental Governance: The Strive Towards a Comprehensive, Coherent, Effective and Efficient International Environmental Regime', *Colorado Journal of International Environmental Law and Policy*, **16**(1), 1–25 at 2.

[81] Roch, Philippe and Franz Xaver Perrez (2005), 'International Environmental Governance: The Strive Towards a Comprehensive, Coherent, Effective and Efficient International Environmental Regime', *Colorado Journal of International Environmental Law and Policy*, **16**(1), 1–25 at 2–6.

[82] Roch, Philippe and Franz Xaver Perrez (2005), 'International Environmental Governance: The Strive Towards a Comprehensive, Coherent, Effective and Efficient International Environmental Regime', *Colorado Journal of International Environmental Law and Policy*, **16**(1), 1–25 at 18.

human development and well-being, and international environmental governance is somewhat less comprehensive than global environmental governance.

Hierlmeier[83] considers global environmental governance against the more general backdrop of governance, which she defines as 'encompassing decision- and policy-making processes as well as the institutional structure for implementing these decisions and policies'. It has to do with systems of rule which are 'backed by shared goals' instead of by formal authority. Global environmental governance in this context 'is comprised of governments, institutions and agreements that form a complex decision- and policy-making network, focused on environmental issues', and it has a distinctly public governance character with the primary actors being the UN and other inter-governmental organizations.[84] This clear public focus, however, is increasingly being distorted by the inclusion of a wide range of non-state actors to operate alongside the 'highly formalized state mechanisms of international governance', with the result that global environmental governance is assuming a network character in a multi-dimensional and non-hierarchical setting.[85] Hierlmeier[86] makes an interesting further point with respect to the reciprocal relationship between national environmental governance and global environmental governance ('global' is seemingly used by the author in this context as meaning 'international'). She finds that as long as environmental governance maintains its public character with the state and inter-governmental agencies playing the predominant roles in this respect, the manner in which global environmental governance systems will be designed and practised will depend largely on the manner in which national systems are designed and operated. This implies that states remain the predominant parties which will determine the architecture and execution of global environmental governance. There is also a very real possibility that states will be able to transplant national environmental governance innovations to various other levels in a global context, thereby significantly influencing global environmental governance in a bottom-up approach, a possibility which was mooted earlier in this chapter.

---

[83] Hierlmeier, Jodie (2002), 'UNEP: Retrospect and Prospect – Options for Reforming the Global Environmental Governance Regime', *Georgetown International Environmental Law Review*, **14**, 767–805 at 769.

[84] Hierlmeier, Jodie (2002), 'UNEP: Retrospect and Prospect – Options for Reforming the Global Environmental Governance Regime', *Georgetown International Environmental Law Review*, **14**, 767–805 at 769.

[85] Hierlmeier, Jodie (2002), 'UNEP: Retrospect and Prospect – Options for Reforming the Global Environmental Governance Regime', *Georgetown International Environmental Law Review*, **14**, 767–805 at 770.

[86] Hierlmeier, Jodie (2002), 'UNEP: Retrospect and Prospect – Options for Reforming the Global Environmental Governance Regime', *Georgetown International Environmental Law Review*, **14**, 767–805 at 803.

Moreover, as is argued elsewhere in this book, much of the success of global environmental governance will depend on the achievements of domestic environmental governance, as this often is the level closest to environmental problems.[87]

Haas[88] follows a similar generalist approach to that of Hierlmeier. He describes the 'architectonics of global environmental governance' in terms of a governance system which is cast in constitutional terms:

> Governance entails a set of commitments that command obedience (rights and responsibilities, conventions, principles and norms), actual rules and procedures by which these commitments are to be realized, a set of authoritative actors who may participate in decision-making (rules of suffrage), a set of formal institutions through which activities are coordinated, and a procedure for adjudicating disagreements and challenges.

Global environmental governance does not have a strong centralized global leadership. It is instead based on a community of interests and consensus among a wide variety of state and non-state actors. It is exercised through political and administrative processes, institutions and actors by means of legislative, executive, and judicial authorities which make norms, administer bureaucratic matters, and enforce norms (the so-called *trias politica* doctrine).[89] In this way, it is very similar to any domestic governance effort. Global environmental governance furthermore consists of norms that 'establish expectations against which states are willing to be judged', mostly in the form of soft law and more formal treaty law. Norms in Haas' view are therefore evidence of the global community's shared intentions, they shape and describe the global community's commitments, and they place broader obligations mostly on states to give effect to their intentions and commitments. Global environmental governance also consists of general principles (such as the polluter pays and the no-harm principles) and values which form the basis of these norms.[90] Another component of global environmental governance is rules which are more specific than the foregoing norms, values and principles, and they provide focused 'regulatory injunctions administered through a combination of numerical targets, procedural permits, and reporting

[87] See Chapter 6.

[88] Haas, Peter M. (1995), 'Global Environmental Governance' in Commission on Global Governance, *Issues in Global Governance*, London: Kluwer Law International, 334.

[89] Thus described, global environmental governance has a substantive and procedural component.

[90] Haas, Peter M. (1995), 'Global Environmental Governance' in Commission on Global Governance, *Issues in Global Governance*, London: Kluwer Law International, 335.

systems'[91] established in the many environmental regimes that deal with specific global environmental issues. These rules are directed at national governments and are concrete means to translate supra-national governance into national and sub-national terms.

Finally, as far as pluralistic perspectives are concerned, Köck[92] explains that global environmental governance is a normative concept which has been developed in answer to the many regulatory problems that arise and will arise in a supra-national context. It has subsequently been transformed from primarily a national and sub-national concern and enterprise into one which today is characterized by a complex multi-actor constellation; an equally complex, diverse, multi-layered and multi-level institutional fabric; and a complex mass of crisscrossing forms of interaction between these levels and actors. Moreover, rules are increasingly being set and enforced by non-state actors, and the scientific community is now playing an important role in agenda-setting and problem solving, even at the political level. An increase in the number and types of regulatory instruments that are used is accompanying these foregoing developments, which cumulatively could be said to form the fabric of contemporary environmental governance as a significant part of global environmental politics.

11. GLOBAL ENVIRONMENTAL GOVERNANCE AS ADMINISTRATION

The recent mushrooming of international organizations and other global actors and the growing development of concepts such as 'global administrative law', the 'law of international organizations' and 'international institutional law' suggests that the internal and inter-institutional administrative (or bureaucratic) functions of global environmental institutions, most notably intergovernmental environmental organizations, are increasingly recognized as forming part of the broader construct of global environmental governance.[93]

---

[91] Haas, Peter M. (1995), 'Global Environmental Governance' in Commission on Global Governance, *Issues in Global Governance*, London: Kluwer Law International, 338–40.

[92] Köck, Wolfgang (2006), 'Governance in der Umweltpolitik' in Gunnar Folke Schuppet (ed), *Governance-Forschung*, Baden-Baden: Nomos Verlag, 325 *et seq.*

[93] Among the many writings in this respect see Klabbers, Jan (2008), 'The Paradox of International Institutional Law', *International Organizations Law Review*, **5**, 151–73; generally, Von Bogdandy, Armin *et al.* (eds) (2009), *The Exercise of Public Authority by International Institutions: Advancing International Institutional Law*,

In fact, Kingsbury[94] has already suggested that the term 'global environmental governance as administration' and the propagation of terms such as 'international bureaucracies' reinforce the belief that there is a separate body of law and governance activities that is increasingly manifesting in the broader global (environmental) governance paradigm.[95]

To what extent does global administration contribute to or form part of global environmental governance? The link between them can be traced to the debate on institutionalism discussed in Chapter 4. Interdependent states who wish to cooperatively address global environmental problems will attempt to do so beyond their borders by means of institutions in the form of international organizations, regimes and networks. These institutions would then act as a form of 'international administrative agency'.[96] In other words, intervention through the medium of such institutions not only makes global environmental governance possible but also creates a distinct new arena in global environmental governance where certain administrative functions are performed, which performance makes global environmental governance possible. Mitchell and Farnik[97] argue that it is increasingly possible to observe a 'global administrative space' which has been created:

Heidelberg: Springer Verlag; Klabbers, Jan (2009), *An Introduction to International Institutional Law* 2nd edn, Cambridge: Cambridge University Press; Schermers, Henry G. and Niels M. Blokker (2011), *International Institutional Law: Unity within Diversity* 5th edn, Leiden: Martinus Nijhoff Publishers.

94 Kingsbury, Benedict (2007), 'Global Environmental Governance as Administration: Implications for International Law' in Daniel Bodansky, Jutta Brunnée and Ellen Hey (eds), *The Oxford Handbook of International Environmental Law*, Oxford: Oxford University Press, 63.

95 Venzke states that 'bureaucracy' should be understood in the Weberian sense as a distinct organizational form where bureaucracies exercise authority within larger organizational and normative structures, which process is 'an apparent rational-legal process of administration that fosters the belief in the rightness of the authority exercised'. Venzke, Ingo (2009), 'International Bureaucracies from a Political Science Perspective: Agency, Authority and International Institutional Law' in Armin Von Bogdandy *et al.* (eds), *The Exercise of Public Authority by International Institutions: Advancing International Institutional Law*, Heidelberg: Springer Verlag, 78.

96 Boyle, Alan E. (1991), 'Saving the World? Implementation and Enforcement of International Environmental Law through International Institutions', *Journal of Environmental Law*, **3**(2), 229–45 at 229. See also, Churchill, Robin R. and Geir Ulfstein (2000), 'Autonomous Institutional Arrangements in Multilateral Environmental Agreements: A Little-noticed Phenomenon in International Law', *American Journal of International Law*, **94**, 623–59.

97 Mitchell, Andrew D. and John Farnik (2009), 'Global Administrative Law: Can it Bring Global Governance to Account?', *Federal Law Review*, **37**, 237–62 at 238.

> ... through the coordination of transnational regulation in response to the increasing interconnectedness and interdependence of nation states flowing from the 'globalisation' movement towards economic and social integration ... Regulation and administration is no longer chiefly the domain of national governments with a domestic focus; these bodies now coexist alongside a complex global system or field of governance.

One could thus identify a distinct, developing area that specifically concerns administrative regulation or bureaucratic (technical and technocratic) aspects and tasks of global environmental governance that are performed by states, international organizations, and global networks. While regimes, organizations and networks provide states and non-state actors with the opportunity to govern globally, these institutions cannot be left to their own devices. They require 'administration' themselves, and they perform administrative tasks with a view to regulating interdependence and fulfilling the objectives of global environmental governance.

International organizations are usually responsible for this operationalization of global environmental governance; specifically the administrative or bureaucratic elements thereof. An international organization therefore contributes to the executive branch of global environmental governance (in addition to the legislative and judicial or dispute resolution branches discussed earlier),[98] and could be considered 'the clearest and most conventional example of a transnational administrative body'.[99] International organizations were discussed at length in Chapter 4 and it was shown that they are material entities usually consisting of offices, personnel, and a whole range of administrative apparatus and functions which are used to achieve or administer global environmental governance – to make global environmental governance work, as it were.[100] Most of them have their own legal personality (they are *sui generis* international persons)[101] and a distinct institutional structure and bureaucratic machinery separate from their members, which are usually states. Examples of these organizations include the UN bodies, regional bodies such as those of the EU, and various specialized agencies such as the World Bank and the WTO. Administrative tasks usually handled

---

98 Haas, Peter M. (1995), 'Global Environmental Governance' in Commission on Global Governance, *Issues in Global Governance*, London: Kluwer Law International, 343.

99 Mitchell, Andrew D. and John Farnik (2009), 'Global Administrative Law: Can it Bring Global Governance to Account?', *Federal Law Review*, **37**, 237–62 at 239

100 Young, Oran R. (1994), *International Governance: Protecting the Environment in a Stateless Society*, Ithaca, NY and London: Cornell University Press, 28–9.

101 Amerashinghe, Chittharanjan F. (2008), 'International Institutional Law: A Point of View', *International Organizations Law*, **5**, 143–50 at 148.

by international organizations include, for example, the arrangement of meetings; compliance and enforcement tasks; information gathering and information dissemination; the specification and coordination of obligations; various monitoring activities; and technical, bureaucratic and financial assistance.[102] All of these are tasks which make global environmental governance possible in real terms.

The foregoing generally concerns the implementation and administration of international and regional environmental law at the supra-national level as opposed to the implementation and administration of international and regional environmental law at the domestic level, the latter of which is reserved for the organs and functionaries of domestic governments.[103] In this way it is mostly international organizations and treaty bodies specifically, and to a lesser extent networks, that are responsible for supra-national implementation, which 'deals with the organizational infrastructure and the institutional design [of organizational procedures] which aim at supervising the conduct of states (and sometimes other actors) at the international level'.[104] However, in the light of the reciprocity of global environmental governance discussed earlier, the important role that national administrative bureaucracies play in the administration or implementation of supra-national environmental law, norms and standards must not be underestimated as these are the agencies that are essentially responsible for operationalizing global environmental governance at the infra-national level.[105] In fact, the historical administrative law foundation of some domestic environmental law systems, such as South Africa's, explains the close connection between administrative law and environmental governance.[106] While the functions and activities of national environmental agencies cannot be considered to form part of supra-national environmental administration in the strict sense, they do contribute to the

---

102 Beyerlin, Ulrich and Thilo Marauhn (2011), *International Environmental Law*, Oxford: Hart Publishers, 258.

103 Beyerlin, Ulrich and Thilo Marauhn (2011), *International Environmental Law*, Oxford: Hart Publishers, 257.

104 Beyerlin, Ulrich and Thilo Marauhn (2011), *International Environmental Law*, Oxford: Hart Publishers, 258.

105 A very tangible example of the extent to which national agencies could be instrumentally involved in global administration is where domestic courts would be asked to review decisions by a transnational administrative body. See further Mitchell, Andrew D. and John Farnik (2009), 'Global Administrative Law: Can it Bring Global Governance to Account?', *Federal Law Review*, **37**, 237–62 at 247–50. Another is where a national department of environmental affairs implements international treaty provisions that have been translated into national legislation.

106 Kotzé, Louis J. (2002), 'The Application of Just Administrative Action in the South African Environmental Governance Sphere: An Analysis of Some Contemporary Thoughts and Recent Jurisprudence', *Potchefstroom Electronic Law Journal*, **2**, 1–42.

global environmental administrative effort to the extent that they translate the work of supra-national organizations into infra-national terms. National environmental agencies are therefore part of the global environmental administrative effort, although they would not be regulated by global administrative law but rather by national administrative law.

Global environmental governance through administration has a distinct public-governance flavour to the extent that it is performed by states and state actors. However, the important role that non-state actors increasingly play in influencing especially the manner in which procedural aspects of global environmental governance are dealt with must also be noted.[107] They are less formally constituted than state actors and they sometimes do not have a permanent secretariat and institutional framework, nor are their norms and decisions binding on their members.[108] Yet non-state actors, especially NGOs, often serve as independent sources of information about the quality of environmental and governmental practices. They offer the opportunity to provide expert knowledge and to improve administration, and could act as observers during treaty negotiations and standard setting, for example. Non-state actors and epistemic communities acting through transnational networks fulfil similar functions. More explicitly, non-state actors are responsible for the administration of their own internal affairs which would allow them, in turn, to fulfil their objectives and tasks as part of the broader hybrid global environmental governance effort.

Following Kingsbury's[109] classification of five different types of global administration in the global environmental governance context and the discussion above, the connection between global administration and global environmental governance is further clarified. His classification is seemingly based on the types of actors (state or non-state) involved in performing the administration. These types of administration are distributed administration (performed by organs of national government); international administration (performed by intergovernmental organizations); intergovernmental network organization (performed by less formal but not informal networks of national governments); hybrid administration (performed by transnational state and non-state

[107] Haas, Peter M. (1995), 'Global Environmental Governance' in Commission on Global Governance, *Issues in Global Governance*, London: Kluwer Law International, 344.

[108] Mitchell, Andrew D. and John Farnik (2009), 'Global Administrative Law: Can it Bring Global Governance to Account?', *Federal Law Review*, 37, 237–62 at 240.

[109] Kingsbury, Benedict (2007), 'Global Environmental Governance as Administration: Implications for International Law' in Daniel Bodansky, Jutta Brunnée and Ellen Hey (eds), *The Oxford Handbook of International Environmental Law*, Oxford: Oxford University Press, 64–5, 72–83.

actors); and private administration (performed exclusively by non-state actors). A pluralistic view of multi-actor and multi-level global environmental governance as presented earlier in this book would lead one to believe that all of these forms of global administration are involved in global environmental governance to a greater or lesser extent. The classification also suggests that global administration is part of global environmental governance to the extent that environment-related administrative functions are performed within a state and beyond the borders of a state by state and non-state actors.

What is the contribution of global administrative law to global environmental governance? One definition of the concept suggests that global administrative law is similar to domestic administrative law, with the important difference that it operates in the global context:

> This nascent body of law, unlike domestic or national forms of administrative law, does not operate within the bounds of unitary nation states, and unlike traditional accounts of public international law, it does not arise exclusively between nation states. Instead it operates in a transnational or global space occupied by a vast variety of administrative actors responsible for trans-governmental regulation and administration; the field of 'global governance'.[110]

Although it is still an unsystematized and fragmented body of law, some general principles are developing which form the core of global administrative law, including the procedural participation of interested and affected parties, transparency, the justification for decisions, the standards of reasonableness and proportionality, access to judicial review, and the principle of legitimate expectations, among others.[111] These principles suggest that the value of global administrative law for global environmental governance lies in the measure of accountability and legitimacy that these principles could bring to global environmental governance, especially to the extent that global administrative law could provide the normative means to ensure that the general principles of good governance and administration that are usually found in domestic legal systems guide the global environmental governance actions of state and non-state actors. While it is beyond the scope of this book to canvass this issue any further, it must nevertheless be pointed out that global administrative law could significantly contribute to improving the effectiveness of global environmental governance, especially insofar as the principles of good environmental governance could be used as part of the global administrative law paradigm to improve the accountability, legitimacy, transparency and

[110] Mitchell, Andrew D. and John Farnik (2009), 'Global Administrative Law: Can it Bring Global Governance to Account?', *Federal Law Review*, **37**, 237–62 at 237.

[111] Mitchell, Andrew D. and John Farnik (2009), 'Global Administrative Law: Can it Bring Global Governance to Account?', *Federal Law Review*, **37**, 237–62 at 245.

participative practices in global environmental governance. More importantly, the critical role of global administration in global environmental governance and the idea that global administrative law could ameliorate 'bad' global environmental governance, again emphasizes the procedural aspects of global environmental governance as prerequisites for the achievement of its substantive aspects and objectives (for example, improvement of environmental quality). It also suggests that global administrative law is part of that body of law (which consists mostly of environmental law as Chapter 8 argues), that forms the legal foundation of global environmental governance.

12. NEXT-GENERATION GLOBAL ENVIRONMENTAL GOVERNANCE

While global environmental governance is itself an emerging and amorphous concept, its dynamism and fluidity are simultaneously giving rise to new global manifestations. Three examples are 'earth system governance', 'ecosystem governance' and 'new environmental governance'.[112] According to Biermann *et al.*,[113] earth system governance 'stands at the interface of ... governance theory and earth system analysis', and they define it as:

> ... the interrelated and increasingly integrated system of formal and informal rules, rule-making systems, and actor-networks at all levels of human society (from local to global) that are set up to steer societies towards preventing, mitigating, and adapting to global and local environmental change and, in particular, earth system transformation, within the normative context of sustainable development.

Earth system governance links the social or institutional aspects of governance (situated in social sciences) to earth system analysis (a natural science discipline) by investigating global transformations of the entire earth system.[114]

---

112 The rationale behind the development of the next manifestation of global environmental governance could be attributed to the fact that '[N]ew perspectives and research are needed to understand the complex relation between global transformations of social and natural systems, including accelerating economic integration, globalization in all its forms, internationalization of policy processes, and the multi-scale consequences of ecological transformation.' Biermann, Frank *et al.* (2010), 'Earth System Governance: A Research Framework', *International Environmental Agreements: Politics, Law and Economics*, **10**(4), 277–98 at 279.

113 Biermann, Frank *et al.* (2010), 'Earth System Governance: A Research Framework', *International Environmental Agreements: Politics, Law and Economics*, **10**(4), 277–98 at 279.

114 Biermann, Frank and Philipp Pattberg (2008), 'Global Environmental Governance: Taking Stock, Moving Forward', *Annual Review of Environment and*

Earth system governance thus seems to be a new and developing theoretical approach that seeks to marry social science constructs such as law and governance with natural science-based quantification and computer-based modelling with a primary view to understanding global environmental change in terms of the 'totality of processes in nature and human civilization'.[115] Its focus is global and it is as all-encompassing as many of the definitions of environmental governance discussed above. Yet it significantly departs from social-science and law-based conceptions of global environmental governance by including a natural science focus as well.

Another closely related emerging form of global environmental governance is 'ecosystem governance'. Karkkainen[116] suggests that ecosystem governance is based on the assumptions that the ecosystem context matters in environmental decision-making; ecosystems are complex and dynamic systems; and ecosystems are influenced by causally connected and interactive human actions. The respective implications of these are that ecosystem governance is not uniform and governance must be flexible and fluid in the same way that ecosystems are; ecosystem governance is a complex arrangement which seeks to address complex nonlinear ecosystem problems and will require an extremely high degree of scientific sophistication; and the focus of ecosystem governance, while it might itself manifest globally, must be decidedly localized, yet holistic, and must take into account the complex web of intertwined human actions and their effects on ecosystems.[117] Global *ecosystem* governance thus seeks to 'go beyond' global *environmental* governance to the extent that it is an institutional response which recognizes and is based on the infinite

---

Resources, **33**, 277–94 at 288. For brief reference to the role of global environmental law in earth system governance, see Chapter 8.

115 Biermann, Frank *et al.* (2010), 'Earth System Governance: A Research Framework', *International Environmental Agreements: Politics, Law and Economics*, **10**(4), 277–98 at 279.

116 Karkkainen, Bradley C. (2001/2002), 'Collaborative Ecosystem Governance: Scale, Complexity, and Dynamism', *Virginia Environmental Law Journal*, **21**(2), 189–243 at 194–9.

117 A narrower and perhaps less preferable view of ecosystem governance describes it by focusing on the value of ecosystem goods and services for human well-being:

> The 'ecosystem approach' consists of a strategy for the management of land, water and living resources in an integrated manner, thus promoting both conservation and sustainable use in an equitable way. It recognises that humans are a component of ecosystems and aims to apply the appropriate scientific methodologies to the management of live processes within ecosystems.

Blanco, Elena and Jona Razzaque (2011), *Globalisation and Natural Resources Law: Challenges, Key Issues and Perspectives*, Cheltenham: Edward Elgar Publishing, 117.

complexity of ecosystems instead of more narrowly-viewed environmental issues.[118] The central proposition of ecosystem governance is thus that because ecosystems are dynamic, complex and non-linear phenomena, governance arrangements must be equally accommodative of these dynamic, complex and non-linear characteristics in an integrated and holistic way. Ecosystem governance would in all likelihood require fewer changes with respect to the institutional architecture of global environmental governance and instead more tinkering with the *manner* in which global environmental governance is executed. Yet, ultimately it will have to overcome an important hurdle, namely, it must be sellable to traditionalists who must be convinced that it is a viable transformative (and reformative) development of the current form of global environmental governance, especially since it is often considered to be 'messy, elaborate, cumbersome, ad hoc, and defiantly unconventional'.[119]

'New environmental governance' is another emerging form of global environmental governance that is situated in the context of the 'new governance' paradigm.[120] New governance is a highly experimental form of governance and is a response to three realities: the increased global dimension of decision-making in the absence of a traditional form of centralized global government; the continuing demise of the state and the shift from Westphalian modes of governance to private governance in which global civil society is playing an increasingly important role; and a growing dissatisfaction with the orthodox, inflexible and coercive approaches to governance.[121] In essence, new governance is the opposite of orthodox or 'old' governance. It departs from the traditional state-centred, centralized, coercive, Leviathan and hierarchical notion of governance. Instead 'it is seen as a highly pragmatic and flexible approach to and modality of regulation, a method for ensuring maximum responsiveness and adaptability, with an emphasis on open-ended and provi-

---

118 By definition, 'natural resource governance' is arguably even narrower than ecosystem and environmental governance because it relates only to the natural resource components of the environment and thus excludes complex ecological and even human-centred cultural processes. See an example of its use in literature, among others, Blanco, Elena and Jona Razzaque (2011), *Globalisation and Natural Resources Law: Challenges, Key Issues and Perspectives*, Cheltenham: Edward Elgar Publishing, 65–82.

119 Karkkainen, Bradley C. (2001/2002), 'Collaborative Ecosystem Governance: Scale, Complexity, and Dynamism', *Virginia Environmental Law Journal*, **21**(2), 189–243 at 235.

120 See, for example, Durant, Robert F. *et al.* (2004), 'Toward a New Governance Paradigm for Environmental and Natural Resources Management in the 21st Century', *Administration and Society*, January, 643–82.

121 De Búrca, Gráinne and Joanne Scott (2007), 'Introduction', *Columbia Journal of European Law*, **13**(3), 513–17 at 513–14.

sional goals, and ensuring revisability and corrigibility'.[122] New governance's objectives can broadly be summarized as including to promote participation by all interested and affected parties; to coordinate multi-level governance; to allow increased diversity and decentralization; to establish and promote deliberative arenas; to allow for greater flexibility and revisability; and to foster experimentation and knowledge creation with respect to regulation.[123] In the environmental context, the foregoing could be accomplished through heterachy; networks; participation by all interested and affected parties; reflexive, revisable and fluid environmental standards; voluntary agreements and mutual recognition instead of legislation; the use of a broad range of non-coercive environmental governance techniques such as voluntary codes and guidelines; and alternatives to judicial involvement in environmental dispute resolution such as mediation, conciliation and arbitration.[124]

New environmental governance is understood to be a reorientation of traditional forms of environmental governance and as such it is still evolving, which means that its precise architecture remains open to debate and further analysis.[125] It is nevertheless possible to draw some general conclusions with respect to the phenomenon: new environmental governance could involve as many actors as could potentially have an interest in achieving a common societal goal and an actor need not be political; participation, dialogue and deliberation are important elements of new environmental governance; it is decentralized and thus multi-level and involves devolved decision-making; and it is flexible and revisionary as well as revisable, transparent, inclusive and based on consensus building.[126] In short, it is a concept which heavily relies on the 'governance without government' rhetoric, and it is neatly situated in the current deterritorialized globalization discourse with a predominant focus on the initiative being taken by global civil society. New environmental governance is the ultimate expression or result of a reformative process of global environmental governance that has already begun and which could best

---

122 Walker, Neil and Gráinne De Búrca (2007), 'Reconceiving Law and New Governance', *Columbia Journal of European Law*, **13**(3), 519–37 at 522.

123 Trubek, David M. and Louise G. Trubek (2007), 'New Governance and Legal Regulation: Complementarity, Rivalry and Transformation', *Columbia Journal of European Law*, **13**(3), 539–64 at 542.

124 Kingsbury, Benedict (2007), 'Global Environmental Governance as Administration: Implications for International Law' in Daniel Bodansky, Jutta Brunnée and Ellen Hey (eds), *The Oxford Handbook of International Environmental Law*, Oxford: Oxford University Press, 72.

125 Gunningham, Neil (2009), 'Environmental Law, Regulation and Governance: Shifting Architectures', *Journal of Environmental Law*, **21**(2), 179–212 at 203.

126 Gunningham, Neil 'Environmental Law, Regulation and Governance: Shifting Architectures', *Journal of Environmental Law*, **21**(2), 179–212 at 203.

be described as next-generation hybrid global environmental governance. It acknowledges that:

> ... although much of the 'rowing' is to be done locally by a variety of stakeholders acting collaboratively, nevertheless, certain central 'steering' functions remain with the state. What is involved is 'collaboration in the shadow of hierarchy' with the state underpinning community-based initiatives in a variety of ways ... without which they are unlikely to succeed. In this combination collaboration provides local knowledge, ownership and legitimacy while the state provides essential steering functions and resources.[127]

A cursory survey of these descriptions of 'new' forms of environmental governance, suggests that their 'newness' is primarily determined by their gradual shift away from state-centred public governance authority to multi-actor, multi-level and deterritorialized forms of governance with wider regulatory scope and mechanisms, and an increasing number and variety of actors. In other words, new environmental governance is perceived to be an even more pluralistic, open, fluid, multi-level, multi-actor and disaggregated mass than global environmental governance currently is.

13. SUMMARY

It is impossible to describe global environmental governance according to a detailed classification which comprehensively and exhaustively provides for all possible manifestations of this construct. This is evident from the multitude and multiplicity of descriptions that this chapter has analysed. At the most general level, global environmental governance refers to the disaggregated, yet interdependent, enmeshed mass of global regulatory arrangements which collectively aim to solve the world's common environmental problems. It is a social institution which has been created by people to regulate behaviour and the impact of human behaviour on the global environment.

More specifically, it is a means to order and regulate inter-state interdependence insofar as this interdependence relates to common global environmental problems. It is a means to achieve cooperation by state and non-state actors alike in a global arena where cooperation is patently difficult and interdependence is a given. Global environmental governance is a political process that is used to dictate who gets what with respect to the environment and to resolve global power struggles as far as the environment is concerned. It is a reforma-

---

[127] Gunningham, Neil 'Environmental Law, Regulation and Governance: Shifting Architectures', *Journal of Environmental Law*, **21**(2), 179–212 at 207.

tive strategy to improve existing global environmental governance arrangements to the extent that significant changes are accomplished in impacting behaviour, and environmental quality is improved or environmental degradation is halted in real terms. While the focus of global environmental governance is supra-national, it has a decidedly vivid impact on infra-national environmental governance arrangements. Moreover, global environmental governance would be meaningless without an effective infra-national environmental governance effort. There is clearly a reciprocal relationship between what happens in terms of environmental governance at a supra- and infra-national level. Global environmental governance is thus sub-national, national, regional and international. While there is a gradual move away from state-centred global environmental governance, the state and the institutions it acts through at the supra-national level remain the most important actors in global environmental governance, with the UN and its agencies being the predominant actors.

Law plays a decidedly important role in global environmental governance. It contributes to the institutionalization of global environmental governance in the sense that law is a source of the norms and structures of global environmental governance. In turn, global environmental governance is also responsible for the creation of (international environmental) law.

In addition to facilitating supra-national cooperation, regulating interdependency, changing behaviour as far as the environment is concerned, and improving the environment in real terms, global environmental governance also aims to achieve sustainability or sustainable development. The term is sometimes (confusingly) used interchangeably with 'governance for sustainability', and it seems as if the latter is a broader and more encompassing concept than the former. This conceptual confusion and differentiation seems, however, to be mostly academic, because it is clear that the only intention in coining the new term is to situate global environmental governance in the sustainability paradigm, or to show that global environmental governance is centrally concerned with the *problématique* of sustainability, namely achieving an equitable balance between social, economic and environmental considerations. The achievement of sustainability could thus be considered an overarching, idealistic objective of global environmental governance.

The administrative or bureaucratic functions of international organizations are increasingly thought to form part of the broader global environmental governance paradigm, and today global environmental administration is an element of global environmental governance. 'Global environmental governance as administration' is that which makes global environmental governance work, as it were. Global administrative law is also now considered to be a part of the legal foundations of global environmental governance.

From a phenomenological point of view, global environmental governance is not static. It is developing into new manifestations, or at least it is being transformed by emerging forms of governance such as earth system governance, ecosystem governance and new environmental governance. These forms could collectively be described as 'next generation' global environmental governance, with their emphasis on the need to link social sciences, law and natural sciences in global governance strategies, the need to incorporate ecosystem and earth systems approaches to global environmental governance, and the need to further elaborate and develop the non-traditonalist characteristics of global environmental governance to make it even more suitable for facilitating environmental governance in a globalized age.

8. Law and global environmental governance

> ... it is increasingly obvious that we need to broaden our concept of 'the law' when it comes to analysing environmental legal development ... Trying to analyse environmental law without reference to the wider context in which it is embedded risks an incomplete understanding of this branch of legal knowledge. Moreover, a growing number of scholars recognise that the conventional boundaries between disciplinary areas of study are dissolving and reforming as interdisciplinary areas focused on broader topics like regulation or governance.[1]
>
> (Lee Godden and Jacqueline Peel, 2010)

1. INTRODUCTION

Chapter 5 discussed in some detail the relationship between law and governance. It showed that law has a constitutive, regulative, legitimizing, and steering role to fulfil in the governance paradigm. The penultimate chapter of this book reflects on the role that law plays specifically in global *environmental* governance. As a point of departure, it focuses on the conceptual implications of the 'environment' for law and governance and argues that on the one hand, law and governance require an extended, holistic and comprehensive vision of the environment, whereas on the other hand, an extended vision of the environment requires an equally comprehensive view of law and governance.

The foregoing enquiry into an expanded and holistic vision of the environment, law and governance suggests that it is possible today to recognize the existence of some form of 'global environmental governance law', if not *de iure* then at least *de facto*. Global environmental governance law derives from global law, the idea of 'many environments', and a comprehensive view of pluralized and disaggregated law and governance in a globalized age, which include state and non-state forms of law that are situated on multiple levels and that are made, interpreted and enforced by a diverse range of state and non-

[1] Godden, Lee and Jacqueline Peel (2010), *Environmental Law: Scientific, Policy and Regulatory Dimensions*, Melbourne: Oxford University Press, 2.

state actors. This chapter attempts to formulate broad parameters within which to conceptualize the nature of global environmental governance law.

2. THE ENVIRONMENT AND DEFINITIONAL COMPLEXITIES

True to their nature and their affinity for definition, lawyers, and more specifically environmental lawyers, have been continuously attempting to define the 'environment' for the purpose of transposing it into the legal and regulatory domain. Godden and Peel[2] point out that:

> One of the greatest challenges facing environmental law today concerns the scope of what is encompassed by the notion of environment. Lawyers are fond of definitions, and environmental legislation and the decisions of judges contain many attempts to give a firm legal shape to environmental concepts. The way these definitions have changed over time is itself revealing, evidencing broader transformations in scientific understanding, philosophical approaches, economic models and awareness of cultural diversity. A constant interplay between the law and other disciplines has done much to broaden understanding of the environment that is subject to different forms of legal regulation and management.

Lawyers and regulators have attempted to define the environment and continue to do so in an effort to concretize and shape their regulatory efforts and to try to understand what it is they seek to influence through the institutions they establish and rules they develop, interpret and enforce. There is, however, little agreement on some form of a generally acceptable definition of the environment for the purpose of law and governance. As some commentators put it: '[D]ifferences of basic meaning ... pervade the implications of the term "environmental" ... The usage of this term is key in determining what it is we want to explain.'[3]

2.1 The Society/Environment Interface

Seeking to clarify the 'environmental' concept for the purpose of law and governance is simultaneously a straightforward and complex matter. It is straightforward because the environment can be anything one wants it to be

---

2 Godden, Lee and Jacqueline Peel (2010), *Environmental Law: Scientific, Policy and Regulatory Dimensions*, Melbourne: Oxford University Press, 5.

3 Paterson, Matthew, David Humphreys and Lloyd Pettiford (2003), 'Conceptualizing Global Environmental Governance: From Interstate Regimes to Counter-hegemonic Struggles', *Global Environmental Politics*, **3**(2), 1–10 at 3.

and as such, it should be intuitively straightforward to determine the parameters and content of the legal and governance responses to environmental issues. An extended view of the environment, for example, would mean that global environmental governance could include *all* institutional arrangements which seek to change human behaviour towards the environment and which idealistically attempt to achieve sustainability. A narrower view would mean that the institutional response, including its laws and governance arrangements, would also be narrower, more focused or less comprehensive. For example, the institutional arrangements responsible for global environmental governance would be considerably more comprehensive than natural resource protection or water governance in a specific country. The latter are issue-specific and geographically bound because the conception of the environment as including only natural resources (water) is equally constricted.

Yet the foregoing exercise in arriving at a definition is also a complex matter, because the notion 'environment' and its relationship with society (in other words the society/environment interface) is complex. The relationship or interface between society and the environment is key in understanding a) the societal conflicts that surface when environmental 'problems' arise in society, and b) the type of institutional response to these problems and conflicts that we seek to resolve by means of law and governance. Put differently, it is not only the notion of what the environment is that will determine the law and governance response, but also the society/environment *interface* which will dictate how we will respond to environmental problems through social institutions such as law and governance. The society/environment interface is important for understanding the law/governance/environment relationship because law can regulate only those environmental problems that arise from and within society (as a result of the actions of people). In other words, as a social construct and institutional response to environment-related social problems law has no direct control over the environment, nor can it directly improve the environment or environmental quality. Law can regulate only human conduct, and by doing so endeavour to influence the environment or environmental quality. For example, law cannot cause global temperatures to stabilize by directly influencing ocean currents. It can attempt to address climate change only by preventing people from emitting greenhouse gases or by encouraging and rewarding those people who modify their behaviour in such a way that the greenhouse gas emissions for which they are responsible are reduced. In other words: '[I]t is these *human-induced changes* that ... law seeks to address.'[4] While this statement is self-evident, it is nevertheless

---

4 Bodansky, Daniel (2010), *The Art and Craft of International Environmental Law*, Cambridge, Massachusetts: Harvard University Press, 10. Emphasis added.

important to make it, as it suggests that law and governance are both institutional responses that change *human behaviour* with respect to the environment and that society will use law to achieve a certain (eventual) environmental outcome. In the words of Bothe:[5]

> None of these [environmental] problems can be addressed directly by [legal] prohibitions or orders. To give an example pertaining to the field of environmental protection: An 'order' given to a river to be clean is not a valid legal rule – it is devoid of a valid addressee. Law can only determine human behaviour, it cannot change nature. Thus, if law is to contribute to the solution ... it has to direct or induce human behaviour in a way that the problem is solved. As these are very complex problems, the behaviour of many actors must be determined in a coherent way so that the factual end result is the one which was desired. Thus, the impact of law on the solution of those problems will always be an indirect one. This being so, the question has to be asked where and how precisely law should trigger which type of human behaviour in order to solve a problem.

It is important to realize in this context that 'environmental problems are not automatically social problems. There is an "ecological difference" ... between the natural conditions which sustain life and the artificial conditions which determine institutional reproduction [and response].'[6] In other words, environmental problems do not automatically become problems of governance which society will seek to regulate by means of law, for example. Environmental problems will become problems of governance only if and when society perceives them to be problems. Law is a social intervention that can be applied only to those environment-related issues which society regards as problems. Furthermore, the society/environment interface will be influenced by the way people regard themselves vis-à-vis the environment and how they value the environment. These perceptions and values, in turn, would have an influence on the design and execution of institutional responses to environmental issues. In other words, the values a society places on the environment will very directly determine the design of the laws that a society uses to address environmental issues. For example, whereas deep ecologists decry the pervasive role of humans as dominators of the environment, anthropocentrists instead emphasize the value of the environment insofar as it serves human needs, and promotes health and well-being. Deep ecologists might thus

---

5 Bothe, Michael (2005), *Environment, Development, Resources: Collected Courses of the Hague Academy of International Law*, Leiden: Martinus Nijhoff, Brill, Publishers, 351.

6 Smith, Sean C. (1994), 'How Law Hides Risk' in Gunther Teubner, Lindsay Farmer and Declan Murphy (eds), *Environmental Law and Ecological Responsibility: The Concept and Practice of Ecological Self-Organization*, Chichester: John Wiley and Sons, 118.

support efforts to incorporate the rights *of* the environment in a state constitution, for example, whereas anthropocentrists would rather advocate for the adoption of a human right *to* a specific environmental quality. It can therefore be expected that the manner in which deep ecologists perceive and design environmental governance would differ markedly from that of anthropocentrists.[7]

Another governance or regulatory consequence of the environment/society interface is that, as our perceptions of the environment change over time, as they do, so too will the conception of and accordingly the construction of our environmental governance response:

> Our notions of environment are constructed against a backdrop of changing issues, problems, perceived solutions, groups and institutions ... The environment, while clearly grounded in empirical understandings, nonetheless exists as a mediated construct within a social, political and cultural context.[8]

The foregoing suggests that there is a deep social element inherent in society's perceptions of the environment and the design and implementation of institutional responses (law and governance) designed to address issues/problems that arise in connection with society and its relationship with the environment. Another important insight is that law and governance do not apply directly 'to the environment', as it were. These social institutions would rather seek to change human behaviour vis-à-vis the environment and the manner in which and extent to which they would do so are determined partly by the way in which society views and values the environment.

2.2 The Environment and Environmental Law

Environmental law has emerged as a distinct body of law that must deal with the general interconnected, multifarious and cross-cutting aspects of the society/environment interface:

> Environmental law is special ... Environmental law deals with special problems of ecological and economic interconnectedness and hence with the ubiquitous side effects of any intervention. It deals with long time horizons and complex and uncertain risks, with shared externalities and diverse sources, and with hard tradeoffs between competing values ... the very characteristics that make it 'special also make it more 'general' than much mainstream law. Whereas constitutional law, criminal law, contracts and commercial law ... deal only with human-human interactions,

7 Perez, Oren (2004), *Ecological Sensitivity and Global Legal Pluralism: Rethinking the Trade and Environment Conflict*, Oregon: Hart Publishing, 13–17.

8 Godden, Lee and Jacqueline Peel (2010), *Environmental Law: Scientific, Policy and Regulatory Dimensions*, Melbourne: Oxford University Press, 57.

> environmental law deals with interactions among humans and the other several million species on the planet, in complex interconnected systems, over long time horizons. Because human systems are nested within larger and more diverse ecological systems, environmental law in a very real sense embraces all other areas of law.[9]

Other commentators put it thus: 'environmental law is concerned not only with the relationship of humans with each other but also with the inextricable connection between humanity and the common exterior world – the global environment as a whole and its component parts'.[10] While environmental law has developed in recent years as a distinct body of law that focuses specifically on these complex environmental issues, many of its definitional parameters remain unclear and are insufficiently determined:

> ... when it comes to trying to define the boundaries of the subject [environmental law], it is clear that there is little in the way of agreement. Certain commonly agreed elements exist such as the regulation of polluting activities by man and the protection of natural assets such as wildlife or landscapes, and these fields of law are what many environmental lawyers would describe as their core concerns. However, it is equally clear that there are many other areas of regulatory law ... which have substantial environmental implications, even if environmental protection, as many would understand it, is not their sole focus.[11]

While the conceptual parameters of environmental law remain vague and less determined than, say, contract or family law, having a broadly inclusive definition of the environment would helpfully mean that environmental law could embrace all areas of law. Considering environmental law as including all those rules which affect human behaviour vis-à-vis the environment would usefully

---

9 Wiener, Jonathan B. (2000/2001), 'Something Borrowed for Something Blue: Legal Transplants and the Evolution of Global Environmental Law', *Ecology Law Quarterly*, **27**, 1295–1372 at 1366.

10 Yang, Tseming and Robert V. Percival (2009), 'The Emergence of Global Environmental Law', *Ecology Law Quarterly*, **36**, 615–64 at 623–4.

11 Macrory, Richard (2008), *Regulation, Enforcement and Governance in Environmental Law*, London: Cameron May, 421. The 'pervasive interrelatedness' of the environment also contributes to definitional complexities:

> The pervasive interrelatedness among elements of the environment makes the environment a highly complex system ... The complexity and pervasive interrelatedness of the environment ... make it extremely difficult to decide which activities need to be regulated to what extent in order to achieve a desired balance.

Aagaard, Tod S. (2009/2010), 'Environmental Law as a Legal Field: an Inquiry into Legal Taxonomy', *Cornell Law Review*, **95**, 221–82 at 269 *et seq.*

broaden the scope of environmental law and its substantive reach to include various other sub-disciplines such as trade law, humanitarian law, and investment law, for example. Such a definition would make it possible for law to be considered environmental law if it regulates human activities that affect a very broadly conceived environment and a very wide range of legal rules (both state and non-state) could therefore be considered to be environmental law.[12] As far as legal taxonomy is concerned, such a broad interpretation may be problematic. Yet from a functional/regulatory/instrumental perspective in the global environmental governance paradigm, the suggestion that all law could be considered environmental law insofar as it influences human behaviour that impacts on a comprehensively defined environment is less problematic, because it links the regulatory purpose of law with the central regulatory tenet and broad scope of *global* environmental governance. In other words, a broadened view of environmental law is especially accommodative of a broadened view of the global.

Such an extensive approach also accommodates a broader view of the role of environmental law in the global environmental governance effort. More importantly, it suggests that a restricted and traditional view of environmental law is too narrow and issue-specific to be the only legal sub-discipline that fulfils a function in global environmental governance. The 'globalness' of global environmental governance is sufficiently comprehensive to include administrative law, international environmental law, ancillary sub-disciplines of international law such as trade law, regional laws, and numerous non-traditional or non-state forms of law, among others. Moreover, the multi-level and multi-actor implications of the 'global' also mean that law on all levels of governance (national, regional and international) made by all relevant actors (state and non-state) has the potential to play a role in global environmental governance. When the disaggregated mass of institutional and normative arrangements that result from the foregoing is pitched against a broadly defined environment, clearly then environmental law becomes only a small

---

12 This does not mean that environmental law does or necessarily must reflect environmentalism:

> Environmentalism does not predominate in current environmental law, and there is little prospect of that changing significantly in the future. Instead, environmental law reflects a balance among a variety of competing values and interests, which include environmentalism but also other, arguably more powerful, values such as maintaining traditional patterns of resource exploitation and resistance to government regulation.

Aagaard, Tod S. (2009/2010), 'Environmental Law as a Legal Field: an Inquiry into Legal Taxonomy', *Cornell Law Review*, **95**, 221–82 at 256.

part of the larger legal rubric that fulfils an instrumentalist/regulative/functionalist role in global environmental governance. The foregoing suggests that it might even be possible to speak of 'global environmental governance law'; an issue that is further explored below.

2.3 The Environment and Governance

If there is uncertainty with respect to the parameters of environmental law and the relationship between law and the environment, one can expect that this uncertainty would be replicated and compounded within the more amorphous, fluid and vague governance paradigm. Conceptual clarity with respect to the environment would thus be as important for governance as it would be for law. This is so because our conception of the environment will influence our conception of the legal and regulatory responses to those environmental problems or issues we seek to regulate. It will determine the nature, levels and types of the different actor constellations involved in legal and governance processes and also the nature, levels and types of the actor constellations involved in the environmental governance effort. In other words, the 'environment' will inform the conceptual and pragmatic conception, design and ultimately the implementation of the law and the execution of environmental governance.

In a societal setting, the environment is one of many 'problems of governance'.[13] 'Problem-solving' is one of the objectives of governance and the primary purpose of environmental governance is to achieve a certain environmental objective by influencing the behaviour of people in a particular way with a view to changing that behaviour according to certain standards or an agreed-upon set of rules that should contribute to solving environmental problems. The objective of regulating human behaviour could be to prevent environmental harm, to minimize or mitigate environmental harm, to maintain environmental quality, to improve environmental quality, and/or to provide protection and adaptation solutions for environmental degradation and change. In this way our conception of a specific environmental issue or problem will influence how we define, create and shape the governance response with respect to whatever it is we want to address. For example, climate change is a global environmental problem with global, intra- and inter-jurisdictional, intra-generational, and inter-generational aspects. It truly affects the entire global environment, including all living things on earth, all of the surroundings within which people exist – the land, water and atmosphere of the earth;

---

[13] Koskenniemi, Martti (2004), 'Global Governance and Public International Law', *Kritische Justiz*, **37**, 241–54 at 254.

micro-organisms, plant and animal life; the physical, chemical, aesthetic and cultural properties and conditions of the foregoing that influence human health and well-being in all of the countries of the world simultaneously; any part or combination of these; and the inter-relationships among and between them.[14] If the concept of the environment is sufficiently broad, our concept of the institutional response to governing the climate change component of environmental governance (or climate governance) would be equally expansive and encompassing. The sheer magnitude and complexity of the current global climate governance regime bears testimony to this.

2.4 Towards a Uniform Definition of the Environment?

The nature, extent and severity of environmental problems today require of us to rethink our institutional responses to these problems. Environmental threats nowadays do not occur in and affect the people in a single country only; they have become truly global, a point which has been made throughout this book. Because legal and governance structures 'must adjust to accommodate broader notions of environment',[15] we also need to be innovative and sufficiently comprehensive in our definitional endeavours that seek to understand the environment. This could lead one to potentially limitless descriptions of a concept that until recently related mostly to man-made surroundings and natural elements, media, resources and ecosystems,[16] but which now entails much more:

> The boundaries of what constitutes an 'environmental' issue have already become blurred ... our understanding of what constitutes an environmental issue must grow to encompass economic, social, and trade policy. Indeed, if, as some claim, everything is interconnected, then everything becomes an environmental problem.[17]

---

[14] This expansive notion of the 'environment' is based on the definition of 'environment' in section 1 of South Africa's *National Environmental Management Act* 107 of 1998.

[15] Godden, Lee and Jacqueline Peel (2010), *Environmental Law: Scientific, Policy and Regulatory Dimensions*, Melbourne: Oxford University Press, 6.

[16] An example of a restrictive definitional approach is the popular trend to distinguish between environmental and natural resources and therefore to view the environment by means of a compartmentalized and silo-based approach. The environment does not only consist of natural resources but also of environmental media, chemical and biological processes, and socio-cultural elements, among others. This approach is evident in, for example, Durant *et al.*'s use of the term 'environmental and natural resource management'. Durant, Robert F. *et al.* (2004), 'Toward a New Governance Paradigm for Environmental and Natural Resources Management in the 21st Century', *Administration and Society*, January, 643–82.

[17] Bodansky, Daniel (2010), *The Art and Craft of International Environmental Law*, Cambridge, Massachusetts: Harvard University Press, 10–11.

Or as Caldwell[18] states:

> At the end of the 20th century, the world is in unprecedented transition. The adaptability of present institutions to emerging challenges is being widely questioned. In a broadly encompassing context, these areas of challenge – social, ethical, economic, and technological – have environmental implications. However, this assertion is credible only if the *environment* is understood in its holistic dimensions – comprising complex dynamic interrelationships from cosmic to microcosmic, extending beyond ordinary perceived human experience, yet nevertheless interacting with humanity, and thus shaping the parameters of life on Earth.

What then would be the most useful idea of what the environment is for the purpose of law and governance? According to Von Moltke:[19]

> From a theoretical [institutional] perspective 'the environment' is a construct that has no direct institutional equivalent. Since 'the environment' is by definition everything that lies outside human institutions, there can be no single institution that adequately reflects it. The environmental agenda is in fact an agenda of several issues that exhibit distinctively different problem structures.

This description validly asserts that the environment could be anything and that any conception of the environment would depend on the perceptions of people, which, in turn, would be influenced by preconceived foreknowledge (such as environmental radicalism, rationalism, religion, and so forth).[20] This would mean that no single social institution (including law and governance) could comprehensively and on its own encapsulate the environment, or more precisely, entirely could address the *environmental* problem. Instead, the environment's dynamism, amorphousness and multi-dimensionality by necessary implication require that the environmental governance agenda be equally dynamic, amorphous, and multi-dimensional.

The rather uninspiring conclusion is therefore that there probably cannot be a single universally accepted definition of the environment. For the purpose of law and global environmental governance, what would be important is to

---

[18] Caldwell, Lynton K. (1999), 'Is World Law an Emerging Reality? Environmental Law in a Transnational World', *Colorado Journal of International Environmental Law and Policy*, **10**(2), 227–43 at 229.

[19] Von Moltke, Konrad (2005), 'Clustering International Environmental Agreements as an Alternative to a World Environment Organization' in Frank Biermann and Steffen Bauer (eds), *A World Environment Organization: Solution or Threat for Effective International Environmental Governance?*, Aldershot: Ashgate, 176.

[20] For a comprehensive discussion of some of these concepts, see Godden, Lee and Jacqueline Peel (2010), *Environmental Law: Scientific, Policy and Regulatory Dimensions*, Melbourne: Oxford University Press, 16–39.

acknowledge that over-inclusiveness is arguably better than under-inclusiveness. Thus, an all-inclusive definition of the environment would make better provision for the inclusion of the entire range of issues, levels, actors and mechanisms that disaggregated, polycentric global environmental governance requires. For example, describing the environment as referring only to the natural environment for the purpose of global environmental governance would be inadequate and tantamount to ignoring the complexity, reciprocity and disaggregated yet holistic reality that the 'global' necessitates. An expansive definition of the environment would also be particularly accommodative of 'new' forms of next generation global environmental governance discussed in Chapter 7.

In this context (even though their treatment of the 'global' is less extensive than what this book proposes), Godden and Peel's[21] notion of 'many environments' is appealing because it helps to situate the environment and environmental problems in the global context of global environmental governance:

> ... it is possible to conceive of multilayered, multidimensional, (and potentially mutually exclusive) environments that intersect and overlap to make up a unitary phenomenon. These environments might range from the local to the national, to the regional and global scale; from a single species to world climate trends; from indigenous cultural heritage to partnerships between environmental non-governmental organisations and multinational businesses to reduce industrial waste.

Attributing the meaning of 'many environments' to the environment in global environmental governance would render it sufficiently reconcilable with the global in global governance, and it would be particularly accommodative of the indeterminability of the concept. Moreover, the notion of 'many environments' in the context of the 'global' helpfully points to the interrelatedness of all environmental components, whether they are natural, man-made or cultural; situated in a single country or where they traverse the borders of many countries; even where they are part of the global commons. The interrelatedness of all of the foregoing suggests some form of environmental transnationality (globalness) where the destruction of the rainforests in Brazil, for example, would affect the whole of global society, because global warming would be exacerbated. In fact, 'the collective global interest in a clean planet is far more diffuse than the nation's collective interests in a clean country. The benefits ... of preventing climate change would be spread globally and be enjoyed well into the future.'[22] One could even reframe global environmental

---

21 Godden, Lee and Jacqueline Peel (2010), *Environmental Law: Scientific, Policy and Regulatory Dimensions*, Melbourne: Oxford University Press, 54.

22 Wiener, Jonathan B. (1998/1999), 'On the Political Economy of Global Environmental Regulation', *Georgetown Law Journal*, **87**, 749–94 at 761.

interrelatedness and causality as an example of the well-known butterfly effect, which finds expression in terms of chaos theory. In the same way that a butterfly flapping its wings somewhere in the world could cause a tornado in another part of the world, a localized 'environmental event' has global implications. To misquote Wiener:[23] '[T]he causal pathway is [also] through the globally shared environmental medium, not [only] through the direct effects of the source's pollution on nearby individuals or the neighbouring jurisdiction.' This contributes to discrediting the idea held by some that global environmental governance is restricted only to issues such as stratospheric ozone depletion, climate change, transboundary water pollution and the loss of biodiversity.[24] The global environment, and thus global environmental governance, includes all of these 'environments'; but also many others at various different levels (from the sub-national to the supra-national), whether these environments are natural, cultural and/or man-made.

3. TOWARDS GLOBAL ENVIRONMENTAL GOVERNANCE LAW

An extended view of the environment, of governance, and of the body of laws that regulates human behaviour vis-à-vis the environment allows one the opportunity to further explore the possibility of a newly emerging body of law; one which in this context could be termed 'global environmental governance law'.

3.1 Globalization, Transnationalization, the 'Global' and the Law

Law does not operate in a safe house where it is isolated and protected so that it can act independently from other social institutions, phenomena and the broader processes of change that permeate the world and global society. Because it is a social institution, law necessarily depends on society and it is influenced by social change, especially those changes brought on by globalization. Conversely law also influences society and is itself responsible for initiating or further facilitating change in society. Society and law are thus interconnected. More pertinently, law has been and continues to be deeply affected by the expansion of what Allot[25] calls the 'public realm':

23 Wiener, Jonathan B. (1999), 'Global Environmental Regulation: Instrument Choice in Legal Context', *Yale Law Journal*, **108**(4), 677–800 at 690.

24 See, for example, Wiener, Jonathan B. (1999), 'Global Environmental Regulation: Instrument Choice in Legal Context', *Yale Law Journal*, **108**(4), 677–800 at 686 *et seq*.

25 Allot, Philip (2000), 'The Concept of International Law' in Michael Byers

> International institutional processes proliferated as simulacra of national constitutional processes – deliberative, administrative, arbitral. They took on systematic integrity and organic life, each a social system with its own constitutional structure and process, but systematically linked to national systems, with the social outputs of the external systems flowing back into the national systems as social inputs ... In this way, national processes were *communalized externally* to form an informal and rudimentary international public realm of increasing complexity (of organization) and density (of outputs), and national processes began to be *co-ordinated transnationally* with national decision-making processes coming more and more to be conditioned by products of international decision-making processes.

The expanding and increasingly interconnected national and supra-national public realms, which could collectively be referred to as 'transnationality in the global', are a product of globalization. In fact, the expanding public realm in many ways is globalization. More importantly, the increased transnationality of law and institutional processes would imply that law has become global. It is 'out there' and it is subject to being influenced by global social changes. The concept of transnational law is not new. In fact, in his seminal 1956 work, *Transnational Law*, Jessup[26] develops a theory of transnational law which he describes as 'all law which regulates actions or events that transcend national frontiers ... [including] public and private international law ... [and] other rules which do not wholly fit into such standard categories', which collectively is based on the idea of the 'universality of [the] human problems'.[27] His conception of transnational law admittedly is narrower than more contemporary views, yet the relevance of the concept of transnational law is continuing and growing, specifically in the environmental domain.[28] It is not always entirely

---

(ed), *The Role of Law in International Politics: Essays in International Relations and International Law*, Oxford: Oxford University Press, 79.

26 Jessup, Philip C. (1956), *Transnational Law*, New Haven: Yale University Press, 2 *et seq*.

27 This early description of transnational law is similar to what Jenks calls the 'law of the world community':

> The law of the world community is the common law of mankind; its ambit extends to all the varied activities and forms of social organization in which the life of man has overleaped the boundaries of the state and now defies any possibility of effective national regulation or control.

Jenks, Wilfred C. (1972), 'Multinational Entities in the Law of Nations' in Wolfgang Friedmann, Louis Henkin and Oliver Lissitzyn (eds), *Transnational Law in a Changing Society*, New York: Columbia University Press, 71.

28 Transnational environmental law is also a growing scholarly enterprise as the recent establishment of a journal exclusively devoted to transnational environmental law issues suggests (*Transnational Environmental Law*). See Cambridge University Press http://journals.cambridge.org/action/displayJournal?jid=TEL [accessed 24 January 2012].

clear what the differences are, if any, between global and transnational law, and most commentators seem to use the terms interchangeably.[29] What is clear is that these terms clearly do *not* and should not describe international only (i.e., the relations between two or more states). In all probability, transnational and global law have the same meaning, especially when they are used in a globalized context to denote polycentric, multi-level and multi-actor global governance.[30]

In the same way that governance has become global, so too has law been freed from its national and state-centred shackles in the attempt to deal with or regulate globalization and its consequences.[31] To be more precise, law has become global because, first, it is created and enforced at various levels including the sub-national (for example, by a local government), the national (for example, the government of India), the regional (for example, the EU, and the international (for example, the UN). In many instances, these levels are either connected or are at least mutually receptive to reciprocal influences that flow from the national to the supra-national and vice versa. For example, international law influences the design and content of national legal developments and its success largely depends on effective national implementation.[32] Conversely, domestic legal rules have the potential to influence international law. The same reciprocity exists between national laws and regional laws and between regional and international laws. Second, law is global because today it is created and enforced by multiple actors operating in the predominantly public or state-centred domain, and increasingly in the private or non-state actor domain. Law is thus global because the actors in law are global to the extent that they are state and non-state and they are interdependent and enmeshed, both with respect to the actors that create, interpret and enforce law,

---

29 See, for example, Peters, Anne (2010), 'Transnational Law Comprises Constitutional, Administrative, Criminal and Quasi-private Law' in Pieter H.F. Bekker, Rudolf Dolzer and Michael Waibel (eds), *Making Transnational Law Work in the Global Economy*, Cambridge: Cambridge University Press, 154–73.

30 In keeping with the central theme and focus of this book, the remainder of this chapter employs the concept global law.

31 This is also true for environmental law. See Verschuuren, Jonathan (2012), 'Overcoming the Limitations of Environmental Law in a Globalised World' in Frank Wijen *et al.* (eds), *A Handbook of Globalisation and Environmental Policy* 2nd edn, Cheltenham: Edward Elgar Publishing, 616–40.

32 Although one must be conscious of the fact that 'the existence of an international provision does not automatically imply similar provisions at the national level, because there is usually much leeway in international treaties as well as deficient implementation of supra-national law'. Holzinger, Katharina, Christopher Knill and Thomas Sommerer (2008), 'Environmental Policy Convergence: the Impact of International Harmonization, Transnational Communication, and Regulatory Competition', *International Organization*, **62**, 553–87 at 557.

and the actors on whom law is imposed. Third, law is global because, as a result of the plurality of the actors involved with law at multiple levels, the nature and types of legal rules have changed from being exclusively state-centred legal rules in the strict sense to being a mixture of state and non-state law which has a private character and which has been created by non-state actors such as the global self-regulatory rules of multinational enterprises.[33]

In this context, the rise of global law clearly answers the need to regulate globalization. Stern[34] proposes that globalization can be regulated in three ways: by means of unilateral regulation by a state through the worldwide (meaning global) extension of its national laws (the frequent attempts of the United States in this respect are an example); multilateral regulation through private or non-state actors and non-state regulatory systems; and multilateral regulation by states through the creation of a worldwide international legal system of regulation (the emerging regional legal system of the EU is often cited as an example in this respect). Realizing that the global system needs the globalization of legal rules, and thus of legal control, as no system can work in the long term without rules and control, enables one to understand the globalization of law and the subsequent emergence of global law as the confluence of the three ways in which globalization could be regulated. Consequently, the means to regulate globalization do not act separately, as Stern seems to suggest. They should rather be considered a collective phenomenon consisting of simultaneous efforts that cumulatively lead to the formation of a body of global law. In short, law could be considered increasingly global to the extent that it 'contains all legal phenomena everywhere, overcoming the artificial separation of the national and the international realms, and removing the anomalous exclusion of non-governmental transnational events and transactions'.[35]

3.2 The Emergence of Global Law

The foregoing gives rise to various pertinent questions: is there something like global law and global environmental law; what law at which level is the law that forms part of global environmental governance; and would it be possible to discern some form of emerging *de facto* global environmental governance

---

33 For an extensive discussion see Chapter 5.

34 Stern, Brigitte (2000), 'How to Regulate Globalization?' in Michael Byers (ed), *The Role of Law in International Politics: Essays in International Relations and International Law*, Oxford: Oxford University Press, 255–66.

35 Allot, Philip (2000), 'The Concept of International Law' in Michael Byers (ed), *The Role of Law in International Politics: Essays in International Relations and International Law*, Oxford: Oxford University Press, 88.

law? Answering these questions is not a mere academic exercise. Determining whether or not some form of global environmental governance law exists also tells us something about the manner in which law operates in the global environmental governance paradigm, because '[W]e designate legal fields – environmental law, labor law, criminal law – on the premise that those designations identify something important about how the law operates.'[36] Moreover, it tells us something about the legal foundations and legal rules that constitute, legitimize, prescribe, proscribe, and guide global environmental governance.

In answering these questions, as a point of departure one must again appreciate the role of law in the global context by restating the meaning of 'global', as it is explained elsewhere in this book.[37] Global does not only mean international. Instead it evinces geographical, causal and temporal characteristics ranging from the sub-national to the supra-national. For example, the success of international law depends on the extent to which national legal regimes will incorporate and implement it. Conversely, national law also has the potential to affect international legal developments and the development of international law is often preceded by a specific domestic event. By virtue of the process of legal transplants, the content and design of national laws often depend on the dictates and content of international law. So too it is possible that international law could 'borrow' from national legal regimes, some examples being the global climate regime, the precautionary principle, which stems from the German legal system (*Vorsorgeprinzip*), and the laws of the EU, which could be seen to have been borrowed (at least in part) from their Member States.[38] In a very direct and concrete way, national law could thus inform supra-national law through the 'global accretion of consistent national law [which] can also eventually ripen into the recognition of "customary international law" applicable to all states, regardless of the states' specific consent'.[39] Universal human rights are arguably examples of national legal inventions which have achieved global *ius cogens* status that set out *erga omnes* obligations.[40]

---

36 Aagaard, Tod S. (2009/2010), 'Environmental Law as a Legal Field: an Inquiry into Legal Taxonomy', *Cornell Law Review*, **95**, 221–82 at 224.

37 See Chapters 1, 2, 4–6.

38 Wiener, Jonathan B. (2000/2001), 'Something Borrowed for Something Blue: Legal Transplants and the Evolution of Global Environmental Law', *Ecology Law Quarterly*, **27**, 1295–1372 at 1302–1303, 1305.

39 Wiener, Jonathan B. (2000/2001), 'Something Borrowed for Something Blue: Legal Transplants and the Evolution of Global Environmental Law', *Ecology Law Quarterly*, **27**, 1295–1372 at 1302.

40 De Wet, Erika (2006), 'The International Constitutional Order', *International and Comparative Law Quarterly*, **55**, 51–76.

While 'global' has some geographical dimensions in the sense that it implies transnationality and an interplay between national, regional and international law, it does not exclusively refer to one of these levels but rather seeks to describe the interdependence, interconnectivity and reciprocity between national, regional and international levels. In this sense, national, regional and international law are all smaller parts of a comprehensive conceptual construction of global law where the 'global' provides an opportunity to resituate law in a broader, more encompassing, reciprocally interconnected and causal 'legal space'.[41] So too are the different forms of state and non-state law that are created and enforced by multiple state and non-state actors at these different levels inherently part of this global construction.

While opinions on the existence of global law vary, it is now generally accepted that the realities of globalization (including the disaggregated pluralistic enmeshment of the global legal order as described in Chapter 5) offer strong support in favour of the formalization of some kind of global law. The existence of global law is underpinned and supported by the prevalence of global legal pluralism. It is a body of law that has peculiar characteristics different from those of traditional state law, and it can be explained in terms of the phenomenon of differentiation within world society, which results from strong globalized socio-economic processes. It is not a-political, as one would expect, but as some suggest it is rather a body of law which will become re-politicized by means of non-traditional processes outside the orthodox political realm.[42] Global law has neither a single authoritative centre and source nor a distinct territorial boundary, and it is produced by means of the 'coupling' of law to the globalizing process as a reaction to and a result of, globalization.[43] Global law is therefore not a universal type of law that applies to everyone everywhere (although it arguably has the potential to assume characteristics of universalism, or at least common elements that apply everywhere, as the example of the general legal prevalence of a particular set of universal human rights suggests). It is also not global 'in the sense that everyone on the planet can be sure that wherever he or she goes on the planet, human relationships will be governed by some law, even if not by a law that is everywhere the

---

41 Anders, Gerhard (2004), 'Lawyers and Anthropologists: A Legal Pluralist Approach to Global Governance' in Ige F. Dekker and Wouter G. Werner (eds), *Governance and International Legal Theory*, Leiden: Martinus Nijhoff Publishers, 50–51.

42 Teubner, Gunther (1997), '"Global Bukowina": Legal Pluralism in the World Society' in Gunther Teubner (ed), *Global Law without a State*, Aldershot: Dartmouth, 4.

43 Teubner, Gunther (1997), '"Global Bukowina": Legal Pluralism in the World Society' in Gunther Teubner (ed), *Global Law without a State*, Aldershot: Dartmouth, 8.

same'.[44] Even less likely is the assumption that there is a body of universal law that, in addition to traditional international law that applies *between* nations, also applies *within* nations to everyone everywhere.[45] Global law instead implies, for example, that even if its laws do not apply outside the borders of a country, the national laws of that country have some effect on the supra-national legal order, regionally and/or internationally. So too does international and regional law affect national legal systems. Global reciprocity in this context is evident from Richardson's[46] statement that 'local regimes should come to act globally by recognizing the extent of the local effects from global issues, by managing local environmental issues as regional issues, and by integrating the social, economic and environmental issues of their locality'.

In addition to processes of harmonization, cross-pollination, legal convergence and integration (all collectively understood in the context of the 'globalization of law'), some legal rules do in fact apply universally. These could, for example, include those elements of customary international law which could be considered as setting out *erga omnes* obligations and which have *ius cogens* status. Universal human rights are examples of global constitutional constructions which are recognized as *ius cogens* norms setting out *erga omnes* obligations. They have a strong ethical underpinning and hierarchical standing.[47] In the environmental context the customary international law norm of *sic utere tuo ut alienum non laedas* is arguably the best example of a universal legal rule that applies to all states and which sets out universal obligations on all states not to cause transboundary environmental harm.[48]

The emergence of global law is further evident where different national jurisdictions increasingly borrow from one another in a steady process of horizontal legal borrowing, thus resulting in the creation of a truly *inter*-national, or inter-jurisdictional system of law where distinct national jurisdictions display considerably more similarities than ever before.[49] In a globalized

---

44 Shapiro, Martin (1993/1994), 'The Globalization of Law', *Global Legal Studies Journal*,**1**(37), 37–64 at 37.

45 Caldwell, Lynton K. (1999), 'Is World Law an Emerging Reality? Environmental Law in a Transnational World', *Colorado Journal of International Environmental Law and Policy*, **10**(2), 227–43 at 229.

46 Richardson, Benjamin J. (2000), 'Environmental Law in Postcolonial Societies: Straddling the Local-Global Institutional Spectrum', *Colorado Journal of International Environmental Law and Policy*, **11**, 1–82 at 62.

47 De Wet, Erika (2006), 'The International Constitutional Order', *International and Comparative Law Quarterly*, **55**, 51–76.

48 This rule was formulated in the famous Trail Smelter Arbitration Case. See Trail Smelter Arbitration Reports of International Arbitral Awards 16 April 1938/ 11 March 1941 Vol III, 1905–1982.

49 Yang, Tseming and Robert V. Percival (2009), 'The Emergence of Global Environmental Law', *Ecology Law Quarterly*, **36**, 615–64 at 616.

world, the *inter*-national and national and supra-national are more interwoven and interdependent than ever before, especially because of increased transnational legal transplants and legal borrowing, as a result of the interdependency of these legal systems on each other for their effective realization and enforcement, and because of the disaggregation of law-making, administration and enforcement in polycentric global governance. Global law further implies that the sources of law in the global (including national, regional and international levels) have become multifarious and disaggregated where these are spread among a wide range of state and non-state actors operating at multiple levels. These hybridized sources in turn imply that the nature of law in the global has also changed from being strictly coercive, top-down state-made law to being more reflexive, soft, and flexible forms of non-state law.

In a nutshell, global law is a result of globalization and more specifically the need to govern the effects of globalization. Global law is not geographically limited and it is disconnected from a central locus of authority. Global law traverses borders and includes all levels of governance ranging from the national to the supra-national. Global law is made, interpreted and enforced by a wide variety of state and non-state actors and therefore ranges from being strict, coercive state-based law to more flexible and reflexive forms of non-state law. Global law is inherently reciprocal and causal to the extent that it is an enmeshed mass of legal arrangements in the global arena that are mutually dependent and interrelated.

3.3 Emerging Global Environmental Law

If one accepts the existence of some form of global law, the question arises if it would be possible to discern a distinct body of global *environmental* law (otherwise expressed as transnational environmental law). While scholarship on the conceptual field and legal taxonomy of global environmental law is underdeveloped, some definitions thereof do exist. For example, Wiener[50] sees global environmental law as 'a marriage of international and national environmental law; something old, something new, something borrowed for something blue'. With reference to the growing regime of global production and chemical regulation, Tseming and Percival[51] define global environmental law as an *emergent* system which is:

---

50 Wiener, Jonathan B. (2000/2001), 'Something Borrowed for Something Blue: Legal Transplants and the Evolution of Global Environmental Law', *Ecology Law Quarterly*, **27**, 1295–1372 at 1371.

51 Yang, Tseming and Robert V. Percival (2009), 'The Emergence of Global Environmental Law', *Ecology Law Quarterly*, **36**, 615–64 at 616–17, 619 *et seq.*

> ... the set of legal principles developed by national, international, and transnational environmental regulatory systems to protect the environment and manage natural resources. As a body of law, it is made up of a distinct set of substantive principles and procedural methods that are specifically important or unique to governance of the environment across the world. It includes: (1) public international environmental law ... (2) national environmental law ... and (3) transnational law, which describes the set of legal principles used to regulate the cross-border relationships between private individuals and organizations.

In the authors' view, global environmental law is therefore national, international and transnational; a view that resonates well with the understanding of 'global' presented in this book. Their definition is also instructive to the extent that it illustrates an important albeit manifestly evident point: one of the ways through which environmental law has become global is through the internationalization of environmental law. This has to do with the process by means of which environmental laws are manifesting beyond state borders to apply to global environmental problems (mostly the environmental commons, common public environmental goods, and transboundary environmental pollution issues). The internationalization of environmental law involves not only the actual creation of international environmental laws but also the interactive political and diplomatic process through which state and non-state actors engage to create these laws.[52] Presumably, these processes present rich opportunities for cross-fertilization which has the potential to influence the creation of common (and possibly even universally similar or generic) global legal rules that are at least based on the same ideas and influences, if not exactly on the same content. However, in terms of the theory of 'the global' described earlier in this book, internationalization is only part of a much larger project of the globalization of law. The *nationalization* of international environmental law, the inter-jurisdictional transplantation of laws (or the *inter*-nationalization of laws), the regionalization of national environmental laws and the nationalization of regional environmental laws also play a part in environmental law becoming global or in the emergence of global environmental law. Such an extended view sits well with the concept of *transnationalization*, which is explained as the 'legal regulation of the full gamut of economic, cultural, social, and, in this context, environmental interaction between and across nations'.[53] Global environmental law is therefore the national environmental

---

52 Yang, Tseming and Robert V. Percival (2009), 'The Emergence of Global Environmental Law', *Ecology Law Quarterly*, **36**, 615–64 at 646.

53 Ong, David M. (2010), 'From "International" to "Transnational" Environmental Law? A Legal Assessment of the Contribution of the "Equator Principles" to International Environmental Law', *Nordic Journal of International Law*, **79**(1), 35–74 at 44.

laws of states, national environmental laws between states, and supra-national (including regional and international) environmental laws beyond states.

Global environmental law could also be understood in terms of the geography of law coupled with an expansive view of the environment proposed above. Kysar[54] explains that '[L]aw contains its own geography', and that:

> ... the geography implicit in law will over time come to resemble that of the earth sciences. As the category of environmental pathways acknowledged by law expands and diversifies, and as the operations of those pathways come to be seen as hemispheric or global in scale rather than national or regional, then eventually, the claims of deep interconnection so prominent in environmental science, and so urgently pressed in environmental politics, also will find concrete expression in environmental law.

Arguments for an expanded geography of law to more closely fit the expansive reach and interconnected global nature of the earth system sit particularly well with the concept of earth system governance referred to in Chapter 7. It was argued in Chapter 7 that earth system governance refers to the global system of formal and informal rules, rule-making systems, and actor-networks that steer societies towards preventing, mitigating, and adapting to environmental change and earth system transformation, and it thus relates to transformations of the entire earth system.[55] Global environmental law is part of this 'global system of rules', it has a more expansive geography and it has the potential to even further expand its geography to more closely resemble that of the earth system. In other words, to see environmental law through the lens of the earth system (or earth system governance), provides one with the opportunity to expand its geography (and as a result its reach and influence) to a truly global one.

While substantive law certainly would be part of global environmental law, especially insofar as it dictates the objectives of the law and governance response, global environmental law, as with any national legal system, also includes procedural laws which dictate how substantive laws must be enforced or, even more broadly, how governance must be performed. In this sense, global environmental law also consists of procedural rules such as those related to administrative justice, access to justice and dispute resolution, due process, participative governance and transparency (collectively referred to as good environmental governance), which are necessary to realize the substantive

---

[54] Kysar, Douglas (2010), *Regulating From Nowhere: Environmental Law and the Search for Objectivity*, New Haven: Yale University Press, 123, 124.

[55] Biermann, Frank *et al.* (2010), 'Earth System Governance: A Research Framework', *International Environmental Agreements: Politics, Law and Economics*, **10**(4), 277–98 at 279, 288.

objectives of global environmental law. Global administrative law, and the more general principles of good governance enshrined in the *Convention on Access to Information, Public Participation in Decision-Making and Access to Justice in Environmental Matters*, June 25, 1998, 38 I.L.M. 517 (1999), for example, serve as examples of procedural global environmental laws. Global administrative law is thus also part of global environmental law. In short, therefore, global environmental law consists of various substantive and procedural laws that are focused on achieving some substantive 'environmental' result and that prescribe the manner in which to achieve this result.

More recently Shaffer and Bodansky[56] (correctly) explained that transnational environmental law is much broader than international environmental law and that it subsumes the latter legal sub-discipline. In the authors' view, transnational environmental law most usually involves inter-state cooperation in a transboundary setting; and it relates to the 'migration and impact of legal norms, rules and models across borders ... [and] ... encompasses all environmental law norms that apply to transboundary activities or that have effects in more than one jurisdiction'.[57] They seem to imply with this that transnationalism involves trans-jurisdictionality, a possibility which is reinforced by their reliance on the idea of cross-nationality as employed by Holzinger, Knill and Sommerer[58] to study the cross-national convergence of environmental policies. The legal norms of transnational environmental law are broadly defined as those that 'lay out behavioral prescriptions issued by an authoritative source in a written form, whether or not mandatory or backed by a dispute settlement or other enforcement system'. It includes national environmental law norms that 'horizontally' affect other jurisdictions as well as 'private' norms made by non-state actors.[59] Their description helpfully explains that transnational envi-

---

[56] Shaffer, Gregory and Daniel Bodansky (2011), 'Transnationalism, Unilateralism and International Law', University of Minnesota Law School Legal Studies Research Paper Series Research Paper No. 11-34, August available at http://papers.ssrn.com/sol3/papers.cfm?abstract_id=1920470 [accessed 21 December 2011].

[57] Shaffer, Gregory and Daniel Bodansky (2011), 'Transnationalism, Unilateralism and International Law', at 1 University of Minnesota Law School Legal Studies Research Paper Series Research Paper No. 11-34, August available at http://papers.ssrn.com/sol3/papers.cfm?abstract_id=1920470 [accessed 21 December 2011].

[58] Holzinger, Katharina, Christopher Knill and Thomas Sommerer (2008), 'Environmental Policy Convergence: the Impact of International Harmonization, Transnational Communication, and Regulatory Competition', *International Organization*, 62, 553–87.

[59] Shaffer, Gregory and Daniel Bodansky (2011), 'Transnationalism, Unilateralism and International Law', at 1–2 University of Minnesota Law School Legal Studies Research Paper Series Research Paper No. 11-34, August available at http://papers.ssrn.com/sol3/papers.cfm?abstract_id=1920470 [accessed 21 December 2011].

ronmental law is national and supra-national. While one can find little fault with such a comprehensive description, the authors do seem to suggest that 'transboundary-ism' must be a condition or element of transnational environmental law, which in turn suggests that their understanding of transnationality is quite literal and geographically limited, and thus more restricted than what this book envisages. The foci of transnational environmental law are states *inter se* and the result is that attention is diverted from the important contribution of a wide variety of state and non-state actors situated on various levels that act in global environmental governance. Such a focus might also accentuate the inter-state nature of transnational environmental law at the expense of a more global view in which, for example, the global commons also assume a prominent position and in which international and regional environmental law play a more fundamentally substantive normative role instead of being relegated to only disciplining unilateral action by states in their transnational environmental relations.[60] By the authors' own admission, global environmental law is 'another variety of transnational environmental law'.[61] If the authors mean to imply that transnational law usually has a transboundary focus, the point must be made that transnational environmental law could then be considered a part of global environmental law.

The general criteria to measure the emergence of 'global' law, in addition to the fact that it must be multi-level to a greater or lesser extent, is whether or not it 'has moved beyond the inter-state paradigm'.[62] Has environmental law moved beyond the state? In the light of this chapter's earlier analysis it is possible to conclude that the law that regulates environmental issues today is a mixture of state and non-state law that manifests at various levels and that comprises a whole range of different legal sub-disciplines that might influence peoples' behaviour towards the environment.[63] Environmental law in the

---

[60] Shaffer, Gregory and Daniel Bodansky (2011), 'Transnationalism, Unilateralism and International Law', at 8 University of Minnesota Law School Legal Studies Research Paper Series Research Paper No. 11-34, August available at http://papers.ssrn.com/sol3/papers.cfm?abstract_id=1920470 [accessed 21 December 2011].

[61] Shaffer, Gregory and Daniel Bodansky (2011), 'Transnationalism, Unilateralism and International Law', at 3 University of Minnesota Law School Legal Studies Research Paper Series Research Paper No. 11-34, August available at http://papers.ssrn.com/sol3/papers.cfm?abstract_id=1920470 [accessed 21 December 2011].

[62] Hey, Ellen (2010), 'Global Environmental Law and Global Institutions: A System Lacking "Good Process"' in Roland Pierik and Wouter Werner, *Cosmopolitanism in Context: Perspectives from International Law and Political Theory*, Cambridge: Cambridge University Press, 45.

[63] On the role of non-state law in global environmental regulation, see Verschuuren, Jonathan (2012), 'Overcoming the Limitations of Environmental Law in

context of 'many environments' has thus moved beyond the state, both in a geographical sense and in terms of the levels and actors involved. It would thus be possible to speak of global environmental law to the extent that environmental law embraces the 'many environments', the various sources of law which have to do with these environments, and the many actors which create and enforce these laws. It consists of those rules at the national, regional and international levels that are made by state and non-state actors with the explicit and implicit purpose of influencing human behaviour towards the globally conceived 'many environments'. It aims to change human behaviour in the global arena and the effect of human behaviour on the entire global environment, which is holistically construed to be an intransigent, interconnected and interacting whole, or a 'multilinear, multi-loop interactive feedback system'.[64] As determined by this context, environmental law has become global horizontally (between the different national, regional and international levels), vertically (ranging between nations *inter se* and between regions *inter se*); in terms of its sources of authority, to the extent that it is both private and public due to the numerous state and non-state actors involved; and with respect to the global nature of the 'many environments' to which it applies. Such a broad definition implies that a very wide range of laws could be considered global environmental law, and it admittedly brings with it taxonomical anomalies. Yet, typifying a wide selection of laws as being part of global environmental law usefully integrates environmental concerns into the specific legal sub-disciplines that govern various other aspects of global activity which are related to the human/environment interface. These include, for example, trade, commerce, travel and leisure, and construction law. The benefits of such an expanded view are obvious: '[S]ince almost every form of international activity – from humanitarian aid to warfare – has environmental implications, environmental protection would be enhanced if environmental concerns were incorporated into the law governing these activities.'[65]

3.4 Emerging Global Environmental Governance Law

The emergence of global environmental law against the backdrop of globalization, perhaps more than anything else, emphasizes the point that (interna-

---

a Globalised World' in Frank Wijen *et al.* (eds), *A Handbook of Globalisation and Environmental Policy* 2nd edn, Cheltenham: Edward Elgar Publishing, 616–40.

64 Caldwell, Lynton K. (1999), 'Is World Law an Emerging Reality? Environmental Law in a Transnational World', *Colorado Journal of International Environmental Law and Policy*, **10**(2), 227–43 at 228.

65 Dunoff, Jeffrey L. (1995), 'From Green to Global: Toward the Transformation of International Environmental Law', *Harvard Environmental Law Review*, **19**(2), 241–301 at 281.

tional) environmental law cannot be the sole component of the legal response that seeks to address the global arena's 'many environments' (or the global environment) today. Neither could regional laws or national environmental law systems be the only legal institutional responses that seek to change human behaviour towards the environment. Put differently, international environmental law has become inadequate to fill the shoes of global environmental governance's legal foundation. The regulatory consequences of globalization instead involve polycentric global environmental governance, which is multi-actor and multi-level. This means that there must also be a body of law that makes global environmental governance work, as it were. Presumably this body of law would consist chiefly of global environmental law. A broad view of the existence of the 'many environments' also suggests that it could include other legal disciplines such as trade law, administrative law, constitutional law, for example, insofar as these bodies of law could be used to influence human behaviour towards the environment. If global environmental governance is understood as an institutional response to global environmental problems, which includes the entire collection of normative arrangements (including state and non-state forms of law) at national, regional, and international levels, which are created, maintained, and enforced by state and non-state actors, then it might be possible to describe the collection of these normative arrangements that manifest in the global environmental governance milieu as global environmental governance law. It includes national, regional and international law. It is hard and soft, coercive and reflexive, and it is made, interpreted and enforced by states and non-states actors. Importantly, global environmental governance law could include environmental law (on all levels, made by all actors); pure public international law and its many divisions; economic law, trade law, global administrative or institutional law, and so forth. In fact, it is an emerging body of law, as amorphous as its parent concept global environmental governance is, and it could include any sub-discipline of law to the extent that it is relevant to facilitating global environmental governance or to achieving the objective of global environmental governance, namely to change human behaviour vis-à-vis the environment with the idealistic hope of achieving sustainability. It thus transcends and recasts the traditional disciplinary boundaries within law; the traditional geographical delineation of national, regional and international levels with respect to law; and the traditional sources of law, changing them into global rhetoric which requires 'changing the boundaries and building the linkages between local, national and international institutions'.[66] It also necessitates

[66] Richardson, Benjamin J. (2000), 'Environmental Law in Postcolonial Societies: Straddling the Local-Global Institutional Spectrum', *Colorado Journal of International Environmental Law and Policy*, **11**, 1–82 at 82.

rethinking the regulatory link between law (broadly conceived, as is suggested by the foregoing) and the objectives of law in the global environmental domain.

This would mean that global environmental governance law consists of all the laws that seek to influence human behaviour with respect to the global environment and which have some substantive global environmental objective. It is all the laws that seek to regulate the procedural aspects of global environmental governance by dictating the manner in which global environmental governance occurs; it is all the laws that provide for the creation and revision of the entire institutional framework of global environmental governance; and it is all the laws that facilitate the ongoing process of the further institutional and normative growth of the ongoing global responses to global environmental problems. Global environmental governance law is therefore created through global environmental governance, it is used to achieve the objectives of global environmental governance, it upholds and maintains global environmental governance and, conversely, it is used to create and execute the institutional, substantive and procedural elements of global environmental governance. It is an interconnected phenomenon with reciprocal vertical and horizontal flows ranging among national, regional and international legal systems, among specific sectoral environment-related issues, and among the various state and non-state actors that are involved with global environmental governance on these different levels. It explicitly discards legal 'boxing' and the silo-based approach to categorizing and fragmenting the environment and legal sub-disciplines and is instead inclusive, cross-cutting and general.

While such a broad definition and general approach may seem not particularly useful to legal taxonomy and to pragmatic considerations, it forces us to resituate the role of law in the global environmental regulatory context and to face the modern realities and challenges that the 'many environments' in the globalized context require us to do. It also enables us to understand the steady emergence of a *de facto* mass of laws that forms the basis of the pluralistic, dynamic, multi-level, multi-actor process of change through global environmental governance, which idealistically aims to sustainably optimize environmental benefits and use while at the same time seeking to protect environmental capital for the sustainable benefit and use of present and future generations.

4. SUMMARY

Law has an important role to play in global environmental governance. This is so because law (whether state or non-state law or both) is one of the primary institutional responses that society uses to address environment-related problems that arise within that society. Law changes behaviour and it thus attempts to influence the behaviour of people vis-à-vis the environment. How society views and values the environment will largely determine the design, purpose, and extent of the laws and the entire governance response to solve environment-related problems that arise in society. A broad and comprehensive view of the environment in the global context is preferable to a narrow and restricted view and more compatible with the complexity of the nature of global environmental governance.

To date, environmental law has traditionally played the predominant role in regulating human behaviour with respect to the environment. Yet the realities of globalization, the causal effect of global reciprocity, and the interconnectedness of the existing regulatory processes (global governance), coupled with an extensive view of what constitutes the environment, means that environmental law cannot continue to serve as the sole set of legal rules in global environmental governance. Global environmental governance instead requires all those laws that aim to change human behaviour with respect to a broadly conceived environment in the global context. This global body of laws already exists. Each one of them has some environmental objective in mind. Global environmental law is made, interpreted and enforced by all state and non-state actors involved in and responsible for global environmental governance on all levels of governance, ranging from the national to the international; it is based on and exudes the characteristics of global law; it consists of substantive and procedural elements; it is simultaneously national, inter-national (or inter-jurisdictional), regional, and international; and it consists of 'hard' and formal state-based law and softer, more informal non-state law.

The existence of this body of global environmental law suggests the *de facto* emergence of global environmental governance law. Global environmental governance law is the legal foundation of global environmental governance. It constitutes global environmental governance; it legitimizes it; it determines who should govern what and provides governance actors with legal personality; it sets out the minimum standards which should be achieved through the governance of a specific environmental problem (for example emission reduction targets); it provides the means to change human behaviour vis-à-vis the environment; and it determines how global environmental governance actors should govern. It also provides the means to interpret legal rules and to resolve legal and governance disputes that might arise during governance and those environment-related disputes that arise in society. In addition to serving as a vehicle for global environmental governance that enables governance, global environmental governance law also applies to the regulators or governors in their capacity as the governed or regulated to the extent that these entities are bound to abide by laws in the same way as traditional regulated subjects are bound by them.

9. Reconstructing global environmental governance

> What is only rarely realised is that it is indeed structurally impossible to define, in a comprehensive manner, something which is a social creation to begin with.[1]
>
> (Jan Klabbers, 2009)

1. INTRODUCTION

If Klabbers is to be believed, governance, and by implication, global environmental governance, are difficult (impossible even) to define and describe because they are social institutions created by man. This is also true for law. Yet the difficulties of definition do not diminish the need thereof and the need for a description of a concept or phenomenon: '[P]erhaps it is some innate instinct for orderliness which leads the human mind endlessly to establish and to discuss classifications and definitions and to evolve theories to justify them.'[2] The previous chapters have attempted to describe, to situate and to understand the social institutions of law and global environmental governance. What remains in this final chapter is to synthesize the main insights from these chapters with a view to formulating a reconstructed concept of global environmental governance.

2. GOVERNANCE

How does governance apply in the environmental regulatory domain? Kjaer[3] states that 'no clear and positive definition of governance has yet been

[1] Klabbers, Jan (2009), *An Introduction to International Institutional Law* 2nd edn, Cambridge: Cambridge University Press, 6.

[2] Jessup, Philip C. (1956), *Transnational Law*, New Haven: Yale University Press, 7.

[3] Kjaer, Poul F. (2010), *Between Governing and Governance: On the Emergence, Function and Form of Europe's Post-national Constellation*, Oxford: Hart Publishing, 2.

produced, nor has a general theory of governance yet been developed.' This view emphasizes that the complexity, fluidity and amorphous nature of governance arguably make it impossible to formulate a generic definition of governance that would be universally applicable and useful across the scientific spectrum. Yet despite this uncertainty and complexity it is nevertheless intuitively possible to postulate 'universal truths' about governance. What are they?

We understand governance to be primarily concerned with the regulation of human behaviour. It is thus a social institution, intervention, phenomenon and/or construct through which society aims to intervene and influence human behaviour, social processes and the effects of human behaviour, and in so doing to achieve a social outcome different from the one which would have arisen without this intervention. Governance facilitates regulatory intervention and cooperation to protect and promote common interests and is mostly concerned with adjusting human behaviour in an interactive setting where the achievement of common goals and solving of collective problems are primary concerns. The various actors involved are coerced and/or encouraged to change their behaviour according to what is perceived to be legitimate, acceptable, and in their common interests. Because of its emphasis on adjusting human behaviour, governance is therefore focused on human agency in the institutional context, which means that it has to do with people's ability to choose and to make decisions and to impose these decisions on themselves and on other people, mostly by means of rule setting, rule interpretation, rule application and rule enforcement.

People could act individually to achieve a certain outcome or they could act collectively if it were in their common interest to do so. In fact, in some instances the nature of a governance problem or issue is such that people are forced to act together to address their problem. Environmental degradation is an example of a governance problem which forces people to take collective action, since a degraded environment, whether it is within the borders of a particular country or spans a specific region and thus includes many countries, affects everyone. Individuals in a country, for example, would elect a government through which they would aim to promote their collective interests within the country's borders, including peace and order, economic prosperity and, for our present purposes, environmental protection. Just as individuals in a state would form a government to govern, a collection of states will protect and promote their common interests outside their national borders through supranational institutions such as regimes and international organizations. Whereas states play the primary role in governance, both in and outside their borders, today the forces and effects of globalization make it increasingly difficult for states to effectively promote and protect common interests and solve common problems of governance, such as global environmental degradation, outside their borders. Non-state actors are therefore gradually emerging as important and increasingly influential agents of governance to assist the state in achieving the objectives of a specific governance effort. Globalization is therefore leading to the disaggregation of global governance, which invites the participation in governance of numerous non-state actors such as NGOs, MNCs and epistemic communities, for example, with the object of solving collective problems and/or promoting common interests. In this way, state-centred public governance has mutated into multi-level and multi-actor hybrid governance by virtue of non-state, private actor involvement on the national, regional and international levels. This suggests that governance occurs everywhere. It is performed by individuals in a country, in and by national governments, NGOs, corporations, regional organizations such as the EU, and internationally by the UN, for example.

Governance also has to do with power and authority, whether derived from states (public authority) or from non-state actors (private authority) or from both of these sources simultaneously (private-public or hybrid authority). Governance is concerned with relations between states; relations within states; relations between state actors and non-state actors; and relations between non-state actors. Governance is both government (understood here to include state and non-state governance) and the process of governing, and it therefore has materialistic and functionalist or procedural characteristics which cumulatively aim to achieve the substantive dictates of a specific government and a governance effort. As the following section explains, law contributes to providing the rules related to the substantive content and the procedural aspects of governance. In other words, law mostly provides the 'what' and the 'how' of governance.

3. GOVERNANCE AND LAW

Governance is clearly a social phenomenon because it involves people, it is institutional because it provides the 'rules of the game' and material institutions such as government, and it is normative because it is based on and uses normative arrangements (or rules) to achieve a certain outcome. In terms of the normative basis of governance, and more specifically the rules of governance, law (broadly viewed as including state legal rules and non-state, law-like rules) plays a critical role because law is the constitution of governance; law legitimizes governance; law creates agents of governance and allows them to govern; law provides the authority to these actors to govern; law prescribes how to govern and what to govern; and law provides the minimum thresholds for what is deemed acceptable or unacceptable behaviour in society. Law therefore ultimately fulfils a distinct constitutive, legitimizing, prescriptive, proscriptive, instrumentalist and guiding function in and of governance. In short, '[G]overnance can be accomplished by law'[4] and the regulative objectives of law are simultaneously accomplished through governance. For example, a state's constitution establishes the state, it determines the composition of a state's government, it delimits the powers of that government, and it places certain obligations on the government with respect to the citizens of the state. The Charter of the UN has a similar constitutive function; so too do the rules that establish a NGO. These examples illustrate the extent to which law, through a constitution, constitutes or establishes the institutions (or actors) that must govern and the manner in which law prescribes to these institutions which substantive legal prescriptions and proscriptions to accomplish through governance. Law therefore provides the parameters or minimum thresholds for what is deemed to be acceptable and unacceptable behaviour (in other words, law proscribes and prescribes), and the minimum goals which must be achieved through governance. In addition to constitutions, various laws would also determine and instruct institutions or actors how to govern by means of provisions related for example to transparency, democracy, deliberation and participation, administrative justice and access to justice.[5]

While the foregoing examples illustrate the extent to which law applies to the governor, law also applies to the governed, which would generally consist of people or the institutions through which they act collectively (such as states and international organizations), especially in the public space where individuals or a group of individuals (such as the citizens of a state) operate. Law will prescribe to these individuals or groups of individuals what is permissible and what is not, how their behaviour should conform to what society deems to be acceptable, the punishment if their behaviour does not conform to this standard, and/or the rewards if it does. In addition to state-based law, non-state law-like rules such as codes of conduct and behavioural principles are increasingly important in the 'governance without government' setting, especially insofar as they provide non-coercive, reflexive guidance to the governed and the governor with respect to the human-environment interface. For example, because a society places a high premium on its water resources, that society would create laws that must prescribe the conditions in which and the extent

---

[4] Keohane, Robert O. and Joseph S. Nye (2002), 'Governance in a Globalizing World' in Robert O. Keohane (ed), *Power and Governance in a Partially Globalized World*, London: Routledge, 203.

[5] A domestic example is South Africa's Promotion of Administrative Justice Act 3 of 2000, whereas the *Convention on Access to Information, Public Participation in Decision-Making and Access to Justice in Environmental Matters*, June 25, 1998, 38 I.L.M. 517 (1999) operates supra-nationally. The principles of good environmental governance would be applicable similarly.

to which people in that country will be allowed to carry on industrial activities that have the potential to pollute water resources. If people do not heed these provisions, they might incur the civil, criminal and/or administrative liability which is provided for in the law. In addition to these state-based laws, individuals or corporations could voluntarily decide to subscribe to corporate practices with respect to 'managing' their activities in such a way that water pollution is avoided or minimized, or the water is rehabilitated. The ISO 14001 EMS is a concrete example of this. Also, numerous legal arrangements exist regionally and internationally, most of which apply to states (collections of individuals) and operate in the same way as domestic laws. An example is the host of multilateral environmental and environment-related agreements that exist today.

The relationship between law and governance, notably, is a continuously reinforcing, interlinked and reciprocal one. While law enables governance, state and non-state actors would through performing acts of governance, create law, interpret law, and apply and enforce law with a view to changing human behaviour, solving collective problems that arise in society and protecting and promoting collective interests.

4. ENVIRONMENTAL GOVERNANCE

What do the universal truths of governance mean for environmental regulation? It was suggested above that people could act individually to achieve a certain outcome or they could act collectively if it would be in their common interest to do so. Environmental degradation is an example of a governance problem which forces the taking of collective action since a degraded environment affects everyone, whether that environment is situated within the borders of a country or spans a region and therefore includes the environments of various countries. Clearly then the environment, arguably more than anything else, is an example of a shared social issue or a problem which requires collective action by state and non-state actors alike.

How far do the boundaries of the definition of the 'environment as a collective governance problem' extend? Answering this question is important, because the answer would influence the scope, depth, extent and nature of the environmental governance response. Understood in its broadest possible form, the environment relates to everything that people perceive to exist around them including people themselves; the natural environment; the human-made environment; water, soil and air; all forms of life including biological and chemical processes; and the manner in which people interact and experience the aesthetic (including the socio-cultural) and utilitarian aspects of the environment. Because the grasp of the nature of 'the environment' is wholly conditional on human perceptions, any idea of what it is will be influenced by differing ecological and socio-economic conditions; the geographical space wherein people find themselves; and a host of cultural, ethical, and political factors. For example, the environment would be very different for a destitute single mother of four children living in a township in a corrugated iron shelter without water, sanitation and electricity somewhere on the outskirts of Cape Town from what the environment would be for someone living in Munich. This reality and the extraordinary variety in the assumptions people make about their environments admittedly renders the making of choices with respect to the scope, depth, extent, and nature of the environmental governance response extremely difficult. The diversity in people's concepts of the environment would also suggest that environmental governance responses might be different in the different geographical, socio-economic, political and ecological contexts in which they occur. For example, while the performance of environmental governance in South Africa is predominantly anthropocentric in nature, the German approach to environmental governance would arguably be more ecocentric. It is because many environments coexist simultaneously that the performance of environmental law and governance differs so starkly from place to place – in this example, in South Africa and Germany. This malleability and diversity in the concept of the environment demands that the design of environmental governance should be equally malleable and diverse.

What is also clear is that human actions affect the environment. Human behaviour depletes environmental resources, it produces new environmental components and harms the environment. Environmental governance is a strategy that people use to alter human behaviour with a view to achieving a type of environment or environmental quality or level of environmental protection that they perceive to be more acceptable. People design institutions and act through them to change human behaviour with respect to the environment. For our present purposes it is unnecessary to reflect on the underlying motivations for people to do so: it could be to optimize economic benefits, to gain competitive advantage, to gain greater political power, or even for genuinely altruistic ecological purposes. A more important point is that human behaviour towards the environment can be changed: '[H]uman nature is somewhat malleable, its shape determined in limited but important ways by whether the prevailing social, economic, and political systems are designed to bring out cooperation or conflict, ecological awareness or consumer fetishism.'[6] Whether acting individually, collectively through

[6] Hempel, Lamont C. (1996), *Environmental Governance: The Global Challenge*, Washington: Island Press, 21.

states, networks, regional governance bodies or international organizations, people will use law as an institutional mechanism to change behaviour vis-à-vis the environment.

Viewed thus, the objectives of environmental governance also become clear. Generally speaking, environmental governance has a pragmatic objective and an idealistic objective. Its pragmatic objective is to change human behaviour, often by means of law, with a view to addressing those environmental issues that society perceives to be problematic. If governance is an institutional response that seeks to change human behaviour, then environmental governance aims to change human behaviour with respect to a comprehensively conceived environment. The idealistic objective of environmental governance is the achievement of sustainability, and in this sense the pragmatic objective of changing human behaviour vis-à-vis the environment is a prerequisite and first step to be taken en route to that end. Yet, the achievement of sustainability (meaning an equal balance between social, financial and ecological capital) is arguably an impossible task, and instead of ever hoping to achieve it one can hope that the attempt to do so will play a guiding role in the performance of environmental governance. Thus, while the value and use of sustainability should not be unrealistically overstated, it remains an important conceptual framework or organizing principle for the design of those institutional responses through which people seek to influence behaviour with respect to the environment:

> Sustainability is ultimately about ideas and forms of human organization that cohere ecologically and that do not require linear notions of time for their validation – only a deep sense of harmony and connectedness. By providing the organizing framework for this sense to develop, sustainable development ... offers a means of collective hope and transcendence that help make the personal sacrifices required for future environmental improvement more worthwhile ... As with the postmaterialist notion of progress, sustainable development refers to development that is largely qualitative or self-limiting in nature. It can conceivably encompass most of the important objectives of global environmental governance. And despite suffering from abstraction and oversimplification in day-to-day usage, it offers a useful bridge for connecting environmental concerns with social and economic well-being.[7]

Sustainability is important not only for the design of these institutions themselves in the sense that they must be sustainable, but also more importantly for the results they seek to achieve. In other words, sustainability must guide institutional responses such as law and environmental governance to achieve outcomes that are sustainable.

---

[7] Hempel, Lamont C. (1996), *Environmental Governance: The Global Challenge*, Washington: Island Press, 40–41.

Despite its malleability in terms of its scope, depth, extent, and nature, it is still possible to formulate a generic definition of environmental governance, which would be that it is a normative institutional regulatory intervention and social construct that is predominantly based on law and that aims to influence how people interact with the environment. It entails a pluralistic, dynamic, multi-level, multi-actor response and process of change which pragmatically aims to change human behaviour vis-à-vis the environment, and idealistically to optimize environmental benefits and use, while at the same time seeking to protect and preserve sufficient environmental capital for present and future generations.

5. GLOBAL ENVIRONMENTAL GOVERNANCE

Global environmental governance is a normative regulatory intervention intended to respond to environmental problems or issues that arise in the global arena. The global context is not a level but rather a space which is simultaneously national, regional and international. It consists of specific individual countries (national entities), collections of countries in specific regions (regional entities), and the entire international community of states (the international entity). Global governance is thus the sum of governance performed by the national, regional and international entities. It interlinks these phenomena and intertwines the political, social, economic, and legal processes of which they consist. Governance in the global arena thus consists of all governance arrangements that exist on all of these levels; of all state and non-state governance actors variously situated on all of these levels; and the collection of state and non-state rules, or laws, that these actors would use to change human behaviour to such an extent that it would be conducive to their collective interests.

Global environmental governance focuses primarily on governing unwanted environment-related changes brought about by globalization. In doing so, it focuses on changing human behaviour vis-à-vis the environment within and outside states; on relations between states and between states and their subjects; on the changing role of the nation state; on the rise of civil society and the many private forms of governance performed by non-state actors; on the increasing importance of hybrid public-private governance; on new forms of regulating behaviour; and on interacting to achieve a shared purpose or common good. It is through global environmental governance that the conflicted state, in tandem with a wide variety of non-state actors, aims to find an appropriate balance between unbridled economic growth and the need to preserve ecological capital for the present and future generations. In simple terms, global environmental governance is environmental governance in the global context. Global environmental governance is therefore a normative institutional regulatory intervention and social construct that is predominantly based on law and that aims to influence how people interact with the global environment. It entails a pluralistic, dynamic, multi-level, multi-actor response and process of change which pragmatically aims to change human behaviour vis-à-vis the global environment, and idealistically to optimize environmental benefits and use, while at the same time seeking to protect and preserve sufficient environmental capital for present and future generations.

Environmental law remains the predominant body of legal rules through which the institution of global environmental governance would seek to change behaviour and to achieve sustainability. However, because of globalization and the global *problématique* of a widely conceived global environment and global environmental issues or problems, global environmental governance today employs a widely diverse and pluralistic array of state-based laws and non-state (law-like) rules which are increasingly assuming a transnational or global character. This body of laws could be described as global environmental governance law which is a body of law characterized by a broad geography equating to an equally broadly conceptualized environment. Global environmental governance law therefore manifests in a context and reality where:

> We are presented not with discrete natural environments connected only by certain global common substrates, nor with discrete political communities connected only by certain channels of international commerce and environmental impact. Rather, we are presented with a 'complicated tissue of events', both biophysical and sociolegal, in which even conventionally domestic environmental problems must be viewed as global in scope and in which politics and law accordingly must adapt to the challenge of ineradicable interdependence among states.[8]

Global environmental governance law provides the substantive and procedural normative aspects of global environmental governance. Global environmental governance law, more specifically, consists of national, regional and international environmental law; all non-environment-related substantive bodies of law which could contribute to achieving the pragmatic and idealistic objectives of global environmental governance, such as economic law, trade law, and humanitarian law; all procedural laws that prescribe how global environmental governance should be conducted, such as administrative law and the principles of good environmental governance; and all non-

---

[8] Kysar, Douglas (2010), *Regulating From Nowhere: Environmental Law and the Search for Objectivity*, New Haven: Yale University Press, 147.

state based law-like rules created, interpreted and applied by non-state actors, to the extent that these rules aim to achieve the objectives of global environmental governance in a less coercive and more reflexive way. Global environmental governance law is the constitution of global environmental governance; it legitimizes global environmental governance; it creates global environmental governance actors and allows them to govern; it provides the authority to these actors to govern; it prescribes how to govern and what to govern; and it provides the minimum thresholds for what is deemed acceptable or unacceptable behaviour in society as far as the global environment is concerned. Global environmental governance law therefore ultimately performs a distinct constitutive, legitimizing, prescriptive, proscriptive, instrumentalist and guiding function with respect to global environmental governance.

6. CONCLUSION

As an overarching objective, this book has sought to clarify the concept of environmental governance by situating it in the global context. It has endeavoured through a meta-theoretical analysis to describe the theory of governance in the context of globalization, the role of law in governance, and the construct of global governance. In the final instance, the book has described global environmental governance as a phenomenon and has explained certain aspects of the role of law in global environmental governance through a description of what can broadly be understood as global environmental governance law.

Clearly, the bulk of the enquiry was descriptive and many of this book's possible shortcomings may lie in its descriptive approach. Nevertheless, by providing a clearer conceptual framework of the meaning of governance in the environmental regulatory domain and the place and role of law in the global environmental governance paradigm, the book has provided some content to the concept of global environmental governance. This should create opportunities for other commentators to take up the discussion and for future researchers critically to take this investigation further by doing some of the following things, perhaps: by evaluating the successes and failures of global environmental governance; by devising theoretical and pragmatic approaches to ameliorate global environmental governance; by re-evaluating the successes and failures of law in global environmental governance; and by envisaging a new, future paradigm and construct for global environmental governance law.

Global environmental governance has the predominant but not exclusive responsibility to set the world on a sustainable path, and lawyers will continue to play a crucial role in this effort. Our task is inevitably a serious and at the same time a challenging one. While the complexity of the task could understandably cause us to shy away from this obligation, the moral duty we owe to ourselves, our children and the environment is sufficiently weighty to compel us to continue to involve ourselves in conceptualizing, critiquing, and improving the many ways in which we seek to change human behaviour vis-à-vis the environment.

Bibliography

BOOKS

Abbott, Kenneth W. *et al.* (2002), 'The Concept of Legalization' in Robert O. Keohane (ed), *Power and Governance in a Partially Globalized World*, London: Routledge.

Abbott, Kenneth W. and Duncan Snidal (2010), 'Why States Act through Formal International Organizations' in Paul F. Diehl and B. Frederking (eds), *The Politics of Global Governance: International Organizations in an Interdependent World*, Boulder: Lynne Rienner Publishers.

Akhtarkhavari, Afshin (2010), *Global Governance of the Environment: Environmental Principles and Change in International Law and Politics*, Cheltenham: Edward Elgar Publishing.

Allot, Philip (2000), 'The Concept of International Law' in Michael Byers (ed), *The Role of Law in International Politics: Essays in International Relations and International Law*, Oxford: Oxford University Press.

Anders, Gerhard (2004), 'Lawyers and Anthropologists: A Legal Pluralist Approach to Global Governance' in Ige F. Dekker and Wouter G. Werner (eds), *Governance and International Legal Theory*, Leiden: Martinus Nijhoff Publishers.

Bache, Ian and Matthew Flinders (eds) (2004), *Multi-level Governance*, Oxford: Oxford University Press.

Bauer, Steffen and Frank Biermann (2005), 'The Debate on a World Environment Organization: An Introduction' in Frank Biermann and Steffen Bauer (eds), *A World Environment Organization: Solution or Threat for Effective International Environmental Governance?*, Aldershot: Ashgate.

Benford, Robert D. (2011), 'Framing Global Governance from Below: Discursive Opportunities and Challenges in the Transnational Social Movement Arena' in Cerneliu Bjola and Markus Kornprobst (eds), *Arguing Global Governance*, London: Routledge.

Benz, Arthur (2004), 'Einleitung: Governance-Modebegriff oder nützliches sozialwissenschaftliches Konzept?' in Arthur Benz (ed), *Governance – Regieren in komplexen Regelsystemen: Eine Einführung*, Wiesbaden, Germany: VS Verlag für Sozialwissenschaften.

Beyerlin, Ulrich and Thilo Marauhn (2011), *International Environmental Law*, Oxford: Hart Publishers.

Biermann, Frank and Steffen Bauer (eds) (2005), *A World Environment Organization: Solution or Threat for Effective International Environmental Governance?*, Aldershot: Ashgate.

Birnie, Patricia, Alan Boyle and Catherine Redgwell (2009), *International Law and the Environment* 3rd edn, Oxford: Oxford University Press.

Bjola, Corneliu and Markus, Kornprobst (2011), 'Introduction: the Argumentative Deontology of Global Governance' in Cerneliu Bjola and Markus Kornprobst (eds), *Arguing Global Governance*, London: Routledge.

Black, Julia (2004), 'Law and Regulation: The Case of Finance' in Christine Parker *et al.* (eds), *Regulating Law*, Oxford: Oxford University Press.

Blanco, Elena and Jona Razzaque (2011), *Globalisation and Natural Resources Law: Challenges, Key Issues and Perspectives*, Cheltenham: Edward Elgar Publishing.

Bodansky, Daniel (2010), *The Art and Craft of International Environmental Law*, Cambridge, Massachusetts: Harvard University Press.

Bodansky, Daniel, Jutta Brunnée and Ellen Hey (2007), 'International Environmental Law: Mapping the Field' in Daniel Bodansky, Jutta Brunnée and Ellen Hey (eds), *The Oxford Handbook of International Environmental Law*, Oxford: Oxford University Press.

Börzel, Tanja A. (2006), 'European Governance-nicht neu, aber anders' in Gunnar Folke Schuppert (ed), *Governance-Forschung*, Baden-Baden: Nomos Verlag.

Bosselmann, Klaus (2008), *The Principle of Sustainability: Transforming Law and Governance*, Aldershot: Ashgate.

Bothe, Michael (2005), *Environment, Development, Resources: Collected Courses of the Hague Academy of International Law*, Leiden: Martinus Nijhoff, Brill Publishers.

Braithwaite, John and Peter Drahos (2000), *Global Business Regulation*, Cambridge: Cambridge University Press.

Brand, Karl-Werner and Fritz Reusswig (2006), 'The Social Embeddedness of Global Environmental Governance' in Gerd Winter (ed), *Multilevel Governance of Global Environmental Change: Perspectives from Science, Sociology, and the Law*, Cambridge: Cambridge University Press.

Brown Weiss, Edith (1989), *In Fairness to Future Generations: International Law, Common Patrimony, and Intergenerational Equity*, New York: Transnational Publishers.

Bryde, Brun-Otto (2005), 'International Democratic Constitutionalism' in Ronald St. John Macdonald and Douglas M. Johnston (eds), *Towards World Constitutionalism: Issues in the Legal Ordering of the World Community*, Leiden: Martinus Nijhoff Publishers.

Caldwell, Lynton K. (1988), 'Beyond Environmental Diplomacy: the Changing Institutional Structure of International Cooperation' in John E. Carroll (ed), *International Environmental Diplomacy*, Cambridge: Cambridge University Press.

Campbell, Laura B. (2004), 'The Effectiveness of the WTO and WIPO: Lessons for Environmental Governance?' in Norichika Kanie and Peter M. Haas (eds), *Emerging Forces in Environmental Governance*, Tokyo: United Nations University Press.

Cassese, Sabino (2009), 'Is There a Global Administrative Law?' in Armin Von Bogdandy *et al.* (eds), *The Exercise of Public Authority by International Institutions: Advancing International Institutional Law*, Heidelberg: Springer Verlag.

Chambers, Bradnee W. and Jessica F. Green (eds) (2005), *Reforming International Environmental Governance: From Institutional Limits to Innovative Reforms*, Tokyo: United Nations University Press.

Chambers, Bradnee W. and Jessica F. Green (2005), 'Introduction: Toward an Effective Framework for Sustainable Development' in Bradnee W. Chambers and Jessica F. Green (eds), *Reforming International Environmental Governance: From Institutional Limits to Innovative Reforms*, Tokyo: United Nations University Press.

Clapp, Jennifer (2005), 'The Privatization of Global Environmental Governance: ISO 14000 and the Developing World' in David L. Levy and Peter J. Newell (eds), *The Business of Global Environmental Governance*, Cambridge, Massachusetts: MIT Press.

Commission on Global Governance (1995), *Our Global Neighbourhood*, Oxford: Oxford University Press.

Cordonier Segger, Marie-Claire and Ashfaq Khalfan (2004), *Sustainable Development Law: Principles, Practices and Prospects*, Oxford: Oxford University Press.

Crawford, James R. (2007), *The Creation of States in International Law*, Oxford: Oxford University Press.

Crawford, Robert M.A. (1996), *Regime Theory in the Post-Cold War World: Rethinking Neoliberal Approaches to International Relations*, Aldershot: Dartmouth Publishing.

Curtin, Deidre M. and Ige F. Dekker (2005), 'Good Governance: The Concept and its Application by the European Union' in Deidre M. Curtin and Ige F. Dekker (eds), *Good Governance and the European Union: Reflections on Concepts, Institutions and Substance*, Antwerp: Intersentia.

Dekker, Ige F. and Wouter G. Werner (2004), 'Introduction' in Ige F. Dekker and Woulter G. Werner (eds), *Governance and International Legal Theory*, Leiden: Martinus Nijhoff Publishers.

DeSombre, Elizabeth R. (2006), *Global Environmental Institutions*, New York: Routledge.

DiMaggio, Paul J. and Walter W. Powell (1991), 'Introduction' in Walter W. Powell and Paul J. DiMaggio (eds), *The New Institutionalism in Organizational Analysis*, Chicago: University of Chicago Press.

DiMento, Joseph F.C. (2003), *The Global Environment and International Law*, Austin: University of Texas Press.

Drewry, Gavin (1996), 'Political Institutions: Legal Perspectives' in Robert E. Goodin and Hans Dieter Klingemann (eds), *A New Handbook of Political Science*, Oxford: Oxford University Press.

Dunoff, Jeffrey L. (2007), 'Levels of Environmental Governance' in Daniel Bodansky, Jutta Brunnée and Ellen Hey (eds), *The Oxford Handbook of International Environmental Law*, Oxford: Oxford University Press.

Elliott, Lorraine (2005), 'The United Nations' Record on Environmental Governance: An Assessment' in Frank Biermann and Steffen Bauer (eds), *A World Environment Organization: Solution or Threat for Effective International Environmental Governance?*, Aldershot: Ashgate

Ellis, Jaye and Stepan Wood (2006), 'International Environmental Law' in Benjamin J. Richardson and Stepan Wood (eds), *Environmental Law for Sustainability: A Reader*, Portland: Hart Publishing.

Engel, Ronald (2010), 'Introduction' in Ronald J. Engel, Laura Westra and Klaus Bosselmann (eds), *Democracy, Ecological Integrity and International Law*, Cambridge: Cambridge Scholars Publishing.

Erman, Eva and Anders Uhlin (eds) (2010), *Legitimacy Beyond the State? Re-examining the Democratic Credentials of Transnational Actors*, Basingstoke: Palgrave Macmillan.

Esty, Daniel C. (2007), 'Global Environmental Governance' in Colin I. Bradford and Johannes F. Linn (eds), *Global Governance Reform: Breaking the Stalemate*, Washington, DC: Brookings Institution Press.

Fairbrass, Jenny and Andrew Jordan (2004), 'Multi-level Governance and Environmental Policy' in Ian Bache and Matthew Flinders (eds), *Multi-level Governance*, Oxford: Oxford University Press.

Finer, Herman (1949), *Theory and Practice of Modern Government* Revised Edition, New York: Henry Holt and Company.

Finger, Matthias (2005), 'The New Water Paradigm: The Privatization of Governance and the Instrumentalization of the State' in David L. Levy and Peter J. Newell (eds), *The Business of Global Environmental Governance*, Cambridge, MA: MIT Press.

Ford, Lucy H. (2005), 'Challenging the Global Environmental Governance of Toxics: Social Movement Agency and Global Civil Society' in David L. Levy and Peter J. Newell (eds), *The Business of Global Environmental Governance*, Cambridge, Massachusetts: MIT Press.

Friedrichs, Jörg (2004), 'The Neomedieval Renaissance: Global Governance and International Law in the New Middle Ages' in Ige F. Dekker and

Wouter G. Werner (eds), *Governance and International Legal Theory*, Leiden: Martinus Nijhoff Publishers.
Fuller, Lon L. (1968), *Anatomy of the Law*, New York: Frederick Praeger Publishers.
Funk and Wagnalls (1965), *Collier's Standard Dictionary of the English Language: International Edition Volume One*, New York: Funk and Wagnalls Company.
Garner, Bryan A. (ed) (2004), *Black's Law Dictionary* 8th edn, St. Paul: Thomson West.
Gehring, Thomas (1994), *Dynamic International Regimes: Institutions for International Environmental Governance*, Frankfurt am Main: Peter Lang.
Gephart, Werner and Siegfried Hermes (eds) (2010), *Max Weber Wirtschaft und Gesellschaft: Die Wirtschaft und die gesellschaftlichen Ordungen und die Mächte-Nachlaß*, Tübingen: J.C.B. Mohr Paul Siebeck.
Godden, Lee and Jacqueline Peel (2010), *Environmental Law: Scientific, Policy and Regulatory Dimensions*, Melbourne: Oxford University Press.
Goodin, Robert E. and Hans Dieter Klingemann (1996), 'Political Science: the Discipline' in Robert E. Goodin and Hans Dieter Klingemann (eds), *A New Handbook of Political Science*, Oxford: Oxford University Press.
Gunningham, Neil (2008), 'Environmental Regulation and Non-state Law: The Future Public Policy Agenda' in Hanneke Van Schooten and Jonathan Verschuuren (eds), *International Governance and Law: State Regulation and Non-state Law*, Cheltenham: Edward Elgar Publishing.
Haas, Ernst B. (1983), 'Words can Hurt you; or Who Said What to Whom about Regimes' in Stephen D. Krasner (ed), *International Regimes*, London: Cornell University Press.
Haas, Peter M. (1995), 'Global Environmental Governance' in Commission on Global Governance, *Issues in Global Governance*, London: Kluwer Law International.
Haas, Peter M. (2007), 'Epistemic Communities' in Daniel Bodansky, Jutta Brunnée and Ellen Hey (eds), *The Oxford Handbook of International Environmental Law*, Oxford: Oxford University Press.
Habermas, Jürgen (2001), *The Postnational Constellation: Political Essays*, Cambridge: Polity Press.
Habermas, Jürgen (2009), *Geloven en Weten en andere Politieke Essays*, Amsterdam: Boom.
Harlow, Carol (2005), 'Deconstructing Government?' in Tom Ginsburg and Robert A. Kagan (eds), *Institutions and Public Law: Comparative Approaches*, New York: Peter Lang Publishing.
Hart, H.L.A. (1994), *The Concept of Law* 2nd edn, Oxford: Clarendon Press.
Haufler, Virginia (1993), 'Crossing the Boundary between Public and Private: International Regimes and Non-state Actors' in Volker Rittberger (ed), *Regime Theory and International Relations*, Oxford: Clarendon Press.

Heere, Wybo P. (ed) (2004), *From Government to Governance: The Growing Impact of Non-state Actors on the International and European Legal System*, The Hague: T.M.C. Asser Press.

Heinelt, Hubert (2004), 'Governance auf lokaler Ebene' in Arthur Benz (ed), *Governance – Regieren in komplexen Regelsystemen: Eine Einführung*, Wiesbaden, Germany: VS Verlag für Sozialwissenschaften.

Heldeweg, Michiel A. (2005), 'Good Environmental Governance in the EU: Lessons from Work in Progress?' in D.M. Curtin and R.A. Wessel (eds), *Good Governance and the European Union: Reflections on Concepts, Institutions and Substance*, Antwerp: Intersentia.

Hempel, Lamont C. (1996), *Environmental Governance: The Global Challenge*, Washington: Island Press.

Hertogh, Marc (2008), 'What is Non-state Law? Mapping the other Hemisphere of the Legal World' in Hanneke Van Schooten and Jonathan Verschuuren (eds), *International Governance and Law: State Regulation and Non-state Law*, Cheltenham: Edward Elgar Publishing.

Hey, Ellen (2007), 'International Institutions' in Daniel Bodansky, Jutta Brunnée and Ellen Hey (eds), *The Oxford Handbook of International Environmental Law*, Oxford: Oxford University Press.

Hey, Ellen (2010), 'Global Environmental Law and Global Institutions: A System Lacking "Good Process"' in Roland Pierik and Wouter Werner, *Cosmopolitanism in Context: Perspectives from International Law and Political Theory*, Cambridge: Cambridge University Press.

Hirst, Paul (2000), 'Democracy and Governance' in Jon Pierre (ed), *Debating Governance: Authority, Steering and Democracy*, Oxford: Oxford University Press.

Hofmeyer, Ingmar (2009), 'The Evolution of EU Environmental Governance' in Joanne Scott (ed), *Environmental Protection: European Law and Governance*, Oxford: Oxford University Press.

Hood, Christopher, Henry Rothstein, and Robert Baldwin (2001), *The Government of Risk: Understanding Risk Regulation Regimes*, Oxford: Oxford University Press.

Hunt, Alan (2002), 'Legal Governance and Social Relations: Empowering Agents and the Limits of Law' in Michael MacNeil, Neil Sargent, and Peter Swan (eds), *Law, Regulation and Governance*, Oxford: Oxford University Press.

Hunt, Alan and Gary Wickham (1994), *Foucault and the Law: Towards a Sociology of Law as Governance*, London: Pluto Press.

Hurrell, Andrew (1993), 'International Society and the Study of Regimes: A Reflective Approach' in Volker Rittberger (ed), *Regime Theory and International Relations*, Oxford: Clarendon Press.

Hurrell, Andrew (1995), 'International Political Theory and the Global

Environment' in Ken Booth and Steve Smith (eds), *International Relations Theory Today*, Cambridge: Polity Press.

Hurrell, Andrew (2000), 'International Law and the Changing Constitution of International Society' in Michael Byers (ed), *The Role of Law in International Politics: Essays in International Relations and International Law*, Oxford: Oxford University Press.

Hurrell, Andrew and Benedict Kingsbury (eds) (1992), *The International Politics of Envrionment: Actors, Interests, and Institutions*, Oxford: Clarendon Press.

Jachtenfuchs, Markus (2008), 'Institutionelle Struktur und Governance in der EU' in Gunnar Folke Schuppert and Michael Zürn (eds), *Governance in einer sich wandelnden Welt*, Wiesbaden, Germany: VS Verlag für Sozialwissenschaften.

Jann, Werner (2006), 'Governance als Reformstrategie- Vom Wandel und der Bedeutung verwaltungspolitischer Leitbilder' in Gunnar Folke Schuppert (ed), *Governance-Forschung*, Baden-Baden: Nomos Verlag.

Jenks, Wilfred C. (1972), 'Multinational Entities in the Law of Nations' in Wolfgang Friedmann, Louis Henkin and Oliver Lissitzyn (eds), *Transnational Law in a Changing Society*, New York: Columbia University Press.

Jessup, Philip C. (1956), *Transnational Law*, New Haven: Yale University Press.

Johnston, Douglas M. (2005), 'World Constitutionalism in the Theory of International Law' in Ronald St. John Macdonald and Douglas M. Johnston (eds), *Towards World Constitutionalism: Issues in the Legal Ordering of the World Community*, Leiden: Martinus Nijhoff Publishers.

Jürgens, Ulrich (2008), 'Corporate Governance-Anwendungsfelder und Entwicklungen' in Gunnar Folke Schuppert and Michael Zürn (eds), *Governance in einer sich wandelnden Welt*, Wiesbaden, Germany: VS Verlag für Sozialwissenschaften.

Kanie, Norichika and Peter M. Haas (2004), 'Introduction', in Norichika Kanie and Peter M. Haas (eds), *Emerging Forces in Environmental Governance*, Tokyo: United Nations University Press.

Kelsen, Hans (1945), *General Theory of Law and State*, Cambridge: Cambridge University Press.

Kennedy, Paul (2002), 'Global Challenges at the Beginning of the Twenty-First Century' in Paul Kennedy, Dirk Messner and Franz Nuscheler (eds), *Global Trends and Global Governance*, London: Pluto Press.

Keohane, Robert O. (1984), *After Hegemony: Cooperation and Discord in the World Political Economy*, Princeton: Princeton University Press.

Keohane, Robert O. (1993), 'The Analysis of International Regimes: Towards a European-American Research Programme' in Volker Rittberger (ed), *Regime Theory and International Relations*, Oxford: Clarendon Press.

Keohane, Robert O. (2002), *Power and Governance in a Partially Globalized World*, London: Routledge.

Keohane, Robert O. (2002), 'Governance in a Partially Globalized World' in Robert O. Keohane (ed), *Power and Governance in a Partially Globalized World*, London: Routledge.

Keohane, Robert O. and Joseph S. Nye (2002), 'Governance in a Globalizing World' in Robert O. Keohane (ed), *Power and Governance in a Partially Globalized World*, London: Routledge.

Keohane, Robert O., Peter M. Haas and Marc A. Levy (1994), 'The Effectiveness of International Environmental Institutions' in Peter M. Haas, Robert O. Keohane and Marc A. Levy (eds), *Institutions for the Earth: Sources of Effective International Environmental Protection*, Cambridge, MA: MIT Press.

Kickert, Walter J.M. and Jan L.M. Hakvoort (2000), 'Public Governance in Europe: A Historical-Institutional Tour D'Horizon' in Oscar Van Heffen, Walter J.M. Kickert and Jacques J.A. Thomassen (eds), *Governance in Modern Society: Effects, Change and Formation of Government Institutions*, Dordrecht: Kluwer Academic Publishers.

Kimball, Lee A. (2001), *International Ocean Governance: Using International Law and Organizations to Manage Marine Resources Sustainably*, IUCN: Gland, Switzerland and Cambridge, United Kingdom.

Kingsbury, Benedict (2007), 'Global Environmental Governance as Administration: Implications for International Law' in Daniel Bodansky, Jutta Brunnée and Ellen Hey (eds), *The Oxford Handbook of International Environmental Law*, Oxford: Oxford University Press.

Kirton, John (2010), 'The G-20 Finance Ministers: Network Governance' in Alan S. Alexandroff and Andrew F. Cooper (eds), *Rising States, Rising Institutions: Challenges for Global Governance*, Washington, DC: Brookings Institution Press.

Kiss, Alexandre and Dinah Shelton (2007), *Guide to International Environmental Law*, Leiden: Martinus Nijhoff Publishers.

Kjær, Anne Mette (2004), *Governance*, Cambridge: Polity Press.

Kjaer Poul F. (2010), *Between Governing and Governance: On the Emergence, Function and Form of Europe's Post-national Constellation*, Oxford: Hart Publishing.

Klabbers, Jan (2009), *An Introduction to International Institutional Law* 2nd edn, Cambridge: Cambridge University Press.

Klijn, Erik-Hans and Geert R. Teisman (2000), 'Managing Public-Private Partnerships: Influencing Processes and Institutional Context of Public-Private Partnerships', in Oscar Van Heffen, Walter J.M. Kickert and Jacques J.A. Thomassen (eds), *Governance of Modern Society: Effects, Change and Formation of Government Institutions*, Dordrecht: Kluwer Academic Publishers.

Köck, Wolfgang (2006), 'Governance in der Umweltpolitik' in Gunnar Folke Schuppert (ed), *Governance-Forschung*, Baden-Baden: Nomos Verlag.

Kofman, Eleonore and Gillian Youngs (1996), 'Introduction: Globalization – the Second Wave' in Eleonore Kofman and Gillian Youngs (eds), *Globalization: Theory and Practice*, London: Pinter.

Kohler-Koch, Beate and Berthold Rittberger (2009), 'A Futile Quest for Coherence: The Many Frames of EU Governance' in Beate Kohler-Koch and Fabrice Larat (eds), *European Multi-Level Governance: Contrasting Images in National Research*, Cheltenham: Edward Elgar Publishing.

Kooiman, Jan (2003), *Governing as Governance*, London: Sage Publications Limited.

Kooiman, Jan and Kjell A. Eliassen (1987), 'Introduction' in Jan Kooiman and Kjell A. Eliassen (eds), *Managing Public Organizations: Lessons from Contemporary European Experience*, London: SAGE Publications.

Kooiman, Jan and Kjell A. Eliassen (1987), 'Preface' in Jan Kooiman and Kjell A. Eliassen (eds), *Managing Public Organizations: Lessons from Contemporary European Experience*, London: SAGE Publications.

Koppen, Ida (1994), 'Ecological Covenants: Regulatory Informality in Dutch Waste Reduction Policy' in Gunther Teubner, Lindsay Farmer and Declan Murphy (eds), *Environmental Law and Ecological Responsibility: The Concept and Practice of Ecological Self-Organization*, Chichester: John Wiley and Sons.

Kotzé, Louis J. (2009), 'Environmental Governance' in Alexander Paterson and Louis J. Kotzé (eds), *Environmental Compliance and Enforcement in South Africa: Legal Perspectives*, Cape Town: Juta.

Kotzé, Louis J. and Alexander R. Paterson (eds) (2009), *The Role of the Judiciary in Environmental Governance: Comparative Perspectives*, Alphen aan den Rijn: Kluwer Law International.

Kotzé, Louis J. (2010), 'Towards a Tentative Legal Formulation of Environmental Governance' in Tuula Honkonen and Ed Couzens (eds), *International Environmental Law-making and Diplomacy Review 2009*, UNEP Course series 9, Joensuu, Finland: University of Eastern Finland.

Krämer, Ludwig (2006), 'The EU: A Regional Model?' in Gerd Winter (ed), *Multilevel Governance of Global Environmental Change: Perspectives from Science, Sociology, and the Law*, Cambridge: Cambridge University Press.

Krasner Stephen D. (1983), 'Structural Causes and Regime Consequences: Regimes as Intervening Variables' in Stephen D. Krasner (ed), *International Regimes*, London: Cornell University Press.

Kratochwil, Friedrich V. (2000), 'How do Norms Matter?' in Michael Byers (ed), *The Role of Law in International Politics: Essays in International Relations and International Law*, Oxford: Oxford University Press.

Kysar, Douglas (2010), *Regulating From Nowhere: Environmental Law and the Search for Objectivity*, New Haven: Yale University Press.

La Torre, Massimo (2010), *Law as Institution*, Heidelberg: Springer.

Ladeur, Karl-Heinz (2004), 'Globalization and Public Governance: A Contradiction?' in Karl-Heinz Ladeur (ed), *Public Governance in the Age of Globalization*, Aldershot: Ashgate.

Laferrière, Eric and Peter J. Stoett (2006), 'Introduction: Exploring International Ecopolitical Theory' in Eric Laferrière and Peter J. Stoett (eds), *International Ecopolitical Theory: Critical Approaches*, Vancouver: UBC Press.

Lecours, André (2005), 'New Institutionalism: Issues and Questions' in André Lacours (ed), *New Institutionalism: Theory and Analysis*, Toronto: University of Toronto Press.

Lenschow, Andrea (1997), *Transformation in European Environmental Governance: RSC No. 97/61 EUI Working* Papers, Floreance, Italy: European University Institute.

Leonard, Eric K. (2005), *The Onset of Global Governance: International Relations Theory and the International Criminal Court*, Aldershot: Ashgate.

Levy, David L. and Peter J. Newell (eds) (2005), *The Business of Global Environmental Governance*, Cambridge, MA: MIT Press.

Levy, David L. and Peter J. Newell (2005), 'Introduction' in David L. Levy and Peter J. Newell (eds), *The Business of Global Environmental Governance*, Cambridge, Massachusetts: MIT Press.

MacNeil, Michael, Neil Sargent and Peter Swan (eds) (2003), *Law, Regulation and Governance*, Oxford: Oxford University Press.

Macrory, Richard (2008), *Regulation, Enforcement and Governance in Environmental Law*, London: Cameron May.

Mansbach, Richard W. (2010), 'Globalization, East Asia, and the Future of Global Politics' in Peter Yu Kien-hong, Emily Chow and Shawn S.F. Kao (eds), *International Governance, Regimes and Globalization: Case Studies from Beijing and Taipei*, Maryland: Lexington Books.

Marauhn, Thilo (2007), 'Changing Role of the State' in Daniel Bodansky, Jutta Brunnée and Ellen Hey (eds), *The Oxford Handbook of International Environmental Law*, Oxford: Oxford University Press.

Marks, Gary and Liesbet Hooge (2004), 'Contrasting Visions of Multi-level Governance' in Ian Bache and Matthew Flinders (eds), *Multi-level Governance*, Oxford: Oxford University Press.

Matz, Nele (2005), *Wege zur Koordinierung völkerrechtlicher Verträge: Völkervertragrechtliche und institutionelle Ansätze*, Heidelberg: Springer-Verlag.

Mayntz, Renate (2004), 'Governance im modernen Staat' in Arthur Benz (ed),

Governance- Regieren in komplexen Regelsystemen: Eine Einführung, Wiesbaden, Germany: VS Verlag für Sozialwissenschaften.

Mayntz, Renata (2006), 'Governance Theory als fortentwickelte Steuerungstheorie?' in Gunnar Folke Schuppert (ed), *Governance-Forschung*, Baden-Baden: Nomos Verlag.

Mayntz, Renate (2010), *Legitimacy and Compliance in Transnational Governance: MPIfG Working Paper 10/5*, Cologne: Max-Planck-Institut für Gesellschaftforschung.

Messner, Dirk (2002), 'World Society: Structure and Trends' in Paul Kennedy, Dirk Messner and Franz Nuscheler (eds), *Global Trends and Global Governance*, London: Pluto Press.

Morgan, Bronwen and Karen Yeung (2007), *An Introduction to Law and Regulation: Text and Materials*, Cambridge: Cambridge University Press.

Mori, Satoko (2004), 'Institutionalization of NGO Involvement in Policy Functions for Global Environmental Governance' in Norichika Kanie and Peter M. Haas (eds), *Emerging Forces in Environmental Governance*, Tokyo: United Nations University Press.

Najam, Adil (2005), 'Neither Necessary, nor Sufficient: Why Organizational Tinkering will not Improve Environmental Governance' in Frank Biermann and Steffen Bauer (eds), *A World Environment Organization: Solution or Threat for Effective International Environmental Governance?*, Aldershot: Ashgate.

Nel, Johan and Louis J. Kotzé (2009), 'Environmental Management: An Introduction', in Hennie Strydom and Nick King (eds), *Fuggle and Rabie's Environmental Management in South Africa*, 2nd edn, Cape Town: Juta.

Newell, Peter J. (2005), 'Business and International Environmental Governance: The State of the Art' in David L. Levy and Peter J. Newell (eds), *The Business of Global Environmental Governance*, Cambridge, Massachusetts: MIT Press.

Oberthür, Sebastian and Thomas Gehring (2005), 'Reforming International Environmental Governance: An Institutional Perspective on Proposals for a World Environment Organization' in Frank Biermann and Steffen Bauer (eds), *A World Environment Organization: Solution or Threat for Effective International Environmental Governance?*, Aldershot: Ashgate.

O'Brien, Robert (2005), 'Global Civil Society and Global Governance' in Alice D. Ba and Matthew J. Hoffmann (eds), *Contending Perspectives on Global Governance, Coherence, Contestation, and World Order*, London: Routledge.

Ocheje, Paul (1999), 'Exploring the Legal Dimensions of Political Legitimacy: A "Rights" Approach to Governance in Africa' in Edward Kofi Quashigah and Obiora Chinedu Okafor (eds), *Legitimate Governance in Africa: International and Domestic Legal Perspectives*, The Hague: Kluwer Law International.

Overbeek, Henk (2005), 'Global Governance, Class, Hegemony' in Alice D. Ba and Matthew J. Hoffmann (eds), *Contending Perspectives on Global Governance, Coherence, Contestation, and World Order*, London: Routledge.

Parker, Christine *et al.* (2004), 'Introduction' in Christine Parker *et al.* (eds), *Regulating Law*, Oxford: Oxford University Press.

Payne, Anthony (2000), 'Globalization and Modes of Regionalist Governance' in Jon Pierre (ed), *Debating Governance: Authority, Steering and Democracy*, Oxford: Oxford University Press.

Pease, Kelly-Kate S. (2008), *International Organizations: Perspectives on Governance in the Twenty-First Century* 3rd edn, New Jersey: Pearson Prentice Hall.

Percival, Robert V. *et al.* (2009), *Environmental Regulation: Law, Science, and Policy* 6th edn, New York: Aspen Publishers.

Perez, Oren (2004), 'The Many Faces of the Trade-Environment Conflict: Some Lessons for the Constitutionalisation Project' in Christian Joerges, Inger-Johanne Sand and Gunther Teubner (eds), *Transnational Governance and Constitutionalism*, Oregon: Hart Publishing.

Perez, Oren (2004), *Ecological Sensitivity and Global Legal Pluralism: Rethinking the Trade and Environment Conflict*, Oregon: Hart Publishing.

Peters, Anne (2005), 'Global Constitutionalism in a Nutshell' in Klaus Dicke *et al.* (eds), *Weltinnenrecht: Liber amicorum Jost Delbrück*, Berlin: Duncker & Humblot.

Peters, Anne (2010), 'Transnational Law Comprises Constitutional, Administrative, Criminal and Quasi-private Law' in Pieter H.F. Bekker, Rudolf Dolzer and Michael Waibel (eds), *Making Transnational Law Work in the Global Economy*, Cambridge: Cambridge University Press.

Pierre, Jon (2000), 'Introduction: Understanding Governance' in Jon Pierre (ed), *Debating Governance: Authority, Steering and Democracy*, Oxford: Oxford University Press.

Pinto, Moragodage C.W. (1995), 'Reflections on the Term Sustainable Development and its Institutional Implications' in Konrad Ginther, Erik Denters and Paul J.I.M. De Waart (eds), *Sustainable Development and Good Governance*, Dordrecht: Martinus Nijhoff Publishers.

Pinto, Moragodage C.W. (1996), '"Common Heritage of Mankind": From Metaphor to Myth, and the Consequence of Constructive Ambiguity' in Jerzy Makarczyk (ed), *Theory of International Law at the Threshold of the 21st Century: Essays in Honour of Krzysztof Skubiszewski*, The Hague: Kluwer Law International.

Puchala, Donald J. and Raymond F. Hopkins (1983), 'International Regimes: Lessons from Inductive Analysis' in Stephen D. Krasner (ed), *International Regimes*, London: Cornell University Press.

Purvis, Trevor (2002), 'Regulation, Governance, and the State: Reflections on the Transformation of Regulatory Practices in Late-Modern Liberal Democracies' in Michael MacNeil, Neil Sargent, and Peter Swan (eds), *Law, Regulation and Governance*, Oxford: Oxford University Press.

Rechkemmer, Andreas (2006), *International Environmental Governance: Issues, Achievements, and Perspectives – Publication Series of UNU-EHS No. 3/2006*, Bonn: UNU Institute for Environment and Human Security.

Reinalda, Bob (1999), 'International Organizations as Sources of Political Change' in Kees Van Kersbergen, Robert H. Lieshout, and Grahame Lock (eds), *Expansion and Fragmentation: Internationalization, Political Change and the Transformation of the Nation State*, Amsterdam, The Netherlands: Amsterdam University Press.

Rheinstein, Max (ed) (1954), *Max Weber on Law in Economy and Society*, Cambridge, Massachusetts: Harvard University Press.

Rhodes, Rod A.W. (2000), 'Governance and Public Administration' in Jon Pierre (ed), *Debating Governance: Authority, Steering and Democracy*, Oxford: Oxford University Press.

Rittberger, Volker (1993), 'Editor's Introduction' in Volker Rittberger (ed), *Regime Theory and International Relations*, Oxford: Clarendon Press.

Rittberger, Volker (ed) (2009), *Wer regiert die Welt und mit welchem Recht? Beiträge zur Global Governance-Forschung*, Baden-Baden: Nomos Verlag.

Rohstein, Bo (1996), 'Political Institutions: An Overview' in Robert E. Goodin and Hans Dieter Klingemann (eds), *A New Handbook of Political Science*, Oxford: Oxford University Press.

Rosenau, James N. (1992), 'Governance, Order, and Change in World Politics' in James N. Rosenau and Ernst-Otto Czempiel (eds), *Governance without Government: Order and Change in World Politics*, Cambridge: Cambridge University Press.

Rosenau, James N. and Ernst-Otto Czempiel (eds) (1992), *Governance without Government: Order and Change in World Politics*, Cambridge: Cambridge University Press.

Rosenau, James N. and Mary Durfee (1995), *Thinking Theory Through: Coherent Approaches to an Incoherent World*, Boulder: Westview Press.

Rosenau, James N. (1997), *Along the Domestic-Foreign Frontier: Exploring Governance in a Turbulent World*, Cambridge: Cambridge University Press.

Rosenau, James N. (2005), 'Global Governance as Disaggregated Complexity' in Alice D. Ba and Matthew J. Hoffmann (eds), *Contending Perspectives on Global Governance, Coherence, Contestation, and World Order*, London: Routledge.

Rosenau, James N. (2009), 'Governing the Ungovernable: The Challenge of a

Global Disaggregation of Authority' in Dries Lesage and Pierre Vercauteren (eds), *Contemporary Global Governance: Multipolarity vs New Discourses on Global Governance*, Brussels: P.I.E. Peter Lang.

Ruiter, Dick W.P. (2000), 'Legal Institutions as Systems of Legal Norms' in Oscar Van Heffen, Walter J.M. Kickert and Jacques J.A. Thomassen (eds), *Governance in Modern Society: Effects, Change and Formation of Government Institutions*, Dordrecht: Kluwer Academic Publishers.

Sassen, Saskia (2004), 'De-nationalized State Agendas and Privatized Norm-making' in Karl-Heinz Ladeur (ed), *Public Governance in the Age of Globalization*, Aldershot: Ashgate.

Scanlon, John and Francoise Burhenne-Guilmin (2004), 'Executive Summary' in John Scanlon and Francoise Burhenne-Guilmin (eds), *International Environmental Governance: An International Regime for Protected Areas*, Gland, Switzerland and Cambridge: IUCN.

Schermers, Henry G. and Niels M. Blokker (2011), *International Institutional Law: Unity within Diversity* 5th edn, Leiden: Martinus Nijhoff Publishers.

Schneider, David J. (2002), 'Radical or Rational? Reflexive Law as *Res Novo* in the Canadian Environmental Regulatory Regime' in Michael MacNeil, Neil Sargent and Peter Swan (eds), *Law, Regulation and Governance*, Oxford: Oxford University Press.

Schneider, Volker (2004), 'Organizational Governance: Governance in Organisationen' in Arthur Benz (ed), *Governance- Regieren in komplexen Regelsystemen: Eine Einführung*, Wiesbaden, Germany: VS Verlag für Sozialwissenschaften.

Scholte, Jan Aart (1996), 'Beyond the Buzzword: Towards a Critical Theory of Globalization' in Eleonore Kofman and Gillian Youngs (eds), *Globalization: Theory and Practice*, London: Pinter.

Scholte, Jan Aart (2000), *Globalization: A Critical Introduction*, London: Macmillan Press.

Schwöbel, Christine E.J. (2011), *Global Constitutionalism in International Legal Perspective*, Leiden: Martinus Nijhoff Publishers.

Scott, Joanne (ed) (2009), *Environmental Protection: European Law and Governance*, Oxford: Oxford University Press.

Selznick, Philip (1994), 'Self-regulation and the Theory of Institutions' in Gunther Teubner, Lindsay Farmer and Declan Murphy (eds), *Environmental Law and Ecological Responsibility: The Concept and Practice of Ecological Self-Organization*, Chichester: John Wiley and Sons.

Slaughter, Anne-Marie (2001), *Recueil des Cours, Collected Courses of The Hague Academy of International Law, 2000: International Law and International Relations*, The Hague: Martinus Nijhoff Publishers.

Slaughter, Anne-Marie and Thomas Hale (2010), 'Transnational Networks and

Emerging Powers' in Alan S. Alexandroff and Andrew F. Cooper (eds), *Rising States, Rising Institutions: Challenges for Global Governance*, Washington, DC: Brookings Institution Press.

Smith, Sean C. (1994), 'How Law Hides Risk' in Gunther Teubner, Lindsay Farmer and Declan Murphy (eds), *Environmental Law and Ecological Responsibility: The Concept and Practice of Ecological Self-Organization*, Chichester: John Wiley and Sons.

Snyder, F.G. (2002), 'Governing Globalisation' in Michael Likosky (ed), *Transnational Legal Processes: Globalisation and Power Disparities*, London: Butterworths LexisNexis.

Soanes, Catherine and Angus Stevenson (eds) (2005), *Oxford Dictionary of English* 2nd edn revised, Oxford: Oxford University Press.

Speth, Gustave James and Peter M. Haas (2006), *Global Environmental Governance*, Washington: Island Press.

Spiro, Peter J. (2007), 'Non-governmental Organizations and Civil Society' in Daniel Bodansky, Jutta Brunnée and Ellen Hey (eds), *The Oxford Handbook of International Environmental Law*, Oxford: Oxford University Press.

Stephens, Tim (2009), *International Courts and Environmental Protection*, Cambridge: Cambridge University Press.

Stern, Brigitte (2000), 'How to Regulate Globalization?' in Michael Byers (ed), *The Role of Law in International Politics: Essays in International Relations and International Law*, Oxford: Oxford University Press.

Steurer, Reinhard and Rita Trattnigg (2010), 'Nachhaltigkeit regieren: Eine Einleitung im Wissenschaft-Praxis Dialog' in Reinhard Steurer and Rita Trattnigg (eds), *Nachhaltigkeit regieren: Eine Bilanz zu Governance-Prinzipien und – Praktiken*, Munich: Oekom Verlag.

Stone, Randall W. (2011), *Controlling Institutions: International Organizations and the Global Economy*, Cambridge: Cambridge University Press.

Strand, Jonathan R. (2004), 'The Case for Regional Environmental Organizations' in Norichika Kanie and Peter M. Haas (eds), *Emerging Forces in Environmental Governance*, Tokyo: United Nations University Press.

Strange, Susan (1983), 'Cave! Hic Dragones: a Critique of Regime Analysis' in Stephen D. Krasner (ed), *International Regimes*, London: Cornell University Press.

Swan, Peter (2002), 'Governing at a Distance: An Introduction to Law, Regulation, and Governance' in Michael MacNeil, Neil Sargent and Peter Swan (eds), *Law, Regulation and Governance*, Oxford: Oxford University Press.

Swan, Peter (2002), 'Democratic Environmental Governance and

Environmental Justice' in Michael MacNeil, Neil Sargent and Peter Swan (eds), *Law, Regulation and Governance*, Oxford: Oxford University Press.

Swart, Lydia and Estelle Perry (eds) (2007), *Global Environmental Governance: Perspectives on the Current Debate*, New York: Centre for UN Reform Education.

Taekema, Sanne (2008), 'The Point of Law: the Interdependent Functionality of State and Non-state Regulation' in Hanneke Van Schooten and Jonathan Verschuuren (eds), *International Governance and Law: State Regulation and Non-state Law*, Cheltenham: Edward Elgar Publishing.

Taylor, Paul (2003), *International Organization in the Age of Globalization*, London: Continuum.

Teubner, Gunther (1984), *After Legal Instrumentalism? Strategic Models of Post-regulatory Law*, EUI Working Paper No. 100, Florence, Italy: European University Institute.

Teubner, Gunther (1997), 'Foreword: Legal Regimes of Global Non-state Actors' in Gunther Teubner (ed), *Global Law without a State*, Aldershot: Dartmouth Publishing.

Teubner, Gunther (1997), '"Global Bukowina": Legal Pluralism in the World Society' in Gunther Teubner (ed), *Global Law without a State*, Aldershot: Dartmouth Publishing.

Teubner, Gunther (2004), 'Global Private Regimes: Neo-spontaneous Law and Dual Constitution of Autonomous Sectors', in Karl-Heinz Ladeur (ed), *Public Governance in the Age of Globalization*, Aldershot: Ashgate.

Teubner, Gunther, Lindsay Farmer and Declan Murphy (eds) (1994), *Environmental Law and Ecological Responsibility: The Concept and Practice of Ecological Self-Organization*, Chichester: John Wiley and Sons.

Van Heffen, Oscar, Walter J.M. Kickert and Jacques J.A. Thomassen (2000), 'Introduction: Multi-level and Multi-actor Governance' in Oscar Van Heffen, Walter J.M. Kickert and Jacques J.A. Thomassen (eds), *Governance in Modern Society: Effects, Change and Formation of Government Institutions*, Dordrecht: Kluwer Academic Publishers.

Venzke, Ingo (2009), 'International Bureaucracies from a Political Science Perspective: Agency, Authority and International Institutional Law' in Armin Von Bogdandy *et al.* (eds), *The Exercise of Public Authority by International Institutions: Advancing International Institutional Law*, Heidelberg: Springer Verlag.

Verschuuren, Jonathan (2008), 'Introduction' in Hanneke Van Schooten and Jonathan Verschuuren (eds), *International Governance and Law: State Regulation and Non-state Law*, Cheltenham: Edward Elgar Publishing.

Verschuuren, Jonathan (2012), 'Overcoming the Limitations of Environmental Law in a Globalised World' in Frank Wijen *et al.* (eds), *A Handbook of*

Globalisation and Environmental Policy 2nd edn, Cheltenham: Edward Elgar Publishing.

Vogly, Thomas J. *et al.* (2010), 'Identifying Formal Intergovernmental Organizations' in Paul F. Diehl and B. Frederking (eds), *The Politics of Global Governance: International Organizations in an Interdependent World*, Boulder: Lynne Rienner Publishers.

Von Benda-Beckmann, Franz, Keebet Von Benda-Beckmann and Julia Eckert (2009), 'Rules of Law and Laws of Ruling: Law and Governance between Past and Future' in Franz Von Benda-Beckmann, Keebet Von Benda-Beckmann and Julia Eckert (eds), *Rules of Law and Laws of Ruling: on the Governance of Law*, Farnham: Ashgate.

Von Benda-Beckmann, Franz, Keebet Von Benda-Beckmann and Anne Griffiths (2009), 'The Power of Law' in Franz Von Benda-Beckmann, Keebet Von Benda-Beckmann and Anne Griffiths (eds), *The Power of Law in a Transnational World: Anthropological Enquiries*, New York: Berghahn Books.

Von Bogdandy, Armin *et al.* (eds) (2010), *The Exercise of Public Authority by International Institutions: Advancing International Institutional Law*, Heidelberg: Springer Verlag.

Von Moltke, Konrad (2005), 'Clustering International Environmental Agreements as an Alternative to a World Environment Organization' in Frank Biermann and Steffen Bauer (eds), *A World Environment Organization: Solution or Threat for Effective International Environmental Governance?*, Aldershot: Ashgate.

Walker, Rob B.J. (1995), 'International Relations and the Concept of the Political' in Ken Booth and Steve Smith (eds), *International Relations Theory Today*, Cambridge: Polity Press.

Wapner, Paul (1997), 'Governance in Global Civil Society' in Oran R. Young (ed), *Global Governance: Drawing Insights from the Environmental Experience*, Cambridge, Massachusetts: MIT Press.

Weber, Max (1922), *Wirtschaft und Gesellschaft*, Tübingen: J.C.B. Mohr, Paul Siebeck.

Weiss, Thomas G. (2011), 'Governance, Good Governance, and Global Governance' in Thomas G. Weiss (ed), *Thinking about Global Governance: Why People and Ideas Matter*, Abingdon: Routledge.

Weiss, Thomas G. and Ramesh Thakur (2011), 'Framing Global Governance, Five Gaps' in Thomas G. Weiss (ed), *Thinking about Global Governance: Why People and Ideas Matter*, Abingdon: Routledge.

Wiener, Antje (2008), *The Invisible Constitution of Politics: Contested Norms and International Encounters*, Cambridge: Cambridge University Press.

Willetts, Peter (2011), *Non-governmental Organizations in World Politics: the Construction of Global Governance*, London: Routledge.

Williamson, Oliver E. (1996), *The Mechanisms of Governance*, New York: Oxford University Press.
Winter, Gerd (2006), 'Introduction' in Gerd Winter (ed), *Multilevel Governance of Global Environmental Change: Perspectives from Science, Sociology, and the Law*, Cambridge: Cambridge University Press.
Wolfrum, Rüdiger and Nele Matz (2003), *Conflicts in International Environmental Law*, Heidelberg: Springer-Verlag.
Woodward, Barbara K. (2010), *Global Civil Society in International Lawmaking and Global Governance*, Leiden: Martinus Nijhoff Publishers.
World Commission on Environment and Development (1987), *Our Common Future*, Oxford: Oxford University Press.
Young, Oran R. (1983), 'Regime Dynamics: the Rise and Fall of International Regimes' in Stephen D. Krasner (ed), *International Regimes*, London: Cornell University Press.
Young, Oran R. (1994), *International Governance: Protecting the Environment in a Stateless Society*, Ithaca, NY and London: Cornell University Press.
Young, Oran R. (ed) (1997), *Global Governance: Drawing Insights from the Environmental Experience*, Cambridge, MA: MIT Press.
Zürn, Michael (2006), 'Global Governance' in Gunnar Folke Schuppert (ed), *Governance Forschung: Vergewisserung über Stand und Entwicklungslinien*, Baden-Baden: Nomos Verlag.

NATIONAL LAWS AND REGULATORY INSTRUMENTS

Constitution of the Republic of South Africa, 1996
National Environmental Management Act 107 of 1998
Promotion of Administrative Justice Act 3 of 2000

SUPRA-NATIONAL LAWS, REGULATORY INSTRUMENTS AND CASE LAW

African Charter on Human and Peoples' Rights, adopted June 27, 1981, OAU Doc. CAB/LEG/67/3 rev. 5, 21 I.L.M. 58 (1982)
Convention on Access to Information, Public Participation in Decision-Making and Access to Justice in Environmental Matters, June 25, 1998, 38 I.L.M. 517 (1999), *entered into force* Oct. 30, 2001
Convention for the Protection and Development of the Marine Environment of the Wider Caribbean Region, 24 March 1983, in force 11 October 1986, 22 I.L.M. 221 (1983)

Convention for the Protection, Management and Development of the Marine and Coastal Environment of the Eastern African Region, 1985

Global Ministerial Environment Forum *Malmö Ministerial Declaration 2000* available at http://www.unep.org/malmo/malmo_ministerial.htm [accessed 16 March 2011]

Johannesburg Plan of Implementation of the World Summit on Sustainable Development at 14 available at http://www.un.org/esa/sustdev/documents/WSSD_POI_PD/English/WSSD_PlanImpl.pdf [accessed 20 October 2012]

Kyoto Protocol to the United Nations Framework on Climate Change, 37 I.L.M. 22 (1998), *entered into force* Feb. 16, 2005

Montevideo Convention on the Rights and Duties of States, 1933

Trail Smelter Arbitration Reports of International Arbitral Awards 16 April 1938/11 March 1941 Vol III, 1905–1982

United Nations Framework Convention on Climate Change 31 I.L.M. 849 (1992)

Vienna Convention on the Law of Treaties, May 23, 1969, 1155 U.N.T.S. 331; 8 I.L.M. 679 (1969), *entered into force* Jan. 27, 1980

INTERNET SOURCES

Badrinarayana, Deepa (2007), *A New Environmental Order: Laying the Legal and Administrative Foundation for Global Environmental Governance* (S.J.D. dissertation, Pace University School of Law, November), available at http://digitalcommons.pace.edu/cgi/viewcontent.cgi?article=1007&context=lawdissertations [accessed 14 March 2011]

Biermann, Frank (2004), *Global Environmental Governance: Conceptualization and Examples (Global Governance Working Paper No 12 November, Amsterdam, Berlin, Oldenburg, Potsdam: The Global Governance Project)*, available at www.Glogov.org [accessed 26 February 2011]

Cambridge University Press, http://journals.cambridge.org/action/displayJournal?jid=TEL [accessed 24 January 2012]

Carbon Disclosure Project, https://www.cdproject.net/en-US/Pages/About-Us.aspx [accessed 24 January 2012]

Ivanova, Maria H. (2003), *Partnerships, International Organizations, and Global Environmental Governance* available at http://www.gppi.net/fileadmin/gppi/Ivanova_Article.pdf [accessed 11 March 2011]

King, Alexander and Bertrand Schneider (1993), *The First Global Revolution: A Report by the Council of the Club of Rome* (Orient Longman), 114–115, available at http://www.archive.org/details/TheFirstGlobalRevolution [accessed 25 February 2011]

Najam, Adil, Mihaela Papa, Nadaa Tayjab (2007), 'Global Environmental Governance: A Reform Agenda (e-book)' in Cutler J. Cleveland (ed), *Encyclopedia of Earth*, Washington, DC: Environmental Information Coalition, National Council for Science and the Environment), available at http://www.eoearth.org/article/Global_Environmental_Governance:_A_Reform_Agenda_(e-book) [accessed 18 March 2011]

OECD, *Environment and Globalisation: Background Report for Ministers – Meeting of the Environment Policy Committee at Ministerial Level, Environment and Global Competitiveness* [ENV/EPOC(2007)18/FINAL], available at http://www.oecd.org/dataoecd/3/59/40511624.pdf [accessed 21 April 2011]

Perez, Oren (2010), *Private Environmental Governance as Ensemble Regulation: A Critical Exploration of Sustainable Business Indexes and the New Ensemble Politics* (Theoretical Inquiries in Law, Forthcoming; Bar Ilan Univ. Pub Law Working Paper November), available at http://papers.ssrn.com/sol3/papers.cfm?abstract_id=1710639 [accessed 14 March 2011]

Shaffer, Gregory and Daniel Bodansky (2011), 'Transnationalism, Unilateralism and International Law', August, University of Minnesota Law School Legal Studies Research Paper Series Research Paper No. 11-34, available at http://papers.ssrn.com/sol3/papers.cfm?abstract_id=1920470 [accessed 21 December 2011]

Späth, Konrad (2005), *Inside Global Governance: New Borders of a Concept*, available at http://www.cpogg.org/paper%20amerang/Konrad%20Spaeth.pdf [accessed 26 February 2011]

Strand, Jonathan R. (2004), *The Case for Regional Environmental Organizations: Regional Integration and Multilateral Environmental Governance* (United Nations University, Institute of Advanced Studies Working Paper), available at http://www.ieg.earthsystemgovernance.org/sites/default/files/files/publications/Strand_The%20Case%20for%20REOs_2002.pdf [accessed 4 October 2011]

Trubek, David M. and Louise G. Trubek (2006), *New Governance and Legal Regulation: Complementarity, Rivalry, or Transformation* (University of Wisconsin Law School Legal Studies Research Paper Series No 1022), available at http://papers.ssrn.com/sol3/papers.cfm?abstract_id=908229 [accessed 4 January 2012]

United Nations http://www.uncsd2012.org/rio20/about.html [accessed 25 February 2012]

UNEP Governing Council *Decision 21/21: International Environmental Governance 2001*, available at http://www.un.org/documents/ga/docs/56/a5625.pdf [accessed 16 March 2011]

JOURNAL ARTICLES

Aagaard, Tod S. (2009/2010), 'Environmental Law as a Legal Field: an Inquiry into Legal Taxonomy', *Cornell Law Review*, **95**, 221–82.

Abbott, Kenneth W. (2004/2005), 'Toward a Richer Institutionalism for International Law and Policy', *Journal of International Law and International Relations*, **1**(1–2), 9–34.

Alkoby, Asher (2003), 'Non-state Actors and the Legitimacy of International Environmental Law', *Non-state Actors and International Law*, **3**, 23–98.

Amerashinghe, Chittharanjan F. (2008), 'International Institutional Law: A Point of View', *International Organizations Law*, **5**, 143–50.

Armstrong, Kenneth and Claire Kilpatrick (2007), 'Law, Governance, or New Governance? The Changing Open Method of Coordination', *The Columbia Journal of European Law*, **3**(13), 649–77.

Auer, M.R. (2000), 'Who Participates in Global Environmental Governance? Partial Answers from International Relations Theory', *Policy Sciences*, **33**, 155–80.

Barnett, Michael N. (1997), 'Bringing in the New World Order: Liberalism, Legitimacy and the United Nations', *World Politics*, **49**(4), 526–51.

Benner, Thorsten, Wolfgang H. Reinicke and Jan Martin Witte (2004), 'Multisectoral Networks in Global Governance: Towards a Pluralistic System of Accountability', *Government and Opposition*, **39**(2), 191–210.

Berman, Paul Schiff (2005), 'From International Law to Law and Globalization', *Columbia Journal of Transnational Law*, **43**(2), 485–556.

Bernstein, Steven (2005), 'Globalization and the Requirements of "Good" Environmental Governance', *Perspectives on Global Development and Technology*, **4**(3/4), 645–79.

Bernstein, Steven (2005), 'Legitimacy in Global Environmental Governance', *Journal of International Law and International Relations*, **1**(1–2), 139–66.

Betsill, Michelle M. and Harriet Bulkeley (2006), 'Cities and the Multilevel Governance of Global Climate Change', *Global Governance*, **12**, 141–59.

Biermann, Frank (2007), '"Earth System Governance" as a Crosscutting Theme of Global Change Research', *Global Environmental Change*, **17**, 326–37.

Biermann, Frank (2010), 'Beyond the Intergovernmental Regime: Recent Trends in Global Carbon Governance', *Current Opinion in Environmental Sustainability*, **2**, 284–8.

Biermann, Frank and Philipp Pattberg (2008), 'Global Environmental Governance: Taking Stock, Moving Forward', *Annual Review of Environment and Resources*, **33**, 277–94.

Biermann, Frank, Olwen Davies and Nicolien Van der Grijp (2009), 'Environmental Policy Integration and the Architecture of Global

Environmental Governance', *International Environmental Agreements*, **9**, 351–69.

Biermann, Frank *et al.* (2010), 'Earth System Governance: A Research Framework', *International Environmental Agreements: Politics, Law and Economics*, **10**(4), 277–98.

Blackett, Adelle (2001), 'Global Governance, Legal Pluralism and the Decentered State: A Labor Law Critique of Codes of Corporate Conduct', *Indiana Journal of Global Legal Studies*, **8**(2), 401–47.

Bodansky, Daniel (1999), 'The Legitimacy of International Governance: A Coming Challenge for International Environmental Law?', *American Journal of International Law*, **93**(3), 596–624.

Boyle, Alan E. (1991), 'Saving the World? Implementation and Enforcement of International Environmental Law through International Institutions', *Journal of Environmental Law*, **3**(2), 229–45.

Branna, Tessa (2007), 'From "Antipolitics" to "Anti-politics": What Became of East European "Civil Society"?', *East European Human Rights Review*, **13**(2), 225–370.

Breitmeier, Helmut (2006), 'Die Output-orientierte Legitimität des globalen Regierens: Empirische Befunde aus der quantitativen Erforschung internationaler Umweltregime', *Zeitschrift für Internationale Beziehungen*, **13**(1), 39–74.

Buhmann, Karin (2009), 'Regulating Corporate Social and Human Rights Responsibilities at the UN Plane: Institutionalising New Forms of Law and Law-making Approaches?', *Nordic Journal of International Law*, **78**, 1–52.

Caldwell, Lynton K. (1999), 'Is World Law an Emerging Reality? Environmental Law in a Transnational World', *Colorado Journal of International Environmental Law and Policy*, **10**(2), 227–43.

Calliess, Gralf-Peter and Moritz Renner (2009), 'Between Law and Social Norms: the Evolution of Global Governance', *Ratio Iuris*, **22**(2), 260–80.

Carr, Donald A. and William L. Thomas (1997), 'Devising a Compliance Strategy under the ISO 14000 International Environmental Management Standards', *Pace Environmental Law Review*, **15**(1), 85–231.

Castells, Manuel (2008), 'The New Public Sphere: Global Civil Society, Communication Networks, and Global Governance', *The Annals of the American Academy*, March, 78–93.

Churchill, Robin R. and Geir Ulfstein (2000), 'Autonomous Institutional Arrangements in Multilateral Environmental Agreements: A Little-noticed Phenomenon in International Law', *American Journal of International Law*, **94**, 623–59.

Coen, David and Mark Thatcher (2008), 'Network Governance and Multi-Level Delegation: European Networks of Regulatory Agencies', *Journal of Public Policy*, **28**(1), 49–71.

Collins, Lynda M. (2007), 'Revisiting the Doctrine of Intergenerational Equity in Global Environmental Governance', *Dalhousie Law Journal*, **30**(2), 79–140.

Conca, Ken (2004/2005), 'Environmental Governance after Johannesburg: From Stalled Legalization to Environmental Human Rights?', *Journal of International Law and International Relations*, **1**(1)/**1**(2), 121–66.

Cortell, Andrew P. and James W. Davis (2005), 'When Norms Clash: International Norms, Domestic Practices, and Japan's Internalisation of the GAT/WTO', *Review of International Studies*, **31**, 3–25.

De Búrca, Gráinne and Joanne Scott (2007), 'Introduction', *Columbia Journal of European Law*, **13**(3), 513–17.

Detomasi, David Antony (2007), 'The Multinational Corporation and Global Governance: Modelling Global Public Policy Networks', *Journal of Business Ethics*, **71**, 321–34.

De Wet, Erika (2008), 'The International Constitutional Order', *International and Comparative Law Quarterly*, **55**, 51–76.

Diggelmann, Oliver and Tilmann Altwicker (2008), 'Is there Something like a Constitution of International Law: A Critical Analysis of the Debate on World Constitutionalism', *Zeitschrift für ausländisches öffentliches Recht und Völkerrecht*, **68**, 623–50.

Dingwerth, Klaus and Philipp Pattberg (2006), 'Was ist Global Governance?', *Leviathan*, **34**(3), 377–99.

Dittgen, Herbert (1999), 'World without Borders? Reflections on the Future of the Nation State', *Government and Opposition*, **34**(2), 161–79.

Duffy, Rosaleen (2005), 'The Politics of Global Environmental Governance: the Powers and Limitations of Transfrontier Conservation Areas in Central America', *Review of International Studies*, **31**, 307–23.

Dunoff, Jeffrey L. (1995), 'From Green to Global: Toward the Transformation of International Environmental Law', *Harvard Environmental Law Review*, **19**(2), 241–301.

Durant Robert F. *et al.* (2004), 'Toward a New Governance Paradigm for Environmental and Natural Resources Management in the 21st Century', *Administration and Society*, January, 643–82.

Engi, Lorenz (2008), 'Governance: Umrisse und Problematik eines staatstheoretischen Leitbildes', *Der Staat: Zeitschrift für Staatslehre und Verfassungsgesichte, deutsches und europäisiches Öffentliches Recht*, **47**, 573–87.

Esty, Daniel C. (1999), 'Toward Optimal Environmental Governance', *New York University Law Review*, **74**(6), 1495–1574.

Etzioni, Amitai (2001), 'Beyond Transnational Governance', *International Journal*, 595–610.

Falk, Richard (1995), 'Environmental Protection in an Era of Globalization', *Yearbook of International Environmental Law*, **6**, 3–63.

Falkner, Robert (2003), 'Private Environmental Governance and International Relations: Exploring the Links', *Global Environmental Politics*, **3**(2), 72–87.

Finkelstein, Lawrence S. (1995), 'What is Global Governance?', *Global Governance*, **1**, 367–72.

Fisher, Elizabeth *et al.* (2009), 'Maturity and Methodology: Starting a Debate about Environmental Law Scholarship', *Journal of Environmental Law*, **21**(2), 213–50.

French, Duncan (2009), 'Finding Autonomy in International Environmental Law and Governance', *Journal of Environmental Law*, **21**(2), 255–89.

Gehring, Thomas and Sebastian Oberthür (2000), 'Was bringt eine Weltumweltorganisation? Kooperationstheoretische Anmerkungen zur institutionellen Neuordnung der internationalen Umweltpolitik', *Zeitschrift für Internationale Beziehugnen*, **7**(1), 185–211.

Giljum, Stefan *et al.* (2005), 'Environmental Governance in the European Union: Strategies and Instruments for Absolute Decoupling', *International Journal of Sustainable Development*, **8**(1/2), 31–46.

Gunningham, Neil (2009), 'Environmental Law, Regulation and Governance: Shifting Architectures', *Journal of Environmental Law*, **21**(2), 179–212.

Guruswamy, Lakshman D. (2002), 'Cartography of Governance: an Introduction', *Colorado Journal of International Environmental Law and Policy*, **13**(1), 1–13.

Haas, Peter M. (2002), 'UN Conferences and Constructivist Governance of the Environment', *Global Governance*, **8**, 73–91.

Haas, Peter M. and Ernst B. Haas (1995), 'Learning to Learn: Improving International Governance', *Global Governance*, **1**, 255–85.

Hansen, Michael W. (2003), 'Managing the Environment across Borders: A Survey of Environmental Management in Transnational Corporations in Asia', *Transnational Corporations*, **12**(1), 27–52.

Harlow, Carol (2006), 'Global Administrative Law: the Quest for Principles and Values', *European Journal of International Law*, **17**(1), 187–214.

Heyvaert, Veerle (2009), 'Levelling Down, Levelling Up, and Governing Across: Three Responses to Hybridization in International Law', *European Journal of International Law*, **20**(1), 647–74.

Hierlmeier, Jodie (2002), 'UNEP: Retrospect and Prospect – Options for Reforming the Global Environmental Governance Regime', *Georgetown International Environmental Law Review*, **14**, 767–805.

Holzinger, Katharina, Christopher Knill and Thomas Sommerer (2008), 'Environmental Policy Convergence: the Impact of International Harmonization, Transnational Communication, and Regulatory Competition', *International Organization*, **62**, 553–87.

Jones, Candace, William S. Hesterly and Stephen P. Borgatti (1997), 'A

General Theory of Network Governance: Exchange Conditions and Social Mechanisms', *Academy of Management Review*, **22**(4), 911–45.
Karkkainen, Bradley C. (2001/2002), 'Collaborative Ecosystem Governance: Scale, Complexity, and Dynamism', *Virginia Environmental Law Journal*, **21**(2), 189–243.
Kingsbury, Benedict (2005), 'Global Governance as Administration: National and Transnational Approaches to Global Administrative Law', *Law and Contemporary Problems*, **68**, 1–13.
Kingsbury, Benedict (2009), 'The Concept of "Law" in Global Administrative Law', *European Journal of International Law*, **20**(1), 23–57.
Kingsbury, Benedict and Lorenzo Casini (2009), 'Global Administrative Law Dimensions of International Organizational Law', *International Organizations Law Review*, **6**, 319–58.
Klabbers, Jan (2008), 'The Paradox of International Institutional Law', *International Organizations Law Review*, **5**, 151–73.
Koh Kheng-Lian and Nicholas A. Robinson (2002), 'Strengthening Sustainable Development in Regional Inter-governmental Governance: Lessons from the "ASEAN Way"', *Singapore Journal of International and Comparative Law*, **6**, 640–82.
Kornhauser, Lewis A. (2004), 'Governance Structures, Legal Systems, and the Concept of Law', *Chicago-Kent Law Review*, **79**(2), 355–81.
Koskenniemi, Martti (2004), 'Global Governance and Public International Law', *Kritische Justiz*, **37**, 241–54.
Kotzé, Louis J. (2002), 'The Application of Just Administrative Action in the South African Environmental Governance Sphere: An Analysis of Some Contemporary Thoughts and Recent Jurisprudence', *Potchefstroom Electronic Law Journal*, **2**, 1–42.
Krasner, Stephen D. (2000), 'International Law and International Relations: Together, Apart, Together?', *Chicago Journal of International Law*, **1**(1), 93–9.
Kumar, Vidya S.A. (2003), 'A Critical Methodology of Globalization: Politics of the 21st Century?', *Indiana Journal of Global Legal Studies*, **2**(10), 87–111.
Kütting, Gabriela (2004), 'Globalization and the Environment: Moving Beyond Neoliberal Institutionalism', *International Journal of Peace Studies*, **9**(1), 29–46.
Lee, Robert and Elen Stokes (2009), 'Environmental Governance: Reconnecting the Global and Local', *Journal of Law and Society*, **36**(1), 1–10.
Lemos, Maria Carmen and Arun Agrawal (2006), 'Environmental Governance', *Annual Review of Environment and Resources*, **31**, 297–325.
Liverman, Diana (2004), 'Who Governs, at What Scale and at What Price?

Geography, Environmental Governance, and the Commodification of Nature', *Annals of the Association of American Geographers*, **94**(4), 734–8.
Llewellyn, Karl N. (1940), 'The Normative, the Legal, and the Law-Jobs: The Problem of Juristic Method', *Yale Law Journal*, **49**(8), 1355–1400.
Lövbrand, Eva, Johannes Stripple and Bo Wiman (2009), 'Earth System Governmentality Reflections on Science in the Anthopocene', *Global Environmental Change*, **19**, 7–13 at 7, 8.
Lubbe, Willem D. (2007) 'Straddling Borders and Legal Regimes: The Case for Cooperative Transfrontier Biodiversity Conservation in the Southern African Development Community', *Yearbook of International Environmental Law*, **18**, 126–52.
Mitchell, Andrew D. and John Farnik (2009), 'Global Administrative Law: Can it Bring Global Governance to Account?', *Federal Law Review*, **37**, 237–62.
Myint, Tun (2003), 'Democracy in Global Environmental Governance: Issues, Interests, and Actors in the Mekong and the Rhine', *Indiana Journal of Global Legal Studies*, 287–314.
Ong, David M. (2010), 'From "International" to "Transnational" Environmental Law? A Legal Assessment of the Contribution of the "Equator Principles" to International Environmental Law', *Nordic Journal of International Law*, **79**(1), 35–74.
Paterson, Matthew (1999), 'Interpreting Trends in Global Environmental Governance', *International Affairs*, **75**(4), 793–802.
Paterson, Matthew, David Humphreys and Lloyd Pettiford (2003), 'Conceptualizing Global Environmental Governance: From Interstate Regimes to Counter-hegemonic Struggles', *Global Environmental Politics*, **3**(2), 1–10.
Pattberg, Philipp (2005), 'What Role for Private Rule-making in Global Environmental Governance? Analysing the Forest Stewardship Council (FSC)', *International Environmental Agreements*, **5**, 175–89.
Pattberg, Philipp and Johannes Stripple (2008), 'Beyond the Public and Private Divide: Remapping Transnational Climate Governance in the 21st Century', *International Environmental Agreements*, **8**, 367–88.
Peel, Jacqueline and Lee Godden (2005), 'Australian Environmental Management: A "Dams" Story', *University of New South Wales Law Journal*, **28**(3), 668–95.
Pelletier, Nathan (2010), 'Of Laws and Limits: An Ecological Economic Perspective on Redressing the Failure of Contemporary Global Environmental Governance', *Global Environmental Change*, **20**, 220–8.
Percival, Robert V. (2009), 'Fifteenth Annual Lloyd K. Garrison Lecture on Environmental Law: The Globalization of Environmental Law', *Pace Environmental Law Review*, **26**, 451–64.

Pratt, Lawrence, Richard P. Wells and Foster C. Knight (1995), 'Environmental Management: Helping Industry Worldwide Advance toward Sustainable Development', *Review of European Community and International Environmental Law*, **4**(2), 106–12.

Raustiala, Kal (1997), 'Domestic Institutions and International Regulatory Cooperation: Comparative Responses to the Convention on Biological Diversity', *World Politics*, **49**(4), 482–509.

Rhodes, Rod A.W. (1996), 'The New Governance: Governance without Government', *Political Studies*, **XLIV**, 652–67.

Richardson, Benjamin J. (2000), 'Environmental Law in Postcolonial Societies: Straddling the Local-Global Institutional Spectrum', *Colorado Journal of International Environmental Law and Policy*, **11**, 1–82.

Roch, Philippe and Franz Xaver Perrez (2005), 'International Environmental Governance: The Strive Towards a Comprehensive, Coherent, Effective and Efficient International Environmental Regime', *Colorado Journal of International Environmental Law and Policy*, **16**(1), 1–25.

Roht-Arriaza, Naomi (1995), 'Private Voluntary Standard-Setting, the International Organization for Standardization, and International Environmental Lawmaking', *Yearbook of International Environmental Law*, **6**, 107–163.

Rosenau, James N. (1995), 'Governance in the Twenty-first Century', *Global Governance*, **1**(1), 13–34.

Sand, Peter H. (1991), 'Lessons Learned in Global Environmental Governance', *Boston College Environmental Affairs Law Review*, **18**, 213–77.

Schuppert, Gunnar Folke (2007), 'Was ist und wozu Governance?', *Die Verwaltung: Zeitschrift für Verwaltungsrecht und Verwaltungswissenschaften*, **40**(1), 463–511.

Shams, Heba (2001), 'Law in the Context of "Globalisation": a Framework of Analysis', *The International Lawyer*, **35**(4), 1589–1626.

Shapiro, Martin (1993/1994), 'The Globalization of Law', *Global Legal Studies Journal*, **1**(37), 37–64.

Smouts, Marie-Claude (1998), 'The Proper Use of Governance in International Relations', *International Social Science Journal*, **50**(155), 81–9.

Sonnenfeld, David A. (2008), 'Globalisation and Environmental Governance: Is Another World Possible?', *Global Environmental Change*, **18**, 341–2.

Steiner, Achim, Lee A. Kimball and John Scanlon (2003), 'Global Governance for the Environment and the Role of Multilateral Environmental Agreements in Conservation', *Oryx*, **37**(2), 227–37.

Stone, Christopher D. (1996), 'Locale and Legitimacy in International Environmental Law', *Stanford Law Review*, **48**(5), 1279–1291.

Strong, Maurice (1973), 'One Year after Stockholm: An Ecological Approach to Management', *Foreign Affairs*, **51**(4), 690–707.

Strong, Maurice F. (1990), 'What Place will the Environment have in the Next Century – and at what Price?', *International Environmental Affairs*, **2**, 208–16.

Trubek, David M. and Louise G. Trubek (2007), 'New Governance and Legal Regulation: Complementarity, Rivalry and Transformation', *Columbia Journal of European Law*, **13**(3), 539–64.

Trute, Hans-Heinrich, Wolfgang Denkhaus and Doris Kühlers (2004), 'Governance in der Verwaltungsrechtswissenschaft', *Die Verwaltung: Zeitschrift für Verwaltungsrecht und Verwaltungswissenschaften*, **37**, 451–73.

Venter, Francois (2008), 'Die Staat, Staatsreg en Globalisering', *Tydskrif vir die Suid-Afrikaanse Reg*, **3**, 412–24.

Vogler, John (2005), 'The European Contribution to Global Environmental Governance', *International Affairs*, **81**(4), 835–50.

Vogler, John and Hannes R. Stephan (2007), 'The European Union in Global Environmental Governance: Leadership in the Making?', *International Environmental Agreements*, **7**, 389–413.

Walker, Neil and Gráinne De Búrca (2007), 'Reconceiving Law and New Governance', *Columbia Journal of European Law*, **13**(3), 519–37.

Weiler, J.H.H. (2004), 'The Geology of International Law: Governance, Democracy and Legitimacy', *Zeitschrift für Ausländisches Öffentliches Recht und Völkerrecht*, **64**, 547–62.

Wiener, Jonathan B. (1998/1999), 'On the Political Economy of Global Environmental Regulation', *Georgetown Law Journal*, **87**, 749–94.

Wiener, Jonathan B. (1999), 'Global Environmental Regulation: Instrument Choice in Legal Context', *Yale Law Journal*, **108**(4), 677–800.

Wiener, Jonathan B. (2000/2001), 'Something Borrowed for Something Blue: Legal Transplants and the Evolution of Global Environmental Law', *Ecology Law Quarterly*, **27**, 1295–1372.

Winchester, Brian N. (2009), 'Emerging Global Environmental Governance', *Indiana Journal of Global Legal Studies*, **16**(1), 7–23.

Yang, Tseming and Robert V. Percival (2009), 'The Emergence of Global Environmental Law', *Ecology Law Quarterly*, **36**, 615–64.

Young, Oran R. (2003), 'Environmental Governance: The Role of Institutions in Causing and Confronting Environmental Problems', *International Environmental Agreements*, **3**, 377–93.

Young, Oran R. (2007), 'Rights, Rules, and Common Pools: Solving Problems Arising in Human/Environment Relations', *Natural Resources Journal*, **1**(47), 1–16.

Zalasiewicz, J. *et al.* (2001), 'The Anthropocene: a New Epoch of Geological Time?', *Philosophical Transactions of the Royal Society*, **369**, 835–41.

Zarsky, Lyuba (1997), 'The Asia-Pacific Economic Cooperation Forum and the Environment: Regional Environmental Governance in the Age of Economic Globalization', *Colorado Journal of International Environmental Law and Policy*, **8**(2), 323–57.

Index

Dear Duncan

Many thanks for this wonderful opportunity and the great prospect of collaboration. I am really looking forward to working with you and your faculty.

With best wishes and thanks.

Luis Jiang

February 2014